Fifty
Classic Climbs

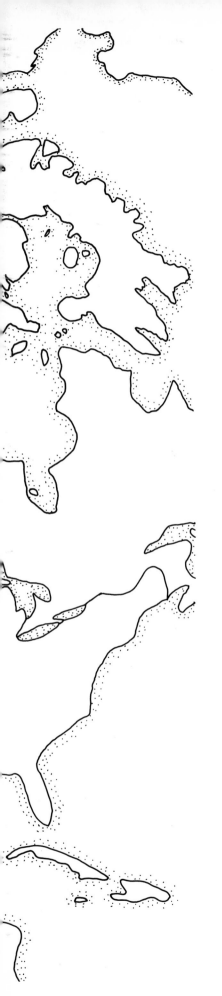

Fifty
Classic Climbs
of North America

Steve Roper & Allen Steck

Sierra Club Books
San Francisco

Library of Congress Cataloging in Publication Data

Roper, Steve.
   Fifty classic climbs of North America.

   Bibliography: p. 315
   Includes index.
   1. Mountaineering—United States.   2. Mountaineering —Canada.
3. Rock climbing—United States.   4. Rock climbing—Canada.
I.   Steck, Allen, joint author.
II.   Title.
GV199.4.R66   796.5′22′097   79-13001
ISBN 0-87156-262-6

Jacket and book design by Marjorie Spiegelman
Maps by Edwin A. Gustafson

Printed in the United States of America
10   9   8   7   6   5   4   3   2   1

Contents

Acknowledgments   viii
Introduction   ix

Alaska and the Yukon

1	Mount Saint Elias, Abruzzi Ridge	5
2	Mount Fairweather, Carpé Ridge	9
3	Mount Hunter, West Ridge	15
4	Mount McKinley, Cassin Ridge	19
5	Moose's Tooth, West Ridge	25
6	Mount Huntington, West Face	31
7	Mount Logan, Hummingbird Ridge	37
8	Middle Triple Peak, East Buttress	43

Western Canada

9	Mount Sir Donald, Northwest Arête	51
10	Bugaboo Spire, East Ridge	55
11	South Howser Tower, West Buttress	61
12	Mount Robson, Wishbone Arête	65
13	Mount Edith Cavell, North Face	71
14	Mount Alberta, Japanese Route	75
15	Mount Temple, East Ridge	81
16	Mount Waddington, South Face	85
17	Devil's Thumb, East Ridge	93
18	Lotus Flower Tower	99

The Pacific Northwest

19 Mount Rainier, Liberty Ridge   107

20 Forbidden Peak, West Ridge   113

21 Mount Shuksan, Price Glacier   119

22 Slesse Mountain, Northeast Buttress   123

23 Mount Stuart, North Ridge   129

24 Liberty Bell Mountain, Liberty Crack   133

Wyoming

25 Devil's Tower, Durrance Route   141

26 Grand Teton, North Ridge   147

27 Grand Teton, Direct Exum Ridge   153

28 Grand Teton, North Face   159

29 Mount Moran, Direct South Buttress   165

30 Pingora, Northeast Face   171

31 Wolf's Head, East Ridge   177

Colorado

32 Crestone Needle, Ellingwood Ledges   187

33 Hallett Peak, Northcutt–Carter Route   191

34 Petit Grepon, South Face   195

35 Longs Peak, The Diamond   201

The Southwest

36 Shiprock — 209

37 Castleton Tower, Kor–Ingalls Route — 217

38 The Titan — 221

California

39 The Royal Arches — 231

40 Lost Arrow Spire — 237

41 Sentinel Rock, Steck–Salathé Route — 243

42 Middle Cathedral Rock, East Buttress — 249

43 Half Dome, Northwest Face — 255

44 El Capitan, Nose Route — 261

45 El Capitan, Salathé Wall — 269

46 Mount Whitney, East Face — 277

47 Fairview Dome, North Face — 283

48 Clyde Minaret, Southeast Face — 289

49 Charlotte Dome, South Face — 295

50 Lover's Leap, Traveler Buttress — 301

An Explanation of the Rating System — 306

Notes on Sources — 308

Bibliography — 315

Index — 320

Acknowledgments

During the three-year period that this book was in preparation, numerous mountaineers suggested routes for inclusion. The responsibility for the final selection was ours, of course, but we are grateful for the suggestions offered and would like to thank all who contributed ideas.

Many climbers displayed a long-term interest in our project, helping in countless ways. Our sincere appreciation goes to Monty Alford, Fred Beckey, Glen Boles, Mike Covington, Jim Crooks, Harry Daley, Greg Donaldson, Clark Gerhardt, Mike Graber, Jim Hale, David Isles, Chris Jones, Steve Komito, Alan Long, George Lowe, Leigh Ortenburger, Galen Rowell, Eric Sanford, Paul Starr, the late Willi Unsoeld, and Ed Webster.

Ed Cooper and Bradford Washburn supplied us with many sensational black-and-white prints. Jack Turner spent most of six weeks confined to a darkroom creating about 150 excellent enlargements from slides and negatives ranging in quality from superb to dubious. The dramatic tones in many of the photographs reproduced in this book are testimony to Turner's skill.

Our longtime friend Dick Long was a stalwart companion on many of our trips to the mountains. Uncomplainingly, he led the most difficult sections of our climbs together; without his hyperactive presence, we might have spent more time talking about the climbs than actually doing them.

Editorially, we were helped greatly by four perceptive people who offered cogent suggestions on how to improve our book. Our thanks to Linda Gunnarson, Diana Landau, Chuck Pratt, and Kathy Roper.

Introduction

How many times early in our climbing careers did we hear a surprised mountaineer exclaim, "What? You haven't done such and such a route? You really must, you know. It's a real classic." This book describes fifty such North American climbs—routes which ambitious climbers dream of doing someday.

We chose our climbs from a list which in the early stages of our research topped one hundred. Only fifty routes, we felt, could be described adequately in a book of this size. Uneasy about thus relegating more than fifty routes to the "honorable mention" category, we nevertheless believe that our final selection reflects the wide variety of excellent climbing that can be done on this continent. Our routes are not *the* fifty classic climbs of the continent, but rather our personal choice of the finest routes in several major areas which differ radically in length, type of climbing, and geographical setting.

Experienced climbers have come to recognize—whether from first-hand knowledge, conversations with friends, or accounts in mountaineering literature—that certain routes are "the ones to do." But why? What makes a climb a classic? In our quest for an all-encompassing definition, we solicited opinions from many leading climbers. Their replies tended to emphasize three basic criteria: the peak or route should look striking from afar, have a significant climbing history, and offer excellent climbing. Since few routes meet all three of these criteria, how much emphasis should be placed on each? Is the history of a route more important than its aesthetic appearance? Does fine climbing override history? We decided that, as a rule, excellent climbing should take precedence over general appearance, which in turn should outweigh historical significance. Excellent climbing, we believe, means many things to the receptive mountaineer: challenging rock; pleasant, varied climbing; no unaesthetic loose sections; bold, sweeping ice slopes and ridges; and, finally, an airy and rewarding summit.

Because we established excellent climbing as the prime qualification for including a route in this book, we have omitted a few well-known peaks such as British Columbia's Snowpatch Spire and Colorado's Lizard Head. To imply that these climbs aren't worth doing would be irresponsible, but we feel strongly that such relatively unknown climbs as Bugaboo Spire's East Ridge Route and the South Face Route on the Petit Grepon provide far better climbing.

Other climbs which passed final muster certainly will be controversial. For example, why are we including three routes on the Grand Teton, while leaving out the fine crag climbs in nearby Garnet and Death canyons? Our reasons, if not always apparent or explicitly stated, are not arbitrary. We feel that no matter how popular some of the Teton crag climbs are, they do not represent the essence of climbing in the Tetons. In a region known for its towering alpine peaks, the three Grand climbs are without question more representative of the area than the others.

Predictably, however, after determining that excellent climbing should take precedence over history and appearance, we began to make exceptions. Sometimes a peak or cliff looks so architecturally perfect from a distance that, regardless of the quality of the climbing, the route has to be considered a classic. For example, the Matterhorn's Hörnli Ridge contains little excellent climbing, yet it is unquestionably a classic because of its appearance and history. Closer to home, the North Face Route on the Grand Teton falls into the same category. Although the climbing on the north face is not extraordinary, the fame, history, and ruggedness of the wall made it obligatory for our list.

One should not infer that we have chosen the most difficult climbs in North America. To be sure, the younger climbers we consulted suggested super-difficult routes. Older climbers, however, tended to nominate moderate routes which were difficult during the "storm years" of their own youth. We attempted to eliminate these extremes, and although all the fifty routes included here are technical in the sense that a rope is required, they range from class 4 scrambles to demanding excursions onto sheer rock faces and alpine ridges.

In choosing the climbs we also decided that a number of years should have elapsed since the first ascent of a route so that we could discern whether the route has continued to attract climbers or was simply a passing fad. Thus, virtually all of the routes in this book were first climbed prior to 1970.

We were faced with still another thorny problem while trying to pare our list to fifty routes: Should we establish a lower limit as to the length of a climb? Reluctantly, we decided that climbs shorter than 500 feet would not be considered. Omitting routes in the Shawangunks, in southeastern New York, the Needles of South Dakota, and West Virginia's Seneca Rocks because of their length proved especially vexing, for we regard each of these areas as a climber's paradise. Unfortunately, so many fine two- and three-pitch routes are found in North America that their representation would have been limited to only a paragraph and a photograph for each. True to form, however, we found exceptions. Devil's Tower and the Lost Arrow, for example, were simply too wonderful and too well known to omit.

During our combined total of sixty years' climbing experience, we have either ascended, attempted, or at least seen nearly all of the routes selected. No one person has yet climbed even half these routes, a situation we attribute to the provinciality, poverty, bad luck, and short climbing careers of most North American mountaineers. Fifteen of the routes we have climbed together, beginning with the third ascent, in 1966, of El Capitan's Salathé Wall. It was on this magnificent cliff that we first conceived of writing a book about the classic climbs of Yosemite Valley. Ten years later, the project, which had grown considerably more ambitious in scope, finally got under way.

Our not having climbed all the routes ourselves bothered us at first, but we soon realized that we lacked both the time and resources for such a stupendous effort. For those climbs with which we were not personally familiar, we interviewed perceptive mountaineers who had done the routes, reviewed existing literature, and sought out photographs.

As we assembled the photographs for this book, we discovered that mountaineers who accomplish alpine ascents are usually so concerned with the necessity for speed and alertness that their cameras, if taken at all, tend to remain in their packs. The storms and frigid temperatures encountered on such climbs also hinder photographic endeavors. In a climatically benign area such as Yosemite, however, an unhurried climber might easily spend an hour casually shooting an entire roll of film. Not surprisingly, then, for every photograph we received of a Canadian climb, we were given twenty from persons who had climbed in Yosemite. Although readers consequently will enjoy more visual impressions of Yosemite than they will of Canadian climbing areas, we hope our narrative conveys the awesome qualities of the less photographed region.

We attempted to avoid emphasizing technical terms in this book, but the use of some technical climbing terminology is unavoidable. Such esoteric designations as Grade VI, 5.8, or A3, which are used to indicate the difficulty of a route, are especially necessary to describe rockclimbing.

Readers who are unfamiliar with the meaning of these designations may find it helpful to consult the brief "Explanation of the Rating System" included at the end of this book.

Technical information concerning each climb follows its descriptive account. Most of the headings in these technical sections are self-explanatory, but four require elaboration. For each "Time" listing we indicate how long an experienced pair of climbers might take to make the climb under optimum conditions. That most of the routes can be done in half the time noted is indisputable; some parties, however, may take twice as long if problems arise or weather conditions deteriorate.

Under "Maps" we list two major types. Canadian maps can be ordered from the Canada Map Office, Department of Energy, Mines, and Resources, 615 Booth, Ottawa, Ontario K1A 0E9. Maps from the United States Geological Survey (abbreviated USGS throughout) can be ordered from the USGS Branch Distribution Center, Box 25286, Federal Center, Denver, Colorado 80225.

In each "Useful Reference" section we mention the title of a guidebook (occasionally more than one) which contains practical information about the route. When this heading is omitted, one can assume that no guidebook is available. Full publication data for these books can be found in the bibliography, which also includes books on climbing history and technique, memoirs of prominent climbers mentioned herein, and periodicals used in our research.

In the "Equipment" listing we indicate only the special or unusual gear one should carry; we do not wish to bore the reader with an extensive list of standard impedimenta. When a climb does not include an equipment heading, one can assume that nothing out of the ordinary is required.

Some of the quoted material in this book has been altered slightly to conform to modern spelling and punctuation. Readers who wish to know the sources of quotations can find this information in the "Note on Sources" at the end of this book.

The climbs in Alaska, the Pacific Northwest, and Wyoming, as well as the Mount Waddington account, were researched and written by Allen Steck; the remaining climbs were written by Steve Roper.

Some mountaineers are proud of having done all their climbs without bivouac. How much they have missed! And the same applies to those who enjoy only rock climbing, or only the ice climbs, only the ridges or the faces. We should refuse none of the thousand and one joys that the mountains offer us at every turn. We should brush nothing aside, set no restrictions. We should experience hunger and thirst, be able to go fast, but also know how to go slowly and to contemplate.

Gaston Rébuffat
Starlight and Storm

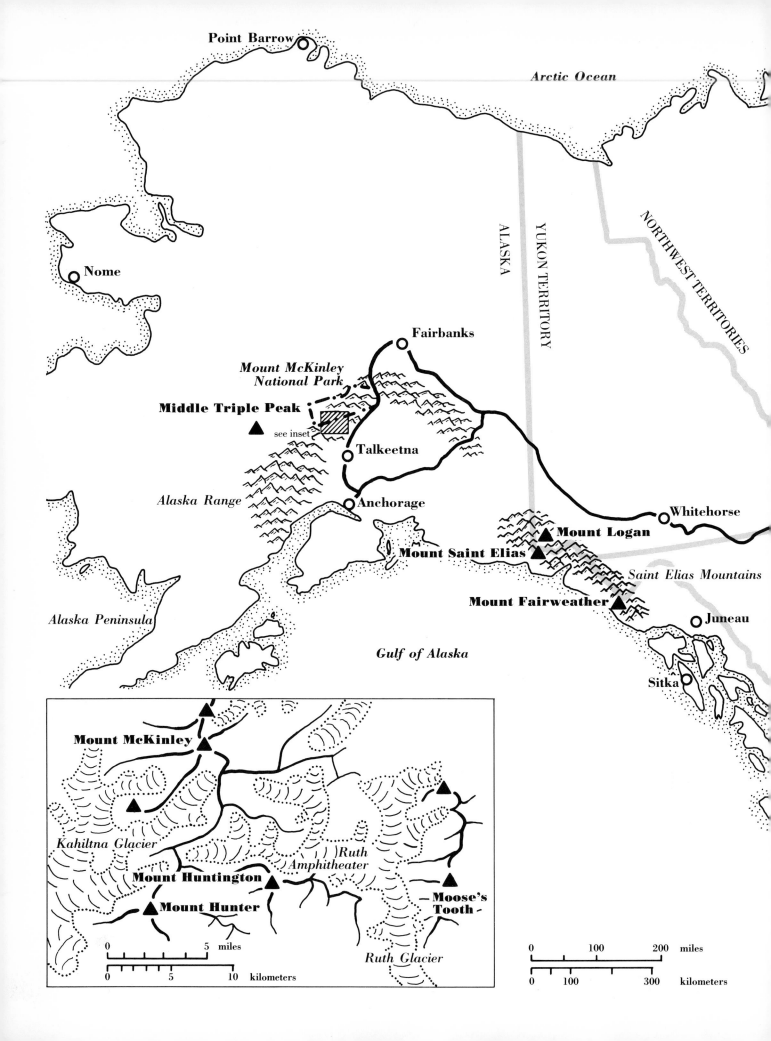

Point Barrow

Arctic Ocean

Nome

ALASKA

YUKON TERRITORY

NORTHWEST TERRITORIES

Fairbanks

Mount McKinley National Park

Middle Triple Peak ▲

see inset

Talkeetna

Alaska Range

Anchorage

Whitehorse

▲ **Mount Logan**

Mount Saint Elias ▲

Saint Elias Mountains

Mount Fairweather ▲

Juneau

Alaska Peninsula

Gulf of Alaska

Sitka

Mount McKinley ▲

Kahiltna Glacier

Ruth Amphitheater

Mount Huntington ▲

Mount Hunter ▲

Moose's Tooth ▲

Ruth Glacier

0   5   miles

0   5   10   kilometers

0   100   200   miles

0   100   300   kilometers

Alaska and The Yukon

The Alaska Range and the Saint Elias Mountains form an 800-mile arc of peaks and glaciers north of the Gulf of Alaska and roughly paralleling its coastline. Within this remarkable cordillera lie many of North America's highest summits, including the continent's highest peak, 20,320-foot Mount McKinley. Both ranges contain numerous glacial systems, and the Saint Elias Mountains may have the greatest number of interconnecting icefields and glaciers outside Antarctica and Greenland.

The climbing history of the Alaska–Yukon region is rich and varied. After the first ascent of Mount Saint Elias in 1897, mountaineers concentrated their efforts on Mount McKinley; after many epic attempts to climb the peak, four Alaskans, led by the Reverend Hudson Stuck and Harry Karstens, finally reached its summit in June 1913. The introduction of ski-equipped aircraft in the early 1930s revolutionized mountaineering in the far northern latitudes by eliminating arduous overland approaches, which had deterred all but the most hardy and determined explorers.

The dedicated explorer–mountaineer and geographer Bradford Washburn participated in the first ascents of several important peaks in the Saint Elias and Wrangell Mountains in the 1930s and has continued to influence Alaskan mountaineering through his aerial photography and mapmaking. In the past thirty years few parties have set off to climb Alaskan peaks without first consulting Washburn's material. Many climbers were inspired originally by the first-ascent possibilities revealed by Washburn's photographs and outlined in detail in his vividly descriptive articles.

Mountaineering in Alaska and the Yukon is characterized by far greater objective dangers—natural hazards as opposed to risks more under control of mountaineers themselves—than exist elsewhere in North America. The climate is subarctic, with intense cold and vicious storms that sweep in from the Gulf of Alaska, occasionally dropping as much as ten feet of snow in a seven-day period. Many expeditions have been defeated, sometimes with tragic loss of life, by this harsh environment, which is comparable to that found on higher Himalayan peaks thirty-five degrees of latitude farther south. Such hazardous conditions require careful attention to logistics, particularly with regard to the selection of expeditionary equipment. But despite these difficulties, mountaineers find that the rewards of climbing in Alaska and the Yukon outweigh the hazards and are arriving in increasing numbers to seek Himalayan-type mountaineering without its characteristic long approaches and inevitable porter problems. The Alaska–Yukon mountains are immense, the climbing routes long and challenging, and the scenery utterly magnificent.

BRITISH COLUMBIA

Mount Saint Elias
Abruzzi Ridge

1

It was not by chance that nineteenth-century voyagers used Mount Saint Elias as a beacon during their explorations of the northwest coast of America. Visible from the sea at a distance of more than one hundred miles, the mountain is starkly beautiful. Its ridges and buttresses rise out of an extensive glacial labyrinth that flows for twenty miles to the tidewater of Icy Bay, resulting in a zone of perpetual glaciation more than 18,000 feet high, one of the highest in the world.

The first recorded observation of Mount Saint Elias is found in the log of the explorer Vitus Bering's ship, the *Saint Peter*. On July 17, 1741, the peak and its satellites were seen, from a distance of some 120 miles, as "high, snow-covered mountains . . . among them a high volcano N by W." Bering named a nearby point of land Cape Saint Elias in honor of the patron saint of

◀ *Mount Saint Elias as seen from the east.* Boston Museum of Science photo by Bradford Washburn.

the day (July 20) on which he and his crew set anchor. The mountain acquired its name from this landmark in 1778, during a visit to these waters by the English explorer and navigator, Captain James Cook.

More than a hundred years passed before efforts were made to explore and attempt to climb Mount Saint Elias. In 1888, W. H. Topham and his party penetrated the defenses of the mountain, reaching 11,400 feet on its southern flank before being turned back by the difficulty of the route. In 1890, Professor Israel Russell, a geologist from the University of Michigan, arrived at Mount Saint Elias with a six-man party. Although his objectives were primarily scientific, he found time to explore and name the Agassiz and Newton glaciers as he searched for a feasible route to the summit on the peak's southeast side. It was on this trip that Russell made the first sighting of an immense mountain to the north which he named Mount Logan. He returned to the Saint Elias region the following year. Starting from Icy Bay, Russell followed his earlier route up the Newton Glacier and ascended to the foot of a large col between Mount Newton and Mount Saint Elias. During a severe storm, so much snow fell that Russell and his party were trapped at their high camp for days. When the weather finally cleared, the expedition was able to ascend to the saddle now known as Russell Col and climb to 14,500 feet on the north ridge of Saint Elias before being turned back by approaching darkness. Once again a long storm set in, and the

party eventually was forced to return to Icy Bay. Here Russell took measurements and calculated the elevation of the mountain to be 18,100 feet, a figure remarkably close to its presently accepted altitude of 18,008 feet.

Besides nearly climbing Mount Saint Elias, Russell's party was the first to view the colossal glacial wilderness to the north of the mountain and paved the way for an elaborate Italian expedition led by the wealthy Duke of the Abruzzi.

His Royal Highness, Prince Luigi Amedeo of Savoy, Duke of the Abruzzi, was twenty-four years old when he arrived in Yakutat, a small native settlement southeast of Mount Saint Elias, in June 1897. The duke was an alpinist of moderate ability, an adventurer who desired more from mountaineering than the familiar ascents his native Italian Alps could offer. His military training had made him a leader of men, and he possessed the charisma to attract people whose devotion to him would be lifelong. The Mount Saint Elias expedition he organized included: Umberto Cagni, a lieutenant in the Italian Army; Francesco Gonella, an official from the Italian Alpine Club; Vittorio Sella, famous photographer and alpinist; Filippo de Filippi, medical doctor and scientist; Erminio Botta, an assistant to Sella; and four mountain guides from Italy.

Following the maps and suggestions provided by Professor Russell, the duke crossed Yakutat Bay and established base camp near the eastern margin of the Malaspina Glacier. De Filippi estimated the size of this vast piedmont glacier at close to 1500 square miles. Leaving the lush vegetation of the coast on July 1, the climbers spent three difficult days crossing the Malaspina northward to the Seward Glacier. Their supplies, including several "light folding iron bedsteads" destined to be jettisoned early, were hauled on four specially constructed sledges by a crew of porters hired in Seattle.

"If the Malaspina Glacier resembles a placid lake," wrote de Filippi, "the Seward is like a stormy sea." The duke and his party labored six days along the eastern edge of this chaotic jumble of ice. But there were rewards: occasionally, in the rocky valleys next to the ice, they joyfully ascended "couloirs full of snow, and steep grassy inclines" covered with flowers in full bloom. At the top of the icefall, the mountaineers left the Seward Glacier and turned west, their passage dominated more than ever by the bulk of Saint Elias looming over them. Their wild location was described vividly by de Filippi: "On the precipitous flanks of Mount Augusta hang glaciers which look like torrents of frozen foam. Mount St. Elias, clearly in view, looks diminished by the vast proportions of

everything around, and we can scarcely realise its true height. Fantastic clouds curl around the summits. . . ."

On July 12 the party crossed a gentle pass leading to the Agassiz Glacier and reached its junction with the Newton Glacier. The porters were sent back for additional supplies, while the climbers spent the next fifteen days struggling through a maze of crevasses to gain the foot of the col reached by Russell six years earlier. For two weeks the expedition had averaged only half a mile a day. De Filippi's description of their ordeal remains valid today: "Enveloped in a blinding mist, we toiled laboriously through the powdery snow in which we often sunk to our waists, patiently seeking our route among a labyrinth of ice blocks, over insecure ice bridges, amid the deafening roar of the avalanches and the crash of falling stones that resounded almost incessantly on the edges of the glacier."

On July 28 the duke and his men explored a route through the crevasses guarding Russell Col and later established their high camp at the 12,280-foot saddle. Early on the morning of July 31, the weather was clear and cold as they prepared for the long ascent to the summit. Climbing conditions were nearly perfect. "We ascended rapidly," wrote de Filippi, "at an even pace. . . . As the light grew stronger the peaks around us shone

In perfect weather, climbers ascend the Abruzzi Ridge. From Russell Col at the extreme lower left, a thin snow crest leads back toward the summit of 13,810-foot Mount Newton. Twenty miles distant, across the Seward Glacier, is Mount Logan, Canada's highest peak. Lou Reichardt.

like silver. We reached the first rocks, black broken masses of diorite, and, while we skirted about a crooked crevasse above them, sudden gusts of icy N. wind drove the fine snow against our faces." The climbers were excited to be nearing the goal whose defenses had drained their energy for so many weeks. At about 16,000 feet they began to suffer the effects of high altitude, but they continued on. Around noon, de Filippi saw the two lead guides move aside to let the duke step first onto the summit: "In another moment the Italian flag fluttered on an ice axe, and we crowded round our chief to join with all our might in his cheer for Italy and the King."

The climbers descended to their camp in four hours and the following day began to retrace their route to the edge of the Agassiz Glacier, where three days later they were reunited with their porters. On August 10 the victorious party reveled in the perfume of the wildflowers on the shore of Yakutat Bay.

Although Sella was disappointed that many of his photographic plates had been damaged by moisture, the Saint Elias expedition was a remarkable success and was destined to become a classic in the history of mountain exploration. The duke had organized and managed his first major expedition well; later he would visit even more exotic ranges.

Aside from the historic ascent of Mount Logan in 1925, the Saint Elias Mountains were visited infrequently during the decades that followed. Then, in 1946, Mount Saint Elias became the goal of another well-organized expedition. Maynard Miller's climbing party landed in Icy Bay, sixty miles northwest of Yakutat, and relayed loads to an advance base camp below their projected route along the

Mount Saint Elias from the east. The Abruzzi Ridge forms the right skyline. Tim Treacy.

south ridge. Above this camp the climbers received additional supplies by air, which greatly facilitated the establishment of their high camp at 15,600 feet. Miller's team, composed of technically skilled mountaineers from the American Alpine Club, managed to reach the summit under less than optimum conditions: a temperature of zero degrees Fahrenheit and a wind of thirty miles per hour.

Mount Saint Elias was not ascended again until 1964. That year two parties planned to climb the Abruzzi Ridge; both groups approached the mountain from the north, landing

ski-equipped aircraft on the Seward Glacier. The first expedition failed in its attempt to reach Russell Col via the unclimbed north ridge of Mount Newton. A Japanese group, however, negotiated the delicate cornices and ice cliffs that had stopped the earlier party and reached the summit on July 17.

Two important variations on the northern approach to Saint Elias were made by expeditions in 1968 and 1972. These groups traversed over the col between Mount Jeannette and Mount Bering. One complicated and devious route involved a 3000-foot ascent and an equally long descent through difficult and heavily crevassed terrain to reach the Newton Glacier.

The last ascent of Mount Saint Elias via the Abruzzi Ridge was accomplished in 1971 by a group of Canadians using the southern approach. Landing by float plane on a lake just south of the Agassiz Glacier, they moved up the Newton Glacier and, on reaching Russell Col, were hit by a five-day storm that deposited seven feet of snow on the mountain. The climbers started for the summit on July 29, but conditions were such that they were forced to bivouac at 15,300 feet and did not reach the summit until the following day.

Although the use of aircraft, including helicopters, has greatly facilitated the approach to Mount Saint Elias, the mountain has had only ten ascents. Six of these have been on the popular Abruzzi Ridge. While the weather pattern in the Saint Elias Mountains has not improved over the years—storms can last for as long as seven days, with snowfall up to ten feet—climbers seeking to test their skills on great Alaskan peaks will find the duke's 1897 route a rewarding and exciting adventure.

First ascent

Prince Luigi Amedeo of Savoy, Vittorio Sella, Filippo de Filippi, Francesco Gonella, Umberto Cagni, Guiseppe Petigax, Antonio Croux, Antonio Maquignaz, Andrea Pelissier, and Erminio Botta. July 1–31, 1897.

Elevation

The summit is 18,008 feet above sea level.

Time

Three to four weeks from a base camp at Oily Lake.

Maps

For standard southern and northern approaches, USGS quadrangle: Mt. St. Elias, Alaska–Canada, scale 1:250,000. For approaches from Icy Bay, USGS quadrangle: Bering Glacier, scale 1:250,000.

Route description

Charter aircraft can be flown to the northeast corner of Oily Lake from Yakutat, Alaska, fifty-four miles to the southeast. The lake lies between the Malaspina Glacier and the Samovar Hills at an elevation of 1500 feet, and its level fluctuates wildly depending on the outflow through its glacial dam. After crossing a 3700-foot col in the Samovar Hills, descend to the Agassiz Glacier and ascend it to its junction with the Newton Glacier. Proceed up the Newton about a mile beyond its upper icefall at 8500 feet. A camp placed here, just opposite the base of the east ridge, will be relatively free from avalanche danger. To minimize exposure to avalanches sweeping the northeast face of Saint Elias, carry loads to Russell Col during the midnight hours, when conditions are more stable. Keeping close to the prominent north ridge, ascend the remaining 5800 feet to the summit over easy snow and ice.

To descend, retrace the ascent route.

Remarks

Parties who wish to climb in the Saint Elias Mountains must register with park authorities. Information can be obtained from the park warden at Kluane National Park, Haines Junction, Yukon Territory, Canada Y0B 1L0.

Mount Fairweather Carpé Ridge

Mount Fairweather is the northernmost and highest summit in Glacier Bay National Monument. The 15,320-foot mountain lies just fifteen miles from the Pacific Ocean, and the huge Fairweather Glacier that flows along the southern escarpment of the peak reaches to within a half mile of the open sea. Allen Carpé, a member of the first party to climb Fairweather, described the mountain in 1931: "It is an uncommonly beautiful peak, standing clear of its neighbors and head and shoulders above them, its flanks mantled in magnificent glaciers that flow to the ocean. Its highest portion swings aloft in graceful curves from broad, white shoulders, but below these its slopes are formidable."

Although the captain of one of Vitus Bering's ships, the *Saint Paul*, sighted Mount Fairweather in 1741, it was Captain James Cook who named the peak during his voyage along the northwest coast of America in 1778. Cook viewed the mountain under rare and optimum conditions; thus the name he gave it is misleading, belying the continual

cloud layers that hide the Fairweather Range. A modern visitor to the region describes it thus: "The Fairweather Range is subject to tremendous and almost continual snowfall. Avalanches constantly pour off the mountains, sometimes with a deafening roar. . . . From thick icefields flow numerous glaciers, jumbled, active and crevassed. To the west, major glaciers enter the not-so-peaceful Pacific, while to the east they push into the quieter waters of Glacier Bay."

Though prospectors had explored the coastal areas near Mount Fairweather, the approach inland to the mountain was virtually unknown when Canadian climbers Allen Carpé, William Ladd, and Andy Taylor arrived at Juneau in the early summer of 1926. Like several other prominent figures in the history of North American climbing, Carpé had acquired his love for mountaineering during his school years in Germany. All three team members had climbed extensively in Canada, and in 1925 Carpé and Taylor, a Canadian, had participated in the impressive first ascent of Mount Logan.

Carpé's group traveled by power launch from Juneau north to Lituya Bay, a beautiful natural harbor on the otherwise unbroken coast. On June 1 their small launch landed at a tiny cove north of Cape Fairweather, and the climbers began the laborious trek toward the west ridge of Mount

Two climbers ascend a rocky buttress on the middle section of the ridge, leading to the south shoulder.
David Coombs.

Fairweather. After crossing low, timbered hills to reach the glacial ice, they became the first explorers to enter Fairweather's icy wilderness. The team spent several days working slowly up a complicated icefall that led to a deep notch in the ridge crest at 9200 feet. Here they were stopped by the difficulty of the climbing and their dwindling supplies. The three climbers reluctantly abandoned their attempt and began the retreat to Cape Fairweather to await the return of their launch. Ladd, a physician from New

York, was especially impressed with their exploratory expedition: "Fairweather is a glorious mountain," he wrote, "the most beautiful, the most fascinating, the most difficult mountain problem I have tackled." Five years were to pass before the men returned to this marvelous mountain.

The second attempt to climb Fairweather was made in 1930, when Bradford Washburn was encouraged by climbing friends to attempt the formidable west ridge. Assembling a group of his Harvard classmates, Washburn began organizing the first of his many expeditions. Since their boat was unable to land at Cape Fairweather because of heavy seas, the youthful climbers were forced to hike to Fairweather from Lituya Bay. Unfortunately, Washburn chose a difficult approach along a glacial valley paralleling the coast; the approach consumed so much valuable time that the climbers reached only 6700 feet on the west ridge before being compelled to retreat. Their expedition, however, provided much new information about the region, and maps of the area were greatly improved.

The growing interest in Mount Fairweather prodded Carpé, Ladd, and Taylor into returning for another attempt, and they landed at Lituya Bay on April 18, 1931. This time

◀ *The south face of Mount Fairweather.* Boston Museum of Science photo by Bradford Washburn.

they were accompanied by Terris Moore, a young climber with whom Taylor and Carpé had climbed the 16,420-foot Mount Bona the previous year. Heavy seas again prevented a landing at the Cape. Avoiding Washburn's interior valley, the four climbers began relaying loads thirteen miles up the coastline to the broad Fairweather Glacier. Carpé described the difficulties: "Ladd and Taylor now spent two days cutting a path through a vile thicket of alders and scrub growing at first on the moraine, then in loose surface débris overlying the live ice." The expedition eventually reached compact, white ice, and the interminable relaying of loads became easier. Five weeks after their departure from Lituya Bay the climbers set up camp on a snow-covered area behind a moraine at the 2000-foot level.

At this point the four mountaineers decided that the most promising route to the summit lay on the mountain's south side, so they turned east and started moving supplies up the Fairweather Glacier. On May 24 base camp was established at 5000 feet. Although rain and fog had accompanied their travels for most of May, on this day the mountain lived up to its name. Beyond their camp a dark crest of rock rose out of the ice, soaring to the summit 10,000 feet above. Carpé was elated: "It seemed to me that this was altogether the most beautiful place I had ever seen; but I confess to that perennial impression."

Food supplies were becoming alarmingly low, so it was necessary to move quickly. The weather remained stable, and at 9000 feet the team established a high camp on a small shoulder of the forty-degree ridge. On May 26 the climbers were in position for a summit attempt, but a sudden snowsquall forced them to retreat to base camp. Heavy snowfall persisted over a six-day period, compelling the men to clear their tents frequently to save the camp from burial. When the storm ended late on May 31, cold, arctic air swept down on the Fairweather Range. Carpé recalled the change of mood: "Northern lights flared through the pale half-light of the Alaskan night. The morning of June 1 was gorgeous: warm sun, a few high clouds drifting lazily, snow and mist blowing off the ridges. . . . Avalanches thundered on all sides."

The four climbers regained their high camp on June 2 and started for the summit at midnight. A biting wind arose as they ascended the steepening arête below the prominent south shoulder. Ladd cut steps across a steep ice face, and soon the group stood on the broad shoulder. The men gazed at the summit pyramid, whose "twisting cracks and strange extruded masses emphasized by the slanting light" were illuminated by the rising sun. Carpé and his companions moved across the broad crest to the base of the pyramid and started up the summit crest as cirrus clouds began moving in quickly from the southeast. Moore, who was leading, began the laborious task of cutting steps up a steep ice bulge, now known as the Ice Nose, on the ridge, while a cloud cap was forming on nearby Mount Crillon. By the time Moore had finished his pitch, Fairweather also was enveloped in the burgeoning storm. With visibility reduced to a few yards, the climbers' hopes for the summit that loomed so close were crushed, and the four men desperately retreated to the shoulder, where they followed their willow markers back to high camp.

Since the storm seemed likely to continue, Ladd and Taylor decided to retreat to base camp so their friends would have a better chance for the summit. With their food reserves thus doubled, Carpé and Moore waited out the storm and on the evening of June 7 decided to make one last effort to reach the summit. The ascent to the south shoulder through the freshly fallen snow was much more arduous than it had been four days earlier. On the ridge crest beyond, the climbers were amazed to find newly formed cornices where before there had been only firm crust. The sky was clear as they reached the Ice Nose, which they climbed easily by clearing the snow from their previously cut steps. After threading through a series of beautiful, wind-sculpted ice turrets, they arrived at the top in a bitterly cold wind. Carpé and Moore enjoyed the rare privilege of viewing the ocean's crashing surf from their lofty Alaskan summit. The two climbers slowly began the

long descent to high camp, then to base camp, not yet comprehending that they had climbed the most demanding and technical route yet done in North America.

Mount Fairweather remained unvisited for the next twenty-seven years. Then, in 1958, a Canadian expedition was organized to repeat Carpé's route on the peak. The venture was part of a centennial celebration for the province of British Columbia, and the expedition flew to its base of operations at Lituya Bay courtesy of the Royal Canadian Air Force. The eight-man party, led by Paddy Sherman, departed Lituya Bay on June 18, leaving their headquarters in charge of two radio operators. The first day's trek along the coast to Fairweather Glacier followed well-used bear and prospector trails through patches of flowers and wild strawberries. Once on the glacier the expedition moved quickly to the 4500-foot level. Here, a base camp was established on June 22, and the climbers picked up additional supplies that had been dropped by parachute.

Conditions on the mountain were far different from those in 1931. Light winter snows had left much of the lower ridge exposed, and there was extreme rockfall danger. Where Moore had indicated easy snow traverses, the present group discovered chaotic icefalls and crumbling rock. Nonetheless, the expedition split into two groups which reached the summit independently on June 26 and 27—the remarkable ascents had required only five days from

The summit of Mount Fairweather as seen from 12,500 feet during an ascent to the south shoulder, at the right. The Ice Nose is the steep, icy crest just below the top.
David Coombs.

base camp. The climbers returned to Lituya Bay on the afternoon of July 9, at which point the decision to have radio operators manage their camp assumed a fateful importance.

On contacting Juneau, Sherman learned that since coastal fog would prevent the scheduled pickup the following morning, their pilot was coming to get them that evening. An hour after their departure from

Lituya, a tremendous earthquake shook the Fairweather region, dislodging ninety million tons of rock into Lituya Bay. The resulting 100-foot wave scoured a nearby bluff to an elevation of 1700 feet, stripping the heavily timbered base camp area to bedrock.

The Fairweather Fault has remained quiet since then, and mountaineers still use beautiful Lituya Bay as a point of departure for Mount Fairweather. There have been only eight ascents of the peak; four of these have been over new routes pioneered since the 1958 Canadian expedition. The fourth ascent of the challenging Carpé Ridge was made in 1976, when two strong climbers reached the summit in twenty-eight hours from a base camp on Fairweather Glacier.

Because of the ban on ski landings and air drops within the boundaries of Glacier Bay National Monument, present-day climbers have the opportunity to enter a glacial wilderness that has changed little since the arrival of the first explorers in the region more than two hundred years ago.

First ascent

Allen Carpé and Terris Moore. April 18 – June 8, 1931.

Elevation

The summit is 15,320 feet above sea level.

Time

Five to eight days after establishing base camp.

Maps

USGS quadrangles: Mount Fairweather, scale 1:250,000; Mount Fairweather—D-5 and D-6, scale 1:63,360.

Route description

Aircraft can be chartered in Juneau for the flight to Cape Fairweather. From the landing site follow the Fairweather Glacier for approximately fifteen miles to a base camp opposite the foot of the Carpé Ridge at the 5000-foot level. Ascend the 40-degree ridge to a prominent shoulder at 13,800 feet, climbing first on rock and ice and later mostly on ice. From the shoulder, climb half a mile to the base of the summit pyramid. About 600 feet below the summit, an ice bulge—now known as the Ice Nose—can be passed in two leads in a gully on the left. Above this obstacle, follow the ridge to the summit.

The leader struggles against fierce winds as he encounters the first difficulties of the Ice Nose pitches. David Coombs.

Remarks

Regulations established by Glacier Bay National Monument forbid ski landings and air drops within monument boundaries. Expeditions to climb Mount Fairweather must be registered with park authorities. For information, write to Glacier Bay National Monument, Box 1089, Juneau, Alaska 99801.

Mount Hunter
West Ridge

3

The Alaska Range, located 150 miles north of the port city of Anchorage, extends across the forty-ninth state in a broad arc. The range is split into two sections by the Nenana River Valley, through which pass the Alaska Railway and the new George Parks Highway, both heading north to their destination in Fairbanks. The Mount Hayes group lies east of the Nenana; to the west of the valley, extending nearly 150 miles toward the Aleutian Peninsula, lies the magnificent McKinley Range. This group of subarctic mountains, whose highest summit is the 20,320-foot Mount McKinley, is exposed to the fury of storms coming up from the Gulf of Alaska. The resulting summer snowfall sustains a vast glacial system whose southern lobes extend more than forty miles toward the sea.

◀ *The west ridge of Mount Hunter. Brian Okonek.*

Clustered around McKinley are many smaller peaks of intensely beautiful character. Mount Hunter, whose elevation of 14,570 feet renders it the third highest peak in the Alaska Range, is one of these remarkable mountains. Its twin summits are separated by an icefield two miles long, and no easy route leads to this isolated plateau. Many of Hunter's ridges are long and heavily corniced, while its 5000-foot faces are swept by avalanches and collapsing séracs from hanging glaciers on the fringes of the ice plateau.

In 1954 Mount Hunter was the highest unclimbed peak in the range and curiously had never been attempted. Its isolated position in relatively unknown country nine miles south of McKinley meant that approaches to its ridges and faces would be lengthy and difficult. Hence, exploration of the peak was neglected while climbing interest was focused on its lofty neighbor to the north.

No individual was more directly involved with the exploration of the McKinley Range than Bradford Washburn, whose aerial-photo surveys between 1936 and 1938 were merely the beginning of a lifelong fascination with this great range. Washburn was a skilled mountaineer whose later predictions for new lines on important peaks of the range were unprecedented in climbing literature. In 1953 he wrote an unusual article for the *American Alpine Journal* entitled: "Mount Hunter Via the West Ridge, a Pro-

posed Ascent." Relying mainly on his remarkably clear photographs, Washburn described the untouched route up the five-mile-long ridge in painstaking detail, enumerating the many obstacles that might befall a potential climber along the way.

Having described the route so expertly, Washburn—who seemed to enjoy his mountaineering in a safer, more vicarious form—expected that the appropriate climbers inevitably would appear. On June 29, 1954, a small airplane landed on the smooth surface of the Kahiltna Glacier near Mount Hunter. On board the plane were Fred Beckey, Henry Meybohm, and Heinrich Harrer, a group fresh from the first ascent of Mount Deborah, an exquisite 12,540-foot peak in the Hayes group. As the plane flew down the glacier, neither the climbers nor the pilot could have dreamed that mountaineering activity in the McKinley area would become so intense in the next few years. On this day, however, the party was entirely alone, each member engaged with the chores of setting up base camp. Less than half a mile distant, and sweeping upward in long, graceful undulations, rose the snow-laden west ridge of Mount Hunter. Beckey and Meybohm conferred about the initial difficulties of the ridge while Harrer went over his equipment list to be sure nothing had been left behind. Harrer was still thinking about the chance meeting with Beckey in Fairbanks which resulted in the Deborah climb and the plan to attempt the unclimbed Hunter. Harrer already had achieved fame for participating in the 1938 ascent of the north face of the Eiger, a bold and dangerous adventure he had sought not only for its own sake but also in the hope (eventually fulfilled) of being selected for the Nanga Parbat reconnaissance expedition in 1939.

On June 30 the three climbers set off to explore the initial part of the route chosen by Beckey and Meybohm. They climbed a headwall of a nearby glacier, traversed along a ridge crest, and then reached a col, passing a rock tower whose probable difficulties had been described carefully by Washburn. The men cached some supplies at the col before retracing their route to base camp.

On July 1, carrying minimum gear and food for eight days, the three men set off toward the summit. On regaining the col, they added the cache supplies to their packs; so it was with great effort that they climbed a short, vertical snow wall near a rounded shoulder on the ridge. From here the climbers cut steps in the ice during their descent to another col, where they built a platform for their first camp. With the first third of the ridge behind them, the trio considered the problems presented by a 500-foot rocky spine that rose just beyond their tent, exploring this complex and difficult section in the late afternoon snow flurry. After leaving fixed lines to facilitate their advance the following morning, the three men returned to camp.

Since Beckey distrusted the unstable surface snow, the group adopted a strategy common in northern latitudes: sleeping during the day and climbing by night, when the snow is firmly crusted. Ample light was available for evening climbing, for the sky was suffused with a soft twilight during the sun's brief passage below the horizon. The climbers remained in their tent for much of the next day as the sun angled toward the horizon; then they moved up the fixed lines and began climbing on a level section of ridge interrupted by several steep ice pitches. It was a beautiful, quiet evening, and the last rays of the sun cast a reddish-orange glow across the cornices. Beckey led through knee-deep snow on the heavily corniced ridge, carefully keeping below the fracture zone. Suddenly a large section of cornice soundlessly disappeared from his view. As the ice and snow plummeted to the glacier thousands of feet below, the muted roar of fragmentation reached Beckey's ears. This unsettling experience halted further climbing, and the three men decided to place a camp on a safe, level portion of the ridge well beyond the danger zone.

Beckey's ability to deal with such hazards came from nearly fifteen years of mountaineering experience. He was most interested in the alpine

Climbers wait at the base of the steep, rocky arête near Peak 9550 while ropes are maneuvered for pack hauling. Brian Okonek.

aspects of mountaineering, in which ice and snow are the principal elements. He also delighted in the unpredictable aspects of climbing; he and his brother, Helmy, had startled North American climbers when in 1942, as teenagers, they made the audacious second ascent of the south face of Mount Waddington, in British Columbia. Beckey's legendary energy in seeking new routes and first ascents on his beloved Cascade peaks could only be described as irrepressible.

The three mountaineers rested in camp for much of the following day and began their summit push in late afternoon. "The long and very exposed ice slope rising from 10,700 feet to 11,500 feet proved the most difficult on the climb," Beckey wrote later. "The surface was unstable, and to climb safely we had to place ice pitons and chop bucket belay stances 13 separate times. . . . Beyond came more cornices, steep and short ice pitches, followed again by still more cornices. . . . Above was the great ice wall blocking the ridge off from the 13,200-foot upper plateau, and beneath it tumbled an array of crevasses in every direction."

The ice wall was the most crucial part of the climb, for as Washburn had noted, an insidious combination of snow conditions and crevasse orientation could easily make the barrier impassable. As Beckey and his friends approached the fractured wall, they were overjoyed to find a slender passage along the sloping edge of a monstrous crevasse that led them to an easier track threading through ice blocks. They plodded across the knee-deep snows of the plateau and reached the summit "in the glorious radiance of the full morning sunshine." The three climbers lingered briefly on the summit, savoring the magnificent panorama of peaks and glaciers that surrounded them, and then began their descent. On returning to their high

Two Mount Hunter climbers approach the steep ice pitches of Peak 10,800, midway along the ridge. Brian Okonek.

camp, the trio rested fitfully and then retraced their route along the ridge by evening light. It was midday when they finally reached their base camp on the level plain of the Kahiltna Glacier.

It is difficult to ascribe the origin of a new mountaineering trend to any one particular climb; yet the ascent of Mount Hunter demonstrated a committing type of mountaineering (later to be called alpine-style climbing) that was quite advanced for its time. Previously, it had been considered too dangerous to under-

take the traverse of lengthy, corniced ridges, for there was very little first-hand knowledge available concerning the fragile nature of these remarkable formations. The first ascent of Mount Hunter was a brilliant climb, accomplished in a manner that set new standards for climbing in subarctic regions.

First ascent

Fred Beckey, Henry Meybohm, and Heinrich Harrer. July 1–5, 1954.

Elevation

The summit is 14,570 feet above sea level.

Time

Seven to ten days, depending on snow and weather conditions.

Maps

Boston Museum of Science: Mount McKinley, Alaska, scale 1:50,000. USGS quadrangle: Talkeetna D-3, scale 1:63,360.

Route description

Climbers use a charter air service in Talkeetna for the seventy-five-mile flight to the Kahiltna Glacier at the foot of Mount Hunter. From here, there are several ways to reach the crest of the west ridge at 9100 feet. The difficulties can be assessed properly only after a reconnaissance of the small glaciers that lead up to the broad ridge crest.

Climb along the ridge crest and traverse over a small tower by climbing through a blocky area and then making three rappels to a col at the eastern side of the tower. Moderate climbing on snow and ice leads up and across Peak 9550 to a tiny col just below a 500-foot arête that is very steep, narrow, and rocky.

Climb the arête; then follow a snow crest which offers moderate climbing, including two steep and difficult ice pitches at about 10,000 and 10,600 feet. Next, proceed along the level, corniced ridge for almost a mile, passing over a difficult ice pitch to surmount Peak 10,800 along the way. A good camp can be placed safely at either side of this gentle dome.

The next 700 feet entail difficult and exposed ice climbing. A crest becomes a broad snow ridge that steepens into an ice arête just before merging into the final sérac barrier guarding the summit plateau. The conditions of the séracs and crevasses here vary with each season; the way through these obstacles may be easy or extremely difficult. Once past this barrier, a half-mile walk across the plateau takes one to the summit pyramid, which is climbed via its west face or southwest ridge.

The descent is made by rappelling and downclimbing the ascent route.

Remarks

Climbers who arrive in early May generally find stable snow conditions but low temperatures. Those who climb in July experience warmer temperatures and deteriorating snow conditions on south- and west-facing slopes below 12,000 feet. The route is ideally suited to an alpine-style ascent, even to the extent of using snow caves rather than tents for shelter.

A mountaineer pauses on the last section of steep ice before the west ridge merges with the sérac barrier guarding the summit plateau. Mike Kennedy.

Mount Hunter lies within the newly created Denali National Monument, and those who plan to climb the peak must register with park authorities. A pamphlet outlining requirements can be obtained from Mount McKinley National Park, Box 9, Mount McKinley, Alaska 99755.

Mount McKinley
Cassin Ridge

From the conception of a great expeditionary route to its creation lies a vast network of human thought and activity. There is an arduous battle with paperwork and logistics, as well as the acquisition of funds and their ultimate disbursement. A growing mass of file folders subdues the spirit until it can be revived by the unfolding kinesthetic delight of the ascent itself. If the game has been played well, humans ultimately stand on a strangely anticlimactic summit, clinically observing the ice ridge or granite wall they have just climbed. Their mountain was an anonymous entity until given human perspective by their presence. Mountains are "façades without shape or dimension until they are flood-lit by human effort," as the English climber Harold Drasdo has so poetically described them.

The south buttress of Mount McKinley, which leads directly to the 20,320-foot summit, the highest point in North America, was such a façade until the publication of the 1956–57 volume of *The Mountain World.* Appearing in this volume is

a comprehensive article on Mount McKinley by Bradford Washburn, the celebrated geographer and Alaskan explorer. Toward the conclusion of his essay, Washburn outlined possibilities for several new and difficult lines to the summit of McKinley. Among the proposed routes were two lines on the seldom-visited south side of the peak: the western rib of the south face and the south buttress, an immense spine of granite and ice rising abruptly from the eastern and northeastern forks of the Kahiltna Glacier. Washburn's comment on the latter route was brief and exciting: "Probably the most difficult and dramatic of all potential new routes on Mount McKinley is the great central bulge on the fabulous 10,000-foot South Face of the mountain . . . . This route may be classed as unequivocally excellent climbing from start to finish."

At the time Washburn's article was written, only twelve ascents via four different routes had been made of McKinley's main summit. Exploratory mountaineering was proceeding slowly, for the peak was so massive and the approaches so difficult that trying a new route was a costly and complex undertaking. Another limiting factor was the horrendous weather—climbers had little enthusiasm for living under the appalling conditions imposed by the subarctic environment—and the lack of lightweight equipment to handle it. Washburn suggested that climbing

Ascending the lower section of the slender Japanese Couloir. Chas Macquarie.

McKinley is much like a polar expedition, but in three dimensions. Storms driven by the cold and demoniacal winds were so persistent that out of any fifteen-day period there might be no more than twelve consecutive hours of clear weather. Because of these conditions, McKinley is equivalent to a 23,000-foot peak in the Himalayas. How does one climb a mountain under such conditions? "The best climbing strategy," wrote Washburn, "has always proved to be to maneuver one's party as high as humanly possible in bad or mediocre weather; then to move *fast* both up and down when the clear break comes."

Reaction to Washburn's exciting list of proposed routes was not long in coming. In June of 1959, a group of young Teton guides with modest alpine experience climbed the peak via the western rib, but no American climbers came forward to explore the challenging "central bulge." The Italian Alpine Club, however, at the suggestion of Piero Ghiglione, a well-traveled explorer and alpinist, already had become interested in sending an expedition to Alaska. Carlo Mauri, a talented young mountaineer and alpine guide, was placed in charge of planning, and he immediately enlisted the aid of his old friend and mentor, Riccardo Cassin, then in his early fifties. Cassin and Mauri had participated in the successful 1958 expedition to Gasherbrum IV, one of the 26,000-foot giants in the Karakoram Range. The Italian Alpine Club eventually invited Cassin to lead the Alaskan expedition.

Cassin had come a long way since the days in the mid-1930s when he and his friends had been the first to climb three of the great north-face routes in the Alps: the Grandes Jorasses, Piz Badile, and the Cima Ovest di Lavaredo. All three were bold and dangerous climbs which assured Cassin a place in Alpine

The south face of Mount McKinley. Cassin Ridge is the conspicuous ridge which rises directly from the foreground to the summit.
Boston Museum of Science photo by Bradford Washburn.

history. Cassin's calm, patient nature, matched by his intelligence, had made him a natural choice for leadership of the 1958 Gasherbrum IV expedition. Fosco Maraini, a companion of Cassin's on this expedition, spoke of his friend in a most poetic way: "There is something indestructible about this man; paleolithic and Neanderthalish. Climbing with him you sense an inner force utterly alien to our complicated, mechanized, intellectualized world . . . a supreme and subtle contact with rocks and sky, with ice and wind. Any Zen master would claim him as one of his own."

In consultation with Washburn, and at his suggestion, Cassin and his friends chose the south buttress of McKinley as their objective, and the long struggle with logistics began. By May 1961 preliminary planning had been completed; by late June the party of six Italians had established their base camp on the east fork of the Kahiltna Glacier, at the foot of the buttress. With Cassin were five young and enthusiastic climbers from the Lecco section of the Italian Alpine Club: Annibale Zucchi, Gigi Alippi, Luigi Airoldi, Giancarlo Canali, and Romano Perego. Only Cassin and Canali were experienced in high-altitude climbing. Ironically, at the last moment Mauri suffered a serious skiing accident and was unable to participate in the climb.

Only a few hundred yards beyond the team's base camp, the south buttress rose above the glacier in sweeping, graceful steps. An immediate problem at the very base of the buttress was an 800-foot series of huge, rocky towers leading to a small hanging glacier. The cliffs above were connected by ice-choked couloirs, snowfields, and granite crests—a perilous 9000-foot climb to the highest summit in North America.

Cassin's plan for the establishment of high camps on McKinley followed classic expeditionary strategy. To acclimatize, climbers would carry high and sleep low. Camps would remain in position until the ascent was completed or the ridge abandoned. While one rope of three climbers explored the route, the other three would transport food and equipment. All of them would return frequently to their base camp for a welcome rest.

After nearly ten days, the extremely difficult passage through the initial towers was completed, and Camp I was set up on a tiny snow shelf at 13,400 feet. The next day Camp II was placed on an ample platform at the bottom of the hanging glacier. Progress seemed slow, but on a first ascent of such magnitude the team realized that reconnaissance would consume too much valuable time. There was no prior information indicating the best way to proceed; with constant storms and low visibility delaying their advance, days would go by with little activity.

On July 16 the umbilical cord to base camp was cut, and, in worsening weather, the climbers committed themselves to the ridge. Snow was falling heavily as the group reached Camp II. Surprisingly, a day of clear weather enabled the team to establish and occupy Camp III, their highest camp, at an elevation close to 17,000 feet. Fixed lines had been placed on all the difficult sections to facilitate both the ascent as well as the eventual retreat.

Early on the morning of July 19, the six mountaineers began their epic journey to the summit in two ropes of three climbers each. Although the day was clear, a cold wind scoured the slopes as the two groups found their way through the unknown and difficult terrain above Camp III. After seventeen hours the climbers staggered onto the summit in the subarctic gloom. The altitude had weakened Canali, who also complained of cold feet. "Driven by a hard, desperately cold wind," Cassin wrote later, "gusts of very fine snow continually lash us furiously and penetrate every opening in our clothing." The men felt little joy in the conquest; even their speech had congealed. Canali's feet had started to freeze, and it was imperative to begin the descent.

The six climbers struggled down the ridge, rappelling the difficult sections. Canali, suffering from altitude sickness, his feet useless, fell at one point and was stopped only by the quick reaction of Cassin. It was a forlorn group that finally reached the safety of Camp III, nearly twenty-four hours after leaving it. It was, however, a minor victory, for the group now faced the more difficult task of guiding their injured friend down the remaining 6000 feet. Canali's obscenely swollen feet no longer fit into his climbing boots, so Alippi sacrificed his boots, using extra socks inside his bootcovers to protect his own feet. A storm enveloped the south side of McKinley as the two groups, after a brief rest at Camp III, resumed the descent. Alippi, unable to wear crampons, continually slipped on the steep snow. Even Cassin noticed a loss of feeling in his feet as the exhausted climbers made their way to Camp II. Alippi could go no farther, so he and his ropemates remained at Camp II while Cassin and Zucchi, realizing that they must get Canali to base camp as quickly as possible, immediately left for Camp I, reaching it that night.

The following morning, as the fury of the storm increased, Cassin and his companions began the arduous task of descending the fixed lines through the rock towers, finally reaching the last obstacle, the dangerous couloir leading down to the glacier. Hanging on the fixed lines in the middle of this claustrophobic ice funnel, they were overwhelmed by a powder-snow avalanche, which miraculously did not sweep them away. At last, literally swimming through the porous snow, they reached base camp, and Alippi's group appeared through the mist

A climber at 13,600 feet, between the top of the Japanese Couloir and the prominent hanging glacier on the ridge. Chas Macquarie.

on the following day. Fortune smiled on Canali, for two days later the weather cleared sufficiently for an aircraft to land at a site farther down the glacier. Canali was transported to an Anchorage hospital, where his toes were saved by timely and expert treatment.

It was a joyous group that was re-united in Anchorage to receive the telegraphed congratulations of President Kennedy and the frenzied attention of *Life* photographers. It was, Maraini wrote later, "Another feather in the cap of the old Neanderthal bear!" The Italians had made the most sustained and difficult ascent yet accomplished on Mount McKinley. Underestimating the severity of the weather, they had dared to use clothing and boots designed for alpine conditions; yet the wisdom and skill of Cassin, together with the courage and enormous determination of the entire group, had brought them all back unscathed.

The Cassin Ridge, as it became known, was not climbed again until 1967, when ascents were made by a Japanese and an American party. The Japanese, first on the mountain that season, made an important variation in the route: the Hidden, or Japanese, Couloir, which is used now by all parties since it bypasses the difficult rock towers leading up to Cassin's Camp I. The fourth ascent was made by a French party, and with another successful Japanese ascent in 1974, the expeditionary approach to the Cassin Ridge ended. Future ascents would be made alpine-style and would involve a much greater commitment.

On an alpine-style ascent, in contrast to the expeditionary approach, only one camp is placed, and it is located wherever the climbers happen to be on the route. As the climbers ascend, the camp moves with

Two climbers in a snow gully at 15,500 feet. Gary Fredrickson.

them. No support remains below—neither the sanctuary of a lower camp nor a series of fixed lines. The expedition becomes committed either to the summit or to a long and dangerous retreat.

The first alpine-style ascent of the Cassin Ridge was made in June of 1976. Four British mountaineers reached the summit in a rapid, six-day climb and, after a brief rest, descended to a camp at 12,000 feet on the West Buttress Route the same day. However, of the thirty-two climbers who attempted the Cassin that summer, only twelve reached the summit. The most outstanding ascent was Charlie Porter's solo alpine-style climb, which demanded the utmost in attentive mountaineering. Porter, known for his audacious big-wall climbing in Yosemite Val-

ley, reached the summit ridge in a thirty-six-hour effort from a bivouac at the top of the Japanese Couloir. He found a profusion of abandoned fixed lines in the couloir—so many, in fact, that climbers no longer would face the route in its original state.

As modern mountaineers approach the Cassin Ridge in alpine style, they know that their climb might entail all the anxieties and disasters, as well as the triumphs, that Mount McKinley has to offer. Standing at the base of the impressive south buttress, they are mindful of those who have passed there before, especially the original architect of the climb, Riccardo Cassin, the man most responsible for casting the floodlight of human effort onto McKinley's southern façade.

First ascent

Riccardo Cassin, Gigi Alippi, Luigi Airoldi, Giancarlo Canali, Romano Perego, and Annibale Zucchi. June 27–July 19, 1961.

Elevation

The summit is 20,320 feet above sea level.

Time

Expeditions have taken from six to twenty days to ascend the Cassin Ridge, not taking into consideration the time necessary to establish base camp and to return there after making the ascent. Round-trip times from Talkeetna have taken from twenty-one to thirty-five days.

Map

Boston Museum of Science: Mount McKinley, Alaska, scale 1:50,000.

Useful reference

Mount McKinley Climber's Guide.

Route description

The usual approach to the south side of Mount McKinley is by charter air service from the town of Talkeetna, located 113 miles north of Anchorage on the George Parks Highway. (Talkeetna also can be reached via the Alaska Railroad.) From the landing site on the southeast fork of the Kahiltna Glacier, proceed to the upper part of the east fork and establish base camp at about 11,200 feet. Ascend the prominent couloir containing a steep, narrow ice funnel to Kahiltna Notch and climb east several leads on the level snow crest close to the base of the south buttress. Rappel about 300 feet to the bergschrund at the head of the northeast fork of the Kahiltna Glacier and traverse four leads to the base of the Japanese Couloir. The couloir, considered by most climbers to be the most difficult part of the route, is subject to ice- and rockfall and gains nearly 1000 feet in elevation. It also contains many fixed lines left by previous parties. Without the lines, the couloir presents eleven pitches of hard climbing, varying from pure ice to pure rock, depending on conditions.

From the top of the Japanese Couloir at 13,400 feet, move up and right over mixed ice and rock for two leads to a narrow rock couloir. Climb the couloir and upon reaching a narrow snow ridge, ascend to the prominent glacier and the best campsite on the climb (14,000 feet). Continue up the glacier and climb a ramp of ice and rock, bearing right for 300 feet; then climb directly upward for 700 feet to the base of a rock rib, the most difficult individual lead on the climb. Follow the ridge above the rib to easier terrain at 15,700 feet.

Bearing left, climb easy snow and rock to a steep rock barrier and ascend a nearly hidden rock couloir for 300 feet. Next, traverse about 1000 feet right to a prominent snowfield just to the left of the hanging glacier on the south face. Climb the snowfield, regaining the crest at about 17,400 feet. Ascend easy, mixed terrain to the base of the final buttress, where a system of snow couloirs leading left is followed to the summit crest at about 19,500 feet. Easy walking leads to the summit.

If the ascent is made alpine-style, the descent normally is via the easy West Buttress Route back to the landing site. If not, the more demanding and difficult descent of the Cassin itself must be undertaken. The Italian team employed three camps above base camp; the French group, only two. The condition of the route and the skill of the party dictate the location of camps.

Remarks

Permission to ascend Mount McKinley must be obtained from the National Park Service; expedition leaders are advised to contact park officials well in advance of their departure date. A detailed pamphlet outlining climbing regulations can be obtained from the National Park Service, Mount McKinley National Park, Box 9, Mount McKinley, Alaska 99755.

Moose's Tooth West Ridge

At the modest elevation of 10,335 feet, the Moose's Tooth lies in isolated splendor above the vast plain of the Ruth Amphitheater. This twelve-mile-square desert of ice near Mount McKinley is the temporary reservoir for virtually all the ice and snow flowing from the southeast side of McKinley. At the basin's southern edge the ice surges between the mile-wide walls of the spectacular Ruth Gorge on the journey to its terminus twenty-five miles to the south.

The Moose's Tooth, located just east of the entrance to Ruth Gorge, possesses a topography so convoluted that it presents remarkably different aspects when viewed from the four points of the compass. The mile-wide southern escarpment is a sheer, solid wall broken by several couloirs rising nearly 3000 feet from a small glacial basin. Just beneath the summit is the 9700-foot south col, which forms an impassable barrier between the west side of the mountain and the immense eastern cliffs, where the face towers some 4600 feet above the Buckskin Glacier. On its northern flank the

The southwest face of the Moose's Tooth. From the left, the route ascends to the rounded west summit, then traverses down to the Englishmen's Col and over to the sharply pointed main summit.   Bradford Washburn.

character of the peak changes dramatically, for there its granite core is covered with ice flutings that rise above a large hanging glacier. Above the flutings lie the delicately balanced cornices of the formidable west ridge, which extends from the summit nearly a mile to the western cusp before plunging abruptly toward Ruth Gorge.

The first attempt on the Moose's Tooth took place in July of 1962. Britishers Tony Smythe, son of the well-known author and climber

Frank Smythe, and Barrie Biven had met for the first time a few months earlier in a fish-and-chips cafe in Bristol and within twenty minutes were discussing the possibility of an Alaskan climb. A specific goal didn't matter at this point; it was the adventure of climbing in such a distant and isolated range that attracted the young men. After their arrival in Talkeetna, the two met Don Sheldon, a well-known local pilot, who mentioned an impressive unclimbed peak adjacent to the fantastic Ruth Gorge. Deciding to pursue Sheldon's suggestion, the naive climbers boarded his Cessna. As they approached the Moose's

Tooth, Sheldon banked the plane steeply so that the pair could view the possible routes. Smythe dismissed the 600-foot buttress above the south col as too difficult. Since the east and south faces were unthinkable, the west ridge seemed their only choice, and the climbers directed Sheldon to land close to its base.

The resplendent western summit of the Moose's Tooth loomed above their base camp, and the two climbers could see that the initial part of the route would involve ascending a short icefall to gain the broad snowslopes of the lower part of the ridge. A steeper portion leading to the lower, western summit—they could not see the cornices of the mile-long section of ridge that led east to the main summit—consisted of a beautiful snow arête supported by rock bands and ice flutings.

On July 5, climbing in the cool twilight hours, Smythe and Biven ascended the icefall and placed a camp on a rounded snow crest at 6500 feet. That evening they set out toward the summit, but a sudden snowsquall forced them into an uncomfortable bivouac. The following morning the sky was crystal-clear, and the two men were able to climb over the western summit and move

◀ *The north face of the Moose's Tooth. The West Ridge Route follows the right skyline.* Boston Museum of Science photo by Bradford Washburn.

along wondrous cornices to a huge gap in the crest. Beyond lay a series of wind-scoured cornices and delicate furrows whose apparent fragility forced Smythe and Biven to think of little else but a hasty retreat. Two days later the climbers were back on Ruth Glacier.

The Britishers' alpine-style attempt had been ambitious but naive, and their defeat can be attributed primarily to a lack of experience on heavily corniced Alaskan ridges. Soon the Moose's Tooth began to attract considerable mountaineering interest, and climbers saw the mountain as a highly desirable objective.

In May 1964, an experienced team of German mountaineers—Walter Welsch, Klaus Bierl, Arnold Hasenkopf, and Alfons Reichegger —arrived at the Moose's Tooth. The party had been flown in by the ubiquitous Don Sheldon, who also had transported Lionel Terray's French team for an attempt on the unclimbed Mount Huntington. Welsch, the group's leader, had become interested in Alaskan mountaineering after reading about previous expeditions.

Technically skilled on both rock and ice, the Germans first attempted to climb the Moose's Tooth from the easily reached south col, the route that had been rejected by Smythe and Biven in 1962. However, after establishing a camp on the col, the climbers found the rock so steep and frost-shattered that they abandoned the route and decided to attempt the

west ridge. Transferring their supplies back to base camp, they discovered that another party had arrived on Ruth Glacier. The meeting with American climbers Fred Beckey, Eric Bjornstad, and Robert Baker was cautiously congenial. As the rival parties discussed their respective strategies, it was agreed that the ascent could be carried out jointly, with one important condition: the Germans would make their summit bid first.

Traveling light, the German and American climbers established their camp on the west ridge at the 7900-foot level, 1400 feet higher than the British high camp. The weather during this period was remarkably stable. The sun was low on the horizon as the four Germans, in two separate teams, started for the summit on June 1; the American climbers would follow later. With Bierl and Hasenkopf leading, the two teams traversed to the couloir leading upward to the ridge crest. There was a sense of urgency in their movements, for they were climbing on a strange and unknown peak in an isolated range. The uncertainty, the danger that surrounded them, filled them with an excitement which they knew must be tempered with caution.

On the ascent to the western summit the Germans entered the region of the great cornices, where it was imperative to belay carefully. The unstable layer of snow on the steepening ice caused them difficulties.

After reaching the western summit, they traversed easily to the gap they named Englishmen's Col in honor of Smythe and Biven. Beyond the col, as he neared the top of the next cornice crest, Hasenkopf slipped on the glare ice and plunged toward the southern precipice until he was caught by the rope just above the abyss. Ordinarily, such a fall might encourage a retreat; on this day, however, it merely strengthened the resolve of the Germans. Hasenkopf seemed unaffected by his encounter with fate and, after climbing back to his belayer, continued the ascent.

The climb to the middle summit proved to be the most difficult section of the entire ascent. One lead, in agonizing proximity to the cornices overhanging the northern snow flutings, was referred to as a veritable *Himmelsleiter*—a ladder to heaven. Both teams were intrigued by the beauty of the pitch as they traversed across the glistening ice.

A series of rappels down a perpendicular chimney were needed to reach the gap between the middle and the true summit; here the first team left a fixed line in the chimney to assist the other climbers and the retreat. Welsch and Reichegger were just a short distance behind the lead team and soon arrived at the gap. After a brief rest the four reunited climbers ascended toward the summit over noticeably easier ter-

Traversing through the mists near the west summit. Gary Bocarde.

rain. As they stepped onto the summit cornice, which Welsch likened to the "crests of gigantic breakers," the rising sun bathed sky and snow alike in a reddish glow. Twenty-two hours had passed since the Germans had left their high camp. Far down the ridge they noticed the Americans retreating along the cornices leading back to the western summit. It was a supreme moment, and the four climbers were refreshed by the beauty that surrounded them. Myriad peaks could be seen in the newly illuminated ice wilderness as they prepared for their descent.

With the German party's ascent of the Moose's Tooth, European climbing interest in the McKinley Range waned. Perhaps the greatest reason for this decline was the lack of major unclimbed peaks, which these highly nationalistic teams usually sought. The Moose's Tooth was not visited again until the early 1970s, when various parties unsuccessfully attempted to climb the east face and the buttress above the south col.

Then, in 1974 and 1975, the mountain was climbed by groups tackling the huge couloirs on the south face; one of these parties descended the west ridge rather than face a series of dangerous rappels in the couloirs. Perched serenely above the hanging glacier on the north face, the west ridge of the Moose's Tooth, with its magnificent cornices and snow flutings, awaits its second ascent.

First ascent

Walter Welsch, Klaus Bierl, Arnold Hasenkopf, and Alfons Reichegger. June 1–2, 1964.

Elevation

The summit is 10,335 feet above sea level.

Time

Three to four days from base camp; add another day or two if two camps are to be placed above base. The first ascenders were gone for forty hours from their high camp.

Map

Boston Museum of Science: Mount McKinley, Alaska, scale 1:50,000.

Route description

Ski-equipped aircraft can be flown to a base camp at the foot of the ridge after a forty-minute flight from Talkeetna.

From base camp, climb the easier of two glacier lobes descending from the northwest side of the Moose's Tooth. A high camp can be placed on the upper snowslope at about 7900 feet, just beneath the steeper wall of the western summit. Enter a large couloir between two rocky ribs slanting up and to the left. On reaching the crest at 9000 feet, continue along the corniced ridge (with occasional ice pitches up to 45 degrees) to the 9780-foot western summit. Traverse along the gently angled but heavily corniced crest to reach the Englishmen's Col. A short rappel may be necessary to reach the col. The most difficult section of the climb consists of the steep, exposed, and heavily corniced ice pitches which lead to the middle summit. Continue traversing to a col (again, rappels may be necessary) located between the middle summit and the final level section of ridge leading to the 500-foot summit arête. This portion of the route is slightly easier, although no less exposed and dangerous. Exercise great caution when climbing the summit cornices.

To descend, retrace the route of ascent.

Remarks

Late May is a good time to start the climb. Because the Moose's Tooth lies within the newly created Denali National Monument, those who plan to climb the peak must register with park authorities. A pamphlet outlining the requirements can be obtained from Mount McKinley National Park, Box 9, Mount McKinley, Alaska 99755.

The undulating, corniced crest leads nearly a mile to the main summit. To the left of the ridge rises the upper north face. Gary Bocarde.

Mount Huntington West Face

6

Mount Huntington is said to be the most beautiful peak in Alaska, although some mountaineers feel the honor might well be shared with its neighbor, the Moose's Tooth. Mountains attract climbers by virtue of their sheer verticality; yet a superb peak owes its fascination to more than just its steepness — an observation that becomes apparent to those who view the snow-encrusted Huntington. This 12,240-foot peak in the McKinley Range is a pyramidal formation whose three somber faces are bordered by ice-clad ridges of unquestioned beauty.

In the late 1950s, Bradford Washburn published an impressive set of aerial photographs of Mount Huntington. At this time little was known of potential routes on the peak, especially since Alaskan mountaineering continued to be focused upon the huge bulk of McKinley just eight miles to the north. To those who studied Washburn's

photographs, it seemed possible to climb a slender buttress leading onto Huntington's west face. However, the sheer granite on the upper part of the face was so discouraging that it was on the lower-angled northwest ridge that the first attempts were made. In 1957 a party led by Fred Beckey reached the ridge crest several thousand feet below the summit, but logistics and the severity of the long, heavily corniced ridge forced a retreat.

Despite the fact that Washburn's beautiful photographs of Huntington's summit crest were circulating among American and European climbers anxious for new adventures in the McKinley Range, the mountain remained untried for six years following the Beckey expedition. Then, in 1964, a French expedition led by Lionel Terray made the first ascent of the northwest ridge. Facing the coldest Alaskan weather in years, Terray and his talented group struggled for twenty days on the long, exposed ridge. Terray later wrote that on a long pitch above his party's first camp he had to fight his way along the crest: "A vertical bulge makes me traverse right. After several meters I find bare ice, and what ice! It is smooth as a mirror and hard as glass. I have never struck such ice!" Alaskan conditions greatly impressed this international mountaineer, who fell to his death the following year while climbing in France.

Many American mountaineers were envious of the French success on Mount Huntington, for they, too,

had nourished hopes of climbing the remarkable peak. Two such climbers were Harvard students Dave Roberts and Don Jensen. Both were seasoned mountaineers with good alpine judgment and in 1963 had participated in the bold ascent of the 14,000-foot north face of Mount McKinley. With Huntington no longer a virgin summit, the two climbers began to visualize a more committing adventure: a route on which they might advance the frontiers of Alaskan mountaineering. Roberts and Jensen could see from Washburn's photographs that the west face of Huntington was the route they were looking for. A slender, corniced snow arête led to two prominent icefields which abutted difficult-looking granite cliffs and buttresses. Above these, gentle-angled snowslopes could be followed until they intersected the upper northwest ridge. No such sustained technical rock problems had been attempted in Alaska; most peaks had been climbed by ridges, which usually were the easiest and safest routes.

Agreeing that a climbing party of four would be most efficient, Roberts and Jensen chose a close friend, Matt Hale, as the third member of their team. Hale, a young climber with great technical ability, had not previously climbed on large mountains. Still, he possessed the tenacity so necessary for enduring the persistent discomfort of long expeditions. Searching for a fourth member, the group hoped to find a veteran Alaskan climber, but no one was available. As their departure time grew near, the climbers finally chose Ed Bernd, another young and enthusiastic climber from Harvard who also was untried on big alpine walls.

During the winter of 1964, the expedition members conferred with increasing frequency and intensity, their eyes riveted on a new series of Washburn photographs that showed their projected route in unnerving detail. The four men openly expressed the hopes and fears that assail most mountaineers prior to a great climb. The bond that joined them grew stronger over the months, and they realized that such closeness would be important to the successful completion of their climb.

In June 1965 the four friends arrived in Alaska; the transition from civilization to the Tokositna Glacier was startling to novice and veteran alike. After their plane had departed, the climbers stood quietly by their packs, their mood greatly affected by the glacial stillness occasionally broken by the dull roar of avalanches. In the distance loomed the brooding west face of Huntington. Bernd and Hale were subdued and awed by their surroundings; in contrast, Roberts and Jensen, who had assumed joint leadership because of their greater knowledge of Alaskan climbing, began to organize the loads for transport to a small col at the base of the route. The foursome constructed an ample

The sunlit west face of Mount Huntington. The fluted snow ridge at the lower right is the Stegosaur.   Bradford Washburn.

snow cave on the col and then decided, on July 4, to attack the first problem of the climb: the route to the lower icefield.

A snow arête, whose cornices resembled the scaly spine of a reptile, rose in the mists above the col; soon it would become known as the Stegosaur, the first of many imaginative names the Harvard climbers applied to the route. Progress was slow, and for each day of leads won there were two days of storm during which the four men dared not move. As they descended the fixed lines each evening, it seemed to the climbers that logistics and endless storms were conspiring to defeat them. It took them nearly twenty

days to establish Alley Camp just above the lower icefield.

Even though they had climbed only a third of the route, the four men began to explore the pitches on the steep rock buttresses—the Spiral and the Bastion—with even greater determination. Roberts and Hale eventually took the lead and pioneered the route to the base of a dark, bulging wall—called the Nose—that forms a barrier below the summit snowfields. They sensed that this single pitch might be the key to the climb. Hale led in fine style, hanging like a spider from pitons driven into the overhang. He worked his way slowly over the coarse rock, finished the lead, and brought up his companion. "We spoke quietly," recalled Roberts in *The Mountain of My Fear,* "discussing the route and our chances rather than the bursting sense of triumph we were beginning to feel."

As the two climbers rappelled to Alley Camp, they encountered Jensen and Bernd, who were ascending fixed lines with equipment for a higher camp. The two teams were self-sufficient, yet they worked together toward the common goal. Jensen congratulated Hale on his lead of the Nose. Everyone seemed to have broken through the cocoon of despair in which they had been climbing for the previous few weeks; Bernd in particular was confident and enthusiastic, for he had learned much about mountaineering and about himself during those weeks.

The climbers had enjoyed five straight days of clear weather, and since a high camp had been placed just beneath the Nose, fewer supplies were needed and the pace quickened. By then it was July 29, and Roberts noted that "the summit dared whisper in our ears." Jensen and Bernd pushed the route through the final band of cliffs and set their tiny bivouac tent behind a rocky outcrop midway up the summit snowfield. They rested there for much of the afternoon and evening before being joined by their two companions, who reached the outcrop with a horrifying story. After leaving Alley Camp in mid-morning, they had fairly sailed over

Ed Bernd follows a steep dihedral on the Spiral. Don Jensen.

the familiar fixed lines to the upper cliff band. There, as Hale was adjusting his crampons, he slipped and fell, pulling Roberts with him. The two climbers slid thirty feet before their rope caught on a rock projection and brought them to a halt. Although deeply shaken by the experience, they slowly continued the ascent.

The reunited team immediately began ascending the remaining few hundred feet to the ridge climbed by Terray. Upon reaching the thin, airy ridge crest, their shapes barely discernible in the evening gloom, the men turned toward the summit. By midnight they were grappling with the steep, frail summit flutings, and three hours later, as the rising sun illuminated the tundra to the north with an "orange wall of flame," they stepped upon the summit of Mount Huntington. Roberts stared into the new day: "All the world we could see lay motionless in the muted

splendor of sunrise. Nothing stirred, only we lived; even the wind had forgotten us." Elated, but tired, the four climbers returned to the rocky outcrop and began a time-consuming series of rappels leading back to their camp below the Nose. Their spirits were higher than the noonday sun as they finished their last rappel.

"Climbing is defined by a purposed completion, the summit," Roberts later wrote, "yet the best of it is never that final victory, for after that there is only the descent. The best moments lurk in the tension just before success." Perhaps it is presumptuous to claim that the worst moments often lurk just after success, but it is a fact that most climbing deaths occur during rappelling, that most dangerous of all mountaineering techniques. The four Huntington climbers, in their state of summit euphoria, had no premonition of the tragedy that awaited them.

After a fitful afternoon nap at Nose Camp, Bernd suggested to Roberts that the two of them continue the descent that evening to Alley Camp to avoid compressing all four men into a single tent. Bernd and Roberts started at about ten o'clock, rappelling and climbing down the fixed lines. In the middle of the Spiral, Bernd was attaching the rappel line to a fixed piton with a carabiner. It was midnight, the darkest hour, and as he stepped toward the cliff edge there was an awful grating sound. Roberts watched in horror as his companion pitched backward into the void and soundlessly disappeared.

Stunned, Roberts struggled to comprehend. The piton was intact; yet the carabiner and rope had vanished with Bernd, who had failed to clip the carabiner through the eye of the piton. It was clear enough what had happened. Seasoned climbers often test their rappel anchors at least twice; Bernd had neglected to test his at all. The possibility of death is inherent in all climbing expeditions, yet it is never expected. Mountaineering is an ultimate game, and few human activities give as much meaning to the aphorism: "Play for more than you can afford to lose, and you will learn the game." Still, few mountaineers understand this wager, around which revolves the endlessly tormenting question: "Why do I climb?"

Roberts gathered his strength and managed to descend to Alley Camp. When the others arrived, he informed them of the accident. Three

The last pitch below the start of the summit snowfield.   Don Jensen.

grieved climbers descended to base camp to await the return of the airplane.

Ten years passed before the west face, now usually known as the Harvard Route, was climbed again. A second-ascent team of two, Dean Smith and Bruce Wehman, spent a total of eighteen days ascending the peak. After setting fixed lines a short distance above their camp on the col, they climbed alpine-style to the summit and back to the col in six days, using small ledges for their bivouacs. A Japanese party made the third ascent in 1976 after avalanche hazards forced them to abandon plans to attempt the south face.

In accordance with the general increase in alpine-style mountaineering in the McKinley Range, Mount Huntington has become the location for several bold adventures. In 1978 two climbers reached the summit via the avalanche-raked north face. On their descent of the west face they found and used the fixed ropes that had been left by the first ascenders. However, as new lines of ascent are exhausted on Mount Huntington, mountaineers may be attracted more frequently to the beautiful mixed climbing of the Harvard Route.

First ascent

Dave Roberts, Don Jensen, Ed Bernd, and Matt Hale. June 29–July 30, 1965.

Elevation

The summit is 12,240 feet above sea level. The climbing route begins at 9200 feet.

Difficulty

Severe snow and ice climbing may be expected, with rock difficulty up to 5.9 and A2.

Time

The first ascent required thirty-two days from the landing site to the summit and three days for the descent. The Smith–Wehman ascent took fourteen days from the landing site.

Map

Boston Museum of Science: Mount McKinley, Alaska, scale 1:50,000.

Useful reference

The Mountain of My Fear.

Route description

The landing site is located on a fork of the Tokositna Glacier about four miles west of the summit. Move supplies to an advance base camp just below the small snow col between Mount Huntington and point 9550. Above the col is the Stegosaur, a corniced snow arête. Ascend this formation in twelve pitches involving easy to moderate rock (one aid section) and some difficult ice climbing. Above the Stegosaur, seven easy mixed pitches lead to the top of the first icefield. After climbing a one-pitch chute known as the Alley, four easy mixed pitches up the second icefield—the Upper Park—end at the steeper rock buttresses of the face.

The route then weaves upward through small ice gullies and rock outcrops to a 300-foot ice couloir leading up and slightly left to the Nose, a huge overhang offering the quickest way to reach the upper snowslopes. These eleven pitches, including the 70-foot aid pitch on the Nose (A2), form the crux of the route and contain hard rock climbing and intricate, mixed snow-and-ice pitches up to 70 degrees. Above the Nose, ascend one mixed pitch; then climb four additional mixed pitches, angling up and right, to the final rock barrier. Above this barrier (A2) ascend seven pitches on the 50-degree summit snowslopes to the northwest ridge. Midway up this snowfield is a 10-foot-high rock outcrop suitable for a bivouac. After reaching the ridge crest, ascend 600 feet toward the summit and then climb past several tricky, unconsolidated cornice flutings for four pitches to the summit.

The descent is made by rappelling and downclimbing the ascent route.

Equipment

Carry alpine-style gear suitable for a Grade VI rock-and-ice climb. A rack of thirty rock pitons should be adequate, unless fixed lines are used.

Remarks

Since Mount Huntington lies within the newly created Denali National Monument, those who wish to climb the peak must register with park authorities. A pamphlet outlining the requirements can be obtained from Mount McKinley National Park, Box 9, Mount McKinley, Alaska 99755.

Mount Logan
Hummingbird Ridge

By the time Alaska was purchased by the United States in 1867, most of the highest peaks in the Saint Elias Mountains visible from the sea had been charted, but nothing was known of the territory beyond this coastal fringe. It fell to Professor Israel Russell to provide the first description of the vast ice peaks to the north, in the inland part of the range. In 1891, during his second expedition to Mount Saint Elias, Russell reached 14,500 feet on the peak's north shoulder. He had expected to see forests and perhaps some trace of human habitation. "What did meet my eager gaze," he wrote, "was a vast snow-covered region, limitless in its expanse, through which hundreds, and perhaps thousands, of barren angular mountain-peaks projected." He named the culminating point of the huge massif after Sir William Logan, the founder and first director of the Geological Survey of Canada.

◀ *The south face of Mount Logan.* Boston Museum of Science photo by Bradford Washburn.

Mount Logan's elevation was established officially at 19,850 feet by the International Boundary Commission survey expedition of 1913. The mountain, second highest in North America, was recognized as the center of a glacial system larger than any outside Antarctica and Greenland. Icefields border the coastal region for nearly 250 miles and extend inland for an average distance of 100 miles. Logan itself is immense and actually may be the largest mountain in the world. Its ridges span some twenty-four miles in an east–west direction and nearly twenty miles north and south, and its summit plateau comprises almost ten square miles above the 17,500-foot level. Its central south ridge, now known as Hummingbird Ridge, is the dominant feature of the 14,000-foot southern escarpment of the mountain. The ridge descends from the summit for nearly six miles before disappearing into the level icefields of the Seward Glacier.

The successful Canadian–American expedition to Mount Logan in 1925 was a remarkable adventure in the annals of North American mountaineering. An eight-man party led by Albert MacCarthy was forced to haul ten tons of supplies 130 miles just to reach the mountain. From their advance base camp, which the climbers reached on June 8 after four weeks of traveling, the summit was still eighteen miles distant and 12,000 feet higher. The weather was unusually fierce as the team pioneered a route up the broad, western slopes of the mountain, past King Col, to a high camp at 17,800

feet. After being trapped by storms with temperatures ranging between zero and minus thirty-three degrees Fahrenheit, six of the party were able to reach the summit on June 23; the two remaining climbers, slightly frostbitten, returned to a lower camp to await their friends. Although enthralled by the magnificent view, the summit party retreated hastily as a new storm approached. Several hours later wind-driven snow forced the men into a wretched bivouac at 19,000 feet; they burrowed like animals into the snow to escape the fury of the new storm. The following day, as they struggled along the plateau with visibility at fifty feet, the climbers chanced upon one of the willow wands they had left as markers during the ascent. The discovery saved their lives, for they were able to follow the remainder of the markers back to their high camp. Suffering from exhaustion and mild frostbite, the group returned to base camp on June 28. Few mountaineering expeditions had encountered such hardships, and the team's ascent was viewed as a unique accomplishment in the history of mountain exploration.

It often happens after the first ascent of a great mountain that many years pass before it is climbed again. And so it was with Logan. In June 1950, climbing parties made the second and third ascents using the 1925 route. In 1953 a small American expedition arrived on the Seward

Glacier to explore the approach to the east ridge of Logan. In the group was Dick Long, a young climber from California. As the team pulled supply sledges across the Seward Glacier, Long gazed at Logan's incomprehensible southern escarpment, which dominated the horizon to the northwest. "Even at a distance of twelve miles, the south ridge was huge," he recalled later, "and it looked impossible. The rocky crest rose out of the Seward six miles from the summit. At about 14,000 feet it leveled into a mile-long series of cornices before rising another 6000 feet to the summit. I couldn't get that apparition out of my mind."

Even ten years later Long, by then a resident physician in Sacramento, California, was still thinking seriously about climbing the ridge. He confided in three close companions—Allen Steck, Jim Wilson, and John Evans—and together they made plans for a series of big-wall training climbs that would prepare them for the sustained mountaineering they anticipated on Logan. They surmised correctly that the south ridge would require a climbing mentality well adjusted to continuous exposure and reliance on fixed lines. By autumn of 1964 the party had grown to six persons, with the addition of engineer Frank Coale and ski racer Paul Bacon.

The six men flew to their base camp at the foot of Logan's south ridge on July 7, 1965, during a period of stable weather. Furious avalanche activity forced them to climb mostly at night, and after ten days they had established Camp 1 on the ridge crest at 9600 feet. It was an incident near this camp that gave the route its name. Steck, waiting his turn to ascend a fixed line, had an encounter that he described later in the *American Alpine Journal:* "Suddenly I am aware of a whirring sound . . . a falling rock! Instinctively I press myself close to the cliff, but the sound persists and as I turn to investigate I notice a tiny hummingbird hovering over my bright red pack. . . ." This unlikely meeting inspired a unanimous decision to call the route the Hummingbird Ridge.

Struggling up the narrow, twisting rock ridge above Camp 1, the team became bogged down in an arduous daily routine: two men led and fixed the lines while their companions, the hauling team, carried the loads—mostly food for the thirty-five days they estimated it would take to climb the peak. As soon as a new campsite was located, the lower camp would be dismantled and the loads carried up to the new camp. Finally, the fixed lines would be removed for use higher on the ridge, for they were essential for the hauling team. The climbing was complex and sustained, and there were many falls.

Camp 2, an exposed and fearsome place. Allen Steck.

On July 22 the tents at Camp 1 were removed before the lead climbers had found a new site higher on the ridge. Steck described the result of this rash decision in his diary: "In the fading light the haulers are forced to huddle in a narrow notch while Evans and Coale are furiously carving the heart out of a huge cornice to make room for the tents. Wilson is brewing tea, sitting on his pack with the stove in his lap, while I am just tired and frightened. I am terrorized by each blow of the shovel. My greatest concern is:

What happens when the cornice goes?" The team was trapped at Camp 2 for seven days, where the exposure, together with an almost continuous blizzard and declining food supplies, contributed to a general depression.

Often there is a moment during a climb when the need to make a difficult decision becomes the pivotal point of the venture. During a discussion at Camp 2 on July 25, it was agreed that defeat was imminent. Half the food had been consumed to climb one-fifth of the route! Long was disconsolate: "Who will climb this ridge," he wondered aloud, "and how will they do it?" Finally it was decided to push the route as far as a prominent snow dome at 13,600 feet. If it seemed impossible to complete the long, horizontal traverse by August 2, then retreat would be in order. The small chance for success that did exist somehow gave the climbers the incentive for continued, aggressive climbing.

A climber descends fixed lines toward Camp 2, located on the corniced ridge silhouetted against the glacier. Allen Steck.

The group forced the route to Camp 3 and on to Camp 4 in just three days. At this point the climbing and the transporting of loads became easier. The use of a lightweight shovel to carve a path for the haulers contributed to the spectacular advance. However, on July 30 another storm was developing, so the lines below Camp 4 were left in place in readiness for the retreat that seemed sure to begin. Miraculously, the following day dawned clear and still.

Evans stared incredulously at the corniced crest stretching out in front of him toward the final buttress of the mountain. "Looks like the beginning of the forward retreat," he mused.

Long and Coale took the lead on the mile-long crest traverse, and by evening Camp 5 had been placed securely on a level stretch halfway across the intricate series of cornices. Evans, burdened by a monstrous load, especially appreciated the lines fixed along the traverse by

the lead team: "Of my many mishaps on that little jaunt one was most memorable. This time I pitched off head-first . . . and thus enjoyed an exhilarating snap when my jumar finally picked me up on the fixed line."

Steck and Evans completed the traverse the following day. Steck was elated at the progress they were making: "I drew the last lead, took the shovel, and bade farewell to

John. The air was still, the sun incredible. The cornices and ice towers were balanced on a slender spine of rock, the culmination of this giant ridge that formed a 7000-foot barrier between two glacial cirques. A soft mist rose to the east of the crest. I turned for a moment and was completely lost in silent appraisal of the beautifully sensuous simplicity of windblown snow."

The climbers continued to the summit plateau, arriving on August 6. The weather was calm and clear and the temperature a mild twelve degrees Fahrenheit as they stood upon the summit, the tenth expedition to have won that honor. The view down the ridge was magnificent, and the six men marveled at the spine's tortuous path south toward the Seward Glacier. Far to the south of Mount Saint Elias they could see the Pacific Ocean, a hundred miles distant. The climbers then began a western descent, which took them to a tiny food cache left thirty-two days earlier near the 1925 team's advance base camp.

Long and his companions not only had climbed the most beautiful and dramatic ridge on Mount Logan, they also had made the first traverse of the mountain. According to one mountaineering historian, the ascent—which has not been repeated—"made demands on technical ability, judgment and endurance not previously encountered in the St. Elias Mountains and perhaps not in North America."

First ascent

Dick Long, John Evans, Allen Steck, Jim Wilson, Frank Coale, and Paul Bacon. July 7–August 6, 1965.

Elevation

The summit is 19,850 feet above sea level.

Time

The first ascent required thirty-two days from the landing site to the summit and three days back to the landing site at the base of the descent route.

Map

USGS quadrangle: Mt. St. Elias, Alaska–Canada, scale 1:250,000.

Route description

For the flight to Mount Logan, charter air services are available in Whitehorse, Yukon Territory. From the landing site at the base of Hummingbird Ridge, ascend the glacier that descends from Logan's southwest face for two or three miles to a base camp.

The route to the ridge crest about 2800 feet above base camp lies on a buttress (some 5.7) to the left of a steep, rocky couloir which leads to a deep notch. The first section of the ridge begins as an exposed, rocky arête and gradually changes into snow and ice. Platforms have to be chopped for camps.

Above Camp 3, climbers descend a small tower as they carry loads to the next camp.   Allen Steck.

At 13,600 feet the long, horizontal corniced ridge is reached. The difficulty of this dramatic traverse varies from year to year. An excellent campsite can be established on a large, level area midway along the traverse. After the horizontal ridge the climbing becomes easier. When 1000 feet below the summit, traverse left onto snowfields to avoid a steep section of the ridge. Next, climb several ropelengths to a saddle just south of the summit; from here it is a short walk to the top.

The summit plateau is so extensive that the descent route should be studied carefully beforehand with the aid of aerial photographs. Either the east ridge or the west buttress can be used; on the latter route there is an easily missed saddle which must be crossed to gain the icefields leading down to King Col.

Remarks

Those who wish to climb in the Saint Elias Mountains must register with park authorities. Information can be obtained from the park warden at Kluane National Park, Haines Junction, Yukon Territory, Canada Y0B 1L0.

Far out on the mile-long cornice traverse, two climbers stand on the site chosen for Camp 5. Closer to the camera, three companions carry loads on the beginning of the "forward retreat." Allen Steck.

Middle Triple Peak *East Buttress*

8

Climbing in Alaska's Kitchatna Range *was* something different, mused Mike Graber as, poised in his aid slings, he peered around an overhang and pondered his next move. His body angled crazily to the left, the hardware sling pulling heavily on his shoulder, as he strained to place the next chock high above his head. Climbing in a precise, methodical way that gave him a feeling of great power, he soon climbed the overhang and, after delicate moves with sky hooks, rurps, and assorted micro-hardware, was able to set anchors to belay Alan Long, his climbing partner from past adventures in this fantastic range. Below, preparing the loads for hauling as soon as the fixed line was set, were their companions, Andy Embick and George Schunk.

◀ *The east buttress of Middle Triple Peak.* Andy Embick.

This was only the first lead of twenty-eight on the east buttress of Middle Triple Peak, at 8835 feet the second highest peak in the Kitchatna Range. The team members knew that they would be living in a vertical world for days—how many they could not be sure—and certainly they would not always experience the pleasurable warmth they were enjoying at the moment. They knew the weather could not hold; at best they could expect only a day or two of sun before being forced to climb on sleet-covered rock as wind and snow swirled along the cliff face. They also were aware that the long Alaskan days would tempt them to climb throughout the twilight hours, foregoing sleep until exhaustion eventually would compel them to rest. Success on an Alaskan Grade VI would not come easily.

But on this beautiful, sunny day the climbers were euphoric. Above them an almost flawless, gently rounded headwall rose nearly 1200 feet to a lower-angled ridge. Higher, the ridge steepened into a pillar which swept upward in a relentless, powerful arc to the summit icefield. A view from across the cirque would reveal the 3300-foot buttress as a gigantic prow of stone, slicing through the glacial seas of the Sunshine Glacier. Embick later wrote: "We were touching the warm, nubbly skin of the grandest mass of rock I'd ever known, immersed in air and half-dancing, half-flying upwards, shirtless on belays . . . breathing deeply the essence of rock climbing."

The story of how the Kitchatna Spires, a subrange located in the Alaska Range, were opened for climbing is a fascinating one. The region was known to geographers working for the state of Alaska, but information concerning its incredible topography—as evidenced by aerial photography—had not yet reached the climbing community. The story of the region's discovery by climbers begins in 1962, when there appeared in an issue of *Summit* magazine a remarkable photograph of fantastic granite peaks called the Riesenstein, said to be located in British Columbia. "Last summer," *Summit* informed its readers, "three Austrians, Machler, Bisserlich, and Kronhofer, bushwhacked up the Klawattl River from the Nass River to climb and explore in the area." The team climbed two summits and then made two attempts to climb the highest peak. The editors of *Summit* concluded the brief article by wondering: "Who will be the first to climb it?"

The peaks were of such obvious alpine quality that mountaineering interest was substantial and immediate. One can imagine the quantity of requests for maps and photos that must have deluged the Canadian Geological Survey authorities. However, it soon became distressingly evident that the information provided by *Summit* in no way

43

matched the topography shown on the maps. Alvin DeMaria, an eastern climber and one of those fascinated by the Riesenstein, eventually concluded that "*Summit* had fallen victim to someone's sense of humor. Yet, there were the pictures; palpable mountains—they must have some existence. But where? Chamonix? Africa? Asia? The moon?"

The mystery finally was solved by a researcher at the American Alpine Club library in New York; the peaks were found to belong to a subrange in the southwestern portion of the Alaska Range, some sixty miles west of Talkeetna. The photo in *Summit* showed the eastern cliffs and glaciers of unnamed and unclimbed peaks in the Kitchatna Range. A massive buttress was the most prominent feature of the highest summit, which eventually would be named Middle Triple Peak.

When DeMaria and five companions flew into the range in June 1965, they became the first climbers to visit the area. As soon as they landed and set foot on the glacier, DeMaria realized that the peaks were larger than he had imagined, for the "immensity of the walls . . . suddenly took on the proportions of an absurd joke. Climb? These walls? Plastered with snow and icy couloirs, rising two to three thousand feet above the glacier, the summits seemed the epitome of inaccessibility . . . one could place the entire Bugaboo group . . . in a single cirque of this Kitchatna range." Not prepared for a long,

A view of the east buttress from the Sunshine Glacier.   Mike Graber.

multi-day ascent, DeMaria and his friends climbed several smaller summits, at the same time discovering that typical Kitchatna weather was little else but "white-out and storm."

After returning home, the group reported that the Kitchatna Range was big-wall country, several Yosemites transplanted to the icing zone of southwest Alaska—a Patagonia of the northern latitudes, where constant storms were simply part of the normal weather pattern.

By 1974 thirteen summits had been climbed in the Kitchatnas, including three of Grade IV difficulty. This same year saw the successful completion of the first Grade VI rock climb in Alaska: the west face of Mount Dickey. The rock on Dickey, however, was in part terribly decomposed, so it was on the clean, substantial walls of the nearby "northern Patagonia" that climbers sought new and challenging routes. In 1975, Grade VI climbs were made on Tatina Spire and on South Middle Triple Peak by a three-man party.

The unclimbed Middle Triple Peak, one of the loftier, more imposing summits of the range, became the objective of two strong parties the following summer. First to arrive were Charlie Porter, fresh from a solo ascent of the Cassin Ridge on Mount McKinley, and his partner, Russ McLean. While Porter and McLean had come to climb the incomparable west face, another team was establishing its base camp near the foot of the tremendous east buttress. In this party were Graber, Long, Embick, and Dave Black, a medical-student friend of Embick's.

The immensity of the buttress overwhelmed Graber's team. The group was obsessed with the desire to attempt this beautiful new climb; yet at the same time, being unsure of the progress of Porter and McLean, they realized they stood a much better chance of reaching the summit first via the easier north ridge. Graber and his friends climbed this ridge and reached the wind- and snow-scoured summit on July 10. Believing that they had made the summit first—they had seen no sign of the other climbers—they were overjoyed. Their elation was short-lived, however; for on returning to Talkeetna after the expedition, they discovered that Porter and McLean had indeed made the first ascent of Middle Triple. Ironically, they had reached the summit on July 1, during the very period that Graber's party had been agonizing over the choice of routes. However, it was a small loss, for the lure of new adventures on the awesome east buttress was enough to ensure the climbers'

return the following year. And so in late May 1977, Graber, Long, Embick, and George Schunk flew into the Kitchatnas and soon were enjoying that auspicious first day of sunshine and euphoria.

Five days later, after a bivouac in a snowy headwall, Graber awoke and brushed the snow from his insulated bivouac suit. He noticed that his friends also were stirring in their snowbound niches at the top of the headwall. At least they had found a reasonable place to bivouac and finally were refreshed. Those first sunny days had been nice, he remembered, but then came the fog and eventually the storm, which continued throughout the final, thirty-four-hour ascent of the headwall. Bivouacs under these conditions do seem more endurable, thought Graber, if one is exhausted. The climbers prepared a small meal with hot drinks while below them lay the white, swirling void.

The following days passed in a haze of exhausting activity; while the climbing on the ridge was moderate, it was extremely difficult to haul the loads along the low-angled traverses. On reaching the pillar the climbers again encountered difficult rock, where they endured yet another bivouac, submitting to gusty winds and spindrift that coated everything with soft, white rime. The following morning—was it the sixth or the seventh?—the four climbers prepared their equipment for what they hoped would be the final push to the summit. Leaving their bivouac equipment behind, they put

Mike Graber ponders his next move on the first pitch.   Alan Long.

on all their windproof clothing, took their hardware slings and ice hammers, and started up the wall, looking like brightly colored mannikins against the dark-gray granite wall. The equipment needed for such an adventure was astounding in its volume and variety: complete Grade VI ice- and rock-climbing gear, bivouac equipment, food, and cooking utensils. Two climbers were fully occupied each day just transporting the huge loads.

The forty-hour struggle to the summit and back to their gear seemed an eternity and left the four climbers dazed and weakened. The weather could not have been worse. A difficult section stood out in Embick's mind: "stark, chilling, and awesome, the rime-encrusted final rib reared up to the vertical, split cleanly by a seven-inch crack we luckily were able to avoid." The climbers reached the summit icefield and, after a few pitches, suddenly realized there was nothing left to climb. The summit? They scarcely could see it through the fog, though Long thought he saw a rock he remembered from the previous ascent. They began the descent immediately, realizing that the climb was far from over.

Like spiders on tiny strands weaving a path back to earth, the climbers spun down the cliff, hammering in rappel anchors. Twenty rappels? Thirty? They lost count as they concentrated on immediate problems, all the while in the grip of an immense fatigue. Finally they reached their base camp on the glacier and collapsed, their strength gone.

Sunshine again. Tents flapped in the soft breeze as the climbers awakened from their sleep of exhaustion. Unpleasant memories already were fading as the four men reflected on their experience. In front of the climbers, in the early morning sun, soared the magnificent buttress, a monument to personal commitment and perseverance.

Alan Long ascends a fixed line on the first pitches of the 1200-foot lower headwall. Mike Graber.

First ascent

Mike Graber, Alan Long, Andy Embick, and George Schunk. June 2–9, 1977.

Elevation

The summit is 8835 feet above sea level. The climbing route is about 3300 feet long.

Difficulty

VI, 5.9, A3.

Time

The first ascent took eight days.

Map

USGS quadrangle: Talkeetna B-6, scale 1:63,360.

Route description

The Kitchatna Range is best reached by charter air service from Talkeetna, 113 miles north of Anchorage. The most convenient landing site is on the Tatina Glacier, from which a pass offers access to the Sunshine Glacier and the start of the route.

The east buttress can be divided into four important features (heights are approximate): the steep lower headwall (1200 feet), a lower-angled ridge (700 feet), the pillar (1100 feet), and the summit icefield (300 feet). The route's difficult aid climbing is confined to the lower headwall, though there are several aid pitches on the upper pillar.

At the foot of the buttress, slightly to the right of its lowest point, ascend a crack system that leads to the left side of an inverted staircase containing four overhangs, 500 feet above the start of the climb. Enter another crack system that splits the third and fourth overhangs and continue to the top of the headwall. The next section, the lower-angled ridge, includes towers, steep slabs, ramps, and knife edges leading to the base of the pillar. Climb the pillar via snow- and ice-filled cracks for about half its height; then traverse to its left side. Ascend a left-facing dihedral four pitches to reach the summit icefield.

The descent requires about twenty rappels. Retrace the route to the base of the pillar and then rappel down the northeast side of the buttress to reach the hanging glacier about 1000 feet above the start of the climb.

Equipment

Take generous racks of pitons and chocks, with several large sizes of both. Expeditionary equipment is mandatory because of fierce storms. Ice axes and crampons are needed for the summit icefield.

A climber removes hardware from a pitch on the ridge section of the route. Mike Graber.

Remarks

This route, which has not yet had a second ascent, is comparable to longer Patagonian climbs. The weather can be cataclysmic. Only climbers of proven Grade VI capabilities should consider the climb, which is one of the most demanding of the fifty routes described in this book.

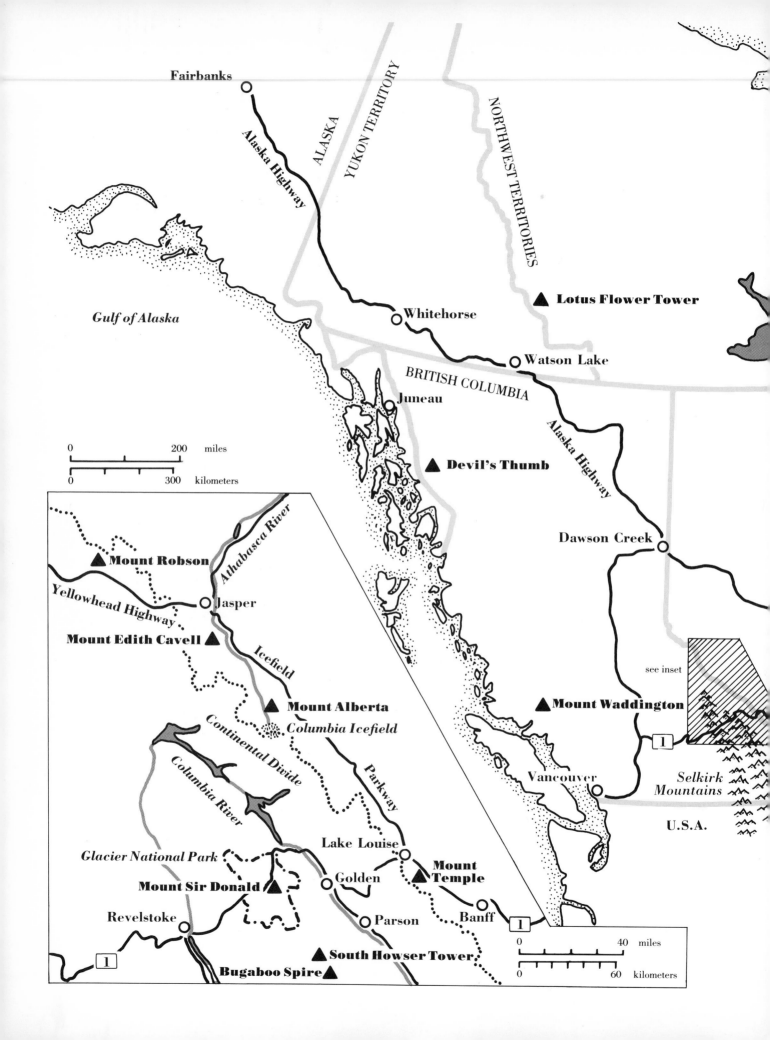

Fairbanks

Alaska Highway

ALASKA

YUKON TERRITORY

NORTHWEST TERRITORIES

Gulf of Alaska

Whitehorse

▲ **Lotus Flower Tower**

Watson Lake

BRITISH COLUMBIA

Juneau

Alaska Highway

▲ **Devil's Thumb**

| 0 | | 200 | miles |
| 0 | | 300 | kilometers |

Dawson Creek

see inset

Athabasca River

▲ **Mount Robson**

Yellowhead Highway

Jasper

Mount Edith Cavell ▲

Icefield

▲ **Mount Alberta**

Columbia Icefield

Continental Divide

Columbia River

Parkway

▲ **Mount Waddington**

1

Vancouver

Selkirk Mountains

U.S.A.

Glacier National Park

Lake Louise

Mount Sir Donald ▲

Golden

Mount Temple

Revelstoke

Parson

Banff

1

| 0 | | 40 | miles |
| 0 | | 60 | kilometers |

1

▲ **South Howser Tower**

Bugaboo Spire ▲

Western Canada

For more than 500 miles, the spectacular Canadian Rockies form a natural boundary between the provinces of British Columbia and Alberta. Along this frontier only four roads cross the Continental Divide, attesting to the rugged character of the range. The Canadian Rockies are justifiably renowned among travelers for their lofty peaks and colossal glaciers; the vistas of serrated ridges and icefalls framed by vast primeval forests are unmatched on the continent. Mountaineers long have been fascinated with this area, and climbing historians regard the Rockies and adjacent ranges as the birthplace of North American climbing.

With the completion of the transcontinental railway across Canada in 1885 came the establishment of the continent's first major climbing centers. Around the turn of the century, Canadian Pacific Railroad officials imported Swiss guides to such majestic alpine locales as Lake Louise and Glacier, and mountain climbing quickly became popular in the region. Over the next few decades, guides and their most capable clients made bold and dramatic first ascents, such as those on Mount Robson and Bugaboo Spire. So thoroughly did these guided parties comb the Rockies and the adjacent ranges to the west that by 1930 virtually no unclimbed peaks remained.

Farther west, in the coastal ranges of British Columbia, mountaineers of the 1930s were just beginning to explore vast expanses of uncharted land. This region is wetter and far less accessible than the Rockies, and before planes were used to reach base camps, the approaches to coastal peaks involved days of struggling, first through brushy lowlands and then across convoluted icefields. The peaks themselves are spectacular and, in general, more difficult to climb than those in the Rockies; mountaineers who stand atop Mount Waddington or Devil's Thumb can consider themselves among the climbing elite.

In the early 1960s a climbing renaissance took place in western Canada as bold and highly skilled mountaineers established Yosemite-style rock climbs as well as grim, Eiger-like routes on formidable north walls. Since the establishment of such high-caliber routes, Canada has offered a full range of mountaineering diversions. Some of the routes chosen as classics for western Canada are relatively easy; for instance, the ridge routes on Mount Sir Donald and Bugaboo Spire have remained favorites among generations of moderately experienced mountaineers. Higher up the scale in difficulty is the Lotus Flower Tower route, surely one of the most spectacular climbs on the planet. Aficionados of mixed rock-and-ice climbing—the type of climbing for which Canada is most noted—will find our routes on Mount Edith Cavell and Mount Robson to be superb.

Great Slave Lake

ALBERTA

SASKATCHEWAN

Edmonton

Calgary

Purcell Mountains

Mount Sir Donald Northwest Arête

9

Although the Canadian Rockies long have been regarded as one of the most famous and best-loved mountain chains in North America, there are ranges not far to the west which offer equally imposing vistas and possibly even finer climbs. The four interior ranges of British Columbia—the Purcells, Selkirks, Monashees, and Cariboos—cover 50,000 square miles, and the terrain throughout this region is rugged and extremely wild, even today.

Of the four mountain chains, the Selkirk Range always has attracted the largest number of climbers. Conspicuous, fine-looking peaks lured the early explorers, but even more important as a drawing card was the range's accessibility. The Canadian Pacific Railroad crosses the central portion of the Selkirks, and when the difficult route over Rogers Pass finally was opened in 1885, mountaineers found they could step from a plush club car into

◄ *Mount Sir Donald. The Northwest Arête Route follows the left skyline.* Ed Cooper.

alpine terrain. An enormous hotel called Glacier House was constructed near the pass the following year, and it was not long before tourists and climbers alike interrupted their journey to gaze at or climb the nearby peaks.

It was obvious to the first explorers that the finest mountain of the central Selkirks was Mount Sir Donald, a 10,818-foot rock pyramid which could be seen from Glacier House. Only two miles distant, the peak rose 6700 feet above the hotel; the final 2500 feet were smooth and airy. Two Swiss Alpine Club members climbed Sir Donald in 1890 by way of its broken south side. Nine years later the railroad recognized the potential for climbing—and for profit—and imported several Swiss guides. The ascent of Sir Donald —part glacier and part class 3 rock—immediately became the goal for adventurous gentlemen climbers, most of whom preferred climbing with a trustworthy guide.

One of the Swiss guides, a man from Interlaken named Eduoard Feuz, will be linked forever to the early climbing history of the Selkirk Range. Feuz ascended Mount Sir Donald repeatedly, establishing several new routes and variations. He guided eight of the mountain's first sixteen ascents, all of which took place on the south side of the peak.

Most of Feuz's clients were eminently satisfied with the standard route on Sir Donald, for it offered pleasant and varied climbing on an

extraordinary mountain. Nevertheless, Feuz was intrigued by the striking arête which formed the left-hand skyline when viewed from Glacier House. The northwest arête, which began at a windswept saddle between Sir Donald and another imposing pyramid called Uto Peak, was unbroken by major ledges or shoulders; indeed, the razor-sharp ridge rose at a forty-five-degree angle for 2500 vertical feet to the pointed summit. Feuz, aware of the angular nature of the Sir Donald quartzite, was not overly concerned about the apparent smoothness of the arête; however, he decided to put off an attempt on the ridge until a competent client came along.

In the late summer of 1903, E. Tewes, a mountaineer from Bremen, Germany, arrived at Glacier House. After a few easy climbs with Tewes, the impressed Feuz suggested attempting the untouched northwest arête, which by then had occupied his thoughts for several years. Tewes agreed, but the pair realized it would be wise to have another guide accompany them on such a bold undertaking.

At 4:30 A.M. on September 3, Feuz, Tewes, and the second guide, Christian Bohren, set out from the hotel. The first part of the journey was familiar to all three men, for it was Sir Donald's standard approach. The climbers moved rapidly along the path paralleling the breathtaking

Illecillewaet Glacier, the premier tourist attraction of the region. After an hour of easy walking, the trio left the path and began toiling up a steep slope below the west face. Wild blueberries were so abundant that a "rest stop" was used as an excuse for a late breakfast.

The gorged, blue-tongued climbers made excellent progress up the slope, soon departing from the standard approach to enter new territory. A long traverse over loose rock slowed the men, but at eight o'clock they stood in the Uto–Sir Donald Saddle, squinting southward into the morning sun. Appalled by the seemingly vertical head-on appearance of their projected route, the pioneers had to remind themselves that the arête was tilted back at a reasonable forty-five degrees.

The first few hundred feet of the ridge were easy, a mere warm-up for the climbers, who scrambled unroped. Pausing once in a while to rest, the three men were delighted with a panorama made splendorous by the brilliant sky. The Illecillewaet Glacier, already far beneath them, could be seen emerging from a vast ice cap which stretched into the distance. Serrated peaks and ridges—many of them unvisited even by the two guides—bordered the gleaming icefield. Closer at hand was the imposing north face of Sir Donald itself, a 2800-foot-high wall no one ever had observed so intimately. This ice-plastered face,

not climbed until sixty years later, reminded the three Europeans of the great rock and ice faces of their beloved Alps.

Soon the exposure increased dramatically; a fall would end fatally below either the north or west face. The guides produced a bulky hemp rope and tied Tewes to its middle. Moving simultaneously, but carefully, the threesome climbed onto the steep portion of the arête. Whenever a steep or smooth section barred easy progress, the two guides stopped to safeguard their client. Following European tradition, the Swiss belayed the rope across their shoulders while standing unanchored, a technique that sends chills through present-day American climbers, who learn the sitting, anchored hip belay on their first day of instruction.

However, the likelihood of a slip on Mount Sir Donald was remote that September day; for not only was Tewes a competent rockclimber, but the flint-hard quartzite offered numerous sharp-edged holds. One reason for the increasing popularity of mountaineering in the central Selkirks, the guides reflected, was the quality of the rock. The fine-grained, greenish quartzite was bonded together so well that the elements had been ineffectual in tearing the mountain apart. Consequently, the siliceous rock was a climber's dream: so solid that even the ledges were free from rubble. The two guides had climbed in other parts of western Canada, and many times they had cursed the rotten,

In the winter Mount Sir Donald is mantled with snow; in this aerial view the prominent northwest arête can be seen in the foreground, between the two faces. Jim Stuart.

dangerous limestone and shale which they had encountered. As Feuz and Bohren gazed at Glacier House, a vertical mile below them, they once again gave silent thanks to the Canadian Pacific Railroad for bringing them to this unusual part of the world.

Hour after hour the three mountaineers worked up the arête. Most of the time they climbed astride the sharp junction of the north and west faces; occasionally, however, steep sections forced them onto slanting ledges and gullies on the sides of the ridge. The trio encountered no single outstanding pitch, for the climbing was remarkably uniform. But what uniformity! The quality of the quartzite seemed to improve with every step, and the exposure, thrilling enough on the lower arête, became exhilarating higher on the ridge.

Two-thirds of the way to the summit, the party discovered it would be easier—and faster—to leave the knife edge and move to the right onto the slabby west face. Just after four o'clock Feuz and Bohren led their client onto Sir Donald's summit. The successful mountaineers waved wildly to those they knew were following their progress from the hotel; then, in a mood of exultation, they gathered around the summit cairn for a late lunch and an appreciation of the view. Fifty miles east lay the great peaks of the Rockies, partly obscured by towering cumulus clouds. Not far to the north rose the icy, unexplored high point of the Selkirk Range, Mount Sir Sandford. To the west were countless ranges and valleys; the hotel and a glinting strip of railway track were the sole signs of civilization. Soon the lengthening shadows suggested retreat, and the three satisfied men descended the familiar south-side route to the comforts of Glacier House.

Tewes was so impressed by the ascent that in an article about his Canadian adventures he warned prospective climbers about the "se-

Even a late summer storm in the Selkirks can deposit several inches of new snow; here, a chilled climber works his way up the angular quartzite of the lower northwest arête.   Steve Roper.

vere climb of the extremely difficult ridge of Sir Donald." But opinions regarding difficulty change quickly in the mountaineering community, and in 1909—the year the entire arête was followed all the way to the summit—one climber commented that the ridge "cannot be considered difficult under favorable conditions."

Mountaineers today concur with this appraisal, and of the fifty climbs described in this book, the northwest arête of Mount Sir Donald is one of the easiest—"under favorable conditions." However, summer storms often deposit several inches of snow on the ridge, and a large percentage of would-be climbers have been deterred by slippery rock, frigid hands, high winds, or various combinations of these factors. Since there are only thirty or forty days a year when conditions are truly favorable on the most popular rock climb in the Selkirks, northwest arête climbers should consider themselves blessed by the gods if they are able to grasp dry, sun-heated quartzite.

First ascent

Edouard Feuz, Christian Bohren, and E. Tewes. September 3, 1903. In 1909, A. M. Bartleet and Val Fynn made the first ascent of the upper third of the ridge, which had been bypassed in 1903.

Elevation

The summit is 10,818 feet above sea level.

Difficulty

III, 5.2.

Time

Many parties make the climb in a single day from the Illecillewaet Campground, but a high camp established at about 6800 feet makes the summit day an easy one.

Map

Canadian Department of Energy, Mines, and Resources sheet: 82 N/6, scale 1:50,000.

Useful reference

A Climber's Guide to the Interior Ranges of British Columbia.

Route description

Mount Sir Donald is located in Glacier National Park, some forty miles west of the town of Golden. The roadhead at Illecillewaet Campground is several miles west of Rogers Pass. From the upper campground (close to the site of the dismantled Glacier House), follow a marked trail two miles toward Perley Rock. Leave this trail at an obvious spot near timberline and ascend a well-defined path which shoots up a very steep slope to the east. At about 6800 feet—and two or three hours from the campground—a level morainal area beneath the Vaux Glacier is reached.

Scramble onto the classically shaped moraine to the north and follow it until it abuts the west face of Sir Donald. An upward traverse across talus and snow couloirs brings one to the Uto–Sir Donald Saddle.

The route on the ridge itself is obvious and should present few problems in good weather. Although there are several easy class 5 sections, most of the route is specimen class 4.

The fastest and easiest descent for those climbers willing to downclimb class 4 unroped is via the arête. The standard route on the south side of the mountain requires a stretch of glacier travel. On this descent, leave the summit and wander down several thousand feet of class 3 slabs and broken blocks. When nearing the steep lower section of the face, work west and drop down onto the Vaux Glacier; follow the glacier and cliffs on its north side back down to the 6800-foot level.

Equipment

Chocks work especially well on the arête; pitons need not be taken. Carry an ice axe if planning a southern descent.

Bugaboo Spire
East Ridge

From the Bugaboo—Crescent Saddle the East Ridge Route closely follows the right skyline. The imposing southeast face lies on the left.   Greg Donaldson.

Conrad Kain is the most fascinating figure in early Canadian climbing. Born in Austria in 1883, Kain became an Alpine guide in his early twenties. But wanderlust soon overcame the young man, and in 1909 he emigrated to Canada to seek another lifestyle, for, as he put it, "guiding itself is only a side-issue, not a real profession. One should and must think of his old age." Through the Canadian Pacific Railroad, Kain arranged a summer guiding job; he arrived in the Rockies hoping to establish a livelihood as a homesteader and trapper.

Kain eventually settled into a comfortable life as a married man with a farm, but he is remembered today for his summer "side-issues." During his thirty-year career as a guide, he ascended numerous excellent peaks; the first ascent of the imposing Mount Robson is regarded by many climbers as his finest accomplishment. Kain's clients were so enthralled with his personality and professionalism that many returned over several seasons to make further ascents with their favorite guide. The Austrian realized early

that being a successful guide required far more than just technical ability, and he once set down his impressions of some other necessary attributes: "First, he should never show fear. Second, he should be courteous to all, and always give special attention to the weakest member in the party. Third, he should be witty, and able to make up a white lie if necessary, on short notice, and tell it in a convincing manner. Fourth, he should know when and how to show authority . . . and should be able to give a good scolding to whomsoever deserves it."

In 1910 Kain was a member of a small group of explorers who set out to investigate a cluster of needlelike peaks in the little-known Purcell Range. The sharp spires had been seen for years from Mount Sir Donald and the Rockies, but so rugged were the central Purcells that no one had ever been near the major mountains. Greatly impressed with his close-up view of the Bugaboo Group, as it came to be known, Kain vowed to return to attempt the *"aiguilles* that will probably not be easy to climb."

Six years passed before the Austrian guide once again scrutinized the towering masses of granite. One of the sharp teeth, which rose abruptly out of an extensive glacier, especially intrigued Kain, for not only was it high and wonderfully shaped, but, unlike many of the other spires, it displayed a ridge which looked climbable. Bugaboo Spire, as it was soon named, is a marvelous piece of granite. The clean, sweeping cracks of the 10,420-foot pyramid are pleasing from every viewpoint, and its finest face—the southeast— rises over 1500 feet from the glacier. The ridge that formed the left edge of this face Kain proposed to attempt with three clients.

On August 29, 1916, the four mountaineers accomplished the first ascent of Bugaboo Spire's south ridge, a route Kain thought equal to his finest Alpine climbs. The Austrian was delighted with his route and the quality of Bugaboo Spire's granite: "When every hold is solid, difficulties are welcome and met with a smile." Present-day climbers rate these difficulties only 5.4, but without question, climbing Kain's famous Gendarme Pitch, high on the route, is a thrilling and rewarding experience.

During the next half-century, countless mountaineers visited the incredible granite needles, and Kain's route on the south ridge of Bugaboo Spire was ascended hundreds of times. Because the other ridges and

Shari Kearney follows one of the first pitches on the ridge; the Bugaboo–Crescent Saddle is seen at the center right. Alan Kearney.

faces on the peak were so intimidating, Kain's ridge was still the only established route to the summit as late as 1958. In that year an array of talented mountaineers gathered at Boulder Camp, the standard camping area for climbs in the Bugaboos.

Two of these climbers were David Isles and Dick Sykes, both students at Princeton, who had embarked on a summer tour of classic North American climbs. Having started

◀ *The east ridge of Bugaboo Spire. Howser Spire rises in the background; South Howser Tower is the prominent left-hand summit. Galen Rowell.*

their adventures by climbing Shiprock, they moved on to Colorado, where the north face of Hallett Peak beckoned. Then they went on to the Grand Teton in Wyoming for another north face. After adding the Durrance Route on Devil's Tower to their growing list of ascents, the two mountaineers drove to Canada and made the four-hour hike into Boulder Camp, where they encountered two acquaintances whom they had not seen in nearly a year. One was John Turner, an Englishman living in Montreal. This unheralded climber was known among the cognoscenti for his daring, unprotected ascents on difficult rock. The other climber, Dave Craft, a relative newcomer to the sport, already displayed traces of the earthiness and cynicism that soon would make him one of the more enigmatic climbing personalities in the United States.

After climbing several standard Bugaboo routes, including Kain's 1916 route, the four men looked for first-ascent possibilities. Feeling that Kain's ridge was essentially a one-pitch climb, the expert rock technicians examined other lines on Bugaboo Spire for a continuous route more commensurate with their abilities. Someone in the group pointed to the ridge at the right edge of the southeast face. Isles later described the further adventures of the young men:

I don't remember who first suggested the east ridge of Bugaboo, but it was an obvious candidate for a new route. Probably it was Turner who supplied the energy. He and I went off one day, climbed up to the col between Bugaboo and Crescent Spire, and could see at once that there was a potential route. We went up a few pitches and found the climbing straightforward and the rock beautiful. By then it was late, so we returned to Boulder Camp in very good spirits. The next day, August 8, we returned with a second rope consisting of Craft and Sykes. The climb went without a hitch. Turner and I went first, and he did most of the leading; I took only a few pitches. It was a fantastic day and an incredible climb. Nowhere was it very hard, but it had a fine position and clean, hard granite. We knew we had a winner. I wish now I had taken more photographs, but I guess my hands were full doing something else.

The views from the summit of Bugaboo Spire were outstanding that day. The air was so clear that the four successful climbers could pick out individual peaks in the Rockies, fifty miles to the east. As the men lounged on the summit, they realized that the 1500-foot climb had taken only five hours from their rope-up ledge. Not only was this time remarkable, but a fine first ascent had been done all free, using only a dozen protection pitons.

A climber faces the route's lower pitches, which lie in long, vertical crack systems. Greg Donaldson.

Much of the climbing had been easy and moderate class 5; they had encountered more difficult rock only once or twice. The men thought laughingly of some of the slow and overly cautious climbers they knew and wondered if such conservative climbers would have been so efficient. Soon the usual afternoon clouds began massing, and the four mountaineers happily descended Kain's ridge, speculating on what the Austrian would have thought of their accomplishment.

Hundreds of mountaineers have since repeated the east ridge, and all of them have discovered the delectable granite that Isles described. Long flakes which look scary and steep can be liebacked quickly and joyfully, for the granite is rough and sharp-edged. Jamcracks which appear smooth and strenuous contain hidden holds, permitting spectacular climbing of moderate difficulty. In the past, climbers could smash a piton rapidly into a perfect crack anywhere on the route; now chocks can be slipped into the same crack quietly and even more quickly.

If east ridge climbers are fortunate enough to make their ascent on a warm day, they will be able to flash up the granite cracks in shirt-sleeves. More likely, however, the skies will be gray and threatening, and climbers must gamble that snow flurries or lightning will not trap them on the summit after their scintillating climb.

First ascent

John Turner, David Isles, Dick Sykes, and Dave Craft. August 8, 1958.

Elevation

The summit is 10,420 feet above sea level.

Difficulty

III, 5.7.

Time

Four to six hours.

Map

Canadian Department of Energy, Mines, and Resources sheets: 82 K/10 and 82 K/15, scale 1:50,000.

Useful reference

A Climber's Guide to the Interior Ranges of British Columbia.

Route description

From the town of Parson, on British Columbia Highway 95, a good road leads south about twenty miles to Bugaboo Creek. Follow the road along the creek fourteen miles to its end. A well-trodden path leads up the valley alongside the Bugaboo Glacier and eventually leads straight up a steep hillside to Boulder Camp. This attractive meadow is located at 7700 feet, not far below the obvious mass known as Snowpatch Spire.

To reach Bugaboo Spire, ascend a steep slope to the north of Boulder Camp until reaching the gentle glacier which lies east of Snowpatch Spire. Ascend this glacier to the col between Bugaboo and Crescent spires.

From the col scramble upward a few hundred feet to the rope-up terrace. Chimney up the left edge of a flake for about 100 feet; then work left into a system of grooves. Ascend these grooves to a good ledge overlooking the impressive southeast face. Next, a fine and varied pitch takes one to the ridge crest. Follow a dihedral on the right side of this crest for a short distance until the difficulties ease. Several class 4 and 5 pitches lead to the top of a small gendarme. Make a short rappel into the notch behind this gendarme; then scramble up to the summit.

To descend, climb down the south ridge in the direction of Snowpatch Spire. A rappel is necessary to descend the Gendarme Pitch on Kain's route.

Equipment

Carry a selection of ten or twelve chocks; take an ice axe for the descent from the Bugaboo–Snowpatch Saddle.

Remarks

August is the preferred month to climb in the Bugaboo Group, although bad weather is common even then.

South Howser Tower *West Buttress*

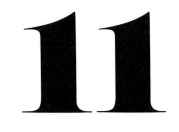

11

Thousands of mountaineers visited the Bugaboo Group during the half-century following Conrad Kain's 1916 exploration, and most of them were content to climb the most obvious and easily accessible prizes, Bugaboo Spire and Snowpatch Spire. In the late 1950s, however, upper-echelon climbers began to realize that other peaks in the vicinity had been neglected. Howser Spire, for example, with its three distinct towers, was climbed infrequently even though it was the highest peak in the group and, as such, should have been more popular. The two lower towers of this peak were ascended even less frequently; indeed, the southernmost summit, South Howser Tower, had not been climbed since 1941. This neglect of Howser Spire is curious, for every mountaineer who climbed the standard Bugaboo routes during the 1950s observed the triple-summited peak looming a few miles

◀ *South Howser Tower as seen from the north. The West Buttress Route follows the right skyline.* Galen Rowell.

to the west. Yet if the visible side rarely was visited, the hidden, or western, face of the peak was totally unknown.

To rectify this situation Fred Beckey and two companions decided in 1959 to explore the massif's back side. When the three men reached Pigeon Col—a saddle near South Howser Tower—they saw the upper portion of steep cliffs. As they descended the west side of the col, immense granite walls came into view. Beckey described the scene later: "Our immediate reaction was: Patagonia. The Howsers looked like FitzRoy and Cerro Torre and their satellites all grouped together. . . . Giant columns of rock soared upward for 2000 feet or more. Couloirs sank to the depths streaked with black ice, and below were icefalls that ended in hanging valleys. . . . We were surely the first humans to stand so close to these awesome walls. . . ."

One prominent feature, the west buttress of South Howser Tower, particularly fascinated the appreciative Beckey, who wrote: "It was apparent that this climb was a classic; from any vantage point the buttress swept up in architectural loveliness. It was the most spectacular route on the western Howser walls." The three explorers ascended the first 300 feet of the buttress, and Beckey discovered that "here was a climb of high Yosemite standards, almost 2500 feet in height, and subject to all the dangers of mountaineering in an alpine range."

After returning from their reconnaissance, the three men discussed their projected route. They had seen enough of the buttress to divide it into four distinct sections for reference purposes. The first section was an 800-foot, relatively low-angled "approach" buttress split by several crack systems. Above this was a 400-foot section of broken rock. The third section looked formidable, and Beckey and his cohorts named it the Great White Headwall. This steep, lichen-free wall, 800 feet high, was split by a single crack that widened as it rose higher. From the top of the headwall, the fourth section, leading to the summit, looked broken and rather easy. Unfortunately, storms prevented the 1959 party from making a second attempt.

Beckey did not forget the sight of Howser's west side, but two years passed before he was able to return; this time he was accompanied by Yvon Chouinard. This diminutive young man had been climbing for five years and was renowned not only for his excellent rockclimbing technique but also for the durable, hand-crafted pitons he had forged from chrome—moly steel alloy. Chouinard and Beckey had been climbing together for much of the summer of 1961, and three weeks before they established their base camp at Pigeon Col, they had made the first ascent of the spectacular north wall of Mount Edith Cavell, an adventure recounted later in this book.

On August 8 Beckey and Chouinard left Pigeon Col and dropped down a glacier to the base of the buttress, where several days earlier the pair had climbed two pitches and left their ropes anchored in place. As Chouinard stepped out of his prusik slings at the ledge where the upper rope was attached, he was horrified to find the rope half severed. After his initial shock passed, Chouinard decided the culprits were rodents attracted to the odor and texture of the rope. The dangerously weakened rope had held Chouinard's weight, but the episode could have had tragic consequences. Fortunately, the men had a spare rope and were able to continue the climb.

The next few pitches made up for the scare, for they were the landscape of a rockclimber's dream. Moderate class 5 jamcracks and liebacks on perfect granite led upward for hundreds of feet; occasionally, the cracks narrowed or steepened, forcing the leader onto direct aid. Superb belay ledges appeared exactly where needed, and to the west, the belayer was afforded views of an array of peaks that stretched to the horizon.

By late afternoon the two climbers arrived on a large, sandy ledge at the base of the Great White Headwall. Thirteen pitches lay behind them; eight had been entirely free, and only one had required extensive direct aid. The climbing thus far had been even more enjoyable than expected, thanks to the quality of the rock and the varied techniques required.

An aerial view of South Howser Tower in winter; the west buttress is the long, sweeping rib which drops down and slightly left from the summit. The highest large snowpatch midway up the buttress covers the ledges at the base of the Great White Headwall. Jim Stuart.

As the climbers had expected, the imposing Great White Headwall was to form the crux section. Beckey described the wall immediately above the ledges: "The exposure and the starkness of the route at this point become unique, as one is climbing on the narrow headwall between the terrible drop to the north couloir and the sweep of the great south face."

Knowing they had a few hours left before dark, Beckey and Chouinard climbed two predominantly aid pitches and rappelled at sunset, leaving their ropes fixed in place. As the men settled into a comfortable bivouac, Beckey congratulated his partner on his pitons, especially the four-inch-wide aluminum "bong-bongs" which the Californian had developed the previous winter. These cowbell-like pitons had been driven numerous times that day to protect long, difficult jamcracks. A horizontal piton with its eye bent at right angles to the blade also had proved useful; appropriately, its trade name was Bugaboo. Chouinard had been working on this versatile item for a year and had great hopes of a commercial success. Alternating between memories of the wonderful climbing and visions of a lucrative manufacturing business, the two men drifted into uneasy sleep.

Muddled gray skies greeted the climbers at dawn, but as they ascended pitch after pitch on the exposed headwall, the clouds dissipated. The single crack the two climbers had been following eventually widened into a chimney, allow-

ing the men to free climb for several pitches. By noon they stood on ledges atop the Great White Headwall, and three hours later, after a few easy class 5 pitches and much scrambling, Chouinard and Beckey became the fifth party ever to stand on the isolated summit.

The two adventurers admired the view for an hour before turning their attention to the tricky descent route. The satisfied climbers reached Pigeon Col before dark and soon were regaling friends who were camping in the col with stories and statistics of their bold new route. The two climbers estimated they had driven about 130 pitons on the twenty-three ropelengths. Direct aid had been used on ten of these pitches, but because of the quality and continuity of the cracks, not a single bolt had been necessary.

The Beckey–Chouinard route on South Howser Tower did not become popular immediately, for talented rockclimbers of the 1960s preferred to establish new routes rather than follow in the footsteps of others. But by the 1970s most of the prominent Bugaboo lines had been ascended, and mountaineers began repeating those routes which were rumored to be special.

As the west buttress became a desired route, direct aid gradually was eliminated, and finally the route was accomplished entirely free. Surprisingly, the buttress contains relatively few extreme pitches; instead, numerous 5.8 and 5.9 leads provide exciting and well-protected climb-

George Homer stems a dihedral low on the route. Chas Macquarie.

ing. The route presently is regarded as one of finest free routes in Canada.

Twenty years have gone by since Fred Beckey turned a corner to be astonished by the gigantic western escarpment of Howser Spire. He encountered not a single human footprint where now hundreds may be found. On a fine August day two parties might well be working their way up the west buttress, and, in the distance, from one of the other "Patagonian" walls, one is likely to hear faint climbing signals and yodels.

First ascent

Fred Beckey and Yvon Chouinard. August 8–9, 1961.

Elevation

The summit is about 10,850 feet above sea level.

Difficulty

V, 5.8, A2. Done free, the route has some 5.10.

Time

The climb can be done in one long day, but most parties prefer to bivouac on good ledges beneath the Great White Headwall.

Map

Canadian Department of Energy, Mines, and Resources sheets: 82 K/10 and 82 K/15, scale 1:50,000.

Useful reference

A Climber's Guide to the Interior Ranges of British Columbia.

Route description

See the Bugaboo Spire account for the approach to Boulder Camp. From the camp, move north onto the glacier east of Snowpatch Spire and follow it to the col between Snowpatch and Bugaboo spires; then work across the Vowell Glacier to Pigeon Col, the saddle between Pigeon Spire and South Howser Tower. From the col, drop down another glacier and traverse to the base of the obvious west buttress of the tower.

For most of the climb, the route is quite obvious. The first eight pitches lie on the low-angled "approach" buttress and involve crack climbing and a few chimneys. The next 400-foot section consists of moderately difficult chimneys and blocks.

The route up the Great White Headwall follows a prominent crack system; this section involves some very difficult crack climbing. Eventually, the angle of the headwall decreases until an easy arête leads to broken rock several hundred feet below the summit.

Descend via the standard route on the south and southeast sides of the peak. Rappel anchors will be found to facilitate the descent to a bergschrund that must be negotiated to reach the snowslopes leading down to Pigeon Col.

Equipment

The climb can be done using a selection of thirty chocks, including several large ones. An ice axe should be carried for the descent.

The upper part of the route lies on clean, white granite.
Chas Macquarie.

Mount Robson
The Wishbone Arête

Clouds drift across the junction of the two ridges comprising the Wishbone Arête. "Gargoyles" can be seen on the upper ridge but are more pronounced on the Emperor Ridge, which forms the left skyline. Ed Cooper.

Mount Robson, the high point of the Canadian Rockies, is a soaring, ice-clad mass which totally dominates its surroundings. The isolated hulk known as "King of the Rockies" is visible from ranges ninety miles distant. Since there are no easy routes to Robson's summit, the peak has retained an extraordinary and well-deserved reputation among generations of mountaineers. Swept by unpredictable and ferocious storms, the mountain rarely is visible, and for decades the phrase "Robson is out of condition this year" echoed throughout climbing centers. During one fourteen-year period—1939 to 1953—the 12,972-foot peak repulsed every party that attempted it. Consequently, Robson acquired an aura of invulnerability for later climbers; in fact, for many climbers the mountain became the ultimate goal, the ascent which would transform a dilettante into a true mountaineer.

Mount Robson first was climbed in 1913 by a three-man party led by the famous guide Conrad Kain. This diminutive Austrian was so overcome by his first view of the peak that he exclaimed: "God made the mountains, but good God! who made Robson?" From the summit he saw "more glaciers than there exist in all Switzerland." Kain's demanding route remained untouched for forty years, and even then the second-ascent party, which included Dmitri Nabokov, son of the novelist, found the route difficult and thrilling.

A few days after Kain's 1913 ascent, a Swiss guide named Walter Schauffelberger started up the southwest side of the mountain with two clients. The southwest face, more than 9000 feet high, was by no means as glaciated as Kain's eastern side, but it was still an awesome alpine wall. Schauffelberger focused his attention on the southwest arête, a prominent feature later called the Wishbone Arête because of its distinctive shape. Studying the route from below, the Swiss guide could see that the two ridges forming the forks of the "wishbone" were so broken as to be poorly defined. Higher, though, the ridges rose steeply and symmetrically until they converged 1500 feet below the top. From here a classically shaped ice ridge shot directly to the summit. Schauffelberger suspected that the lower ridges were climbable, but he was concerned about a series of giant snow pinnacles straddling the final arête.

Leaving camp near Berg Lake one August dawn, the three men traversed upward around the western flank of Robson to the base of the arête. Moving rapidly, they scrambled up the shattered limestone and shale of the easy lower ridge. The numerous ledges they encountered were overflowing with rubble, a sure sign that the nearby

◀ *The southwest escarpment of Mount Robson. The south glacier, the standard ascent route, can be seen to the right of the Wishbone Arête.*   Ed Cooper.

rock was constantly shedding its rotten outer layer. As the ridge became steeper and more exposed, the men uncoiled their hemp ropes and began belaying. Fourteen hours after leaving camp, three tired climbers bogged down at the feared snow pinnacles, called "gargoyles" by later mountaineers. These terribly exposed snow teeth had been simple cornices at one time, but the elements—severe at this altitude—had sculpted them into bizarre shapes.

The summit was only 500 feet away, but darkness and a sudden storm arrived simultaneously; so Schauffelberger and his clients decided to abandon their attempt. They retreated and set up a bivouac, which proved to be especially miserable because of their rudimentary gear. Strong winds howled continuously, and massive quantities of rime formed on the rocks. Fortunately, August nights on the fifty-third parallel are short, and after six hours the half-frozen men continued their descent, arriving exhausted at Berg Lake by nightfall.

Thus ended the most dramatic feat in early North American climbing history. Without pitons or other specialized equipment, the Schauffelberger party had ascended 7000 vertical feet, endured a harsh bivouac, and safely descended interminable, icy slopes. Had the weather been clear, it seems likely

that the climbers would have reached the summit. Basil Darling, one of Schauffelberger's clients, later wrote: "I feel sure that some day the arête will become known as one of the finest rock climbs in Canada, and probably the most sporting route to the top. . . ."

Later climbers surmised that the 1913 group had been able to move so quickly because the lower two-thirds of the arête had been unusually free from snow and ice. Still, it was somewhat odd that Darling had chosen the word *rock* to describe the type of climbing encountered. The 1500-foot section above the junction of the ridges was—and is—the obvious crux, and few rocks ever protrude through the heavy mantle of snow.

Although some thirty parties attempted the Wishbone Arête during the next forty years, many of these endeavors were simple forays which ended low on the ridge. Not one of these groups came anywhere close to the 1913 high point. Meanwhile, mountaineers had established several other routes on Robson, and by the mid-1950s about two dozen parties had reached the wind-scoured summit. One of these groups included an intense young man named Don Claunch.

Claunch was one of the leading ice climbers in the 1950s and did much of his climbing in Washington. He had attempted Mount Robson three times, but only once attained the summit. In 1953 he had seriously considered the Wishbone Arête, but marginal weather had driven him onto the standard route on the south face. In the summer of 1955 he once again made the long drive to the mountain.

The Alpine Club of Canada had established a summer base camp at Berg Lake, and it was there that Claunch persuaded two southern Californians to join him in an attempt on the Wishbone. One of the men was Mike Sherrick, a competent rockclimber who had just been involved in a minor controversy. Two weeks earlier Sherrick had raced up the standard 5.7 route on Snowpatch Spire in the nearby Bugaboos, and in the summit register he had written: "By California standards this route is 5.5." This entry, which infuriated local climbers, was not so much an arrogant gesture as it was a sign that Sherrick was in splendid condition. The other Californian, Harvey Firestone, was a medical student who had had limited climbing experience. He was quite aware of this handicap and accepted the fact that Sherrick would lead the hard rock sections and Claunch would take over on the snow.

On August 7 the three men transported huge packs around the west face to the base of the Wishbone, some 5000 feet below the summit. Late in the day—to no one's surprise—it began to rain, and the climbers morosely took shelter in their tent. Intermittent storms the following day kept the men confined to their camp, but August 9 broke clear and cold. "Within an hour,"

Sherrick later wrote, "we had eaten a hasty breakfast and were setting out on what was to be the greatest adventure, and the longest ordeal, of our lives."

The freshly fallen snow and hail melted quickly as the sun rose, and by noon the mountaineers were battling steep gendarmes streaming with water. Late in the day a more dangerous situation developed: sheets of ice formed as the temperature plunged. Sherrick's rockclimbing skills became apparent to the others as he weaved delicately along the highly exposed arête, stopping occasionally to place pitons. At dusk the trio reached a level patch of snow not far beneath the junction of the "wishbone," and upon this dramatic site they set up their tent. Having made the decision to travel light, the climbers had not carried sleeping bags. Using their ropes as insulation and candles for warmth ("It is surprising how much heat a candle can produce," wrote Sherrick), the shivering men spent a fitful night.

The following day the weather once again was perfect, but the difficulties were such that only 1500 feet were gained. Claunch, the acknowledged ice expert, took over the lead as the trio reached the gargoyles and found they could not be overcome by such conventional methods as step-cutting. Crusty one minute and hollow the next, the strange obstacles were unlike anything Claunch had

ever encountered. He burrowed through, traversed around, or directly attacked the hoarfrost-covered formations as the hours sped by. Sometime in the early afternoon the climbers passed Schauffelberger's high point, wondering if the snow teeth had been in equally wretched condition forty-two years earlier. None of the men slept on the next bivouac, for the cold was intense and they were worried about the final 300-foot section, which clearly was more imposing than the terrain they already had covered.

As they squeezed their numbed feet into totally frozen boots the next morning, the three pioneers stared at the final barrier. A sixty-degree ice chute stretched upward for 150 feet, ending at a dead-vertical headwall. After chopping a hundred steps, Claunch stopped to belay Sherrick and Firestone up to his precarious stance. Then, returning to the lead, the Washington climber inched upward, sometimes hacking steps, sometimes hanging from an ice axe buried for its entire length. A bitter wind arose, swirling ice crystals around the men and creating a magical rainbow effect. "I was almost blinded by this sudden surprise," wrote Claunch in the *American Alpine Journal*, "but managed with considerable effort to climb the remaining five or six feet above the groove, delicately balanced on a thin crust. Sixty or 70 feet more and we were on the summit, greeted by clouds and evidences of an approaching rainstorm. We clasped hands."

The descent via the standard South Face Route was uneventful, though very tiring, for the dehydrated climbers. Arriving at their camp below the arête at dusk, they snuggled into sleeping bags for their first real sleep in three days. The Mountain of the Spiral Road, as the local Indians called Robson, had another route to its icy summit.

Claunch, Sherrick, and Firestone had met relatively few objective dangers on their ascent. Present-day climbers wonder if the Wishbone Arête is not in fact the safest route on a notably dangerous mountain. No hanging glaciers threaten to break off onto helpless mountaineers below, and since the arête is steep-sided, rockfall is minimal. The gargoyles are unstable, to be sure, but experienced climbers can arrange such safe belays that the chances for a long fall are reduced.

Since the easiest—in terms of technical difficulty—way up Robson is via the south face, mountaineers who *must* climb the peak choose this route, even though avalanches are common and hair-raising traverses must be made under unstable ice cliffs. These objective dangers are accepted by most climbers as part of the Robson experience, but few of them are aware that a safer, though more demanding, route lies nearby. Although the Wishbone Arête cannot be called a popular climb, perhaps the day will come when a new generation of mountaineers will enjoy more often the direct route so obvious to Walter Schauffelberger in 1913.

First ascent

Don Claunch, Mike Sherrick, and Harvey Firestone. August 7–12, 1955.

Elevation

The summit is 12,972 feet above sea level. The distance from the high camp below the ridge to the summit is approximately 5000 feet.

Difficulty

V, 5.6.

Time

If one catches the mountain in excellent condition, a one-day ascent can be made. During normal weather conditions, plan on a two- or three-day round trip from high camp.

Map

Canadian Department of Energy, Mines, and Resources sheet: 83 E/3, scale 1:50,000.

Useful reference

Climber's Guide to the Rocky Mountains of Canada—North.

Route description

From the town of Jasper drive west on Yellowhead Highway for about sixty miles to the Kinney Lake turn-off. Take this new road north for a few miles to the lake. Hike north eight miles along a good trail to Emperor Falls, not far below Berg Lake. Leave the trail in this area, wade the stream channels, and scramble up loose couloirs for several thousand feet until reaching a broad shale terrace at about the 8000-foot level. Traverse south on the ledges for a mile until reaching the Fan Glacier. High camp can be established on moraines below the icefield.

The Wishbone Arête is reached easily from here, and once the ridge is attained, there are no more significant routefinding problems. Myriad variations, all short, can be made on the lower section; higher, the route is less complex.

The descent via the standard South Face Route is as follows. Drop down the steep upper south face (staying fairly close to the eastern drop-off) until it is possible to zigzag down the main glacier. An ice cliff not far above the prominent cone known as Little Robson must be descended to reach the lower glacier; follow this icefield down to moraines and gullies. Terraces at the 8000-foot level then can be followed north for a mile to reach high camp. If no gear has been left at the base of the arête, follow paths down to Kinney Lake.

Equipment

Carry a few rock pitons and ice screws along with standard alpine gear. A small shovel can make the gargoyles easier.

Mount Edith Cavell North Face

"It is not a good thing to look at great walls for too long a time." So wrote Yvon Chouinard after waiting for days to try the enormous, snow-plastered north wall of Mount Edith Cavell. To be sure, storms were almost continuous during that week in 1960, but Chouinard's observation of the real reason for the failure of his first attempt is an accurate one, and climbers long have been aware of this psychological phenomenon. Dread of the unknown often takes precedence over desire, and fixating on a wall is hardly the way to allay one's fears. Only when a route is well known does the uncertainty disappear, and if ever the word "unknown" was applicable, it was to describe the great Canadian north faces in the early 1960s.

Although rockclimbing was becoming popular and sophisticated in North America in the 1960s, equaling the stage reached long before in

The north face of Mount Edith Cavell. The Angel Glacier can be seen one-quarter of the way up the route. Ed Cooper.

Europe, very few snow-and-ice climbs approached high-level Alpine standards. For half a century the Canadian Rockies had been known to contain dozens of smaller versions of the Eigerwand. Why hadn't they been climbed? Only one established route, Mount Robson's Wishbone Arête, came close to the Alpine classics of the 1930s. Perhaps the main reason for this curious state of affairs was Chouinard's axiom. Canada's big walls looked horrendous and death-dealing, and besides, there was always a challenging virgin ridge nearby to offer a convenient excuse.

Thus, it was curiosity as well as challenge that brought Chouinard, Fred Beckey, and Dan Doody to Mount Edith Cavell in the midsummer of 1961. What would those ice-covered rocks be like? What about the steep rock bands in the center of the face? Would the rockfall be Eiger-like? Would the weather ever clear?

Beckey already was a legendary figure in the mountaineering world and had done hundreds of new routes. One of these was the bold ascent of Mount Hunter's west ridge, recounted earlier in this book. However, Beckey had done most of his climbing in Washington, a state not known for its Eiger-like formations. Doody, a cinematographer, was a relative newcomer to serious climbing and had climbed mostly in Wyoming. Chouinard, just

beginning his career as a manufacturer of climbing equipment, was fascinated by big mountains, although most of his climbing had been done on rock. All three men were, in their own fashion, somewhat frightened by the wall.

Named after a British nurse who was falsely accused of spying by the Germans and executed during World War I, Mount Edith Cavell is more massive than spectacular, wider than tall. Nearly 4000 feet high, the north face is sliced by numerous ledges which hold snow and ice, as well as perched debris, throughout the year. One-third of the way up the face is a small, beautifully shaped mass of ice known as the Angel Glacier. One "wing" of this icefield hovers ominously over the lower part of the face. On the broad wall above lie two indistinct ribs which terminate on the summit ridge.

The three men quickly chose the direct right-hand rib for their attempt and settled back to wait for a break in the weather. Because of an arrangement with the Canadian National Railways, they were staying gratis at the elite, railroad-owned Jasper Park Lodge, surely another first for impecunious climbers of the post–World War II generation. Owning only one sports jacket among them, the three took turns eating in the rarefied atmosphere of the great dining hall. Outside, during lulls in the ceaseless parade of storms, they tried to avoid staring at the fearsome wall fifteen miles distant.

On July 20 the sky was warm and overcast at three in the morning, but when the climbers checked a few hours later, it had cleared. Despite a forecast of a front moving in, Chouinard, Beckey, and Doody hurried to the foot of the face. Climbing unroped to save time, the trio rapidly ascended the 1000-foot rock wall beneath the glacier, all too aware of the ice mass poised above. Once safely on the lower-angled section of the glacier, they relaxed somewhat and made good time toward the right-hand rib. The face above them, 2500 feet high and tilted at an angle of fifty-five degrees, was alive with rockfall that morning, and the snow was pitted with stones of every size. Cautiously, but swiftly, the team moved onto the rock rib, seeking shelter beneath small overhangs. For many hours the men moved up steep rock interspersed with patches of snow and ice. Creeping out into the "shooting gallery" from their secure belay caves proved traumatic, though the mixed climbing generally was straightforward and not too difficult. Doody, hampered with heavy movie equipment, tried to shoot film, but he was stymied by the necessity of keeping his head and camera under bulges. Stones whizzed by like bullets, and small avalanches swept the nearby gullies. By early evening the climbers were becoming anxious about both the rockfall and the approaching bivouac, which burgeoning clouds threatened to make memorable. It was close to midnight when they settled onto small, protected ledges 1000 feet below the summit.

Fortunately, the clouds held their moisture until dawn, but just as the threesome began moving again they were embroiled in a furious thunderstorm. "Clouds moved back and forth," Chouinard wrote later, "unveiling ghastly views of the ice-plastered wall to the right and left of us." Moving efficiently, nonetheless, the climbers soon reached the ice slope which mantles the upper part of the north face. The storm let up somewhat, but as if to maintain the Eiger-like mood, the fifty-degree slope was found to consist of several inches of granular snow pellets on top of rock-hard ice. Hundreds of steps had to be chopped, steps which would instantly fill with the mothball-sized pellets. The sibilant sound of ice slithering down the slope added to the eerie, lonely atmosphere.

At the very top of the face the climbers encountered a final challenge: a band of incredibly loose shale. Unable to protect himself and powerless to keep the rope from dislodging plates of rock onto the pair below, Chouinard struggled up the last few feet to the summit ridge. Fifty feet away stood the summit cairn built by those who had taken easier routes in the past. It was early afternoon, and Chouinard finally was able to relax: "Never have I felt so happy as on that day on the summit with my friends."

Five years passed before the next ascent was made. Gray Thompson and Dennis Eberl encountered little life-threatening rockfall but found the summit icefield in the same wretched condition. The team bivouacked higher than the first group and made the top early on the second day. In his account of the climb, Eberl stated: "Under the right conditions, the objective dangers are not great, and it is certainly one of the great face climbs in North America."

The third ascent, made in 1967, was an audacious one, for during a long summer day Royal Robbins climbed the face alone. Known primarily as a brilliant rockclimber, Robbins proved to both himself and others that a good rockclimber using good judgment can ascend an alpine wall safely and in admirable style. Robbins was especially impressed with the quality of the climb, finding that the one-foot-on-ice, one-foot-on-rock method of climbing required a certain rhythm which was extremely stimulating.

Two more ascents took place in 1967. One of these was a new route, the left-hand rib mentioned earlier. This line is about equal in difficulty to the original route, even though it is more continuous since there is no glacier travel along the way. The rib terminates on the eastern summit, a few hundred yards from the true high point. During the past decade both routes have become quite popular and presently can be regarded as warm-ups for the really grim *Nordwands* which abound in the Rockies.

From the Angel Glacier, at the lower left, the North Face Route follows the left skyline. Glen Boles.

First ascent

Yvon Chouinard, Fred Beckey, and Dan Doody. July 20–21, 1961.

Elevation

The summit is 11,033 feet above sea level. The north face is approximately 4000 feet high.

Difficulty

IV, 5.7.

Time

Small, competent parties can do the route easily in one day.

Map

Canadian Department of Energy, Mines, and Resources sheet: 83 D/9, scale 1:50,000.

Useful reference

Climber's Guide to the Rocky Mountains of Canada—North.

Route description

From the town of Jasper drive south on the Banff-Jasper Highway for about seven miles to a junction. Turn right on Astoria River Road and drive another seven miles or so to the end of the road, close under the north face of Edith Cavell.

Less than an hour is required to approach the wall. Climb the class 4 face below the Angel Glacier for 1000 feet; then surmount a steep ice cliff which gives access to the lower-angled part of the glacier. Cross the bergschrund and climb onto the inobvious rock rib which lies above. A few 5.7 sections are found in the next 800 feet, but most of the climbing is much easier. Soon one is climbing more in ice gullies than on rock, though sheltered belay spots usually can be found on the rock. Eventually the upper ice slope is reached—one can climb it directly to the final shale band or diagonal left to avoid the very loose shale.

The descent is long but quite simple. Class 2 and 3 gullies drop down 4000 feet on the southwest slopes of the mountain. After reaching Verdant Creek follow it north a few miles and intersect the trail along the Astoria River. Three miles east lies the roadhead. Allow about four hours for the return from summit to car.

Equipment

Carry a few chocks and ice screws along with standard alpine equipment.

Mount Alberta
Japanese Route

The Columbia Icefields are the culmination of the Canadian Rockies,
as well as a mandatory tourist stop
on the Banff–Jasper Highway. Although the Rockies' highest peak is
not located here, one-third of the
range's forty-five mountains exceeding 11,000 feet ring the 100-
square-mile ice plateau. One of
these soaring peaks, Snow Dome, is
a unique watershed apex, for meltwater from its summit ice cap drains
into three oceans. To the north, the
waters of the Athabasca River eventually reach the Arctic Ocean.
Streams flowing southwest from
Snow Dome join the mighty Columbia River on its circuitous journey to
the Pacific, while water draining
southeast finally empties into Hudson's Bay and the Atlantic.

A few miles north of Snow Dome
rises one of the most notorious peaks
in the Rockies—Mount Alberta.
This 11,874-foot mountain is well
known for having no easy route to its
icy summit. Inclement weather, falling stones, and ice-covered rocks
have intimidated scores of mountaineers even before they have come

An aerial view of the northwest face of Mount Alberta in winter. Although the climbing route lies on the opposite side of the peak, one can see the formidable cliff band which bars easy access to the summit on all sides. Jim Stuart.

to grips with Alberta's major climbing problems. For every party that has reached the summit—perhaps ten in all—there have been many that have turned back disappointed.

Viewed from the east—the direction from which prospective climbers approach the peak—Mount Alberta is not particularly impressive. It does not have a sharp, craggy summit, nor do hanging glaciers hover above its flanks. In fact, Alberta resembles the famous stratified peaks of Montana's Glacier National Park more than it does most of the other peaks bordering the Columbia Icefields. Only the peak's north face is truly alpine; its other three sides are composed primarily of dark rock notable for its shattered nature. Observant mountaineers in search of a viable route immediately notice several formidable bands of rock encircling the mountain. So steep are these somber black cliffs that even in midwinter, when Alberta's environs are reminiscent of Alaska, they remain free from snow. Especially conspicuous is the final tier, which guards access to the summit ridge. Varying in height from 300 to 600 feet, this menacing cliff band is unbroken by a single low-angled couloir.

◀ *The east side of Mount Alberta.* Ed Cooper.

In 1898 Mount Alberta's spectacular ramparts greatly impressed J. Norman Collie, the famed Scottish mountaineer and the first person to observe the peak at close range. From a neighboring mountain Collie found that Alberta "towered frowning many hundreds of feet above us. It is a superb peak, like a gigantic castle in shape, with terrific black cliffs. . . ." Collie named the peak but made no effort to climb it, although he did accomplish the first ascent of nearby Snow Dome.

Although the area became better known in the early years of the twentieth century, it was not until 1924 that an expedition finally set forth on a serious attempt to reach Alberta's summit. Deciding to spare no expense in their bid, Howard Palmer and Joseph Hickson engaged Conrad Kain, the Austrian whose exploits on Mount Robson and Bugaboo Spire already had made him the best-known guide in Canada. Kain's expertise was never put to use on the 1924 trip, however, for the weather was so stormy that the three men never once saw the summit during the week spent at the base of the peak. Palmer was "abysmally dejected" as the party made the long journey back to Jasper. Later, he described the mountain's topography: "It possesses no easy side, being built after the fashion of the mythical Tower of Babel. . . ."

In 1921 Palmer had written a climber's guide to the Canadian Rockies with J. M. Thorington. The frontispiece consisted of a photograph of

Mount Alberta, a constant reminder to climbers of the challenge offered by the highest unclimbed summit in the Rockies. It is curious that in the next few years, apart from the Palmer–Hickson attempt, no North American climbers responded to the subtle taunt. However, interest in the peak was aroused in a distant land—Japan. Yuko Maki, an experienced mountaineer and assistant to the Crown Prince, had obtained a copy of Palmer's guidebook and was amazed to discover that so fine and high a peak as Alberta was still unclimbed. With the blessing of the Crown Prince, Maki organized an expedition to Canada, and in early July of 1925 he and five other Japanese stepped off the train in Jasper. Maki, well respected in the mountaineering world for his bold ascent of the Eiger's Mittellegi Ridge four years earlier, had brought along the latest mountaineering equipment, including pitons and silk ropes. Hiring two Swiss guides and an amateur Swiss climber, the first Japanese expedition ever to climb in North America headed south along the Athabasca River with supplies for twenty-five days.

The sixty-mile approach along the gentle river valley took only a week, and on July 20 the expedition members established their high camp on a beautiful meadow at 6800 feet, just beneath the mountain's beetling south face. The weather during July had been exceptionally warm and dry, and in marked contrast to the depression felt by Palmer's party the previous year, the enthusiasm of the Japanese party was unbounded. But clear skies alone do not ensure success, and as several of the men reconnoitered the peak, they concluded that the great upper cliff barrier might well be impregnable. On the southeast flank of the mountain, the cliff band was more broken than it was elsewhere, but it was still frightfully steep. The climbers reluctantly agreed that the southeast side was the only feasible place to launch their attack.

Well before first light on July 21, 1925, the nine climbers emerged from their tents. Jean Weber, the Swiss amateur, claimed in his lengthy account of the climb that "had anyone seen the sleepy expression on the faces, he would not have been convinced by everybody's assertion of having had a wonderful rest. . . ." By the time the sun's rays struck Alberta, the mountaineers had overcome the easy lower slopes; however, cliff bands and narrow couloirs soon slowed their progress. The guides knew that leading a party of six clients was not the fastest way up a difficult mountain, but it was obvious that no one wished to remain behind.

The climbers' earlier reconnaissance had indicated that they might encounter loose rock, but early in the day the nine men discovered to their horror that the mountain was fragmented beyond description. Every hold was loose, and ledges were covered with tons of rubble. At one point a small falling rock struck one of the Japanese; stoically ignoring his gashed face, he greatly amused the group by declaring that the mountain had drawn its "first blood."

Hours passed as the guides belayed their clients on a roundabout system of ledges and chimneys. Every hold, wrote Weber, "had the tendency to remain in the hand. . . ." At last the team reached the final tier of black cliffs, where progress slowed drastically. Heinrich Fuhrer, the chief guide, made several brilliant leads up the steep rock. In one spot he was the top man of a three-man stand, a maneuver that caused the other climbers to grip the rock with all possible strength, "in case that terrible thing should happen none dare think of."

Late in the afternoon the nine mountaineers emerged onto the summit ridge, expecting to find easier going. But the ridge proved to be sharp and exposed, and it wasn't long before they were threading through delicately perched cornices overhanging the east face. The climbers finally reached Alberta's airy summit at 7:30 in the evening, sixteen hours after leaving their camp. As the ecstatic men constructed a sturdy cairn, Maki composed a brief note to leave behind. After writing the names of the party and giving thanks to the "three Swiss gentlemen," Maki closed his remarks with a respectful statement: "We came from Japan so far called by this charming great mountain." Leaving a ceremonial ice axe protruding from the cairn, the tired men retraced their ascent route, bivouacking along the way.

Many mountaineers attempted Mount Alberta after its historic first ascent, but not one stood atop the peak until 1948, when two Americans, John Oberlin and Fred Ayres, repeated the Japanese route. During the twenty-three-year span between the first and second ascents, the ice axe left in the summit cairn became part of the climbing folklore of the Rockies. Rumors spread that the axe was made of pure silver, and that the Emperor himself had told Maki to plant it on the summit. If the rumor had persisted a few more years, the axe "would have been of gold set with rubies," Oberlin later wrote. The experienced second ascenders were well aware of the hearsay concerning the axe but were not overly disappointed when they finally encountered an ordinary Swiss axe, slightly rusted, sticking out of the summit cairn. (Both the axe and Maki's well-preserved note were removed by the 1948 party and are on display in the museum of the American Alpine Club in New York.)

Oberlin and Ayres took nearly fourteen hours ascending the peak, finding the conditions far different from those reported by the Japanese. The "rock" part of the route proved to involve alpine climbing, and the summit cornices were enormous and continuous. The two

Americans also had expected the summit ridge to be easy, but they spent several nerve-racking hours working along the ridge with mists swirling about them.

On the fourth ascent of Alberta, in 1958, Brian Greenwood and Dick Lofthouse became the first party to avoid a bivouac; the two Canadian guides found the peak in reasonable condition and arrived back at their camp before dark. Further ascents were made in the late 1960s, when several consecutive years of relatively dry weather cleared the peak of excess ice and restored it to approximately the condition enjoyed by the Japanese.

No one ascends or attempts Mount Alberta expecting superlative climbing. Present-day climbers are well aware that the approach is arduous, the weather foul, and the rock dangerously loose. Yet, like the north face of the Eiger, Mount Alberta continues to attract ambitious mountaineers who regard the challenge of a difficult route simply too great to resist.

First ascent

Heinrich Fuhrer, Hans Kohler, Jean Weber, Yuko Maki, S. Hashimoto, M. Hatano, T. Hayakawa, Y. Mita, and N. Okabe. July 21–22, 1925.

Elevation

The summit is 11,874 feet above sea level.

Difficulty

IV, 5.6.

Time

If the weather is decent, a competent party can complete the route from high camp in one day.

Map

Canadian Department of Energy, Mines, and Resources sheet: 83 C/6, scale 1:50,000.

Useful reference

Climber's Guide to the Rocky Mountains of Canada—North.

Route description

Leave the Banff–Jasper Highway at Milepost 57, some eight miles north of Sunwapta Pass. Ford the stream channels of the Sunwapta River; then follow a steep, well-trodden game trail on the brink of gravelly cliffs which border the south side of the creek leading west. After two miles, pass through a jumble of morainal material. Later, ascend northwest onto a grassy slope; then follow an easy glacier and several scree couloirs to Woolley Col, a 9300-foot pass not far to the southeast of Mount Woolley. From here Mount Alberta can be seen three miles to the west. The approach continues with a descent to a flat glacier which turns a ridge known as Little Alberta on its north. Allow a long day for this tiring approach.

Begin the ascent at the southeast base of the peak. Scramble up several thousand feet of rubble, keeping on the east side of the mountain; then diagonal up and right through the many cliff bands and chimneys (there are several possible routes in this area), aiming for the summit ridge just right of the right-hand notch of two prominent notches. Upon reaching the ridge, the route to the summit is obvious.

To descend, retrace the ascent route, rappelling when necessary.

Equipment

Carry ten pitons and ten chocks, as well as ice axes for the summit ridge.

Mount Temple East Ridge

15

Lake Louise, located in the central Canadian Rockies, is a world-famous resort rea, but mountaineers who spend time there generally shun such activities as lakeside strolls and powerboat excursions. To the minority who seek out high terrain, the wide spectrum of climbing available within a few miles of the stately Lake Louise Chateau is almost unrivaled on the continent. The quartzite towers near Moraine Lake have proven irresistible to rockclimbers, while the short approaches in this scenic area further tempt those who enjoy warm, steep cliffs. Adventurers who are more at home on exposed ice walls have discovered that the north face of Mount Fay is similar to such famous Alpine ice climbs as the Triolet and Les Courtes. Mountaineers who prefer less intimidating

The East Ridge Route of Mount Temple follows the right skyline. The Black Towers can be seen astride the level section of ridge halfway to the summit. Glen Boles.

ice climbing have found Mount Victoria to be one of the most rewarding climbs in Canada. This heavily glaciated peak, which dominates the skyline above Lake Louise, is justifiably one of the most popular climbs in the region. The knife-edged summit ridge provides a dramatic finale to a long and interesting snow climb.

The Lake Louise district obviously offers classic climbs for all tastes. In addition to the aesthetic climbs mentioned above, there are dozens of mixed snow-and-rock climbs in the area. Many mountaineers prefer such challenges, for changes in terrain and climbing technique guarantee a high level of enthusiasm throughout a climb. Five miles south of the Lake Louise Chateau lies one such route—the east ridge of Mount Temple.

At 11,636 feet, Mount Temple is the highest peak in the area; indeed, only ten peaks in the 450-mile-long Canadian Rockies rise higher. More impressive than Temple's height, however, is its stupendous bulk. Located three miles east of the Continental Divide, and with no other peaks nearby, the isolated mass dominates this section of the range. Among mountaineers Temple is renowned for its sinister, 4500-foot north face, the most awesome sight in the area. A hanging glacier atop the shadowed wall threatens climbers presumptuous enough to attempt the Eiger-like formation, and the face has been climbed only by skilled—and lucky—mountaineers.

Climbers fascinated by mountain topography also are drawn to Temple's east ridge. This two-mile-long formation can be divided into three distinct sections: a forty-five-degree rock ridge containing a few steep steps; a relatively level but serrated section known as the Black Towers; and a long snow ridge—the upper part of the glacier atop the north face—that rises to the summit.

Other facets of Mount Temple are less spectacular; the southwest flank, for example, is composed largely of scree. It was up this seemingly endless slope that three American mountaineers made the first ascent of the peak in 1894. Their ascent was noteworthy primarily because it was made without guides, an unusual occurrence in those days. Lake Louise was for years the premier guiding center of the Rockies, and the "tourist route" on Temple's southwest side was guided regularly for decades following its first ascent. The peak's east ridge, however, was considered too tough by the guides, and it was not until 1931 that climbers first attempted to reach the summit via this route.

Nineteen thirty-one was a vintage year in the history of North American climbing, especially in Wyoming's Teton Range, where a flurry of climbing activity was taking place. Among many excellent new Teton routes, the Black Dike Route on

Mount Moran was established in June by professional guide Hans Wittich and a client of his named Otto Stegmaier. Wittich was impressed with Stegmaier's competence, and after the pair completed a few more Teton routes, Wittich suggested that they motor to Lake Louise to try peaks more alpine in character.

In mid-August, after climbing several traditional routes in the Lake Louise area, Wittich and Stegmaier began to consider the east ridge of Mount Temple. After eight continuous weeks of mountaineering, the two men were in top condition, and since the weather had been mild during their stay, the ridge also was in good shape. It seemed an auspicious time to attempt the untouched ridge; so at dawn on August 17 the guide and his client set out from their camp at Moraine Lake.

As Wittich and Stegmaier toiled up easy slopes beneath the east ridge, they were pleased at the profusion of wildflowers and intrigued by the discovery of fresh grizzly tracks. Soon, however, all traces of the organic world vanished, and the men entered a barren region composed solely of rock. Three hours after leaving camp, the two climbers reached their first major obstacle, a 300-foot vertical step on the ridge. Although the firm quartzite was pleasant to climb on, the route-finding was difficult and time-consuming. Wittich later recalled one desperate spot where "an overhanging rock forced [him] almost down to the abyss. Abundant energy

The north face of Mount Temple; the East Ridge Route follows the left skyline. Ed Cooper.

only can overcome such moments." It was eleven o'clock when the guide pulled himself onto the top of the Big Step, communicating his triumph with a hearty yodel.

Although progress over the shale-covered slopes above was much faster than over the quartzite cliff, quantities of loose rock caused Wittich to describe this area as "disgusting and most dangerous." Soon the Black Towers were encountered. Traversing around some of these pinnacles and ascending others directly, the men climbed for hours

among dark, loose gendarmes. Wittich reached the top of the final spire at six o'clock and later described his experience in jubilant words: "I roared like a loud-speaker down to Otto 'Oh!' and 'Oh!' and 'Mensch, ist das wunderbar!' Right in front of me, wonderful in the evening sun, shone the hanging glacier. . . ."

Selecting a safe path between the cornices overhanging the south face and the bergschrund at the top of the north-face glacier, Wittich and Stegmaier slowly pushed on, pausing at times to take in the stunning view. At an elevation of nearly 11,000 feet, they were higher than all but a few of the hundreds of peaks visible to them. The vast Waputik Icefield, in nearby Yoho National Park, glistened in the evening light.

After about an hour the two men were forced onto a snow arête so narrow that Wittich "hewed a saddle on the very crest and swung . . . on the saddle in cowboy fashion." The tired mountaineers traversed a succession of false summits, wondering if they could finish the climb before dark. The possibility of having to bivouac astride a snow saddle spurred Wittich into frenzied activity, and swinging his ice axe "like a demon," he finally hacked his way to the summit. The two men had been climbing continuously for fifteen hours.

Total darkness enveloped the victorious climbers just after they began their descent, and a memorable bivouac ensued. So frigid were the hours after midnight that the climbers "danced on the narrow ledge for two hours to limber up. . . ." But the night was short, and it was not long before Wittich and Stegmaier were racing down the tourist route "like devils."

It cannot be said that the east ridge instantly became a classic, for only two more ascents were made in the next thirty years. In 1962 Brian Greenwood and two friends made the fourth ascent, also taking about fifteen hours. Greenwood, a well-known Canadian guide, was so impressed with the quality of the climb that he published a lengthy note in the *Canadian Alpine Journal*. "I make no apologies," he wrote, "for this account of a 1962 climb up a ridge first ascended in 1931. . . . It is a climb that deserves to be done much more frequently."

Greenwood's evaluation of the neglected route spurred other mountaineers into action, and by the mid-1960s the ridge had been ascended a number of times. Few parties, however, were able to better the time of the first-ascent party; indeed, bivouacs midway up the route were common. When Chris Jones, author of a distinguished history of North American climbing, ascended the ridge in 1977, he expected a routine climb. Using several protection pitons at the Big Step and the Black Towers, Jones and his companion encountered only a few sections where they could dispense with their rope. Although the two climbers were slowed by foul weather, they spent parts of three days achieving the summit, and Jones later cautioned: "Never underestimate a route done in the 1930s; mountaineers back then were often fast and competent."

With mist blanketing the wall above, Chris Jones begins climbing the steep quartzite of the Big Step. R. D. Caughron.

One of the early ascent parties established a major variation which bypasses the lower ridge and the Big Step. At the extreme left edge of the north face lies a steep, 1500-foot-high snow couloir which leads to the east ridge just beneath the Black Towers. Since the couloir is remarkably uniform and attractive, some recent parties have preferred to use this variation rather than struggle up the vertical quartzite of the Big Step. One wonders if Wittich and Stegmaier would have approved of this alternative to their uncompromisingly direct line.

First ascent

Hans Wittich and Otto Stegmaier. August 17, 1931.

Elevation

The summit is 11,636 feet above sea level.

Difficulty

IV, 5.6.

Time

If conditions are favorable and the party is strong, a one-day ascent is possible.

Map

Canadian Department of Energy, Mines, and Resources sheet: 82 N/8, scale 1:50,000.

Useful reference

Climber's Guide to the Rocky Mountains of Canada—South.

Route description

From Lake Louise follow a paved road south for about ten miles to Moraine Lake. At the north end of this lake, follow a trail leading north for about two miles and then head up arduous slopes, aiming for a

Nearing the double-corniced summit ridge.   R. D. Caughron.

400-foot-high rock tooth at the base of a series of couloirs. To the left of the tooth lies an easy couloir. Climb it to its top; then move right into the next couloir. Climb this to its top; then move right once again. Ascend the third couloir to the ridge crest.

Scramble up the ridge to the Big Step; several medium class 5 pitches lead to its top. Another step is encountered higher, but it is shorter and easier than the Big Step. Above, easier climbing on shale- or snow-covered slopes brings one to the serrated ridge known as the Black Towers. This section involves complicated routefinding and is time-consuming. From the final tower to the summit, the route over the remaining snow ridge is obvious.

To descend, follow the summit snow ridge southwest until reaching the 11,000-foot level; then work down easy but tedious couloirs and slopes to Sentinel Pass at 8600 feet. From here a rough trail leads three-and-a-half miles to Moraine Lake.

Equipment

Take along a small selection of chocks and a dozen pitons. Also carry ice axes and at least one pair of crampons.

Mount Waddington South Face

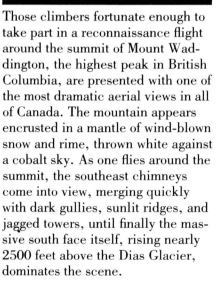

Those climbers fortunate enough to take part in a reconnaissance flight around the summit of Mount Waddington, the highest peak in British Columbia, are presented with one of the most dramatic aerial views in all of Canada. The mountain appears encrusted in a mantle of wind-blown snow and rime, thrown white against a cobalt sky. As one flies around the summit, the southeast chimneys come into view, merging quickly with dark gullies, sunlit ridges, and jagged towers, until finally the massive south face itself, rising nearly 2500 feet above the Dias Glacier, dominates the scene.

The early explorers who approached Mount Waddington on foot were equally impressed by this masterpiece of mountain architecture. W. A. D. Munday, with his wife, Phyllis, approached the mountain in 1926 and described its lower cliffs as being "camouflaged into an appearance of inviting ruggedness by their patchwork pattern of white, black, light and dark grey, which is fantastically arabesqued by innumerable pinkish aplitic dikes intruded into the old

The central tower of Mount Waddington, described by W. A. D. Munday as "the great spire poised in the void, an incredible nightmarish thing that must be seen to be believed." Phyllis Munday took this historic photo in 1928.

85

stratified rocks." The couple's expedition into the heart of the Waddington Range resulted in many discoveries, notably the vast Franklin Glacier flowing southwest from Mount Waddington some twenty-five miles to a point close to the sea at Knight Inlet. Using this glacier system as a means of access, the Mundays returned for further reconnaissance in 1927 and the following year were the first to ascend Mount Waddington's northwest peak.

During the early years of its exploration, Mount Waddington was known only as "Mystery Mountain." Though Captain Robert Bishop sighted and triangulated the mountain in 1922, his report was lost among the voluminous files of the Canadian Geological Survey. Three years later the Mundays rediscovered Mount Waddington from a peak on Vancouver Island, and their 1926 expedition finally confirmed the location, indeed the very existence, of Mystery Mountain. Sometime around 1930 the mountain officially was named after Alfred Waddington, who had secured a charter in 1893 to build a toll road from the coast up through the Homathko Valley to the interior plateau of British Columbia—a road that fortunately was never constructed. Not only did the region's terrain and climate cause difficulties, but Waddington also met with severe resistance from the Chilcotin tribe. Fearing that

their territory was about to be invaded by white settlers, the Chilcotins attacked and killed nearly all of the members of Waddington's surveying crew one night as they slept in their tents. The project ultimately was abandoned, and the Homathko Valley remains to this day a dense, forested wilderness of roaring glacial streams and matted paths of grizzly bears.

The Mundays continued exploring their beloved Waddington Range, mapping and climbing many of the fine peaks of the region, which covers some 400 square miles and also contains innumerable active glaciers and icefalls. In 1934 the Mundays and their companions, Henry Hall and Hans Fuhrer, became the first party to make an attempt on the unclimbed south face. This attempt met with little success, for as Munday commented later, "various patches of snow and ice hung in niches in the face above us but blank cliffs forbade linking them into a practicable route. At about 11,500 feet we turned back. . . ."

After being stymied by the complexities of the imposing south face, the group went on to make the second ascent of the northwest peak. Inspired by the vast panorama before them, the Mundays again turned to Waddington's awesome summit tower, searching the peak's nightmarish accumulation of rime for the key to its ascent. Directly in front of them, "only a few hundred

feet distant, the great spire poised in the void, an incredible nightmarish thing that must be seen to be believed, and then is hard to believe; it is difficult to escape appearance of exaggeration when dealing with a thing which in itself is an exaggeration."

During the course of their explorations that summer, the Mundays were unaware that just a few weeks before their attempt on the south face, another party had arrived at the mountain by means of a new route from the east, via the Tiedemann Glacier. The approach itself later became a classic in Canadian bushwhacking, leading from Tatlayoko Lake down the wild Homathko River to the Tiedemann. In the party were Ferris Neave, Roger Neave, and Campbell Secord. During the climbers' extraordinary four-week expedition they nearly conquered the northeast face of the summit tower, turning back 600 feet from the top because of approaching darkness and a persistent snowfall. It was a remarkable attempt, accomplished with meager supplies and incredible audacity. The Neave party not only found a new way to Waddington over the Tiedemann and Bravo glaciers, but also discovered that the northeast face was climbable.

With the publication of the Mundays' information and a photograph of the summit tower, along with Ferris Neave's account of his party's bold attempt on the north side of the peak, Mount Waddington became the most sought-after ascent in

◀ *The south face of Mount Waddington.* Barry Hagen.

Canada. Strangely, subsequent expeditions continued to come to the south side; the approach from the east was forgotten and would not be tried again for another seventeen years.

The strong Sierra Club party that approached Mount Waddington in 1935 was decisively defeated by the weather, and the climbers were unable even to set foot on the mountain. Bestor Robinson was the leader of that group and, commenting on the chances of reaching the summit, noted prophetically: "The Bavarian two-rope technique for overhangs, pitons for direct aid, rope traverses and other phases of technical rock climbing will probably be necessary." But, as these young climbers from sunny Yosemite were to discover, it would take more than mere technical ability to reach the summit of Waddington. Several members of the expedition returned in 1936, and though there were a few changes in the party, all were highly qualified rockclimbers, again under the leadership of Robinson. The Sierra Club party had joined forces in Vancouver with climbers from the British Columbia Mountain Club, resulting in an unwieldy team of nine persons.

To complicate matters, a party composed of four climbers from the eastern United States—Fritz Wiessner, William House, Alanson Willcox, and Betty Woolsey—soon appeared at base camp on the Franklin Glacier. At this point there were too many climbers to operate safely on such a demanding alpine

face, so the Wiessner party waited while the Sierra Club climbers and their Canadian friends made their attempt. During the next two days, the nine climbers made several valiant efforts to find a way to the summit, but each time they were unable to master the difficulties of the terrain. They were learning that alpine climbing rarely involves optimum conditions and found they were unprepared for rock that was loose, cold, wet, and often covered with ice or rime. Climbing of this nature, which requires a great sense of commitment, was only just emerging in North America.

Wiessner and House then prepared for their attempt. They had climbed together many times on local rock in the East, and while it was House who suggested the attempt on this majestic peak, it ultimately fell to Wiessner to provide the knowledge for its successful completion. The experience that Wiessner brought to this remote mountain in western Canada was remarkable. He started climbing at an early age on cliffs—the famous Elbsandsteingebirge—near his home in Dresden. In the early 1920s he began serious climbing on the marvelous limestone walls of the Kaisergebirge in north-central Austria, where he excelled in long alpine routes. One of these, a daring line up the southeast face of the Fleischbank, involved free climbing of the highest order. By

1930 Wiessner had acquired the knowledge necessary for solving the complex problems often encountered on major alpine peaks and was ready to seek new challenges in more distant ranges.

The two climbers—Willcox and Woolsey remained at a lower camp as a support team—left their small tent on the Dias Glacier shortly before three in the morning. By seven o'clock they reached a prominent, triangular snowfield some 1500 feet above their camp. The climbing then became extreme, as everyone had predicted, and Wiessner changed into a pair of rope-soled *Kletterschuhe* he had brought from Bavaria for difficult rock work. He studied the terrain carefully: "Above us extended the last 1000 feet of the south face in sheer forbidding-looking rocks, but the possibility of climbing it could be detected by anyone looking at it with a trained eye. I knew that the objective dangers could be overcome, if this part of the climb was attacked intelligently and cautiously."

The men moved confidently over the ice-covered rock, with Wiessner leading and House struggling with the troublesome pack. They finally reached the crest and stepped onto a summit so small that only one of them could stand there at a time. It was four in the afternoon. As is often the case with a successful climb, the joy of achievement, acquired through a combination of speed and technical excellence, was all too brief. The two climbers realized that

A climber ascends to the belay station at the upper edge of the triangular snowfield. Jack Tackle.

the descent would entail hours of intricate and dangerous rappelling, much of it in the dark, perhaps demanding even greater skill than was needed on the ascent. At two in the morning they finally reached the safety of their Dias Glacier camp, exhausted but content with the conclusion of a brilliant ascent, one of the finest technical climbs yet accomplished in North America.

Six years passed before the face was climbed again. In 1942 teenage brothers Fred and Helmy Beckey mastered the face with the same speed and daring exhibited by Wiessner and House. They also pioneered a new line on the last 500 feet below the summit when ice-choked chimneys forced them onto steeper rock. Youth and skill were perfectly matched on this ascent, which was all the more astonishing because the climbers' summit footgear consisted of "felt pullovers on tennis shoes."

The character of climbing on Mount Waddington changed dramatically with the opening of the Southeast Chimney Route by a strong and capable Sierra Club team in 1950.

Most subsequent ascents would be accomplished over this shorter and easier line to the summit by approaching the peak along the route taken by the Neave expedition in 1934. It is understandable that the desire to reach the summit was stronger than the desire to continue the tradition on the south side of the mountain. However, it is ironic that climbers in the mid-1960s undoubtedly were directed to the Southeast Chimney Route by a note in the climber's guide to the range advising that the south face is "not recommended because of rockfall hazard and rotten rock." By 1969, when the second edition of this guide was published, big-wall climbers in other Canadian ranges already were tackling greater problems and objective dangers than those found on Waddington's south face. By then, rockfall was accepted as one of the common characteristics, however unpleasant, of alpine climbing.

The third ascent of the south face was made in the summer of 1977 by Jack Tackle and Ken Currens, who added yet another variation to the original route by ascending 5.9 rock from the triangular snowfield directly into the amphitheater just below the summit. From this point they proceeded directly upward to a prominent notch in the northwest ridge only two ropelengths from the top.

The number of expeditions to the south side of the peak undoubtedly will increase as it becomes known that the southern rocks are a reasonable risk after all, particularly in view of the unstable nature of the Bravo Glacier on the northeast side. Attracted by the immense southern rampart, an international cast of climbers continues to be drawn to Mount Waddington, whose snow-covered buttresses and towers, crowned by the golden masonry of the upper cliffs, fascinate those who prefer their climbs difficult, varied, and remote.

First ascent

Fritz Wiessner and William House. July 21, 1936.

Elevation

The summit is 13,177 feet above sea level. The climbing route is approximately 2500 feet long.

Difficulty

V, 5.7.

Time

Ten to fourteen hours from a high camp at 11,700 feet, depending on conditions. Because the descent consists of numerous complicated rappels and much downclimbing, a bivouac can be avoided only by an extremely early departure from high camp.

Map

Canadian Department of Energy, Mines, and Resources sheet: Mount Waddington 92N, scale 1:250,000.

Useful references

A Climber's Guide to the Coastal Ranges of British Columbia. A brief history of Mount Waddington, including a bibliography and photo essay, can be found in the 1969 issue of *Ascent.*

Route description

Mount Waddington is located 180 air miles northwest of Vancouver, British Columbia. The southern side is approached most easily by float plane from either Vancouver or the Campbell River on Vancouver Island. At the head of Knight Inlet, logging roads lead to within a few miles of the terminus of the Franklin Glacier.

Ascend the Franklin Glacier past Icefall Point to a high camp on the Dias Glacier just beneath the south face. Allow four to five days from Knight Inlet to establish this camp.

Cross the bergschrund and ascend a large, slightly hidden couloir that descends from the notch between the summit tower and the Fang. When the couloir forks, take the left branch, which leads to rock bands giving access to the prominent, triangular snowfield directly in line with the summit and halfway up the face. From the upper left edge of this snowfield, continue past several ridge towers for four ropelengths into a small amphitheater about 500 feet below the summit. On the left side of this final wall are two distinct, parallel chimneys. Climb the left chimney for one pitch and then begin an ascending traverse to the right to reach the southeast ridge near the summit. The Beckey variation exits the amphitheater at its right edge, eventually reaching the crest at approximately the same place as Wiessner's original route.

To descend, rappel more or less directly to the triangular snowfield and then return to camp along the ascent route.

Equipment

Carry standard alpine gear. Crampons and an ice axe are essential. In 1977 there was much residual snow, and crampons were used on all but five pitches. Take five each of angles (small- to medium-sized) and horizontals, as well as ice screws and extra webbing for rappel anchors. Hard hats provide much peace of mind.

Remarks

To minimize the danger of falling ice and rock, the couloir at the start of the route only should be climbed early in the morning or late at night. Although snow conditions vary from year to year, there always is an accumulation of rime on the summit ridges. After a storm it is wise to wait three or four days for the rocks to clear before beginning an ascent.

Devil's Thumb
East Ridge

17

"It's the hardest climb I've ever done." This concise—if too often heard—statement should be considered seriously only if the reputation of the speaker warrants it. Fred Beckey had been pioneering difficult routes for a decade when he used these words to describe his 1946 first ascent of Devil's Thumb, and his appraisal was well respected by mountaineers who remembered he had climbed the fabled south face of Mount Waddington as well as many daring routes in the Cascades. It is entirely possible that his valuation was a prime reason why the summit of the Thumb was not revisited for nearly a quarter of a century.

Devil's Thumb is well known to the residents of Petersburg, Alaska, for during the very few clear days enjoyed by the village each year, the 9077-foot-high fang dominates the mountainous eastern horizon. Most

Devil's Thumb viewed from the southeast. The East Ridge Route follows the right skyline.
Greg Donaldson.

present-day mountaineers are vaguely aware of "a huge tower somewhere up on the southeastern Alaska coast," but few of them have seen the peak at closer range than the villagers.

Beckey decided while in the army during World War II that his first postwar climbing trip would be devoted to attempts on Devil's Thumb and other peaks in the mysterious region known as the Stikine. The Stikine River had been traveled extensively by early prospectors, but little was known about the nearby icefields and ragged peaks straddling the Alaska–British Columbia boundary. Fritz Wiessner had visited the area a year after his first ascent of Mount Waddington but had attained no summits. Other than this 1937 venture, no mountaineers had explored the district; indeed, it was quite likely no human ever had set foot within five miles of the Stikine's most spectacular summit, the towering Devil's Thumb.

Beckey easily convinced Wiessner to return to the fabulous untouched region, and in early July 1946 the two men, along with Donald Brown, left the coast and traveled by motor launch up the Stikine River. Dropped off seventy miles inland, the three mountaineers began transporting their copious supplies through luxuriant brush and morainal deposits. It took a week to relay loads the thirteen miles from the river to the beginning of the icefields, but just as the group caught sight of their objectives, Wiessner

badly sprained his knee. The expedition ground to a halt, and a few days later the three men retreated to the coast.

Not about to abandon climbs dreamed about for so many years, the indefatigable Beckey had cached most of the expedition's supplies at a base camp near the icefields. When he reached civilization, his first act was to telegraph climbing friends in Seattle, asking them to hasten north. Only a week passed before two experienced climbers, Bob Craig and Cliff Schmidtke, arrived on the ferry to greet the anxious Beckey.

When the newly formed group arrived back at the cache a few days later, they were astonished to find gear strewn all over the landscape. "After superficial investigation," Beckey wrote in the 1947 issue of the *American Alpine Journal*, "we indicted some sagacious goats, now browsing on a distant hillside, safe from castigation. The main losses were some cheese, salami, butter and sugar. The greedy beasts even chewed an empty Klim can." Undeterred by this pilferage, the pioneers proceeded on skis into uncharted territory.

The weather was continually bad during the next two weeks, but the men managed to struggle up the region's highest mountain, lovely Kate's Needle. Foremost in their thoughts, however, was the great tower looming in the west. Beckey thought that Devil's Thumb "looked terrific—like a truncated Matterhorn, only steeper. Verglas and ice patches clung to the granite diorite at amazing angles." On August 15 the trio skied five miles across the icefields and set up camp at the eastern base of the Thumb.

Through binoculars, Beckey, Craig, and Schmidtke studied route possibilities. The south face was out of the question, for it swept upward to the summit in a steep, unbroken line. Much of the north side of the mountain was hidden from their view, but they guessed from the topography of nearby peaks that it must be huge and alpine. It took the group just a few minutes to reach the conclusion that their sole chance for success was on the face directly in front of them. The southeast flank, only a few thousand feet high, would be a snow climb for two-thirds of its height, after which it seemed possible to attain the east ridge and follow its serrated course over rock and ice to the summit.

On August 16 the men left camp at three in the morning, intent on making a serious reconnaissance despite threatening weather. Ascending forty-five-degree snowslopes, the climbers made slow progress to a saddle at 8000 feet. Just above this point, however, whirling mists enveloped the peak, and the men fled to camp in an icy downpour. A second attempt two days later was interrupted by darkness after much demanding climbing. The adventurers settled into a miserable bivouac at 8700 feet; by dawn it was snowing, and the disappointed trio once again struggled downward to their camp.

Devil's Thumb as seen from base camp on the glacier southeast of it. The two steps of the east ridge can be seen on the right skyline. Greg Donaldson.

A four-day blizzard kept the mountaineers confined to their tents, and it was not until August 25 that the fresh snow on the Thumb had melted sufficiently to justify another attempt. All three men realized that this effort would be their last, for the food was nearly gone and the weekly boat down the Stikine River was due in two days. It was again three in the morning when the trio departed camp; this time, however, the weather prospects looked wonderful. The climbers reached their previous high point by noon, then set out along the severely exposed summit ridge. To the north an ominous 5000-foot wall plunged abruptly to the Baird Glacier. The drop on the opposite side of the arête was not as extreme, but it was impressive enough that the threesome belayed carefully as they navigated the cornices and rock towers guarding the approach to the top. At two in the afternoon the three mountaineers stood on the wildly exposed summit. For once the sky was totally clear, and the climbers could pick out Mount Fairweather, 220 miles to the northwest. It had taken nearly fifty days to realize his goal of climbing Devil's Thumb, thought Beckey, but to stand upon such a magnificent summit on a pristine day was worth all the thrashing through brush and endless days cooped up inside a leaking tent.

The descent was complex and dangerous, but the jubilant mountaineers were back in camp before dark. The next day the trio journeyed twenty miles to the Stikine River, arriving on its banks just hours before the boat appeared around a bend.

During the summer of 1970, a Canadian party consisting of Dick Culbert, Paul Starr, and Fred Douglas skied across the icefields toward Devil's Thumb, intent on forcing a new route up the peak, which had not been climbed a second time. Like Beckey's party, however, the

A climber works his way up the first step of the east ridge. Greg Donaldson.

Canadians were intimidated by the awesome north and south faces. Under the mistaken impression that Beckey, Craig, and Schmidtke had ascended the east ridge for its entire length, the three men resigned themselves to repeating this 1946 route, although the lower part of the ridge contained two formidable rock steps.

Leaving their camp before first light, the Canadians worked up steep snowslopes to the first step. Soon the three climbers were tackling moderate class 5 rock. "Most of the first six pitches," wrote Culbert in his

account of the climb, "were extremely steep and went free only because of the fabulous rock, split almost to the point of being loose." The men spent much of the day on the excellent rock of the two steps, with daylight fading as they labored along the icy summit ridge: "Occasionally we were forced out onto the north face by ice-slush plumes glued to gendarmes. Wild!"

After a bivouac on the summit ridge the Canadians finally reached the top, extremely impressed with the route they supposed had been established by Beckey's group. They reached camp exhausted at midnight, having spent forty hours on the mountain.

Thousands of feet above the ice cap, a climber emerges onto the summit ridge.   Greg Donaldson.

The line climbed by the Canadians was far safer, more direct, and more aesthetic than the original, but the 1970 climbers were not to know they had pioneered a new route until months later, when Beckey pointed out his route on photographs. Soon other mountaineers traveled to Devil's Thumb, and for the majority there was no question of which route to try. Greg Donaldson, who climbed the direct ridge in 1971, wrote that the climb "passed in a real dream: warm but not hot, clear with dry rock—never a moment when the going was really easy, never exceptionally hard."

Donaldson's party was fortunate to encounter such good conditions on its summit bid, for the Stikine has a reputation among present-day mountaineers as being one of the wettest areas on the continent. Those who enter the icefields for short trips are fully aware that they may never even glimpse the peaks they have come so far to climb. The mountaineer who spends a month on the icefields, however, probably will open his or her tent door one morning to discover the Thumb shimmering with meltwater and etched against a sky alarmingly blue compared to its usual gray.

First ascent

The upper third of the east ridge was first climbed by Fred Beckey, Bob Craig, and Cliff Schmidtke on August 25, 1946. The lower ridge, containing the two rock steps, was ascended for the first time in the summer of 1970 by Dick Culbert, Paul Starr, and Fred Douglas.

Elevation

The summit is 9077 feet above sea level.

Difficulty

IV, 5.6.

Time

The round trip from a camp at 6000 feet has been made in one day, but this is possible only by a very skilled party climbing in good weather.

Maps

For an overall view of the region and its various approaches, see the USGS topographic sheet: Sundum, scale 1:250,000. For a more detailed look at Devil's Thumb, see USGS quadrangles Sundum A-1 and Sundum A-2, both with a scale of 1:63,360.

Route description

From the coastal city of Prince Rupert, British Columbia, take a ferry 200 miles north to Wrangell, Alaska. In this town it is possible to charter an aircraft that, depending on surface conditions, can land on Flood Lake, Shakes Lake, or the Stikine River. Before being dropped off, have the pilot overfly the area to select the most efficient approach to the peak. Allow two or three days for the ski journey over the icefields to the eastern base of Devil's Thumb.

The route is quite obvious and follows the ridge crest closely, with a few excursions onto the south side at the two rock steps.

The best way to descend is to follow the 1946 route instead of retracing the ascent path. The southeast face requires several rappels and some tricky downclimbing.

Lotus Flower Tower

18

"I think as soon as we came over a rise and caught our first glimpse of Lotus Flower Tower, many miles away, we knew instantly that it was the route to do." As Jim McCarthy stared at the 2200-foot-high pillar of granite, he realized that if he and his two partners could manage to climb the obvious crack system on the southeast face, it would become an instant classic. Sandy Bill, one of McCarthy's companions, later described the group's first glimpse of the tower: "A great wall grasps our eyes and casts its spell. . . . The closer we get the more beautiful it becomes—simple, elegant, yet gentle." The third man, Tom Frost, immediately began photographing the pillar; when he developed his film weeks later, he was surprised to find that many rolls contained little else besides shots of the awesome granite shaft.

◀ *The southeast face of Lotus Flower Tower.* Tom Frost.

The three men stood mesmerized in an area known as the Cirque of the Unclimbables, the culmination of the Logan Mountains, a range which stretches along the Yukon–Northwest Territories border at the sixty-second parallel. Only half a dozen parties had ever visited the Cirque, and even though its major peaks had been climbed by these groups, innumerable virgin walls remained to challenge competent adventurers. Arnold Wexler, member of a 1955 expedition, had experienced a "feeling of frustration engendered by these peaks with their sheer faces of flawless granite. They looked impregnable and impossible. . . . I know of few mountain ranges in Canada that offer such a challenge to the rock enthusiast."

As McCarthy, Frost, and Bill relaxed in camp that evening in August 1968, they recalled Bill Buckingham's unequivocal words in the *American Alpine Journal:* "Here are some of the finest mountains in North America, a compact range of jagged spires and towering granite walls offering routes of every conceivable difficulty. . . . This single cluster of peaks is at least the equal of any of the more famous areas. . . ." In 1960 Buckingham's group had accomplished numerous excellent routes, including the "back side" of the great pillar they named Lotus Flower Tower.

Several months before the 1968 expedition, Jim McCarthy, having climbed in the Cirque once before, had cajoled Frost and Bill into visiting the climbing nirvana he recalled

so well. Since midsummer offered the most stable weather, the three men and a coterie of followers gathered in early August at Dawson Creek, British Columbia, the lower terminus of the Alaska Highway. Several days later, after an interminable dusty drive through the monotonous boreal forest, the group reached Watson Lake, a small outpost in the southern Yukon. Chartering two aircraft, they flew 150 miles north over totally wild country and landed on Glacier Lake, just east of the Cirque. A short but strenuous approach through alder and talus led the climbers to Fairy Meadow—a delightful, moss-covered campsite near the entrance to the Cirque.

As the three mountaineers reminisced about the climbs and zeal of their predecessors, they began to consider their own strategy. McCarthy and Frost, who were experienced big-wall climbers, estimated that the wall would take several days. Not only did the steep pillar look as if it would require much direct aid, but weather would be an important factor. McCarthy reminded his partners that on his previous two-week trip he had seen the sun only a few times. Although vicious weather was unlikely in August, a drizzle could make the climbing slow, cold, and unpleasant. After packing wet-weather gear, a four-day supply of food, and many quarts of water, the climbers' duffel bag reached monstrous proportions.

Leaving camp at noon on August 10, the three men made the short hike from Fairy Meadow to the base of the southeast face.

That afternoon McCarthy and Bill fixed ropes over the first two pitches; the climb began in earnest at dawn the following day, August 11. Bill, who was to haul the bag the first day, waited shivering in the talus as the others mounted the ropes. Looking upward, he watched the "sunbeams play like butterflies around the flower of stone."

The route on the first half of the pillar was obvious, for a single crack split the wall. To the surprise of all three men, much of the climbing was moderate class 5. The granite was not overly steep, and the rock was so rough that holds were plentiful. Late in the day the climbers faced the sole routefinding decision to be made on the 2200-foot wall. If they continued along the same crack system, they would ascend up and left along wet grooves that eventually arrived at the summit. But from the ground the men had spotted a striking set of clean, parallel cracks on the right side of the face which shot straight to the summit. The three men conferred on the matter. McCarthy was convinced that the logical and easiest path lay in the main crack system. The other two climbers, realizing they were ahead of schedule, opted for the parallel cracks of the direct route and finally managed to persuade their recalcitrant friend, who later stated simply: "They were right."

Sandy Bill leads a dihedral above the first ascenders' bivouac ledge; above him lie the parallel cracks leading to the summit.   Tom Frost.

Sandy Bill and Jim McCarthy at a belay station high on the southeast face. Tom Frost.

In the subarctic gloom at ten o'clock that evening, Frost manteled onto the first real ledge of the route. McCarthy, anxious about the forthcoming bivouac, yelled up to Frost, inquiring if the newly found site was adequate. "It looks all right," floated back the reply, "if you happen to like flat grass." Bill, relieved to have dragged his immense burden for the final time that day, also was captivated by their bivouac site: "Indeed it is a palace, a few square feet of the meadow perched in the sky. . . . We break out our best German salami and Edam cheese to celebrate. . . ."

One more pitch the following morning brought the men to a ledge at the base of the parallel cracks that soon were to become fabled in the mountaineering world. Bill gazed at "a long, long crack hanging straight, like a thread, from the very peak of the tower—the Great Line." There actually were several perfectly formed cracks, each an inch or two wide and twenty or thirty feet apart; all of them shot straight to the summit, 1000 feet above. None of the climbers had ever seen such a sight, not even in Yosemite Valley, a place renowned for its continuous crack systems. It was, they realized, perhaps the finest series of cracks ever encountered by climbers, and once again Frost began snapping pictures.

Choosing the most accessible crack, the leader began hammering pitons. "The climbing is not difficult," Bill stated later, "its greatness is its esthetic purity. All day we creep up this line." Although the golden granite was sprinkled liberally with knobs, the angle steepened gradually throughout the day, and most of the team's progress was made by means of direct aid. McCarthy cursed the coin flip that had doomed him to the role of hauler that day and enviously watched his joyful teammates.

Nightfall caught the men in one of the wildest positions imaginable. Frost had just surmounted an overhang about 400 feet below the summit; the exposure was tremendous. By the time all three men were reunited at Frost's hanging belay station, it was nearly dark, and an hour went by before the climbers were settled into their hammocks. When McCarthy's hammock began to make small ripping sounds, he moved about restlessly, wondering what was happening. As the noise grew louder, it became clear that the seams were parting. "Jim serenaded Tom and me to sleep," Bill wrote later, "with his slowly disintegrating hammock and curses."

Straining to place his foot in an aid sling, Sandy Bill leads a pitch along the Great Line. Tom Frost.

The weather had been perfect for two days, but the third day dawned gray and sullen. An hour later, however, the sky suddenly cleared—a fine omen on a fine climb, the men thought. McCarthy was overjoyed to be rid of the duffel bag and to take his turn on the Great Line. He and Bill nailed upward quickly, finally exiting the 1000-foot crack just below the summit. By noon the three climbers were sitting around the cairn built eight years earlier by Buckingham's group. Bill was ecstatic: "It has been a beautiful crack—a beautiful climb. We lounge in the warm sun and savor

the peaks around us. We have eaten lotus and known its power on this Wall of Forgetfulness. We linger long before descending the back side."

So compelling were the photographs Frost published of the upper crack that the very next year a small group drove to Watson Lake with the express purpose of repeating the route, a testimony to the climb considering the many other untouched walls in the area. Although this party never left Watson Lake because of foul weather, other groups soon followed. The second ascent of the route was made by three Frenchmen in 1971. They climbed the lower section mainly free but, like their predecessors, nailed most of the Great Line.

In the early 1970s many European mountaineers visited North America, and the Cirque of the Unclimbables became a popular destination. Within a remarkably short time span, Swiss, Austrian, and French parties repeated the southeast face of the Lotus Flower Tower; American ascents were a decided minority. However, one group of climbers from the United States—Steve Levin, Mark Robinson, and Sandy Stewart—ascended the pillar in 1977 without recourse to direct aid. The crux, a difficult jamcrack, led through the overhang where the first ascenders had slept.

The 1977 American party noticed that previous climbers had left vast amounts of trash, both at Fairy Meadow and, surprisingly, on the Tower itself. "We were also greatly distressed," Levin later wrote, "at the practices of [one party], for shooting mountain goats and marmots, cutting down trees unnecessarily and incompetent waste removal. The Cirque of the Unclimbables is a magnificent and beautiful area. *Please* let's keep it that way."

First ascent

Jim McCarthy, Sandy Bill, and Tom Frost. August 10–13, 1968.

Elevation

The summit is about 7500 feet above sea level.

Difficulty

V, 5.8, A2. Done free the route is 5.10.

Time

The climb can be made in two days if the weather is good.

Map

Canadian Department of Energy, Mines, and Resources sheet: 95 L/4, scale 1:50,000.

Route description

From Watson Lake, just off the Alaska Highway, one can charter an aircraft for the 150-mile flight north to Glacier (or Brintnell) Lake. From here follow Brintnell Creek west for a mile or two; then head up the steep hillside to the north. The long day's journey to Fairy Meadow is strenuous and unpleasant. An alternative approach is to drive 180 miles north on a gravel road to the mining town of Cantung (or Tungsten); from here a helicopter sometimes can be chartered for the 20-mile flight to Fairy Meadow.

From Fairy Meadow, follow the main stream north for a few miles; then curve west into the last cirque encountered before reaching Mount Sir James MacBrien, the high point of the region. Lotus Flower Tower can be seen at the back of this cirque. (The Cirque of the Unclimbables is a name used to designate several major cirques separated by ridges.)

The first 1000-foot section of Lotus Flower Tower is obvious; the main difficulties are found in the first dihedral. Leave the main crack system at the 1000-foot level and climb up and right to the upper of two prominent ledges. From here it is impossible to lose the route.

To descend, follow the ridge leading northeast to a notch; then descend rotten rock and ice gullies (with several rappels) to easy snowfields.

Equipment

The climb can be made using chocks only; take many larger sizes for the jamcracks along the Great Line.

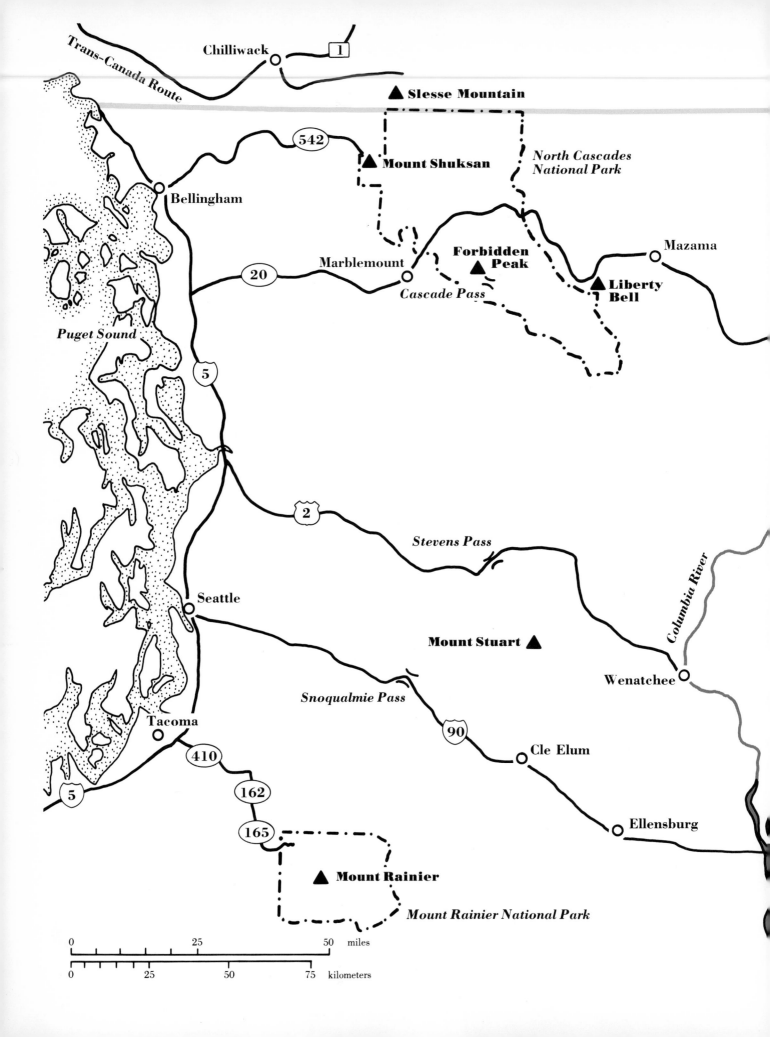

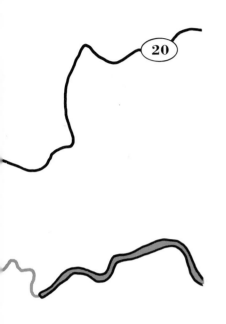

The Pacific Northwest

Most geographers identify the Cascade Range as beginning near Mount Lassen in northern California and ending at the Fraser River Valley, located a few miles north of the United States–Canadian border. Dormant volcanoes and cinder cones are characteristic features of the southern segment of the range, while peaks to the north of Mount Rainier are composed primarily of vast intrusions of igneous and metamorphic rock. The latter region also contains the largest concentration of glaciers in the contiguous United States—an accumulation of ice totaling nearly a hundred square miles. Cascade storms are notorious among climbers, yet it is the precipitation from these storms that endows the range with its enchanting alpine qualities.

Early Cascade mountaineers were attracted first to the region's high, snow-covered volcanoes, and by 1911 all of them had been climbed. After more than a decade of moderate mountaineering activity on the relatively accessible southern peaks, climbers began exploring the little-known subranges to the north, particularly the incredibly wild North Cascades. Several outstanding climbs took place during the 1920s, including the first ascent of Canada's Slesse Mountain in 1927. In the 1930s, the introduction of European climbing techniques and equipment aided climbers in establishing daring routes on Mount Rainier's Liberty Ridge and on the west ridge of Forbidden Peak—two of our classics. Other notable climbs of this period include Mount Rainier's Ptarmigan Ridge Route and the Southwest Chimney Route on lofty Mount Goode.

Around 1938 Fred Beckey first surfaced in the Northwest climbing community; as this book documents, he was destined for great achievements. With Beckey leading the way, an increasing number of climbers explored new frontiers on both familiar and untried Cascade peaks during the next forty years. The number of new routes accomplished was impressive, as was the bold style in which they were done. As Beckey noted in *Challenge of the North Cascades:* "Standards of difficulty steadily rose. The new technical competence, new ideas, new equipment, and the increase in the number of climbers, and the examples of other climbing areas, all contributed to the general surge."

Our choice of classic routes in the Pacific Northwest might have included the north rib of Mount Fury, the Yokum Ridge on Mount Hood, and the graceful northeast buttress of Mount Goode, among others. One of our objectives, however, is to describe climbs representative of the area, and the routes that finally were selected reflect the essence of Cascade mountaineering, encompassing arduous forested approaches, complicated glacier traverses, elegant rocky arêtes and buttresses, and pristine ice slopes that glisten in the afternoon sun.

Mount Rainier
Liberty Ridge

19

Visible for distances in excess of a hundred miles, Mount Rainier possesses the greatest accumulation of glaciers of any peak in the contiguous United States. According to Dee Molenaar, writing in *The Challenge of Rainier*, "Over 35 square miles of ice, including 26 officially named glaciers and numerous unnamed permanent icefields, are distributed across the mountain's flanks and upper summit dome. Six major glaciers flow down the peak directly from the crater rim to well below timberline; eight others originate in vast cirques where they are nourished by the heavy snowfall at these mid-altitudes and by ice avalanching from steep slopes above. . . ."

The English explorer George Vancouver sighted the imposing 14,410-foot mountain in April 1792 and named it in honor of a colleague, Admiral Peter Rainier.

◄ *Mount Rainier as seen from the north.* Austin Post, United States Geological Survey.

Later, an attempt by local residents to change this prosaic name to the generally accepted Indian name for the peak—Tacoma—was thwarted by the powerful U.S. Geographic Board, which recommended that the name given by Vancouver be retained.

The first documented ascent to the summit area of Mount Rainier occurred in July 1857, when a four-man party led by Lieutenant August Kautz reached the crest of the peak close to 14,000 feet. However, the first ascent of the peak, whose highest point was half a mile to the northeast of Kautz's high point, went to Hazard Stevens and Philemon B. Van Trump, pioneers of the now-famous Gibraltar Route, on August 18, 1870. Stevens and Van Trump had arrived on the southern flank of Mount Rainier with the adventurous British mountaineer Edmund Coleman. Their packer had brought them to a place called Bear Prairie, where he had arranged for the three climbers to be guided to timberline by the Yakima Indian guide Sluiskin. The guide attempted to dissuade the trio from the ascent, but the climbers would not abandon their desire to set foot upon the upper slopes of the mountain. As the group struggled up the lower, forested cliffs, Coleman became separated from his companions and was forced to return to Bear Prairie. The other two climbers and their guide pushed on to a timberline camp. Stevens and Van Trump made a reconnaissance climb to 10,000 feet and then, the following

morning, in spite of Sluiskin's pleadings not to enter the terrible upper reaches of the mountain, the two men began their ascent.

Climbing quickly to their previous high point, the pioneers entered more difficult terrain, eventually ascending a huge, steep formation now known as Gibraltar Rock. Late in the afternoon they reached the summit crest only to find that a higher point lay some distance farther to the north. Realizing that a bivouac was inevitable, Stevens and Van Trump proceeded to the summit, where they encountered a large, snow-filled crater with steam vents along its perimeter. As darkness fell, Stevens and Van Trump escaped the harsh wind by entering an ice cave on the inner slope of the crater, where they spent an interminable night alternately warmed by the steam and chilled by the frigid air.

At dawn the two climbers emerged from their shelter into a driving wind and a thick mist; walking a few hundred feet to the highest crest of the crater, they set in place a brass plate inscribed with their names. Through a rift in the clouds the men observed another rounded snow dome to the north which they named Takhoma, later to be called Liberty Cap. Stevens and Van Trump began their descent immediately and, upon reaching their camp in late

afternoon, related their adventures to the anxious Sluiskin, who joyfully embraced the two climbers who had survived the evil forces he believed were dwelling on the slopes of the fearful mountain.

For more than half a century Mount Rainier was climbed primarily by the Gibraltar Route. Ascents were made by persons from all walks of life; geologists in particular were intrigued by this monument to volcanic forces. In 1888, a party that included John Muir and the artist William Keith (who climbed only part way) reached the summit. By the end of 1934, only six routes had been established to the summit of Rainier. The ascent of the Tahoma Glacier by Hans Fuhrer and a client the previous year marked the first time the mountain had been climbed by a new route in fourteen years. As the summer of 1935 approached, a new group of adventurous mountaineers already were planning new and exciting routes to the summit of the huge volcano. One of the possibilities was Liberty Ridge, a huge rib in the center of the awesome north wall of Mount Rainier.

Liberty Ridge rises more than a mile from the Carbon Glacier directly to the summit of Liberty Cap. The ridge is the steepest and most aesthetic of the many alpine ribs on Rainier, and although there are

The north face of Mount Rainier.
Austin Post, United States Geological Survey.

many protrusions of the rotten rock underlying the mountain, the crest is composed mostly of ice and snow. To the east lies the crumbling, 4000-foot Willis Wall, and to the west is the smaller Liberty Wall, both of which are capped by enormous ice cliffs that periodically avalanche onto the Carbon Glacier.

Ome Daiber, an energetic Seattle climber of the 1930s, was so intrigued with the elegant Liberty Ridge that he had started thinking about its ascent in 1933. For two years he had nourished secret hopes for the ascent, studying the terrain on visits to the Carbon Glacier region and acquiring aerial photographs from Bradford Washburn. In September of 1935 he revealed his ambition to climb the ridge to two of his closest climbing companions, Jim Borrow and Arnie Campbell. Both were excited about the daring proposal, and the three climbers agreed to make the attempt later that month.

Daiber, Borrow, and Campbell began their ascent on September 29 from a high camp on Curtis Ridge, located at the eastern edge of Carbon Glacier. A considerable problem existed in reaching the foot of Liberty Ridge, for the Carbon Glacier was severely crevassed, and all snow bridges had melted away. After several false starts, the three climbers found their way down the cliffs of the Curtis Ridge to the edge of the glacier and began the arduous ascent through the crevassed labyrinth. At 8000 feet a particularly broken section of séracs barred the way, but Daiber skillfully cut steps up a vertical ice wall, and the three men finally reached the beginning of the ridge at three o'clock in the afternoon.

The Willis Wall already was in shadow as the concerned climbers started up the crest that rose out of the glacier like a huge cleaver. They had hoped for solid rock, but instead found that the occasional rocky surfaces were composed mostly of bits of pumice held together by coarse dirt and frost. Inclined at forty degrees, the lower part of the ridge offered little difficulty, and the trio climbed rapidly over crusty snow to a small col behind a prominent tower, later called Thumb Rock. There, they decided to make their first bivouac; the hour was late, and the likelihood of finding good sites higher on the crest seemed small. After carving a platform in the frozen pumice, the climbers ate a hasty dinner and then crawled into their homemade bivouac sack to wait out the long night. Inside the crude fabric envelope, the three men, hindered by their packs, struggled for space, while the sputtering, smelly Primus stove—ignited for warmth—was an additional distraction preventing sleep. Outside, avalanches crashed down the slopes of the Willis Wall, and the faint glow of the aurora borealis was low in the northern sky.

From the Carbon Glacier, Liberty Ridge rises for more than a mile to the summit of Liberty Cap. To the left, in shadow, is the Willis Wall.   Alan Kearney.

Dawn finally came. After a meager breakfast the chilled climbers were happy to be moving again. Their first major obstacle was a long, icy chute bordered by dark walls of crumbling rock. Small rock avalanches impeded their progress, and since their crampons did not hold well in the powdery snow covering the ice, more than two hours passed before the cautious climbers emerged onto the slope above the chute. There, the ridge steepened, and the trio, with Daiber in the lead, ascended the icy slopes toward a large prow of unstable rock. Rather than risk a traverse on steep glare ice, the diminutive Daiber climbed the rotten rock. On one occasion he crept nimbly along the ledges as they crumbled beneath him. The men now were level with the ice cliffs overhanging Liberty Wall; as they rested briefly, a huge section of ice broke away and thundered to the glacier below. Soberly resuming the ascent, the climbers crossed an ice slope above the last rock outcrop and saw that an easy snowfield led to the gently rounded Liberty Cap. The trio climbed confidently toward the summit, their crampons biting well in the rough ice.

Just as success seemed assured, the climbers were stopped by a crevasse that split the slope as far as they could see. The crevasse seemed impossible to pass. After a brief reconnaissance, Daiber found a narrow section but still was unable to cross the gap. Campbell later reported the memorable technique that finally won the climb: "The opposite side was above our heads and about eight feet across at our feet but slightly less at our heads. . . . Jim and I each took one of Ome's feet and lifted him nearly to arms' length above our heads. At the arranged signal Ome leaned out and jumped as we shoved, stuck his axe in the easy slope above, and hung on." Daiber set up a belay and pulled his comrades over the edge of the crevasse, and the trio slowly ascended the gentle slopes to the 14,112-foot summit of Liberty Cap.

In the deepening twilight, the group trudged across the ice to the main summit, realizing that another bivouac was inevitable. Again they spread out the bivouac sack and started the stove, but sleep was impossible because of the intense cold. The tired and miserable climbers watched the interminable passage of the stars until at last the first streaks of dawn signaled the end of their ordeal; then they descended quickly and surely along the familiar Gibraltar Route, reaching the roadhead at mid-morning.

Liberty Ridge was Ome Daiber's most significant climb and for twenty-two years remained the only route, other than the Ptarmigan Ridge at the edge of Liberty Wall, that had been accomplished on the immense and precipitous northern flank of Mount Rainier. Though six new routes were established on the mountain in the next two decades, Liberty Ridge was not repeated until August 1955, when a party of four ascended the route in one day. Two climbers made the first ascent of the east side of the frightening Willis Wall in June 1962; present-day climbers have a choice of more than ten routes on the Willis and Liberty walls. It is remarkable, considering the extreme avalanche hazard, that no serious accidents have occurred on these routes. Today, Mount Rainier receives perhaps more ascents than any other peak in the United States. Liberty Ridge in particular remains one of the most popular technical routes on the mountain, offering climbers a direct and challenging line to the summit.

First ascent

Ome Daiber, Arnie Campbell, and Jim Borrow. September 29–30, 1935.

Elevation

The summit is 14,410 feet above sea level. The climbing route gains 5900 feet of elevation.

Time

Eight to fourteen hours from the base of the ridge.

Map

Special USGS topographic sheet: Mount Rainier National Park, scale 1:62,500.

Useful reference

Cascade Alpine Guide: Columbia River to Stevens Pass.

Route description

Enter Mount Rainier National Park at the Carbon River Station via Highways 162 and 165 from the town of Buckley. Drive to Ipsut Creek Campground at the end of Carbon River Road; then follow an old roadway about one-and-a-half miles to a bridge that crosses the Carbon River. Ascend the trail past the snout of the Carbon Glacier and on through Moraine Park to a high camp on Curtis Ridge. Drop down onto the Carbon Glacier (badly crevassed from mid- to late-season) and ascend to the base of Liberty Ridge. Climb up the east side of the ridge for several hundred feet; then traverse across the crest and work up snowslopes and rock outcrops to a col at Thumb Rock (10,775 feet—space for tents).

Climb up and right to a narrow ice gully between steep rock walls. Ascend this gully and then continue toward the ridge crest. Bearing left, climb a snowslope along the crest to the top of a dark prow of rock known as the Black Pyramid. Continue up the ridge until it merges with Liberty Cap Glacier; then ascend several hundred feet and bear west to pass the final crevasses and ice cliffs. Easy climbing then leads to the summit of Liberty Cap.

The difficult descent of Liberty Ridge can be made under optimum conditions; however, the easiest route back to Carbon River Road is to descend the Emmons Glacier— on the northeast side of the mountain—to Steamboat Prow. Next, drop down the Inter Glacier until it is possible to traverse to Curtis Ridge via Saint Elmo Pass and the Winthrop Glacier.

Remarks

Conditions on the ridge are best early in the climbing season, when little ice is exposed and rockfall is at a minimum. The lower glaciers also are easier at this time.

Two climbers ascend the blocky crest of Liberty Ridge toward the jagged spire of Thumb Rock; they may be discerned by the rope that joins them. Phil Leatherman.

111

Forbidden Peak
West Ridge

20

For most of its great length, the Cascade Range consists of isolated, snow-covered volcanoes that rise above gently rolling, forested, lower ranges. However, in its extreme northern segment—the 110 miles between Snoqualmie Pass and the Canadian border—the range undergoes a remarkable transformation. There, igneous and metamorphic rocks form the predominant structure of the range. Many climbers and backpackers who have ventured into the wild North Cascades have described the range as the most sublime in the coterminous United States. Deep, forested valleys lead up to heavily glaciated mountains that often tower more than a vertical mile above adjacent canyons. Storms are common, and an annual precipitation of 200 inches—much of it falling as snow in the higher

The West Ridge Route on Forbidden Peak crosses the glacier, ascends the snow couloir to the base of the ridge, then follows the crest to the summit. Steve Roper.

regions—nourishes an extensive array of glaciers, alpine meadows, and luxuriant valleys. One of the most beautiful of these alpine areas centers around Cascade Pass, a prominent landmark that separates the Cascade and Stehekin river drainages.

Three miles northwest of Cascade Pass, the striking summit of Forbidden Peak rises in near-perfect symmetry to an elevation of 8815 feet. Glaciation has carved three massive ridges from the Skagit gneiss bedrock, giving the peak a classic, sharply pyramidal appearance. Two of the ridges border the cavernous east face, beneath which flows a portion of Boston Glacier, the largest body of ice in the North Cascades. On the west side of Forbidden Peak, an elegant and airy spine of rock ascends smoothly from a prominent saddle to the summit. Viewed from the south, the remarkably triangular peak dominates the huge cirque known as Boston Basin.

Forbidden Peak was still unnamed and rarely seen in the 1930s, when the mysterious mountain became the objective for adventurous climbers seeking new challenges. Hermann Ulrichs was one of these early mountaineer–explorers; in 1932 he applied the name Isosceles to the peak on observing it from Boston Glacier. The following year, a party making the first ascent of nearby Eldorado Peak commented on a beautiful, heavily glaciated peak they noticed to the southeast. Still other explorers referred to it as Forgotten Peak, emphasizing its uncharted

remoteness. Mountaineers found the long, forested valleys difficult and exasperating to penetrate; only the most dedicated mountaineers attempted to reach the peaks through such forests.

On May 30, 1940, Lloyd Anderson, Jim Crooks, Dave Lind, Fred Beckey, and Helmy Beckey—all of whom relished the exploratory nature of Cascade mountaineering—reached the Cascade River roadhead a few miles beyond the small settlement of Marblemount. Anderson was just starting his new business, Recreational Equipment Cooperative, which he operated from the back office of a Seattle gasoline station. The teenage Beckey brothers were just starting their mountaineering careers, while Crooks and Lind had been climbing for several seasons.

The climbers prepared their packs for the sixteen-mile hike to Boston Basin and entered a region characterized by Ulrichs as "steeped in a perpetual cathedral twilight of dim gold and green half-lights. Great pillar-like firs, 250–300 ft. high, abound, with spruce and cedar almost rivalling [*sic*] them in size." Occasionally, the forest thinned out, allowing views of incomparable beauty: the mile-high walls of Johannesburg Mountain loomed across the canyon, while ahead the men could see the gentle slopes leading to Cascade Pass. Higher, past a forested knoll, the climbers caught a glimpse of the mysterious, mist-shrouded pyramid they desired to climb. The hillsides seemed almost vertical as the heavily burdened climbers struggled through the thick alder and the swampy areas near the creeks. Soon they reached the huge trees below Boston Basin. The beautiful green-and-gold light of the forest brightened perceptibly, and the group emerged suddenly into the open slopes of the basin.

Fred Beckey and Anderson easily located the campsite they had used on an approach to the peak six weeks earlier. On that trip, a heavy spring snowstorm had covered the basin as the two men and fellow climber Dwight Watson approached treeline. Beyond the moraine, swirling, snow-filled mists permitted only vague glimpses of the "forgotten" mountain, and the adventure suddenly acquired an oppressive aspect. "The peak's eventual designation came from this veil, for we agreed 'Forbidden' would be a more appropriate name," wrote Fred Beckey years later. Their attempt in winterlike conditions ended in failure when unstable cornices lining the ridge crest prevented the three climbers from even getting close to the summit. During the long hike back to their car, Anderson and Beckey already were planning their return.

Allen Steck and Steve Roper ascend to the base of the snow couloir. Eric Sanford.

Boston Basin lay quiet in the late afternoon light as the five climbers prepared their bivouac in a small grove of alpine fir. After a brief reconnaissance everyone agreed that the inviting west ridge offered the most promising route to the summit. A prominent, snow-filled couloir led from the crevassed glacier to the ridge crest, which, in its partial mantle of spring snow, rose gently 500 feet to the summit, now sharply outlined in the evening sky.

The following morning a chilling mist encircled the climbers' camp, hiding the peak from view. "We started for the peak with the hope things would clear," continued Beckey, "but hours later, on the west ridge, new snow was in the air. There was none of that heartening talk one hears when the worst is surely over, but our cumulative enthusiasm pushed us on." On reaching the crest, the climbers realized the weather held little promise of improvement.

With Lind and Fred Beckey in the lead, the group slowly ascended the exposed, blocky ridge. The arête narrowed at one point, and the mountaineers climbed hand-over-hand along a sharp edge with their feet braced against the slab below.

After passing more slabs and complicated, angular blocks, the men approached a dark tower that loomed over them through the shifting snows and gray mist. With their fingers numbed and their parkas stiff with ice, the five mountaineers decided it was unwise to continue, and they began the retreat to the top of the couloir, where they rappelled over treacherous, snow-covered ledges to the glacier. Two hours later they reached the relative comfort of their timberline camp.

On the morning of June 1 the sun shone intermittently through drifting clouds as the rested climbers prepared for their final attempt on the peak. Although the clouds soon thickened, the persistent climbers retraced the route to their high point. Light snowfall again greeted them as they prepared to force the route past the dark tower. Surprisingly, the rocks retained some warmth from the morning sun, and Lind executed a daring lead along the exposed flank of the forty-foot tower. After placing several pitons for protection, he climbed a short, vertical bulge to the top of the obstacle.

Once past the tower, the team found easier terrain, and even though rime was forming on the rock, the climbers reached the summit by noon. Clouds permitted only veiled views of the surrounding peaks, and the now-persistent snowfall demanded an immediate retreat. The five men descended slowly and cautiously; with careful rope management at the difficult sections, they reached the

A climber ascends the clean, angular rock on the lower part of the west ridge.   Eric Sanford.

gentle slopes of the glacier and, eventually, their treeline camp. "The next day," according to Beckey, "triumph gave us fleet legs, and by noon we reached the car."

After a party of four made the second ascent of the ridge in 1946, more climbers in the Northwest became intrigued by this little-known gem of the North Cascades. Though many new lines were climbed on Forbidden's walls and other ridges, the elegant west ridge continued to be the favored route since one could climb on the crest over its entire length.

Two midwestern climbers found their way into Boston Basin in 1978 with the intention of climbing the west ridge. The trail up the north fork of Cascade Creek had been replaced by a modern gravel road, but the approach to Boston Basin was still through alder and primeval forest. The two mountaineers approached the peak in a period of freakish, stable weather in October, when a dry, warm wind was blowing from the eastern part of the state. The comments of one of the climbers were enthusiastic. She wrote:

The weather was totally un-Cascade. Luckily we had our crampons so the ascent of the glacier and the upper couloir was routine. There were huge holes and corridors in the ice of the couloir; we wandered in and around the chambers, eventually coming out on the ridge crest. The weather was so great that we chose to cache all our things here, including the rope, and go to the summit unencumbered . . . the rock was more solid than we had imagined, with many holds and cracks. We were making short hand-traverses and liebacks over the tremendous exposure of the northwest face—the rock and ice fell away for thousands of feet to Moraine Lake. It took plenty of caution and each move was carefully thought out—without a rope, we couldn't afford any mistakes. We had heard about the blocky tower and found the marvelous traverse along its southern side. We reached the summit about thirty minutes later. It was certainly a satisfying climb on warm, moderate rock.

First ascent

Lloyd Anderson, Dave Lind, Fred Beckey, Helmy Beckey, and Jim Crooks. June 1, 1940.

Elevation

The summit is 8815 feet above sea level.

Difficulty

II, 5.2. Much of the route is class 4.

Time

Four to five hours from Boston Basin.

Map

USGS quadrangles: Forbidden Peak and Cascade Pass, scale 1:24,000.

Useful reference

Cascade Alpine Guide: Stevens Pass to Rainy Pass.

Route description

From the town of Marblemount, on Highway 20, cross the Skagit River and drive approximately twenty-two-and-a-half miles up the Cascade River Road; park at a spur road (3200 feet) angling in sharply from the left. Hike north half a mile to the center of an abandoned mine complex, where an older, narrower road (trail sign) leads up the hill. Follow this road to the second switchback and ascend a little-used climbers' path leading directly up the steep

Near the top of the west ridge, a craggy tower forces the climber to make a delicate, exposed traverse. Steve Roper.

hillside. Higher, the path angles left, crossing two large creeks, and then rises steeply to Boston Basin. Hiking time is about two hours.

Continue north across Boston Basin, heading for the prominent glacier below the south face of Forbidden Peak. Gain the crest of the west ridge by ascending a 500-foot, snow-and-ice-filled couloir at the left edge of the south face. Climb the ridge on solid rock with many ledges and cracks. Occasional difficult sections are climbed by north-side traverses. Two hundred feet below the summit, pass a large blocky tower by airy face climbing on the south side. Easy climbing then leads to the summit.

To descend, retrace the ascent route or downclimb the East Ridge Route back to Boston Basin.

Mount Shuksan
Price Glacier

A well-traveled mountaineer who had seen lofty K2 in the Karakoram Himalaya and had trekked along the remote trails of Peru remarked recently that he had never heard of Mount Shuksan. He may be forgiven for not having traveled to the North Cascades; nevertheless, it is remarkable that the climber had never seen even a magazine photograph of Mount Shuksan. As Harvey Manning wrote in *The North Cascades:* "It is a famous mountain, by photograph if not by name; in magazine advertisements, calendars, and as a Bob and Ira Spring 15 × 60-foot color transparency in New York's Grand Central Station, it has been seen by millions of Americans." Aside from Mount Rainier, Shuksan is probably the most celebrated mountain in the state of Washington; thousands of tourists annually photograph its wondrous northwestern flanks from Picture Lake near Mount Baker Lodge.

◀ *Mount Shuksan as viewed from the north.* William A. Long.

The 9127-foot peak occupies more than ten square miles of Cascade wilderness. Its many glaciers, descending over black, rocky cliffs carved by the elements into grotesque gullies and pinnacles, give the mountain a ragged and ethereal appearance. The striking triangular summit pyramid rises 500 feet above the surrounding glaciers, scarcely deserving of the commentary by Asahel Curtis, who first climbed the peak with W. M. Price in 1906. These two climbers saw "to the north, the black mass of the summit pile. The ascent of this rock pile was a rather difficult piece of rock-work that required over two hours." The marvelous view that the climbers expected from the summit was obscured by smoke from a forest fire. Finding no evidence of a previous ascent, the two men constructed a small cairn and began the descent to their timberline camp.

In 1926 three climbers pioneered a new route on the edge of the northwest face. The following year, C. A. Fisher and E. P. Spearin climbed the now-popular Fisher Chimneys Route on the west face. In 1939 Otto Trott and Andy Hennig, two Europeans who had settled in Washington, made a daring ascent of the peak by climbing directly up the icefall of Hanging Glacier, a prominent ice cascade that overhangs an 800-foot escarpment on the northwest face. The two-day climb was the first made on the northwest side of Mount Shuksan and required technical ice-climbing competence that included the placement of ice pitons. During the next few years,

several parties reached the summit via conventional routes, while more adventurous pioneers began the exploration of new climbing possibilities on a more remote section of the huge mountain.

The seldom-visited northeast flank of Mount Shuksan, including the massive East Nooksack Glacier, is of an alpine character not often encountered by the casual Cascade mountaineer. Of even greater grandeur than the East Nooksack Glacier are the convoluted crevasses and hanging snow masses of the Price Glacier, which plunges 4500 feet from a narrow col near the summit to Price Lake. The approach to these magnificent alpine regions is a typically exhausting Cascade thrash, usually accompanied by persistent rain.

Harvey Manning recalled a rainy hike in the area with his photographer friend Tom Miller: "It was a typical North Cascades weekend . . . the road ended in a muddy mess of bulldozer trails amid a jackstraw of logs and slash." The two hikers wandered through the slash, along an old miner's trail, and around beaver ponds, eventually reaching a broad river channel that led up toward the glaciers. "After nearly two miles of boulder-hopping and channel-leaping," he continued, "we turned the corner. We were impressed. The floor of Nooksack Cirque is a wasteland of glacial violence where new and old moraines mingle with talus and whitewater streams, where sunlight scarcely ever touches the ground . . . Nooksack Cirque is the deepest, darkest, coldest hole that I will ever see in the North Cascades. . . ."

When Fred Beckey, Jack Schwabland, and Bill Granston arrived at the entrance to the Cirque in the gray dawn mist of September 9, 1945, a chilling wind sloughed off the ice slopes into the valley. As the sun rose above Nooksack Ridge, the three men had climbed 2000 feet through the dense forest above the Nooksack River to the crest of an alpine ridge at 5000 feet. There the climbers enjoyed their first close-up view of the upper Price Glacier, which cascaded over the cliffs in front of them. For several years Beckey had wanted to come to grips with the magnificent alpine problem: "The mosaic of the ice gullies on the stupendous walls above had depths of indigo-blue, and soon a blinding-white surface shone in the sun like a glowing curtain. In the morning light the glacier variegated into every conceivable form of intricate grotto with piles of ice masses, seracs, and crevasses. . . . Frail bridges provided another link in this exotic fairyland of ice architecture. Perhaps most wonderful of all was the serene quiet."

The Price Glacier, with its delicate snow flutings, resembles glaciers found in the Andes and the Himalayas. Phil Leatherman.

Beckey and his companions rested briefly while they ate a portion of their day's rations and scanned the ice cliffs for the most promising way through to the summit snowfield. Traversing to the edge of the ice, the trio roped up and climbed onto the glacier. They ascended quickly and easily, their crampons crunching satisfyingly in the newly crusted snow. Creaks and groans emanated from the glacier, and the crash of ice falling from the higher cliffs reminded them of the instability of the ice mass upon which they were climbing. Carefully the trio passed along the base of the monolithic Nooksack Tower and crossed to the chaotic central portion of the

glacier. Above them hovered a series of fractured ice bulges and serrations through which the climbers ascended in a zigzag pattern. Since the ice climbing became difficult and dangerous, the three climbers belayed cautiously through the grotesque formations. A few hundred feet directly above the men lay the bergschrunds spanning the entire width of the glacier. On the right was a steep, rocky cliff, while to the left was a snow wall carved into delicate flutings by the incessant downward path of small avalanches.

Belayed by Schwabland, Beckey attempted to climb through the central section of the huge crevasses, but he failed to gain the top of the upper ice cliff. He then tried to pass the bergschrunds by ascending to the right toward the rocky cliff bordering the glacier: "Climbing onto a narrow band of gneiss I anchored myself to a piton and belayed the others across. Fresh snow clung to the rock. . . . Brushing it off the holds I continued on, edging along little sills above the ice. . . ." It was late afternoon by the time the climbers had ascended the seven pitches leading to a small col overlooking Crystal Glacier. The last, taxing leads had been on steep glare ice in the final chute below the col. Traversing across the upper Crystal Glacier, the three men reached the base of the summit pyramid and ascended the gentle-angled arête to the snow-covered summit. The tired but happy climbers rested among the stones of the summit, appreciating the view of glacier-covered Mount Baker glimmering in the distance and a jagged line of peaks leading north to the Canadian border.

As the sun neared the horizon, Beckey and his companions began the descent toward the south, glissading snow gullies and traversing the easy slopes of the Fisher Chimneys Route. Their early start had given them ample time for the climb, but as they trudged down the talus to the trail above Lake Ann, darkness

Two climbers pause on the upper slopes of Price Glacier. In the background lie the fractured crevasses on the lower part of the route. Don Liska.

121

overtook them. Occasionally falling asleep during brief moments of rest, the climbers finally reached the welcome pavement of the Mount Baker scenic road.

Many mountaineers agree that the Price Glacier is the most beautiful alpine glacier in the lower forty-eight states. Not surprisingly, its ascent was the most difficult ice climb yet made in the coterminous United States, exceeding in complexity even the magnificent ice routes on Mount Rainier.

Climbers have pioneered several new routes on the north side of Mount Shuksan in the intervening years, yet the Price Glacier remains the most serious test for ice climbers seeking adventure on this North Cascade peak.

First ascent

Fred Beckey, Jack Schwabland, and Bill Granston. September 9, 1945.

Elevation

The summit is 9127 feet above sea level.

Time

Eight to ten hours from timberline.

Map

USGS quadrangle: Mt. Shuksan, scale 1:62,500.

Useful reference

Climber's Guide to the Cascade and Olympic Mountains of Washington.

Route description

From the town of Bellingham drive east on Highway 542 toward Mount Baker Lodge. At the Nooksack River Bridge, about seven miles before the lodge, turn left onto Ruth Creek Road and follow it one-and-a-quarter miles; then turn right on a gravel road marked "Ruth Creek" and drive about two miles to its end. Follow an old miner's trail about one-and-a-half miles up the Nooksack River and proceed along gravel bars about half a mile to a point opposite a huge, alder-covered talus

cone on the right. Cross the river and ascend the right side of the cone; then enter a wide gully leading 2000 feet up to the ridge crest east of Price Lake. Ascend an easy route along the crest; then traverse along its west side to slabs at the edge of Price Glacier (campsites).

Ascend the left part of the glacier to about 6500 feet. Traverse to the main glacier through a notch in the rock ridge below Nooksack Tower. Climb through crevasses and séracs (many steep ice pitches) to about 7800 feet, near the base of the bergschrunds guarding the final ice chute. Ascend the bergschrunds directly by steep, sustained ice climbing or ascend diagonally along the edge of the cliff on the right. Above the bergschrunds, climb the ice chute to the col above Crystal Glacier. The 500-foot summit pyramid is climbed easily from the east or south.

The descent usually is made via easy gullies and slopes to the west.

Slesse Mountain Northeast Buttress

Morning sun strikes the east face of Slesse Mountain, throwing the northeast buttress into sharp silhouette. Alan Kearney.

The mountains clustered along the Washington–British Columbia border north of Mount Shuksan are among the most rugged and heavily forested of the northern Cascades. Known by mountaineers as the Chilliwack Group, the peaks display an uncommon vertical relief and often rise more than 6000 feet above their adjacent valleys. The vigorous and luxuriant forest undergrowth, nourished by heavy annual precipitation, presented a nearly impassable barrier to early explorers, particularly the International Boundary Survey crews in the early 1900s. For decades the region remained the most untamed and least penetrated wilderness of the North Cascades.

Situated two miles north of the border, Slesse Mountain is one of the more prominent peaks of the Chilliwack Group. The name of the incomparable mountain derives from the Chilukweyuk Indian word, *sel-ee-see*, meaning fang, a word that perfectly describes the dramatic appearance of the peak's northeastern façade, surely one of the most impressive walls in the Cascades. The huge peak is composed mostly of

gray diorite, although occasional intrusions of lighter colored rock streak the otherwise uniform appearance of the mile-wide escarpment. Buttresses containing cavernous glacial cirques reach high onto the 2500-foot face, conveying the impression of monstrous medieval battlements. It is the northeast buttress, however, that has become a focus of attention for climbers, for this immense rib soars more than 3000 feet in flawless excellence directly to the summit and is so massive and rugged that it was destined to attract mountaineers.

Although Slesse Mountain was first climbed in 1927, not until much later did the northeastern crags come to the attention of climbers seeking technical routes. On one of his many forays into the Cascade wilderness, the ever-exploring Fred Beckey noticed the cliffs on a flight to Chilliwack Lake in 1950: "The rapid succession of east and north faces brought me to feverish attention," he wrote in *Challenge of the North Cascades*. Beckey increased his knowledge of Slesse Mountain's convoluted nature in 1952 when he and two companions climbed the 7850-foot main summit and the towerlike southern peak. The view down the northern precipices was

breathtaking, but Beckey was frustrated when he realized that the broad valley that lay beneath them had no easy access. Beckey first attempted to reach the wall by hiking cross-country from the roadhead near Mount Shuksan. After hours of arduous bushwhacking, Beckey and his companion, Dave Collins, reached the crest south of Slesse Mountain and worked their way down along the eastern cliff. Beckey wrote of the adventure: "On a long descending traverse to the north we kept an eagle eye out for ice blocks that might slide down the slabs from the fragmentary glacier above us, and for any loose currency from the plane wreckage—grim evidence of which lay everywhere." Two years before his hike an airliner with sixty-two persons aboard had crashed near the summit of Slesse Mountain during a vicious December storm.

The two climbers finally reached the foot of the wall but found the scope of the buttresses and cliffs so overwhelming that they could scarcely concentrate on defining a possible route. "A deep, slabbed cirque, dividing buttresses, and the threat of annihilation from sliding seracs stopped us from traversing farther," wrote the unhappy Beckey. He had, however, noted the lines of the immense northeast buttress that rose so smoothly to the summit.

◀ *The clawlike buttresses on the east side of Slesse Mountain loom in front of snow-covered Mount Baker.* Fred Beckey.

In July 1963 the determined Beckey "finally came to grips with the gargantuan face." Ironically, roads bulldozed along Nesakwatch Creek by a logging company, a commercial activity despised by many present-day wilderness travelers, offered a closer approach to the buttress. Beckey and his companion, Steve Marts, crossed the logging slash at the roadhead and struggled through the underbrush toward Slesse Mountain. The two fatalistic climbers prepared to cross beneath the terminus of the rotting glacier to reach the base of the buttress: "We edged our way up and across the exposed slab. . . . Remnants of the hanging glacier, with loose pieces as big as automobiles, were perched precariously on slabs." Once past this obstacle, the two men roped up at the base of the glacier-scoured, slabby wall.

After ascending an open book, Beckey and Marts worked their way up grooves and polished slabs, occasionally using tension in blank areas. Beckey led a particularly unnerving crack filled with wet moss and small cedar bushes. Around midday the climbers reached an easier section of the buttress and gained altitude rapidly. The hours raced by as they worked their way up the narrow edge of the buttress on clean and excellent rock, but when darkness forced a halt, they had ascended half the route. The two climbers prepared their bivouac on a small platform; above them, the darkened spine of the buttress narrowed and steepened.

Mists engulfed Beckey and Marts during the long night, and by daylight they could see little beyond the first few feet of the wall that disappeared into the mists above them. Fearing the arrival of a prolonged storm, the two climbers decided to retreat rather than risk losing their way on the huge buttress. The long series of rappels down the mist-shrouded, confusing cliffs challenged their routefinding ability, but as the fog thinned the two men eventually found their way back to the base of the wall. During the descent Beckey and Marts had anchored ropes at the difficult sections to facilitate their next attempt. The two tired, wet climbers made their way back to the car and drove to the nearby town of Chilliwack, where they basked in the warmth of a coffee shop. They agreed that on their return to Seattle not even their closest friends should be told of this remarkable cliff on Slesse Mountain, for they felt that total secrecy was of vital importance in preventing rival parties from taking this great prize.

A period of typically wet Cascade weather settled over the Chilliwack mountains. Not until August 26 did Beckey and Marts find an opportunity to resume their attempt on Slesse Mountain. Because of the isolated location of the buttress, they invited a third climber, Eric Bjornstad, to join them. Appropriate to the clandestine operation, their companion was not told of their destination until they had crossed the border into Canada. Since Beckey and Marts were familiar with the approach, the three climbers were able to reach the base of the buttress quickly; however, the climbing was every bit as complex as before, and the trio barely reached a bivouac ledge four pitches below the previous high point before nightfall. The audacity of the venture became increasingly apparent to Bjornstad as he warily eyed the beetling crags above.

The next morning was clear and cold as Beckey and his companions ascended the four pitches to the previous bivouac ledge. Marts then began the next lead and found that the climbing became harder and the placement of the pitons more desperate. They had reached the crux of the route, where the rock arched steeply upward to the summit. Beckey and Marts shared leads on three continuously difficult pitches that consumed several hours. After a few short leads, Beckey began a particularly long and difficult pitch. Considerable time passed before he reached the first good ledge the climbers had seen that day. By the time Bjornstad managed to reach Beckey's position, darkness was upon them. Attempting to follow the lead, Marts was unable to remove the pitons in the dark and was forced to spend the night hanging in his aid slings.

Dawn came none too soon for the chilled Marts, who began climbing as soon as there was light enough to permit cleaning the intricate pitch. The reunited climbers soon were bathed in sunlight, and after an ex-

citing traverse on the exposed northeast face, a few pitches over broken terrain led them to the summit. The joyous moment was enhanced by the brilliant sunshine and the jagged array of spires and towers stretching across the horizon. To the south, snow-covered Mount Baker and the pyramid of Shuksan glistened in the sun. Beckey, Marts, and Bjornstad quenched their burning thirst on summit snow and then commenced the rappels down the western crags of Slesse Mountain. Soon the three men were struggling down brush-covered slopes to the logging road on Nesakwatch Creek.

The ascent of the astonishingly beautiful buttress was one of the most daring and sustained alpine climbs yet accomplished in the Cascades. Beckey and his companions had climbed thirty-four pitches, of which twenty-five were class 5. The climb possessed an additional element of drama in that no escape route to easier terrain existed. In the event of bad weather or an accident, the only retreat is a series of complicated rappels down the full length of the buttress, a dangerous undertaking if a party is caught in the steep section of the climb just below the summit.

The second ascent of the buttress was accomplished in 1965 by Hans Baer and Jack Bryan; by 1973 the route had been climbed five times. Still, with less than ten ascents, the austere northeast buttress of Slesse Mountain remains an aesthetically pleasing yet demanding climb for adventuresome mountaineers.

First ascent

Fred Beckey, Steve Marts, and Eric Bjornstad. August 26–28, 1963.

Elevation

The summit is 7850 feet above sea level.

Difficulty

V, 5.9, A2.

Time

Two-and-a-half days from the head of the logging road.

Map

Canadian Department of Energy, Mines, and Resources sheet: Chilliwack, 92 H/4, scale 1:50,000.

Useful references

A Climber's Guide to the Coastal Ranges of British Columbia; Climber's Guide to the Cascade and Olympic Mountains of Washington.

Route description

Turn off Trans-Canada Route 1 at the main Chilliwack exit and drive south three miles to a bridge crossing the Chilliwack River. Turn left just before the bridge and drive about seventeen miles up the Chilliwack River, crossing the river once. Then turn right onto the Nesakwatch Creek logging road and drive about six miles to its end. Hike a short distance south, crossing a major gully; then descend to and cross Nesakwatch Creek. Follow the south side of a prominent stream flowing from the north face of Slesse to a pocket glacier south of the northeast buttress. Head for the base of the buttress, scrambling over slabs exposed to falling ice from the glacier.

The 3000-foot buttress can be divided into three main sections. The lower section is heavily glaciated and slabby; the majority of aid climbing, as well as several hundred feet of easy class 3 and 4 scrambling, is found in this part. At the middle section, the buttress steepens for several pitches and then leans back into a lower-angled area with many bivouac ledges. The final 800-foot section of the buttress is the steepest on the route and forms the crux of the climb. Continuously enjoyable climbing all the way to the summit is found by keeping as close to the well-broken crest as possible and avoiding north-side traverses.

Shari Kearney leading a pitch on the middle section of the northeast buttress. Alan Kearney.

To descend, rappel the northwest face and then traverse the west side of the north ridge about a mile. Cross over the ridge and descend class 3 rock and forested slopes into the Nesakwatch drainage.

Equipment

Carry a rack of thirty chocks and a few pitons.

Remarks

Snow pockets found along the route melt away as the season advances; late-season climbing parties must carry water. It is advisable to check on the use of the logging road in advance.

Mount Stuart North Ridge

23

The Wenatchee Mountains comprise a significant subrange of the Cascades between Stevens Pass and the town of Cle Elum in central Washington. The huge, granitic range lies east of the main crest and thus receives far less precipitation than the mountain areas closer to the sea. Instead of nearly impenetrable deadfall and the horrid spines of the devil's club, climbers approaching these rugged mountains find dry, open forests in which pines predominate; although undergrowth is still prevalent throughout the lower valleys, occasional grassy openings permit enjoyable cross-country travel.

The massive, 9415-foot Mount Stuart is the highest point of the Mount Stuart batholith, which underlies most of the Wenatchee Mountains. Since the peak is one of the highest granitic peaks in the state of Washington, it attracted early geologic

◄ *The north side of Mount Stuart.* Ed Cooper.

explorers. In his *Cascade Alpine Guide,* Fred Beckey mentions that "the famed geologist, Professor I. S. Russell [the same mountaineer who had explored the Saint Elias region in 1890–1891] called the area centering around Mt. Stuart the 'Wenatche Mountains' in 1897, and described results of weathering, which 'produced numerous tapering pinnacles and spires. The light color of the naked granite gives the precipices and crags a seemingly white color when seen from a distance.'"

The mile-wide, moderately inclined southern flanks of Mount Stuart rise 4600 feet above Ingalls Creek and are interspersed with numerous gullies and sharp-pinnacled crests leading to the east–west-oriented summit ridge. Early Cascade climber C. E. Rusk, writing in *Tales of a Western Mountaineer*, described his first view of the peak in 1894: "Directly before us . . . the serrated crags of Mount Stuart stood in menacing ranks, the gullies and depressions seamed with snow, the sharper points black and bare. Stuart . . . stands like a great saw with its teeth pointed to the sky."

It is to the north, however, that Mount Stuart presents its most dramatic configuration, for there the cliffs of the "great saw" approach the vertical. These somber precipices soar above remnant glaciers and contain a grand array of slabs, couloirs, and chimneys that are a delight to mountaineers. The unbroken north ridge rises nearly 3000 feet from the headwaters of Mountaineer Creek and splits the mile-

wide northern façade into two cavernous glacial cirques. Starting as a broad, massive buttress, the ridge narrows to a thin, serrated crest that curves elegantly to the summit. Several hundred feet below the top, a sheer buttress appears to bar access to the blocky summit area.

By the time Rusk reached the summit of Mount Stuart in 1894 by climbing a gully on the southeast side, circumstances surrounding the first ascent already were obscure. Some evidence suggested that Professor Russell had ascended the mountain during one of his trips for the Geological Survey. Rusk mentioned he had heard that Russell "had climbed the peak and had pronounced it the greatest single mass of granite in the United States, if not in the entire world."

Attempts in the 1930s to climb the peak were predictably on the low-angle, south side. In 1933 Louis Ulrich and two companions pioneered a class 3 route—now called Ulrich's Couloir—that led 4000 feet in a direct line to the summit rocks. In 1935 a party climbed the more difficult west ridge. Finally the first north-side route, the northwest buttress, was ascended by Ulrich and two others in 1937. Exploratory climbing on Mount Stuart then ceased for nearly two decades, with the notable exception of the climb of the Stuart Glacier Couloir in 1944. Not until the 1950s did the beautiful north ridge itself attract mountaineers looking for new lines to the summit.

On September 9, 1956, John Rupley, Fred Beckey, and Don Claunch had just finished an exasperating struggle up an extensive talus slope and were resting contentedly on the sandy ledges of Goat Pass, located west of Mount Stuart. The three climbers looked out over the Stuart Glacier, wondering if they would be able to circumvent the huge north ridge that blocked the approach to the northeast face, their intended goal. As Rupley and Claunch were discussing the possibility of climbing the face that day, the impatient Beckey already had descended to the glacier and was strapping on his crampons. Rupley and Claunch joined their friend, and soon the trio was far out on the glacier. Upon reaching the glacier's eastern edge, the men realized the traverse around the immense base of the ridge would be extremely complex. During the ensuing discussion, Rupley and Claunch decided to try the ascent of the north ridge, while Beckey, who by then was not feeling well, returned to their camp on Ingalls Creek.

Rather than attempt the ascent from the base of the ridge, Rupley and Claunch chose a narrow snow gully leading from the Stuart Glacier to the midpoint of the ridge. The two climbers ascended the gully to a small notch at its top. Changing to rockclimbing shoes, the two men followed a succession of angular blocks, airy corners, and narrow spines of rock. Often, they traversed along thin ledges below the ridge crest as well as occasional short cliffs that required the precaution of

Shari Kearney leads a pitch on the lower part of the route. Alan Kearney.

piton placement. The climbing was elegant and beautiful, and the pair ascended many memorable pitches before arriving at the ominous buttress they had seen from the glacier.

As the climbers studied the obstacle, which they named the Great Gendarme, clouds began to cover the peak, and the nearby cliffs began to appear gloomy and unappealing. Realizing that they could not ascend the monolithic formation without resorting to direct aid, Rupley and Claunch chose to attempt a descent into an adjoining couloir which led to easier slabs below the summit. Undeterred by the developing hailstorm, the climbers rappelled from the exposed ridge and found a tiny ledge leading into the darkened, hail-battered couloir. After placing several pitons to safeguard their passage to the low-angled slabs above them, the two men scrambled exuberantly through the swirling mists to the summit rocks.

Had the summit been free of clouds, the victorious climbers would have enjoyed a sweeping view of the surrounding sea of peaks, each wave separated by green park lands and shimmering alpine lakes. After relaxing briefly on the summit, the two climbers began the descent of Ulrich's Couloir, an arduous rock-leaping exercise that took them down 4000 feet to their camp on Ingalls Creek and to the comfort of Beckey's roaring campfire.

Predictably, subsequent climbers made many spectacular first ascents on the north side of Mount Stuart in the years that followed. The steep, lower section of the north ridge was climbed in 1963, and the next year a two-man party climbed the Great Gendarme, a bold undertaking involving three strenuous leads of varying amounts of direct aid. Most present-day Cascade climbers prefer the Stuart Glacier approach to the challenging north ridge and choose to follow the route pioneered by Rupley and Claunch, rather than struggling up the taxing leads of the Great Gendarme.

First ascent

Don Claunch and John Rupley. September 9, 1956.

Elevation

The summit is 9415 feet above sea level.

Difficulty

III, 5.4.

Time

Six hours from the glacier.

Map

USGS quadrangle: Mount Stuart, scale 1:62,500.

Useful reference

Cascade Alpine Guide: Columbia River to Stevens Pass.

Route description

Two-and-a-half miles east of the town of Cle Elum, leave Interstate 90 and drive four miles on U.S. Highway 97 to Teanaway River Road. Continue twenty-three miles, first on pavement and then on gravel (the gravel section is Forest Service Road 232) to the end of the road on the north fork of the Teanaway River. Hike along a broad trail next to the river for half a mile; then turn right on a well-traveled trail to reach Ingalls Pass in two miles. Continue to Ingalls Lake via a faint path that descends into an open, forested basin and then rises to the lake. From the north end of the lake, ascend to the crest and traverse along it to Stuart Pass. Cross to the west side of the crest and hike along steep, grassy slopes, eventually reaching the talus leading to Goat Pass (time: about six hours from the parking area).

From Goat Pass, the north ridge of Mount Stuart appears in profile to the east. Descend onto the Stuart Glacier and traverse across it to the base of a prominent gully (snow or scree) leading to a sharp notch in the ridge crest. From the notch, ascend easily climbed angular blocks, towers, and occasional short walls. The final lead to the Great Gendarme consists of face climbing east of the crest, beneath an overhanging wall. From a bolt at the base of the Gendarme, rappel 75 feet to exposed slabs and traverse into a steep couloir (often icy). Climb up and right on a moderately difficult face to wide ledges. Next, climb a 200-foot, right-ascending crack system to a notch and continue on broken rock to the summit.

Descend via Ulrich's Couloir, visible from the summit area several hundred feet below and slightly east.

Equipment

Carry a rack of ten chocks. Crampons and an ice axe are needed to traverse Stuart Glacier. If there is ice in the couloir west of the Grand Gendarme (early and late season), an ice hammer and a few ice screws are necessary.

Clark Gerhardt prepares to lead one of the many short, steep walls on the north ridge of Mount Stuart. Allen Steck.

Liberty Bell Mountain
Liberty Crack

24

Twenty miles east of the ice-clad peaks of Cascade Pass, dome-shaped Liberty Bell Mountain rises boldly into the sky above the North Cascades, at the end of an isolated, jagged crest forming a remarkable barrier at the head of Early Winters Creek. Across the valley, the ridges of Silver Star Mountain arch down from the summit, exhibiting a startling array of granitic spires and towers. Hermann Ulrichs, who explored and climbed in the area in the 1930s, viewed the unclimbed Liberty Bell Mountain from a nearby peak and observed that its perpendicular spires looked too difficult for him to attempt.

In the 1930s, long before a highway penetrated the pristine pine forests of Early Winters Creek, most climbers approached these mountains from the south by way of Lake Chelan. In 1937 an energetic group of Sierra Club rockclimbers entered

the region north of Lake Chelan and made several outstanding new climbs. Among the four-man team were Kenneth Davis and Kenneth Adam, who had participated the previous year in the ascent of one of Yosemite's classics, the Royal Arches. "Our first choice," Davis later wrote, "was Mount Liberty Bell, which appeared extremely difficult on all sides. . . . On July 20th, we attempted the climb, finding it far less difficult than expected, but the peak itself was spectacular." The climbers ascended the highest summit of the elegant half-mile-long formation identified as Liberty Bell on their map. Later, popular opinion led to a change in nomenclature, and the Californians' peak became known as Early Winters Spire, while a striking granite cone at the northern end of the crest assumed its present name: Liberty Bell Mountain.

Nine years passed before the mountain was challenged by a group of young climbers from the Northwest. In late September 1946, Fred Beckey, Chuck Welsh, and Jerry O'Neil left their car at the start of the Early Winters Creek Trail and began the long hike to Washington Pass, a prominent divide between Liberty Bell Mountain and Cutthroat Peak. "We passed through a most beautiful alp," wrote Beckey in *Challenge of the North Cascades*, "hundreds of acres of perfect meadow occasionally grazed by flocks of sheep. In a few hours the clearly-cut granite helmet forming Liberty Bell came into full view, a sight that shocked us out of our af-

Steve Mitchell aid climbing on the second pitch of Liberty Crack; above him looms the Lithuanian Roof. Alan Kearney.

ternoon trail lethargy." Approaching the pass, the climbers followed meadows and grassy hillsides beneath the awesome 1200-foot east face, whose flawless slabs, broken by several conspicuous overhangs, soared upward for 600 feet. Slicing through the lower half of the massive, seventy-degree cliff was a barely discernible crack that merged with a prominent, dark dihedral midway up the face. Higher, a ramp system composed of small dihedrals and cracks angled steeply upward to the summit.

Impressed by the wall's apparent impregnability, the three men dismissed the possibility of climbing it, just as Yosemite climbers of that time had rejected the idea of ascending El Capitan. Hoping to climb the bell-shaped tower on its easier west side, the trio prepared a stream-side campsite among the spruce trees of Washington Pass.

The following morning Beckey and his partners ascended to the lower southwest cliffs of Liberty Bell. Threading through a series of short buttresses, cracks, and hand-traverses, the men reached the summit after a half-day climb. "The summit was ours!" wrote Beckey. "The climb was just technically right for our mood."

Mountaineers established several new routes on the north and west sides of Liberty Bell in the late 1950s, by which time rumors of spectacular climbs in Yosemite Valley drifted into Seattle climbing circles. The ascent of the northwest face of Half Dome and the forty-five-day siege of the Nose of El Capitan signaled a new and exciting era of big-wall climbing. Concurrent with the establishment of these routes was the development of chrome–moly pitons by Dick Long and Yvon Chouinard. Conventional soft-iron pitons were being replaced by this tough new hardware: knife-blades, the tiny rurp—Chouinard's Realized Ultimate Reality Piton—

and perhaps most important, the large bong-bongs that permitted the ascent of previously unclimbable wide cracks.

Chris Jones, writing in *Climbing in North America*, described Yosemite's influence in Cascade climbing: "The young turks were attuned to the latest in climbing, and in the mid-1960s the latest was Yosemite. They went to the valley and brought home new attitudes and new desires. They found a wall in the Cascades comparable with the big walls of Yosemite. . . ."

Steve Marts, a young climber from Seattle, was intrigued by Yosemite big-wall climbing and invited fellow climber Alex Bertulis to accompany him on an attempt to scale the untouched east face of Liberty Bell. In 1964 the two climbers pioneered two leads on the smooth face, following a thin crack leading to a prominent overhang. The climbing had been consistently difficult direct aid, and the ascent to the edge of the roof represented a significant accomplishment. Returning the following year to the route they began calling Liberty Crack, Marts and Bertulis regained the hanging belay beneath the roof. After hours of effort, Bertulis finished a short lead past the ceiling, finally placing bolts to anchor his belay fifty feet above the lip of the obstacle now known as the Lithuanian Roof in honor of Bertulis' ancestry. Not prepared for a hanging bivouac, the climbers abandoned the route and returned to Seattle, leaving ropes anchored to their high point.

Bertulis was unable to accompany Marts when he returned on July 16 with two other friends, Fred Stanley and Don McPherson. Using the fixed ropes, the trio quickly regained the hanging belay above the roof. Above the climbers stretched the thin, unbroken crack that merged with the dihedral they hoped would offer easier climbing. Marts began climbing the sheer wall, and after a succession of knife-blade, rurp, and bolt placements, he arrived with great relief at a small ledge high above his companions. The arduous lead, the longest of his career, is considered even today to be the crux of the route. The climbers, however, were still unfamiliar with the expertise in piton placement and economy of movement required for such sustained and difficult climbing, and they ascended only one additional pitch before being overtaken by darkness. The trio improvised a hammock bivouac and spent an uncomfortable night suspended like bats above the chasm.

The following morning, the three climbers entered the dihedral, where, as hoped, the climbing became easier. From its top, Marts and his partners looked down for the last time at the solitary crack that had consumed so much time and effort. Climbing up into the disconnected ramp system, they managed four more leads by the end of the day. Their second bivouac, in marked contrast to their first, was

◄ *The east face of Liberty Bell Mountain.* Ed Cooper.

spent on reasonably comfortable ledges high on the ramp. The trio started the last pitches of the climb at dawn and reached the summit in the early morning. Removing the hardware and ropes, the climbers congratulated one another on their triumph, laughing at their grotesque hands, which had been blackened by the constant manipulation of carabiners and pitons. In a joyful mood, they began a series of rappels down the southwest corner.

A year later Bertulis returned to Liberty Crack with three companions, hoping to ascend the route he had helped pioneer. After suffering two falls attempting to climb the crux pitch above the Lithuanian Roof, Bertulis surrendered the lead to one of his companions, who was able to complete the pitch. Two-thirds of the way to the summit, the group decided to establish a more direct line to the top by ascending an overhanging dihedral near the beginning of the ramp system. However, because of the quantity of direct aid required in the dihedral, this variation has not become popular.

Climbers now can approach the east face of Liberty Bell Mountain via a short walk from the Washington Pass Highway, completed around 1968. Still attuned to the current trend in big-wall climbing, most of them carry a large rack of chocks and are particularly intent upon climbing as much of the route as possible without direct aid. In 1974 the route was climbed using only chocks and occasional bolts and

A climber, trailing his hauling line, struggles over the lip of the Lithuanian Roof.   Greg Donaldson.

fixed pitons. Eventually a party of expert climbers ascended the route free except for the nearly flawless expanse of rock above the Lithuanian Roof. Talented aid climbers have pioneered several new lines on the east face, a demonstration that the limits of Cascade mountaineering are continually being tested. For pure kinesthetic enjoyment, however, modern climbers prefer the elegant and challenging leads of the Liberty Crack Route.

First ascent

Steve Marts, Fred Stanley, and Don McPherson. July 16–18, 1965.

Elevation

The summit is 7500 feet above sea level.

Difficulty

V, 5.9, A3.

Time

Fast parties can ascend the route in a long day.

Map

USGS quadrangle: Washington Pass, scale 1:24,000.

Useful reference

Climber's Guide to the Cascade and Olympic Mountains of Washington.

Steve Mitchell follows the aid pitch above the dihedral. Alan Kearney.

Route description

From the town of Mazama, in north-central Washington, drive west on Washington Highway 20 to a parking area one-half mile below Washington Pass. The approach to the obvious east face of Liberty Bell takes about an hour.

Climb a prominent ledge-and-crack system at the base of the wall to reach a solitary crack, which is followed for two leads of difficult aid climbing to a hanging belay 50 feet above the Lithuanian Roof. Continue up the crack for another three pitches of mixed aid (A3) and free climbing to a ledge at the base of a large dihedral capped by a block. Ascend the dihedral in two pitches to a belay spot at the top of the block. More aid and free climbing in steep cracks and small dihedrals leads up and left past occasional stunted trees. After several liebacks and fingertip cracks, a short, easy dihedral leads to a sandy ledge 200 feet below the summit. Easy scrambling leads to the top.

To descend, rappel slabs and chimneys to the southwest.

Equipment

Carry a standard big-wall rack, including many small chocks.

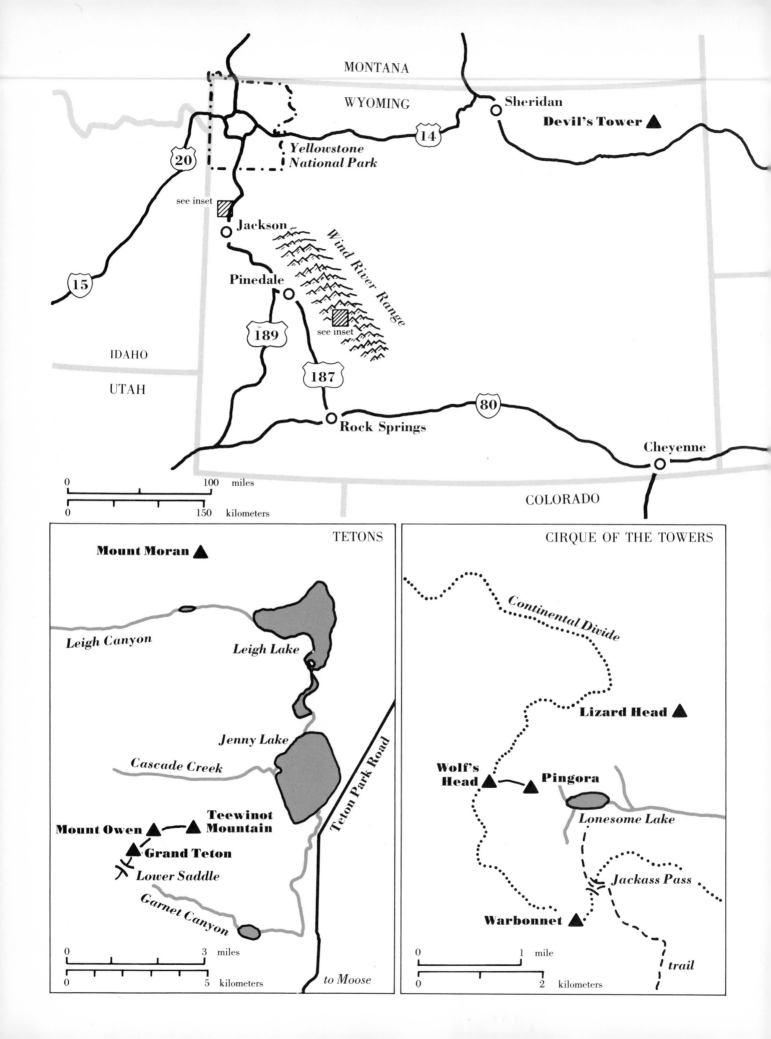

MONTANA

WYOMING

Sheridan

Devil's Tower ▲

14

Yellowstone National Park

20

see inset

Jackson

Wind River Range

15

Pinedale

189

see inset

IDAHO

187

UTAH

80

Rock Springs

Cheyenne

0 ——————— 100 miles

0 ——————— 150 kilometers

COLORADO

TETONS

Mount Moran ▲

Leigh Canyon

Leigh Lake

Jenny Lake

Cascade Creek

Teton Park Road

Mount Owen ▲ ▲ **Teewinot Mountain**

▲ **Grand Teton**

Lower Saddle

Garnet Canyon

0 ——————— 3 miles

0 ——————— 5 kilometers

to Moose

CIRQUE OF THE TOWERS

Continental Divide

Lizard Head ▲

Wolf's Head ▲ ▲ **Pingora**

Lonesome Lake

Jackass Pass

Warbonnet ▲

0 ——————— 1 mile

0 ——————— 2 kilometers

trail

Wyoming

Wyoming's Tetons, a compact range rising to the west of Jackson Hole, have played a disproportionately large role in the history of North American mountaineering. "Almost anyone who has done any mountain climbing in the United States sooner or later visits the Tetons and ascends one or more of the high peaks," wrote Leigh Ortenburger in his *Climber's Guide to the Teton Range*. "These peaks rise steadily at a high angle, bristle with spires and pinnacles, and are topped by sharp summits. . . . There is perhaps no climbing area in the country that can match the Tetons for general mountaineering of an Alpine nature with excellent rock and moderate snow."

The earliest mountaineering efforts in the Tetons focused on the Grand Teton, the range's highest summit, but not until 1898 did four climbers finally reach the top via the now-celebrated Owen–Spalding Route. Technical climbing was introduced in the Tetons by eastern climbers Robert Underhill and Kenneth Henderson in 1929, and in that same year the range acquired national park status. During the following decade, Underhill, Henderson, and others made many significant first ascents, and soon Teton climbers were in the vanguard of technical climbing in North America.

To select a handful of classic routes in a range that so abounds with excellent candidates proved a frustrating task. Our choice of three climbs on the Grand Teton may seem to indicate a prejudice, but the emphasis can be justified. These routes on the Grand are among the most representative of Teton climbing, and the men who accomplished them stimulated the development of equipment and techniques that influenced succeeding generations of mountaineers in every climbing area on the continent.

Mountaineering in Wyoming is not limited to the Teton Range, of course. Two of our classics are located in the lesser-known Wind River Range, which because of its inaccessibility did not attract climbers interested in technical routes until the early 1950s. And no discussion of Wyoming climbing is complete without mentioning Devil's Tower, the isolated formation in northeastern Wyoming that attracts climbers by virtue of its striking appearance and demanding rockclimbing.

Although mountaineers still can find challenging, unclimbed routes in the Wind River Range, increased climbing activity has sharply reduced the number of new routes that can be made in the Tetons and on Devil's Tower. Today, mountaineers concentrate on repeating early, classic routes on the marvelous, sound rock for which these climbing areas are renowned.

Devil's Tower Durrance Route

25

A charming Sioux legend tells of the formation of the marvelous structure in northeastern Wyoming known as Devil's Tower. In the days when the Sioux lived on the plains surrounding this monolith, it was known as both the Mateo Tepee (Lodge of the Bear) and the Bad God's Tower. A group of girls, the story goes, were playing beside a stream when they were attacked by a bear. The maidens fled to the top of a small rock and implored the stone spirits to save them. In answer to their pleas, the rock began to grow taller and bore the girls into the air. As the rock grew to its present height, the bear, which became a giant itself, clawed at the expanding tower in frustration, tearing long, vertical furrows that are clearly visible to this day. The girls eventually became a permanent part of the sky— the seven stars of the Pleiades.

◀ *Devil's Tower viewed from the south.* Ed Cooper.

Literal-minded geologists offer a more prosaic explanation: Devil's Tower is a huge accumulation of phonolite porphyry that was intruded into the earth's crust in a molten state some sixty million years ago. As the intrusion cooled, the wondrous columnar pattern was formed, and during subsequent millions of years the surrounding material weathered away, leaving the present formation standing some 1300 feet above the forested river valley.

Whatever its origin, Devil's Tower makes a dramatic impression when seen for the first time. Following the nature trail around its base, one marvels at the rock's apparent simplicity of form. Many of the huge pentagonal columns rise in near-perfect symmetry all the way to the upper, heavily weathered cap, while others merge and disappear abruptly, transformed into a sheer, smooth wall; still others end suddenly beneath dark overhangs, where columns have collapsed and fallen to the base. Cracks are found between most of the columns, and it was these which eventually enabled climbers to ascend the nearly vertical walls of "Bad God's Tower."

Because of its steep and forbidding sides, it is not surprising that the first ascent of Devil's Tower, in 1893, was made by artificial means. Two local ranchers, William Rogers and Willard Ripley, prepared a crude ladder "by driving pegs, cut from native oak, ash and willow, 24 to 30 inches in length" into a 350-foot continuous crack on the south side of the monolith. Rogers climbed the pegs, which were fastened together with wood strips, and reached the top amidst the cheers of an assembled throng attending a Fourth of July celebration. A handbill specially prepared for this extraordinary first climb announced: "There will be plenty to eat and drink on the grounds," with "dancing day and night." Future climbers of the Tower would never be so well entertained.

It was not until 1937 that the Tower was ascended by a route other than Rogers' ladder. Fritz Wiessner and William House, who had distinguished themselves on Mount Waddington the year before, arrived at the Tower with a climbing friend, Lawrence Coveney. After a brief reconnaissance of the southwest corner of the monolith, the three climbers ascended a fissure between two columns that led to the base of an imposing eighty-foot crack. Tense, but determined, Wiessner climbed the near-vertical pitch in a flawless style that astonished his belayers. After finishing this severe lead, the climbers soon reached the summit, becoming the first to ascend Devil's Tower by using modern techniques.

When Jack Durrance and his climbing partner, Harrison Butterworth, arrived at Devil's Tower in September 1938, they planned to repeat Wiessner's route, which had been described vividly by Coveney in *Appalachia*, the journal of the Appalachian Mountain Club. Durrance, a student at Dartmouth College; was a talented rockclimber who, like Wiessner, had gained his early climbing experience in Germany. From his German companions Durrance learned the art of technical rock work on the steep limestone walls of the Isar Valley and became familiar with the use of pitons and the lightweight *Kletterschuhe*, rope-soled leather boots designed specifically for rockclimbing.

As the two climbers reached the traverse to the base of the Wiessner Crack, a rainsquall forced them to abandon the attempt. The following day it was a sheer whim that led Durrance to try a promising new line he had noticed a few columns left of the one climbed by the Wiessner party. Moving up past a huge, broken column that had fallen against a longer one, Durrance found the climbing to be fairly easy. He momentarily disappeared into a short chimney and emerged for the last moves to the top of the column. As he belayed Butterworth, Durrance marveled at the massive structure they were climbing. The nearby pillars, rounded and weathered, were suggestive of truncated Grecian columns; the climbers felt they could have been ascending the façade of a crumbling ancient temple.

The dihedral above the climbers looked long and difficult, and Durrance realized it would be arduous

Devil's Tower as seen from the southwest. The Durrance Route lies directly to the right of the sunlit face.   Galen Rowell.

The leader emerges from the chimney behind the Leaning Column just before the last moves to its top. Steve Roper.

climbing. He decided to climb by means of a double-rope technique and, taking a generous supply of pitons, moved into stemming position. Placing his right foot in the dihedral and his left in a crack on the face, he slowly pressured his way up the steep pitch. There were moments that called for particular concentration, for, as Butterworth noted, "the avenue up which Jack was climbing became so broad that he had to spread his feet farther and farther apart." Near the top of the crack was a difficult section where "the handholds grew fairly slight, the support for the feet still less convincing." But Durrance persevered, and soon the two climbers were standing on a flat column above what is now called the Durrance Crack.

The route above seemed far less intimidating, and for the first time the men realized they might reach the summit. Several short pitches of crack and chimney climbing brought them to a difficult traverse, which they avoided by rappelling a few feet to an easier traverse that led to the low-angled area known today as the Meadows. The wall above was fractured by chimneys, offering an easy way to the top. Within minutes the two climbers stepped onto the broad summit, which Butterworth found "as unimpressive as any field of weeds and stones in New England. From the center of the little plain the sides of the Tower are naturally invisible, so flat is the top and so sheer the walls one has the sensation of being [on] an island in the sky."

When the second ascent of the Durrance Route was made in 1941, it was in a slightly different style. Seattle climbers Jim Crooks and Sam Heller also had read of the remarkable climbing to be found on Devil's Tower and applied to officials at the national monument for permission to climb it. Since the permit did not arrive by their planned departure date, the pair decided instead to hitchhike and ride freights to the Needles in South Dakota. As they were passing through northeastern Wyoming, they decided to stop at the Tower for a brief look at the famous formation and discovered their permit had been forwarded there by Crooks' parents. The two climbers made a quick decision to attempt the Durrance Route despite having left most of their climbing gear at home. They had brought only a seventy-foot climbing rope and some sling material; they had no carabiners or pitons. Ironically, the usually cautious and conservative park authorities did not ask to examine the pair's climbing equipment, so with youthful enthusiasm Crooks and Heller scrambled up to the start of the Durrance Route. They managed

the short pitch to the top of the Leaning Column without incident. Staring up at the ominous Durrance Crack and thinking of their meager equipment, Crooks was assailed by the classic climber's malady: the sweating palms syndrome. However, he soon recovered his composure and started up the crack. As he came to the pitons left by Durrance, he "clipped" into them by tying small loops of sling rope through the pitons and around the climbing rope at the same time. Near the top of the column Crooks ran out of rope, and so the two climbers finished the pitch by climbing simultaneously. On the descent, without enough rope for full-length rappels, they were obliged to downclimb most of the route.

The third ascent of the Durrance Route proved even more bizarre, with Durrance himself participating in the Hopkins Rescue, the most celebrated event in the Tower's history. In October 1941, professional parachutist George Hopkins floated down upon the broad summit of the Tower, adding to his long list of spectacular jumps. Unfortunately, the 1000-foot coil of rope dropped earlier to facilitate his descent had fallen onto ledges below the summit, well out of reach of the hapless parachutist. Faced with rescuing the stranded Hopkins, park officials dropped supplies to him and then accepted Durrance's offer to lead a group of rescuers to the summit.

Allen Steck stems up the first few feet of the Durrance Crack. There are few resting places along the seventy-foot lead. Steve Roper.

Durrance journeyed by train from Dartmouth to stand once again at the base of the imposing monolith, which truly conveyed the image of a "Bad God's Tower" on that cold, blustery day. This time Durrance had to apply all his skill to complete the ascent, for the crack itself was wet and partially coated with ice. When the rescue group arrived at the summit, they found Hopkins in a cheerful mood despite his six-day ordeal. Durrance and his friends gave Hopkins a quick course in rappelling, and it was not long before everyone was happily back on the ground.

Currently there are more than fifty routes on Devil's Tower, and nearly sixty percent of these are free, many with a 5.10 rating. While there are several 5.7 routes on the south side, the majority of climbers favor the Durrance Route because of its compelling appearance and varied climbing.

First ascent

Jack Durrance and Harrison Butterworth. September 1938.

Elevation

The summit is 5117 feet above sea level. The climbing route is approximately 500 feet long.

Difficulty

II, 5.7. While the route carries an overall rating of 5.6, the length and continuous difficulty of the Durrance Crack elevates it to the 5.7 range.

Time

Two to four hours from the nature trail.

Map

Special USGS topographic sheet: Devil's Tower National Monument, scale 1:48,000.

Useful reference

A Climber's Guide to Devil's Tower.

Route description

Take either the Moorcroft or Sundance exit off Interstate 90 in northeastern Wyoming and follow U.S. Highway 14 to Devil's Tower Junction and on to Devil's Tower National Monument.

A nature trail, marked by numbered viewing stations, completely encircles the monolith at treeline. At the western base of the Tower, leave the trail between stations 2 and 3 and scramble to the top of the talus. Climb up and right over class 3 rock to reach the base of the Leaning Column, at the southwest corner of the Tower. This broken column, one of the very few on the rock, is seen easily from the Belle Fourche Campground, particularly in early morning when the west face is in shadow.

Climb to the crack which forms the left edge of the column and then chimney or stem to its top. Immediately above is the 70-foot Durrance Crack, the crux lead of the climb. Ascend the crack (actually two parallel cracks) using a combination of jamming and stemming techniques. Move into the right-hand crack about 10 feet from the top. The next lead, Cussing Crack, is short. Climb a jamcrack and about halfway up traverse on a good ledge to the right side of the column; then belay on its top. One hundred feet of 5.5 climbing leads past an overhanging chockstone to a solid belay just to the left of the Jump Traverse. This 15-foot traverse, protected by a fixed piton, leads to the west end of the Meadows. A path then leads across this low-angled section to its eastern edge, from which class 4 climbing ends on the summit plateau.

A cairn on the southwestern edge of the summit marks a rappel station 150 feet above the western end of the Meadows. Three long rappels from the Meadows take one to the base of the monolith.

Equipment

Carry a selection of eight medium- to large-sized chocks and two 150-foot ropes for the rappels. There are fixed pitons on every lead.

Remarks

Climbers must register at the visitors' center. Bivouacs are not permitted on any of the routes nor on the summit.

The leader, in about the same position as in the preceding photograph, pressures his way up the Durrance Crack. His companions stand on top of the Leaning Column. Kathy Roper.

Grand Teton North Ridge

26

The 1929 ascent of the east ridge of the Grand Teton by Robert Underhill and Kenneth Henderson was the first new route to be made on the mountain since it was climbed originally in 1898. The climb marked the beginning of renewed interest in the Teton Range and was a precursor to the many new and exciting routes that were about to be done.

In 1930 Underhill was attracted to the unknown northern precipices of the Grand Teton. During one of his excursions along the Teton Glacier he had an opportunity to study the north face but decided that the unconnected ledge systems on the immense wall presented too bold a challenge. He then glanced across the face to the north ridge. This elegant line to the summit showed more promise, and though it was steeper, it was an obvious route that would involve far less climbing. The ridge is a striking formation, and no climber could have looked at it without feeling a twinge of desire to participate in its ascent. Surprisingly, however, not only was the ridge unclimbed, it had never been attempted.

Employing classic stemming technique, Mike Brewer ascends the 100-foot chimney above the Chockstone Chimney Pitch.   Leigh Ortenburger.

147

Already a pioneer of many routes on eastern crags, Underhill was an influential member of the Appalachian Mountain Club. The club was becoming interested in the increased mountaineering activity that was taking place in the Tetons and had appointed Underhill editor of its journal, *Appalachia*. Underhill had sufficient literary energy not only for this project, but also to pursue his career as a professor of philosophy at Harvard University and to contribute articles to other climbing journals. Much of his climbing experience had been acquired in the Alps; his 1928 season in Chamonix included guided ascents of the Peuterey and Brenva ridges of Mont Blanc, as well as the audacious first traverse of the Aiguilles du Diable, led by the well-known French guide Armand Charlet. With this experience and his newly acquired knowledge of the techniques and equipment then popular in Europe, Underhill began to concentrate his energy in further exploring new routes in the Tetons, and in 1931 he made plans for his most daring climb, the north ridge of the Grand.

Underhill first had to solve the problem of the approach to the north ridge. In 1930 he had climbed past the bergschrund on Teton Glacier and made a solo reconnaissance of the Grandstand, a 1200-foot-high massive shoulder that led upward along the base of the north face to

The north ridge of the Grand Teton. Leigh Ortenburger.

the foot of the ridge. Finding the rockfall danger too great, he tried to force a way up to a nearby notch, but this also ended in defeat, and he realized that the Grandstand offered the only reasonable access to the ridge.

Underhill's six-week stay in the Tetons in 1931 resulted in the most noteworthy climbing season in the history of Teton mountaineering. The entire range was in excellent condition because of the moderate winter snows and a summer drought of a magnitude not seen in forty years. Besides other important first ascents, two new routes on the Grand were established by the indefatigable Underhill: the southeast ridge, which now bears his name, and the remarkable north ridge, which he climbed with Fritiof Fryxell.

At dawn on July 19, 1931, just four days after the successful ascent of the southeast ridge, Underhill and Fryxell left their camp at Amphitheater Lake. Fryxell was an excellent climber who was working as a ranger–naturalist in the newly formed Grand Teton National Park. Underhill was wearing tricouni-nailed boots, while Fryxell wore a strange pair of boots indeed: his gear had not arrived in camp, and he was obliged to make the attempt wearing a pair of mismatched work boots, one with a composition sole and the other with a sole of smooth leather. The climbers found the rockfall on the Grandstand much less than they had anticipated. Changing leads as befitted their

footgear—tricounis being much better on snow—they managed to reach the juncture with the north ridge by ten o'clock. To their surprise, the ridge was broken with many ledges and gullies, and they ascended rapidly on moderate rock for 300 feet until they arrived beneath a huge, dark chimney. Underhill described it later as "a vertical pitch under a great chockstone, and we realized that we were facing a difficulty of the first magnitude. . . . The only possible way of ascent lay up the right-hand or inner wall, and this was most unappealing. . . . I set about excogitating reasons why Fryxell ought to assume the lead for this pitch, and I managed to get two excellent ones, based on the necessity of the *courte-échelle* and the desirability of his being the top man in it."

Fryxell not too gently insinuated himself upon Underhill's shoulders and gained an extra foot of reach by stepping on his head. This bizarre attempt to overcome the chimney ended with Fryxell's instantly diminished interest in the pitch because of the scarcity of holds. He returned to the tiny belay ledge. Underhill, controlling his apprehension, studied the wall and the chockstone that hung ominously over their heads: "It was now obviously my turn to try, in the hope that matters might work out more favorably for me, before we definitely

The leader maneuvers into stemming position, protected by a piton driven high on the right wall.

A delicate shift of weight permits the leader to reach holds in the chimney to the left of the huge chockstone.

The last moves in the exit chimney lead to the belay spot. In the background is the base of the 100-foot chimney.

Three rare photos of the crux moves on the Chockstone Chimney Pitch, taken during a 1953 ascent. Photographer Willi Unsoeld stood in aid slings on the wall right of the belay niche.

turned back. In view of our first experience I judged it in order to make use of all the technical means we had at our disposal. I therefore commenced by hammering a piton into a small vertical crack. . . ."

With his nailed boots, Underhill had a tedious time getting up the chimney, which is known now as the Chockstone Chimney and is the crux of the climb. After a frantic series of futile, random kicks accompanied by the horrible noise of tricounis grating over coarse granite, Underhill heeded Fryxell's tense whisper: "Step on the piton!" Eventually, Underhill reached easier ground above, thus accomplishing the hardest lead of his climbing career. The two climbers continued to the summit without further difficulty, though Fryxell led a few of the slab pitches in a curious style, using only his rubber heels and the composition sole of his right boot. The entire climb had taken slightly less than ten hours, an impressive time due in part to the excellent condition of the rock and the favorable weather.

Most climbers credit Underhill with opening the Tetons to pitoncraft by the insertion of his now famous piton. The art of pitoning was in its infancy in America; indeed, there were some eastern climbers who regarded the use of pitons with contempt, as an unfair advantage over the mountain. This conservative element, influenced by the climbing ethics of English mountaineers, soon would complain that with enough pitons one could climb anything. Yet in the short span of thirty years pitoncraft would progress from Underhill's single placement to the nearly 500 required for the ascent of the Salathé Wall on Yosemite's El Capitan.

That Underhill was willing to share his technical knowledge was evidenced by the fact that just a few weeks after completing the north-ridge ascent, he traveled to California to demonstrate pitoncraft and rope management to young and enthusiastic Sierra Club mountaineers.

The second ascent of the north ridge was made in 1936, when the first free passage of the Chockstone Chimney was made by Fritz Wiessner, who led the pitch in a light snowfall. The method commonly used now is a cartilage-rending stemming technique, facing in or out, without the use of direct aid. The chimney still creates apprehension in any climber standing within its darkened confines.

First ascent

Robert Underhill and Fritiof Fryxell. July 19, 1931.

Elevation

The summit is 13,766 feet above sea level. The climbing route is approximately 1200 feet long from the top of the Grandstand.

Difficulty

IV, 5.7.

Time

Ten to twelve hours from Amphitheater Lake; eight to ten hours from the Lower Saddle via the Valhalla Traverse.

Map

USGS quadrangle: Grand Teton, scale 1:24,000.

Useful reference

A Climber's Guide to the Teton Range (Condensed Version).

Route description

The traditional approach to the Grandstand and the beginning of technical climbing on the north ridge is from Amphitheater Lake. Plan a dawn ascent of the Teton Glacier to the base of the north face, and after crossing the bergschrund, turn west and climb the Grandstand all the way to the north ridge. There are many choices of ascent, depending on snow conditions and severity of rockfall.

A shorter and safer approach is via the Valhalla Traverse, discovered in 1960. From a camp on the Lower Saddle, traverse around the west side of the Grand Teton, crossing a snowfield at the lower reaches of the Black Ice Couloir; then ascend an obvious easy shelf that leads up to the north ridge.

Ascend directly up the ridge for 40 feet and then move left on small ledges, eventually reaching gullies which lead to the top of the first buttress. Climb a 15-foot step; then ascend 30 feet over difficult rock to a belay cave at the base of the Chockstone Chimney. Fixed pitons most likely will be found here. Climb a few feet on the right wall; then stem as high as possible, eventually swinging left into the small chimney formed by the chockstone and the left wall of the main chimney. Moderate climbing leads to the top of the pitch.

Next, ascend a 100-foot textbook chimney of moderate difficulty which ends at the belay for the slab pitch that leads left to the exposed corner of the north ridge. Climb the corner to a small ledge which leads back to the west side of the ridge. This point marks the west end of the Second Ledge of the North Face Route. Ascend two obvious chimneys, moderately difficult, just to the right of the ridge crest. A final, difficult, 25-foot face leads to easier climbing and the summit.

The descent usually is made via the easy Owen–Spalding Route. From the summit, descend west over easy slabs, keeping slightly left until a point is reached where it is possible to rappel 120 feet to the Upper Saddle. If conditions permit, it is equally fast to downclimb the class 4 section of the Owen–Spalding Route. Continue to the Lower Saddle via an indistinct route that more or less follows the left side of the central couloir.

Equipment

A selection of ten to twelve chocks, from small stoppers to medium hexes, is recommended.

Remarks

Register for all park climbs at the Jenny Lake Ranger Station. Climbing rangers freely give advice, and photographs of many of the popular routes are available for perusal.

Grand Teton Direct Exum Ridge

Early in the climbing season, when the Teton Range is emerging from its mantle of winter snows, the Direct Exum Ridge is one of the first routes to offer a reasonable approach to the summit of the Grand Teton. Its fortunate southern exposure to the warming rays of the sun throughout the day ensures that ledges and chimneys are quick to clear of snow after a storm. The favorable mixture of sun and stimulating climbing on clean, good rock presents an attraction to climbers that is hard to resist.

As one drives along the road a few miles south of Jenny Lake, the route can be seen in elegant profile: a steep, 800-foot buttress rising above the Lower Saddle merges with the more gently angled rocks of the upper half of the route, which was pioneered by Glenn Exum in 1931.

Paul Petzoldt was the proprietor of a guide service in the Teton Range in the summer of 1931, and he and young Exum were leading two Austrians up the Owen–Spalding

The second lead on the Black Face is continuously steep, but holds and protection points are excellent. Steve Roper.

Route on the Grand—the original route done in 1898. Exum was a newcomer to climbing; still in his teens and a student at the University of Idaho, he had climbed the Grand only once before. As the climbers were making their way up the couloir to the Upper Saddle, Petzoldt pointed out the possibility of using a prominent ledge, later to be known as Wall Street, to reach the unclimbed south ridge at its midpoint and then following the ridge to the summit.

As they reached the level of the striking ledge, Exum decided to follow Petzoldt's suggestion and try this new route. As he was climbing along this wide, sloping formation, he peered down at the steep buttress forming the lower portion of the ridge, wondering if it might ever be climbed. There seemed to be a route part way, but it ended decisively at a large, black wall that appeared devoid of holds. No possible way around that obstacle, he thought, as he continued traversing along the ledge. Just before reaching the ridge

crest, Exum was stopped by a fearfully exposed gap, which he ultimately crossed by an audacious leap.

Having left the security of Wall Street, Exum started up the ridge, climbing smoothly and surely and taking particular care at the more difficult sections, for he was learning that solo mountaineering required the utmost attention. He was surprised by the beauty of the climbing on this marvelous ridge and elated that the climb was going so well. Exum threaded through a succession of chimneys, small knobby faces, and gullies. Midway up the ridge he was stopped by a steep slab, later to become known as the Friction Pitch. Exum fearfully moved up the smooth wall, for the first time losing confidence in his shoes—he was wearing cleated football shoes!—as his feet skittered on the granite. After a few desperate moves, he was able to reach good handholds and soon was resting on a comfortable ledge. As he continued higher, he thought he heard voices—surely it was his imagination. As the voices became louder, however, he realized there were climbers on the ridge just to his right. It was Robert Underhill's party making the first ascent of the southeast ridge.

The Grand Teton as seen from the south. Allen Steck.

When Exum eventually arrived on the summit, he saw Petzoldt and the Austrians coming up the final slabs of the Owen–Spalding Route; soon Underhill and his companions also arrived at the top. Two first ascents of adjacent ridges had been made simultaneously—ridges that would bear the names of the climbers most directly involved in their ascent. Exum was overjoyed to meet the well-known Underhill, whose 1929 ascent of the east ridge had so impressed the young novice.

The Exum Ridge soon became a popular objective for both amateur and guided parties. Not only was the climbing excellent and longer than that found on the Owen–Spalding Route, but the rocks generally were clear of snow after a storm, while the north-facing chimneys of the 1898 route were choked with snow and rime.

Whenever Petzoldt and Exum arrived at the Lower Saddle with a group of clients, they would look longingly at the steep and forbidding buttress that Exum had observed on his solo climb. But while the unclimbed buttress intrigued them, they remained unwilling to make the attempt. The climb would be pioneered by Jack Durrance, a talented and daring climber yet to make his first visit to the fabulous Tetons.

When Durrance arrived at the small encampment near Jenny Lake at the start of the 1936 climbing season, he was already an accomplished rockclimber and had just returned

from an eight-year stay in Germany. He had come to the Tetons to work as a guide for Petzoldt, and during his free time he pondered the possibilities for interesting new routes that he observed while guiding clients to the summit of the Grand. His special talent and love for difficult rock work led him to choose lines that are still aesthetically pleasing and memorable today. Early in August 1936 he opened a route on Symmetry Spire that is known now as the Durrance Ridge; later the same month, accompanied by Paul and Eldon Petzoldt, he led most of the pitches on the first attempt of the unclimbed north face of the Grand.

A few days after the north-face attempt, Durrance roped up with Kenneth Henderson and pioneered the first ascent of the Direct Exum Ridge, adding the difficult lower 800-foot section to the line established by Glenn Exum five years earlier. Durrance liked the steep rock of the lower cliffs, as well as the length of the route, which started just a short distance above the Lower Saddle.

As Durrance and Henderson stood on the splintered rock at the base of the ridge, the climbing line above them appeared painfully indistinct. The massiveness of the rock was impressive; the granite, light-colored and finely textured, was molded into great formless shapes.

155

As they worked their way up the cliff, both climbers delighted in the challenging climbing. Durrance in particular was pleased by the absence of rockfall, an objective danger for which he had a special loathing. Henderson likewise enjoyed the artistry found in pure rockclimbing, having perfected a graceful technique on cliffs and crags near his home in Boston. The two climbers changed leads frequently, with Durrance leading the sensational pitches on the blank wall that Exum had noticed years earlier. This section, now known as the Black Face, was the highlight of their climb. They mastered the buttress in just five hours and then continued to the summit over the easier rock of the Upper Exum Route.

What manner of route was this lower buttress that led Durrance to call it his most memorable climb? The first few leads are moderate enough: after a short, fierce chimney, one arrives near the base of a huge, straightforward chimney—a 130-foot formation visible from the Lower Saddle —complex enough, however, to be worthy of a Durrance–Henderson line. A few leads higher, one reaches the large ledge forming the third step of the buttress. The rock above has the appearance of an immense puzzle; strange, amorphous shapes present intricate routefinding, though only moderate climbing. The exit from a small cave is particularly memorable: one desires to walk upright along a small, slanting crack, but the wall above forces the climber into a comical reptilian slither. After more climbing

The prominent snow-dusted ledge is Wall Street, which leads out to the Direct Exum Ridge. A climber has just reached the top of the Black Face pitches, which begin at the conspicuous short tower. Leigh Ortenburger.

one reaches the base of the celebrated Black Face, a striking, nearly vertical wall composed of massive intrusions of black magma into the light-colored granite. It is a wild place, visually exciting and decidedly airy.

The next two leads, classics in Teton mountaineering, are the most difficult on the route and offer face climbing at its best. Chock placements are excellent, and tiny holds appear as they are needed, as the leader treads cautiously up the eighty-degree face. The last moves of the Black Face take the leader onto the broad ledge near Wall Street, and at this point the hard climbing is finished. Above lies the broken, 1000-foot Upper Exum Ridge. Some climbers coil their rope here and proceed to the summit with the same freedom as Exum experienced in 1931.

First ascent

Jack Durrance and Kenneth Henderson. September 1, 1936.

Elevation

The summit is 13,766 feet above sea level.

Difficulty

III, 5.6.

Time

Four to seven hours from the Lower Saddle.

Map

USGS quadrangle: Grand Teton, scale 1:24,000.

Useful reference

A Climber's Guide to the Teton Range (Condensed Version).

Route description

One-quarter mile south of Jenny Lake Campground turn onto a dirt road leading to the Lupine Meadows parking area. From the parking area follow the trail to Garnet Canyon. Near the head of the canyon the trail switchbacks up a steep hillside until it reaches the moraine of the Middle Teton Glacier. Continue to the bottom of the Lower Saddle between Middle Teton and Grand Teton. Fixed ropes left by the park service facilitate climbing the class 4 section at the base of the saddle.

From the Lower Saddle, hike up to the Black Dike and traverse right to its intersection with the lower part of the ridge. Move up and left along an easy ledge for about 150 feet. Climb up moderate rock and ascend a short, steep, awkward chimney leading to the first step. Just above, enter the prominent 130-foot chimney easily seen from the Lower Saddle. After about 90 feet, make ascending traverses right and then back left to the top of the chimney at the second step. On the left flank of the ridge above, one long pitch with a hard finish ends at a broad ledge at the third step of the buttress.

Climb a short, steep pitch on the wall just to the left of the crest, traverse left into a small cave, and then work out farther left on a narrow, awkward, sloping ledge around a corner to a belay. Move upward over steep rock for about 30 feet; then traverse right to the base of a prominent, short tower just beneath the Black Face. Ascend the tower to a belay at the base of the 80-degree face, which is visible from the Lower Saddle and forms the crux of the climb.

Ascend about 15 feet; then traverse right and up to a belay in the middle of the face 70 feet above the belayer. The face is continuously steep; the holds and protection points are excellent. Next, climb up and slightly left about 80 feet to a belay stance in an alcove. Move left a few feet to a crack leading up to the blocky ledge that marks the intersection of Wall Street and the

Exum Ridge. At this point, one is about 1000 feet below the summit, at the start of the Upper Exum Ridge.

To enjoy the remainder of the climb to its fullest, one must stay on or close to the ridge crest as much as possible. At about the sixth or seventh pitch, one arrives at the base of the 140-foot Friction Pitch, directly on the crest. Fortunately, the most difficult moves are found in the first 20 feet. Moderate climbing and scrambling lead up along the crest to the summit blocks. The summit is reached easily by traversing right for a ropelength on slabs above a prominent snowfield and then scrambling back slightly left and up to the top.

The descent normally is made via the easy Owen–Spalding Route. From the summit descend over easy slabs, keeping slightly left until it is possible to rappel 120 feet to the Upper Saddle. If conditions permit, it is equally fast to downclimb the class 4 section of the Owen–Spalding. Continue to the Lower Saddle via an indistinct route that more or less follows the left side of the central couloir.

Equipment

Carry a selection of twelve small- to medium-sized chocks.

Remarks

Register for all park climbs at the Jenny Lake Ranger Station. Climbing rangers freely give advice, and photographs of many popular routes are available for perusal.

Moderate climbing leads up along the crest to the summit blocks.   Galen Rowell.

Grand Teton
North Face

28

North faces hold a special place in mountaineering, for it is on these sunless walls that a mountain's defenses often are greatest. The immense size and steepness of such walls, caused in part by the harsh environment resulting from the sun's diminished influence over the millennia, present challenges sought by all ambitious mountaineers. In his book *Climbing Ice*, the well-known American mountaineer Yvon Chouinard had this to say about one of the most impressive north faces in the United States:

In the 1950s the goal of every Alpine climber was to do one or more of the great north walls in the Alps—the Matterhorn, Eiger, or Grandes Jorasses. In the States there was but one north wall and that was on the Grand Teton. It had seen very few ascents, and most of these had involved a bivouac somewhere on the mountain. Those fortunate few who managed an ascent came back with stories of terrible rockfall, iced-over

A lieback followed by a fingertip traverse brings the leader to the top of the initial pitch between First and Second ledges.   Steve Roper.

rocks, routefinding problems, and all the usual troubles one finds on a typical big north wall. It was the premier American alpine climb and, of course, was a dream of mine ever since I began climbing. . . .

The north face of the Grand Teton rises nearly 3000 feet above the Teton Glacier and presents a magnificent façade when viewed from the summit of nearby Teewinot Mountain. Several prominent, diagonal ledges on the north face are separated by blank sections that appear overhanging. High on the wall

the ledges disappear altogether, and to early explorers there seemed little possibility of climbing the somber, darkly streaked cliffs that lay just beneath the summit. However, curiosity about a route cannot be satisfied by observation and speculation alone, and so the leading Teton climbers of the 1930s slowly were drawn to the great face.

In the summer of 1933, the guide Paul Petzoldt and fellow climber Sterling Hendricks made the first exploration of the wall. The two

climbers approached the face well above mid-height by traversing across the western face of the Grand Teton on a ledge system that joined the prominent shelf now known as Second Ledge. After reaching the shelf, they descended a large ramp dusted with snow from a recent storm and were tremendously impressed by the 2000-foot drop to the Teton Glacier below. They saw many small ledges and cracks on the wall above but could find no practicable route through the steep cliffs. Realizing that neither of them possessed the technical competence to carry out such daring climbing, they retreated.

Petzoldt waited three years before returning to the wall, this time with his brother Eldon and Jack Durrance. Petzoldt had intended to make the second ascent of Underhill's challenging route on the north ridge of the Grand, but quickly changed his objective after discovering that others had arrived in the Tetons who might be competing with him in the exciting search for a north-face route.

On August 25, 1936, just one week before Durrance was to make his brilliant climb of the Direct Exum Ridge, the three men crossed the bergschrund of Teton Glacier and started up the wall. Climbing rapidly to avoid falling stones, they ascended natural weaknesses in the rock toward the first diagonal ledge

◀ *The north face of the Grand Teton.* Gene White.

on the wall. As the climbing became more difficult, Durrance, an excellent routefinder who was climbing superbly that day, took most of the leads. Ascended for the first time was Guano Chimney, a slanting cleft filled with bird feathers, nests, and fetid slime that even today reminds climbers of long-departed pterodactilian residents. The three men advanced safely to the upper end of Second Ledge, where Petzoldt pointed out to Durrance the steep, 100-foot face which had defeated him three years earlier. Using his last reserves of strength, Durrance struggled up the pitch and arrived at a short ramp now known as Third Ledge.

The climbers' enthusiasm waned rapidly as they stared at the wall above; the difficulties were such that even Durrance was unwilling to challenge them. Dark and repellent in the afternoon gloom, the overhanging rock seemed to forbid any possible line of ascent. An orderly retreat soon was begun, but rather than retrace their route—which would be difficult because of the long, slanting traverses—the climbers rappelled to Second Ledge, traversed over to the north ridge, and followed the easy upper section of that route to the summit.

The team had made a valiant attempt, but the upper north face remained unclimbed. The final 300 feet of the wall required routefinding and climbing abilities of a degree not reached by climbers of that time. Durrance, more of a rockclimber than a mountaineer,

did not consider returning to the face, much preferring direct ridges to tedious traverses along discontinuous ledges.

A decade passed before the wall was attempted again. In 1946 Ray Garner and two others attempted to establish a line up the left portion of the wall, hoping thereby to avoid the traverses along First and Second ledges. But this party was deterred by huge overhangs near the east ridge. It became clear after this attempt that the route to the summit would have to pass along the diagonal ledge systems, including the as yet unknown Fourth Ledge. (What unfortunate nomenclature for these ledges! The naming of mountains and their prominent features offers climbers the opportunity for poetic expression; sadly, these unimaginative names are imprinted forever in Teton climbing history.)

Garner maintained his interest in the north face and in 1949 convinced two friends, Dick Pownall and Art Gilkey, to join forces with him in a new attempt on the route that had defeated Durrance and the Petzoldts. Pownall and Gilkey were among the top climbers in the small mountaineering community residing at Jenny Lake and were working as climbing guides for the Petzoldt–Exum school of mountaineering.

Not until August 13 did favorable weather and a break from guiding assignments coincide. The three climbers ascended Teton Glacier at dawn and embarked on an epic nineteen-hour struggle with the face. They found Guano Chimney not as slimy as reported but encountered sporadic rockfall higher. The routefinding was complex and slow, but Third Ledge finally was reached at four in the afternoon, a rather late hour to begin work on an unknown section. The wall above was not at all appealing, but Pownall was excited to be on unexplored terrain. After examining the cliff face, he took the lead, choosing a shallow chimney leading up from Third Ledge. He climbed fifty feet of strenuous rock and then set up a belay on a narrow shelf just below a bulging wall. Ten feet to his left he saw that his belay ledge disappeared at an abrupt corner. After belaying Gilkey, Pownall began the next pitch and soon found himself unable to pass the corner, which was smooth and tremendously exposed.

Once again a retreat from the north wall seemed inevitable until Pownall, an innovative technician, called for another rope. Clipping his new rope into an aid piton he had placed at the corner, he asked Gilkey to lower him several feet. Then, using a double-rope technique, he swung around the corner and, after placing another aid piton, made a short tension traverse to reach a small chimney. The climbing was easier here; Pownall ascended quickly to a small alcove at the lower edge of Fourth Ledge and belayed his friends across the smooth wall. Considering the altitude— over 13,000 feet—and the fact that

Dick Emerson approaches the principal difficulties on the first free ascent of the famous Pendulum Pitch.   Leigh Ortenburger.

he had been climbing steadily for more than twelve hours, Pownall's skill and determination were remarkable. Even today, many climbers arriving at the Pendulum Pitch in late afternoon are noticeably subdued, with chilled fingers and sagging morale.

The climb was not yet over, however. Garner watched apprehensively as Pownall "went up a shallow chimney a distance of 80′ until he was . . . stopped by a huge chockstone. The exposure was terrific, and the upper section of the chimney was coated with ice. He placed two pitons . . . and then belayed me up to his position. . . . there was no possible chance of continuing upwards."

Twilight was nearly gone. With Gilkey waiting patiently on the ledge below and Garner belaying precariously from a tiny perch, Pownall sought a way out of their desperate situation by a complicated traverse to the right. Garner could hear, but not see, Pownall's struggle up the final moves of the pitch. Shortly,

Pownall's yodel pierced the stillness and Garner knew the climb was over—at least for Pownall. To Garner, at the edge of exhaustion, it seemed as though the ordeal was just beginning. Since he was far to Pownall's left and thus less protected, he had to traverse carefully past a delicately poised, 300-pound slab before he could take tension and pendulum over to Pownall's chimney. Meanwhile, in total darkness, Gilkey waited interminably on Fourth Ledge. With limbs stiffened by the cold, he finally heard the call to climb. After negotiating the shallow chimney, Gilkey traversed cautiously past the loose slab that he had been warned about and then took the final swing into the chimney. He struggled up to Pownall's belay, and the three reunited mountaineers climbed for several leads over low-angled snow and rock, finally reaching the summit at ten o'clock. After bivouacking on the Lower Saddle, Garner and his friends returned triumphantly to Jenny Lake. Pownall took particular delight in describing to his fellow guides how he had managed his now-famous Pendulum Pitch.

The second ascent of the north face was made in 1953 in the fast time of eight hours. Dick Emerson, who figures prominently in the discussion of the Direct South Buttress

Route on Mount Moran, climbed the wall with Teton guides Leigh Ortenburger and Willi Unsoeld. As expected, the Pendulum Pitch proved to be the most exciting part of the climb. According to Unsoeld, Emerson led the pitch free in a marvelous serpentine style, slithering around the corner with the aid of small irregularities that almost could be called holds.

The north face of the Grand Teton is no longer as esteemed as it once was, now that American mountaineers have turned their attention to the ice-clad north faces of Canada and Alaska. However, present-day climbers should not forget that this difficult Teton route can require the utmost in climbing ability and resourcefulness. One hopes that a sense of history will permit those who attempt the climb to recall with admiration the anxious moments of the mountaineers who pioneered this great alpine route.

First ascent

Dick Pownall, Ray Garner, and Art Gilkey. August 13, 1949.

Elevation

The summit is 13,766 feet above sea level. From Teton Glacier, the climbing route is approximately 3000 feet.

Difficulty

IV, 5.8.

Time

Six to ten hours from Teton Glacier and an hour or two longer from Amphitheater Lake.

Map

USGS quadrangle: Grand Teton, scale 1:24,000.

Useful reference

A Climber's Guide to the Teton Range (Condensed Version).

Route description

Plan a dawn ascent of the Teton Glacier to the base of the north face. Cross the bergschrund, climb 60 feet, and then traverse left about one ropelength to the base of a prominent, left-slanting open-chimney system. Ascend for several ropelengths over moderate rock until it is possible to traverse to the right across easy slabs to the base of a deep slot known as Guano Chimney. Ascend this chimney to reach First Ledge.

Scramble upward until just short of the end of First Ledge and climb a shallow open book 60 feet to a good stance on the right. Another lead of moderate difficulty ends at Second Ledge. Climb up and slightly right through a blocky area with a tunnel, ending at Third Ledge. Traverse right until about two ropelengths from the north ridge and ascend a steep, shallow chimney 50 feet to a small ledge with fixed belay anchors.

The next lead (5.8) left along the narrowing ledge to an exposed corner is the Pendulum Pitch, the crux of the route. The pitch is only 40 feet long and ends in an alcove at the lower edge of Fourth Ledge. Ascend this ledge nearly to its end and climb a complicated open-chimney system to a notch. Halfway up this 130-foot lead is a tricky traverse right, past a huge, loose slab, into an adjacent chimney. A 1953 variation avoids this last pitch: about 30 feet left of the open chimney, climb upward to a fixed piton and traverse left over delicate friction (5.7) into the prominent "V" gully at the top of the face. Easy scrambling leads to the summit.

The descent usually is made via the easy Owen–Spalding Route. From the summit, descend west over easy slabs, keeping slightly left until a point is reached where it is possible to rappel 120 feet to the Upper Saddle. If conditions permit, it is equally fast to downclimb the class 4 section of the Owen–Spalding Route. Continue to the Lower Saddle via an indistinct route that more or less follows the left side of the central couloir.

Equipment

A selection of ten to twelve chocks is adequate; fixed pitons are found on many pitches. An ice hammer and crampons also should be taken, and a hard hat definitely is recommended.

Remarks

Those who intend to climb in Grand Teton National Park must register at the Jenny Lake Ranger Station. Climbing rangers freely give advice, and photographs of many popular routes are available for perusal.

Mount Moran Direct South Buttress

Every mountain has impressive and distinctive features, and Mount Moran is no exception. The most prominent feature on the eastern side of the mountain is an immense, vertically oriented black dike, a basaltic intrusion that splits the upper face of the peak. Characteristic of the massiveness of Moran is the south ridge, which descends from the summit in three giant steps for 5000 feet into Leigh Canyon. In spite of its isolated position well north of the Grand Teton, the peak has a long climbing history, including the ascent of the Black Dike Route in 1931. The standard route to the summit—the Colorado Mountaineering Club Route—was established ten years later.

The lower 1500 feet of the south ridge became known as the south buttress, a formation so precipitous that early discussions of its climbing difficulties were gloomy indeed. Many thought that an excessive amount of direct aid would be needed to surmount the buttress; others considered it presumptuous

After completing the double pendulums, Allen Steck begins to ascend the twenty-foot aid crack. Dick Long.

even to make the attempt. Present-day climbers may be grateful, however, that a few members of the Teton climbing community had the desire and ability to explore this challenging route.

During the decade following World War II, new routes in the Tetons were being sought primarily by local climbing guides and a few park-service rangers. These young mountaineers, testing themselves on ever more complicated and difficult rock problems, were laying the foundation for the 1953 climbing season, which was to produce one of the longest and most difficult climbs of the period—the Direct South Buttress of Mount Moran.

Leigh Ortenburger and Bill Buckingham had made an exploratory foray into Leigh Canyon in June of 1953. They returned without having made a serious attempt on Moran, though Ortenburger was able to collect useful information for his forthcoming *Climber's Guide to the Teton Range.* The first actual climbing on the south buttress was organized by Richard Emerson, a climbing ranger at Jenny Lake. Emerson already had scanned the buttress for route possibilities on two earlier trips up Leigh Canyon, and he felt an attempt should be made. As preparation, Emerson had joined Ortenburger and Willi Unsoeld—both Teton guides—earlier in the summer for the second ascent of the

north face of the Grand Teton. At the infamous Pendulum Pitch, Emerson had surprised even himself by accomplishing the first free ascent of the lead.

In mid-August Emerson and his friend Don Decker made a historic attempt on the south buttress. Within a ropelength of the end of the difficult climbing, an eighty-degree blank wall and an approaching storm forced them to retreat. Emerson did not wait long for his second try. On August 30 he and Decker, accompanied by Ortenburger, hiked to the base of the buttress. By the time they roped up, the sun had risen and the cliffs were bathed in golden light. They moved rapidly over the solid, well-fractured rock, marveling at the excellence of the climbing. The wall held a series of textbook moves, and it seemed the trio could climb almost any line by following short jamcracks, chimneys, and an occasional lieback. At every apparent impasse, the climbers somehow managed an improbable hand-traverse left or right to easier rock. Finally Emerson reached his previous high point and once again gazed across the smooth, flawless wall. It obviously was impossible to climb upward, nor could he see a way to reach the large ledge sixty feet to his right.

With the end of the climb so near, Emerson's desire to proceed was overwhelming, but this emotion struggled against his sense of caution and prudence. The exposure was incredible, and he was entirely out of view of his belayer; this was

no place for a miscalculation. The leader pondered his solitary position and then slowly retreated to a belay stance. Perhaps a pendulum could be executed across the blank face. He then belayed Ortenburger, who unsuccessfully attempted to pendulum across the slab forty feet below. Emerson later described the next few minutes:

It appeared as though our "serious attempt" was going to end only 20 feet higher than our reconnaissance had gone! On the way down I scanned the flake for anything that might take a piton and lead to a better place to pendulum. I was successful in getting three wafer pitons in which would hold my weight plus. From the highest of these I was able to reach out about four feet to the right and I could feel a crack which might take another. The crack closed within a half inch, but—by placing an army wafer with its head down, against the flake, I could pound along the edge of the blade. While the entire length of the piton was partially exposed, it was nonetheless quite firm, if the pull on it was down, not out.

Ortenburger lowered Emerson from his amazing wafer piton until he was able to swing across the smooth wall to a small crack, where he placed another piton to anchor a second pendulum. After swinging another ten feet, he climbed a short aid

◀ *The south ridge of Mount Moran.*
Leigh Ortenburger.

crack and sank exhausted onto the belay ledge. Thus ended Emerson's remarkable Double-Pendulum Pitch, a series of maneuvers that involved nearly eight hours of intense effort before his companions were sitting on the ledge beside him. The complexity of this lead remains undiminished to this day.

After the final seventy-five-foot pitch, which included a terribly exposed hand-traverse, Emerson's team found a suitable ledge for their bivouac and the following morning proceeded to the summit. Today few climbers complete the entire route to the summit over the upper 2400 feet of class 4 and 5 ridge climbing, preferring instead to descend to Leigh Canyon after finishing the ten pitches of the south buttress.

This was the first major climb in the Teton Range to combine hard free climbing and fairly extensive use of direct aid. For a number of years it remained the most difficult technical climb in the park, and if one followed the entire ridge to the summit, it ranked as one of the most difficult climbs in the country.

Belayer Steve Roper lowers Dick Long on tension as Long completes the second pendulum of the Double-Pendulum Pitch.   Allen Steck.

First ascent

Richard Emerson, Don Decker, and Leigh Ortenburger. August 30–31, 1953.

Elevation

The summit is 12,594 feet above sea level. The climbing route to the top of the buttress is about 1500 feet.

Difficulty

IV, 5.7, A3.

Time

Ten to twelve hours from a camp near the base of the buttress, which can be approached in half a day from the String Lake parking area.

Maps

USGS quadrangles: Mount Moran and Jenny Lake, scale 1:62,500.

Useful reference

A Climber's Guide to the Teton Range (Condensed Version).

Route description

It is best to camp on the shore of a small lake in Leigh Canyon about one-and-a-half miles upstream from Leigh Lake.

Beyond the Double-Pendulum Pitch, an exposed hand-traverse leads Dick Long to easier climbing.   Allen Steck.

Two prominent, grassy ledges diagonal up and left at the base of the south buttress. Ascend the lower ledge to its end; then traverse 50 feet around the corner and ascend a class 4 chimney system for 200 feet to a good belay stance at the western edge of the upper grassy ledge. Climb up and right 150 feet on moderate rock. Here, traverse left a full ropelength along a narrowing ledge containing awkward moves. Do not go farther left, but ascend directly upward over steepening rock for a full pitch. Climb up and right 60 feet to the base of a severe-looking wall. It is possible to climb the wall directly (5.8) for about 20 feet to a sloping ledge, where a strenuous hand-traverse leads left. An easier alternative lies farther left and ends at the same belay stance.

A large, partially detached flake can be seen 130 feet above. Climb to the flake and enter the crack at its right edge; belay at the top of a chimney. The next pitch continues upward for half a ropelength to a belay spot. A 150-foot pitch then leads to a narrow ledge (5.7) below the bolts protecting the start of the Double-Pendulum Pitch. Directly above are forbidding overhangs. Although the ledge is small and uncomfortable, it is advisable to belay the pendulums from here. Good rope management is important, as there is a short aid section immediately following the second pendulum. From the bolts, descend 20 feet and pendulum to the second anchor (a fixed wafer piton); then either pendulum or tension-traverse right another 15 feet to a narrow ledge at the base of a 20-foot aid crack. Ascend this crack to an ample belay ledge. From here an exposed, 30-foot hand-traverse and 40 feet of easier climbing complete the route.

The remaining 2400 feet to the summit is moderate class 4 and 5 climbing and can be accomplished in five or six hours. The descent from the summit is best made via the Colorado Mountaineering Club Route. For those wishing to return to Leigh Canyon, ascend the left edge of a large bowl until reaching the crest of the south ridge and proceed past several pinnacles (class 3 and 4) to the extreme north end of the level section of the crest. At this point a gully composed of two branches separated by a narrow rib descends to the west. Follow the left-hand gully a short distance; then cross at the first opportunity to the right-hand gully, which leads down into the basin southeast of Thor Peak and eventually into Leigh Canyon.

Equipment

Carry a selection of ten to twelve chocks, from small stoppers to medium hexes.

Remarks

Register for all park climbs at the Jenny Lake Ranger Station, where climbing rangers offer advice and weather reports. Photographs of many popular routes also are available for perusal.

Pingora
Northeast Face

30

Dick Long rests in stemming position before attempting a difficult lieback low on the route.   Allen Steck.

One usually approaches the southern peaks in Wyoming's Wind River Range by following the trail past Big Sandy Lake and hiking north over Jackass Pass to a campsite near Lonesome Lake. Just before the pass, Warbonnet, a peak guarding the southern entrance to the Cirque of the Towers, thrusts a jagged profile to the sky. Dominating the scene as one descends into the heart of the Cirque is the monolithic rock cone of Pingora, whose northeast face sweeps majestically in a clean line from an alpine meadowland to the isolated summit. *Pingora* is the Shoshone word for a high, rocky, in-accessible peak, and eventually the word was attached to this magnificent mountain that rises 1700 feet above Lonesome Lake. The upper cliffs soar abruptly above the lower-angled, massive base of the peak, and the legacy of powerful glacial forces is plainly visible. Pingora, whose lower slabs are as ice-scoured as Yosemite's Glacier Point Apron, epitomizes the grandeur of the granite formations found in the Cirque.

The mystery and fascination of this ring of peaks lie not only in the profusion of unclimbed walls and buttresses, but also in the pristine wilderness of the region, whose remoteness delayed climbing activity until well past the turn of the century. Early mountaineers in the Cirque made the first ascent of the "unclimbable" Lizard Head, the highest peak of the region, in 1933. Orrin Bonney, a Houston attorney and author of the first published guide to the Wind River Range, made several excursions into the Cirque, and in 1940 he and two companions were the first to ascend Pingora, using steep, class 5 slabs on the southeast face. A year later Bonney and another party made the first climb of Warbonnet, the beautifully formed peak he had named because of its remarkable "feathered" appearance.

Modest climbing activity continued throughout the 1940s and 1950s, but the longer and more demanding routes remained untried even as late as 1962. It was in that year that seekers of first ascents—eager climbers from the Tetons, Yosemite, and elsewhere—were beginning to make secretive pilgrimages into the Cirque.

171

In mid-August 1962, two Californians, Harry Daley and Jim Yensan, left their camp at Lonesome Lake and scrambled up grassy ledges leading to the base of Pingora's unclimbed northeast face. The weather had been beautiful for several days, and the peak was in excellent condition for climbing. The pair paused for one last glance at the wall before arranging the belay for the initial lead across some tricky slabs. Daley recalled the first time he had seen Pingora and how he had thought about climbing its marvelous northeast face. He had studied a photograph of the wall so intently that the route already had taken shadowy form in his mind. All would go smoothly, he thought, except for the steep upper section, which looked discontinuous. Without an obvious line, it presented just the sort of problem that makes climbing so fascinating.

Daley took the first lead and moved out across the delicate slabs, taking tension to pass a difficult move. After climbing upward a hundred feet, he reached the base of a long, mossy crack that oozed water deposited by previous thunderstorms. He set his anchors and belayed Yensan, watching with more than casual interest to see how his companion handled the difficulties. Yensan climbed up quickly and then began leading the mossy crack. Experimenting with various contortions in the shallow groove and taking occasional tension, he moved slowly up the pitch to a small belay stance beneath an improbable overhang. Daley overcame this obstacle and the slanting open book above, and the two climbers began to rejoice at their rapid progress. The climb was going well in spite of the rounded edges of the coarse-grained granite that often forced them into awkward and strenuous liebacks.

This was Daley's first climb in the Cirque, and had he known that it was only the third climb of Yensan's career—they had met only the previous month—he might have felt less hopeful of negotiating the unknown difficulties above.

Daley made a brilliant lead over a small ceiling that had been visible since the start of the climb. But then, above this, he faced a difficult-looking lieback which he was able to climb only by using tension. As Yensan reached the ledge on which Daley was belaying, he looked up apprehensively at his next pitch, a thin crack flanked by walls of flawless granite and clogged with hummocks of grass. Yensan devised a technique for this problem that was desperately simple: stepping gingerly onto the first hummock, he plunged all ten fingers into a quivering one higher up and executed a mantelshelf. Repeating the maneuver many times, he eventually reached the top of the vertical garden.

After a short, easy pitch, the two climbers arrived at the base of a high-angled face with two difficult-looking cracks. Yensan sensed that his strength would be severely tested: "I started up the jam crack on the left," he recalled later, "found it tremendously hard and suddenly came flying out. It was Harry's day for belay practice! An attempt at laybacking the smaller crack with buttery fingers had the same dangling outcome and so I came down. . . ." Yensan's arms were cramped, and he could no longer lead. For a moment it seemed as though the pair would have to abandon the climb, but Daley managed to convince his partner that the easiest way off the wall was to continue over the summit.

Daley took over the lead, and the two men ascended several steep cracks and corners, occasionally using direct aid at difficult places. They finally reached the problematical upper section of the route they had noted earlier. The wall steepened dramatically as they climbed to a ledge beneath an ominous ceiling that seemed to bar further progress. The two climbers realized they were facing the most serious obstacle of the climb. Daley was apprehensive as he studied the problem and tried to anticipate possible resting positions. Then, calling for extra caution by his belayer, he climbed on tension to the ceiling, which forced him into an undercling position—a horizontal lieback. After making several quick moves to a corner, he pulled up into a steep, shallow crack only to discover that

◀ *Pingora as seen from the northeast.*
Steve Roper.

173

the difficulties were far from over. Tiring rapidly, Daley desperately placed an aid piton and at last managed to complete the pitch. A lusty yodel reached the tired Yensan, who was relieved that the end of the climb was near. The two men were only minutes from the summit, and they reached it at dark in a mood of quiet elation, having completed a superb line on one of the most beautiful peaks of the Wind River Range.

Daley and Yensan returned to the roadhead the following day to find their car's battery dead. As they were pushing the car, a tallish man in a suit walked up to them and inquired, "You lads been in the back-country—been fishing, or what?" Not recognizing Fred Beckey, the legendary devourer of first ascents, Yensan replied, "Well, we've been doing some climbing in the Cirque," and proceeded to describe their climb on Pingora. "Oh, no!" groaned Beckey, disconsolately. At this moment Beckey's climbing partner, John Rupley, appeared. "They've done it," said Beckey quietly. "Looks like we missed this one by just a few days."

The northeast face of Pingora was the first Grade IV climbed in the Cirque of the Towers. Rumors of the spectacular climbing and the directness of the line spread throughout the climbing community, and soon the route became the most sought-after climb in the Wind River Range. A well-known mountaineer who climbed the route a few years after the first free ascent had

Nearing the top of the grass-hummock pitch.   Dick Long.

174

been made (around 1964) had this to say about his ascent: "Rarely have I enjoyed a climb as much as this one. The rock is sound, the holds are excellent, and the climbing problems varied and interesting. Liebacks, chimneys, and cracks are plentiful. . . . The grass-hummock pitch and the crux with the under-cling are classic leads. It's good to be on a climb without an escape route: once you start the face, you must go over the top."

Orrin Bonney and the region's other early pioneers have retired from climbing, but they probably would be amazed at the current activity in their beloved Cirque, which pres-ently contains seventy or eighty routes. The pristine wilderness of earlier days is being slowly eroded; such is the state of climbing throughout the country. Bonney would be surprised to learn that his route on Pingora, established nearly forty years ago, is regarded by present-day climbers of the north-east face as simply a descent route off the peak.

First ascent

Harry Daley and Jim Yensan. Au-gust 13, 1962.

Elevation

The summit is 11,884 feet above sea level. The climbing route is approx-imately 1300 feet long.

Difficulty

IV, 5.8.

Time

Eight to ten hours from Lonesome Lake.

Map

USGS quadrangle: Mocassin Lake, scale 1:62,500.

Useful references

A Guide to Climbing and Hiking in the Wind River Mountains; also see the *Field Book: Wind River Range*.

Route description

From U.S. Highway 187 at Boulder, twelve miles south of Pinedale, drive east and then southeast on a paved road for eighteen miles. Con-tinue on a gravel road about one mile to a junction; then turn east and drive sixteen miles to another junction. Turn north and continue

for ten miles, past Dutch Joe Guard Station, to a bridge that crosses Big Sandy Creek. When the road forks soon thereafter, follow the right fork one mile to Big Sandy Campground. Many of the road junctions in this forty-six-mile drive have signs indi-cating Big Sandy Opening.

From the campground, follow a good trail six miles to Big Sandy Lake; then turn north onto a less-traveled trail and hike another two miles to Jackass Pass, which forms the south portal to the Cirque of the Towers. An easy descent can be made to Lonesome Lake. The climbing route on Pingora can be seen most clearly from the hillside north of the lake. A prominent feature of the lower sec-tion is a 200-foot, right-facing chimney-and-crack system that be-gins as a curving ledge and ends in a small ceiling. The route then tends to the left, and the upper part fol-lows a line close to the right side of the east face.

Scramble up grassy ledges to the rope-up spot and make a delicate friction traverse left to the start of the curving ledge. Two pitches of steady 5.7 jamcrack and chimney climbing lead to the small ceiling, after which a short traverse left ends at a belay ledge. Difficult stemming followed by a strenuous 5.8 lieback ends at a belay spot below the grass-hummock pitch. Above the hummocks, moderate face climbing mixed with difficult chimneys and corners leads to a flared chimney. Ascend the chimney, or a lieback on the right, and then climb a strenuous lieback above to a belay at a fixed piton. The crux pitch is next and is both strenuous and memorable: climb a 30-foot jamcrack to an overhanging flake; then undercling to the right and handjam a crack that leads to a good belay at the base of a chimney. Climb the short, difficult chimney; then continue over moderate rock to the false summit. After a short rappel (or tricky downclimbing), scramble over to the main summit.

To descend, either downclimb Bonney's Route (5.3) or follow class 3 rock on the south side of the peak to a point where two 150-foot rappels end at easy scrambling on the south shoulder.

The wall steepens dramatically as a climber moves toward the ominous ceiling near the top of the route.   Allen Steck.

Equipment

Carry a selection of twelve to fourteen chocks, as well as half a dozen pitons up to medium angles. Two 150-foot ropes are needed for the rappels.

Wolf's Head East Ridge

31

The monstrous slabs soaring upward from the lower flanks of Wolf's Head seem to compete for dominance on the ridge leading eastward toward Pingora. The summit itself is on the Continental Divide, as are many peaks of the Cirque of the Towers. What distinguishes Wolf's Head is that it is of a ridge than a peak: an east–west spine of rock, appallingly narrow, interrupted by awkward ledges and frustrating, tricky towers that would be simple bouldering problems were it not for the abyss below.

Although not climbed until 1959, the east ridge of Wolf's Head is a moderate route, one that might attract the scorn of present-day hard climbers still in their *Sturm und Drang* years. Nevertheless, it is a climb well suited for weekenders and a fitting objective for new climbers anxious to test themselves on moderate problems. For those who love clean, solid, intriguing granite,

Leading the first pitch of the East Ridge Route, which ascends a narrow, thirty-degree arête.   Alan Kearney.

the kind that invites one to gymnastic revelry under a warm sun, Wolf's Head is an absolute delight. Of all those who come to the ridge, including the hard men, few leave unsatisfied.

In the midsummer of 1977 two climbers who had arrived at Lonesome Lake the previous evening began angling their way up the approach gully to Wolf's Head, located just to the west of Pingora. The sun, still low in the east, cast a sharp light into the Cirque, piercing the coolness of the chimneys and gullies on the eastern walls of the Warbonnet–Warrior crest just across the valley.

"It's going to be a good day, finer than most," the climber known as Doc is thinking as he ambles along, watching the stones ahead of him. He will realize the irony of his prediction later in the afternoon, but at this moment he is enthusiastic about the sun and about the climbing soon to come. Doc's a weekender but keeps very fit. Though in his forties, his lean and wiry frame is that of a much younger man. One should note, too, that Doc is an expert climber, one who can drive to Yosemite for a few days and manage an ascent of the west face of Sentinel or of the Salathé Wall on El Capitan. In fact, he would be among

◄ *Wolf's Head viewed from the south; the East Ridge Route follows the right skyline to the sharp summit tower.* Steve Roper.

the country's top climbers had he devoted his energies totally to the sport of mountaineering. Today, on Wolf's Head, Doc moves up the gully slowly, with casual intent.

The Silver Fox follows close behind. His hair is a lustrous gray, perhaps from too many mountain frights over the years. The Fox also is a weekender, ten years older than Doc and a frequent companion on the latter's rope. The Fox pauses a moment, looks ahead at his friend, and remarks, "So you're wearing your creepers today."

Doc's garish blue-and-yellow running shoes with wide tractor heels rise and fall with squeaky regularity. "Fantastic friction," replies Doc, with a knowing, boyish smile. "Wait, you'll see how they work on this first bit of rock here. Got my EB's in the pack—you know what Messner says about carrying your courage in your rucksack!"

They are traversing now from the gully to a small tower where it is possible to descend to the col at the start of the ridge. In front of them are the first pitches of the climb; it is clear they must ascend a narrow, angular, terribly exposed ridge crest. As it is not too steep, they decide to proceed without the rope. Down to the right are the frightfully sheer northeastern cliffs.

Doc walks upright, slowly and precisely, with hands hanging expectantly at his sides, gunslinger fashion. "Christ!" exclaims the Fox, reaching the narrowest section of the

ridge. He drops onto all fours, like a beast in the field. Using hands and feet, he continues to follow the squeaky shoes, whose soles with their little round disks remind him of octopi. The upper part of the arête then turns into knobby face climbing, the kind that the Fox likes; the climbers proceed over easy rock to the first tower, which they turn on the left.

Streaking clouds move quickly across the crest, casting somber shadows on the rock below. Ahead, a dark chimney leads north across the face of the next tower, the second on the ridge. Beyond the chimney, which the men recognize from the route description, lies the crux of the climb. They pause.

The relaxed expression on the Fox's bearded face belies the hard battles he has fought—and occasionally nearly lost—on mountains and cliffs in distant ranges. He is content this day to play the game with moderation. "You know, Doc," he muses aloud, "I like what Noyce says about contrast and the cult of danger. The implication—no, the hard fact—is that climbers find contrast pleasurable. So do a lot of people, of course. We enjoy calm, but desire and pursue tumult; in the face of starvation, the image of robust feasting obviously is exciting. I don't believe Noyce went so far as to suggest we seek death in order to fully understand our lives, but there was that intimation. What a marvelous psychic geometry of extremes!"

179

"Seems to make sense," says Doc. "Might need some more thought, though. I'm not exactly devoted to suffering, you know." True enough. Doc likes neither hunger nor cold, two conditions that occur with remarkable frequency in mountaineering.

"Well, I know for sure," rejoins the Fox, taking the rope out of the pack, "that I'll find it immediately pleasurable to put on the rope here since it contrasts so nicely with climbing this far without one!" He notices with delight that Doc is lacing up his EBs, the octopi having disappeared. Courage now runs sparkling along the rope.

"Your lead," says Doc smiling, as he maneuvers into a belay at the far edge of the chimney.

The Fox moves out around the top of the chimney and sees a cat-thin ledge cutting across the otherwise smooth wall. Below is the abyss—a constant, compelling presence. As the Fox steps out onto the wall, the tips of his ancient Spiders move along the indistinct holds. He clips into the fixed pin he finds in the crack overhead and then pauses because the Spider toes have strangely missed the sequence of moves. He seems momentarily confused.

Peering out from his awkward belay perch, Doc laughs uproariously at the Fox's apparent dilemma. "Imagine," he chides, "the Fox hung up on a couple of 5.5 moves."

About one-third the distance up the route, the leader nears the top of a steep, knobby face.   Mike Kennedy.

The Fox smiles to himself as he figures the combination and finally passes the tricky section on this second tower. After climbing a short crack he reaches the crest. "On belay, simple orthopedic clown!" he shouts back to the chimney.

Doc emerges from the chimney and climbs quickly and effortlessly across the wall and up to his companion. They climb well together, these two.

At this point, ominous rumblings are heard from the west. The once-blue sky is becoming crowded with clouds: contrast seems to be impinging on the climbers' affairs. The two friends discern another tower through the lowering mists, two parallel cracks leading along its smooth right wall to a corner. It is Doc's lead. Near the corner, forty feet from where they are standing, the upper crack fades and is lost in the smooth granite. Doc gets involved in some complicated face climbing; standing on the lower crack, he makes an awkward move to reach better ledges around the corner, where he sets up a belay. After a few more pitches the two men are past the last obstacle. They unrope and climb unencumbered to the summit block, which they ascend via a short chimney.

As Doc and the Fox reach the summit, static electricity fills the air, and it starts to hail. "No rest for us pagans up here!" cries Doc, as he and the Fox lurch across the ledge and start downclimbing the western side of the peak with greater than prudent haste, in search of safer ground below. A short rappel down a gully that is filling with drifting snow brings them to the traverse which leads to Wolf Jaw Col. Lightning begins crashing into the summit of Wolf's Head, and the Cirque of the Towers erupts into an unearthly cacophony.

Crunching across the snow-covered sod on their way back to camp, Doc is deep in contemplation. "Fox," he says finally, "I've been thinking about your contrast. I'm really not too sure. . . ." He pauses. One can see that Doc is playing with this philosophical paradox. "Perhaps I could enjoy this storm," he continues, "if I could just find some pleasure in it."

The two men's voices fade as they walk into the chilling, wind-driven sleet.

Perched on a tiny crack, the leader is forced into awkward face climbing to reach better ledges around the corner. Alan Kearney.

181

First ascent

William Plummer and William Buckingham. August 28, 1959.

Elevation

The summit is 12,165 feet above sea level. As the climb is primarily a ridge traverse, the elevation gain from the col at the start of the route is only about 400 feet.

Difficulty

II, 5.5.

Time

Five to eight hours, round trip.

A minuscule ledge on the south side of the final tower provides airy climbing. Rich Mathies.

Map

USGS quadrangle: Mocassin Lake, scale 1:62,500.

Useful references

A Guide to Climbing and Hiking in the Wind River Mountains; also see the *Field Book: Wind River Range.*

Route description

See the Pingora account for information on the approach to the Cirque of the Towers. The ridge is reached most easily by climbing a south-facing gully that leads to the notch below the west face of Pingora. Just before reaching the notch, traverse left out of the gully to the summit of the bump known as Tiger Tower and descend short walls to the col between this tower and Wolf's Head.

The first three pitches follow a narrow, 30-degree arête that ends in a steeper, knobby face with cracks. A long level section then leads to the first tower, which is passed on its south side. Descend a short, slightly rotten chimney and enter a larger, deeper chimney on the east wall of the second tower. Proceed to a notch at the top of the chimney. Traverse along a thin ledge on the north side of the tower to a crack leading back to the crest. This traverse is the most difficult climbing on the route. The third tower also is traversed on the north by using a pair of cracks to climb around a tricky corner. The final tower is passed by descending a chimney to the south and then following cracks and an improbable ledge to a chimney which leads back to the crest. Finally, follow a broad ledge on the north side of the ridge and then scramble to the summit block, which is ascended by means of a short chimney.

The descent is made most easily by downclimbing or rappelling the western side of the summit for about 300 feet until it is possible to traverse left across easy slabs to Wolf Jaw Col, located between Overhanging Tower and Wolf's Head. From the col an easy descent can be made back into the Cirque.

Equipment

Carry a selection of eight to ten chocks.

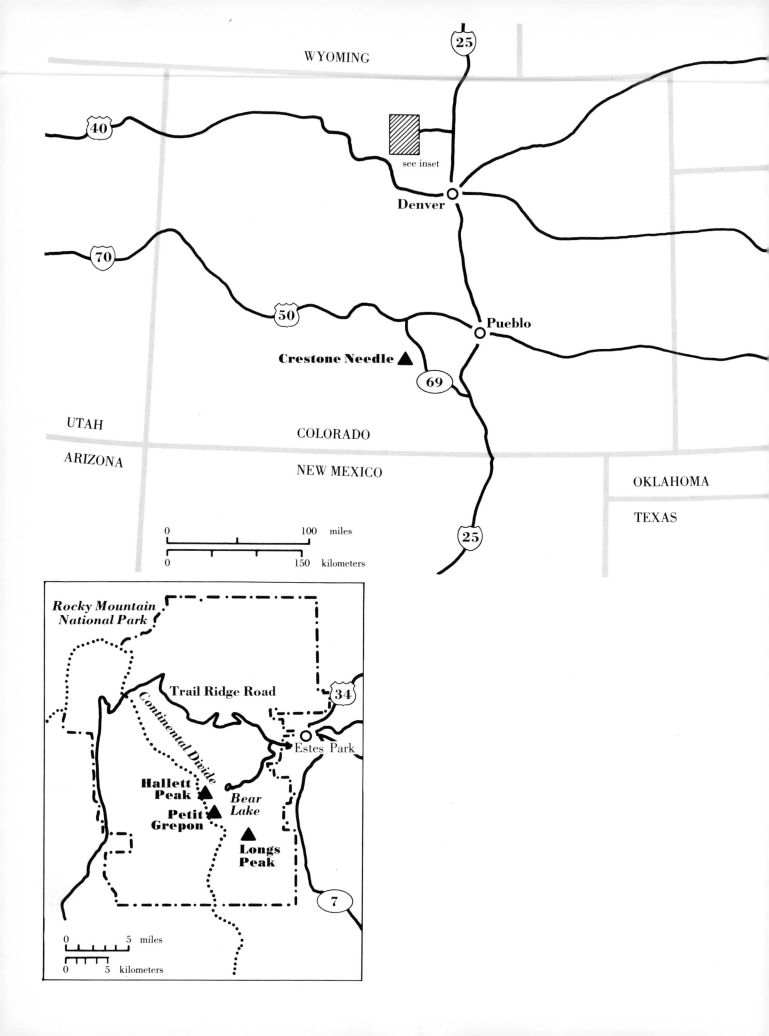

WYOMING

25

40

see inset

Denver

70

50

Pueblo

Crestone Needle ▲

69

UTAH

COLORADO

ARIZONA

NEW MEXICO

OKLAHOMA

TEXAS

25

0   100   miles

0   150   kilometers

Rocky Mountain National Park

Trail Ridge Road

34

Continental Divide

Estes Park

Hallett Peak ▲

Petit Grepon ▲

Bear Lake

Longs Peak ▲

7

0   5 miles

0   5 kilometers

Colorado

The first significant mountain climb in North America took place in 1820 when three men ascended Pikes Peak, a 14,110-foot mass near what is now Colorado Springs. Although this pioneering effort was technically easy, it was a startling achievement for explorers more at home on flatlands and foothills. It is fitting that the first North American climb occurred in Colorado, for a great many Coloradans today are mountaineering enthusiasts.

Colorado's popularity is relatively recent, however; there have been long periods of dormancy when little climbing activity took place. Nearly a century elapsed between the 1820 ascent of Pikes Peak and the day when Professor Albert Ellingwood made the first ascent of the Crestone Needle, the last of the state's 14,000-foot peaks to be mastered. This feat, accomplished in 1916, sparked interest in the technical aspects of mountaineering. Ellingwood later ascended the Crestone Needle buttress; this route was deemed the most difficult in America at the time and paved the way for further significant climbs by the professor and his protégés.

Other climbers also were interested in what the Colorado Rockies had to offer, and in 1927 two recent emigrants from Germany climbed a demanding route on the lower east face of Longs Peak, the most striking geographical formation in Rocky Mountain National Park. Although the route soon to be known as Stettners' Ledges was a superlative achievement for its time, present-day climbers regard it as an indirect and rather unpleasant route; therefore it has not been included in this book.

Interest in difficult rockclimbing waned after 1927, and for the next three decades members of the Colorado Mountain Club sought out unclimbed ridges and couloirs on the state's highest peaks. In the mid-1950s, at a time when Yosemite climbers had established numerous multi-day routes, Colorado's hardest climb was still Stettners' Ledges, a four-hour jaunt. But this condition proved temporary, for during the next decade the course of Colorado rockclimbing changed dramatically.

In the 1960s such talented climbers as Ray Northcutt, Layton Kor, and Bob Culp established dozens of excellent routes in the state, both in Eldorado Canyon (a fine *Klettergarten* near Boulder) and in Rocky Mountain National Park. Longs Peak was a natural candidate for Yosemite-style routes, and in short order the Diamond—the sheerest section of the east face—received numerous ascents. By 1965 the quality of Colorado rockclimbing had become exceptional, and before long a new generation of Colorado free climbers began to influence the sport in every corner of North America.

Crestone Needle
Ellingwood
Ledges

Colorado so abounds with mountains that even by World War I there were still unclimbed 14,000-foot peaks. The state has fifty-three of these giants, and most can be ascended by anyone with a sturdy pair of legs and a functional set of lungs. Only a few of these coveted peaks require use of the hands, and none really demand a rope. Still, many of them are fine-looking mountains, and a few even present spectacular aspects.

For example, hidden in the isolated Sangre de Cristo Range of south-central Colorado lies a cluster of jagged alpine peaks known as the Crestone group. On the afternoon of July 24, 1916, one of these peaks became the last-conquered 14,000-footer in the state. Ranked twenty-first in height, the Crestone Needle proved to be an enjoyable class 3 and 4 scramble for first ascenders Albert Ellingwood and Eleanor Davis. As they descended a couloir on the eastern side of the peak, their

eyes lingered on the northeast side of the Crestone massif. Ellingwood later was to write that this mile-wide wall contained "a superb array of formidable buttresses, seamed by tempting cracks and set off from each other by steep-plunging chimneys that probably have not been free from ice since the glacial era." By far the highest and most impressive of these buttresses was the 2000-foot prow which led directly to the summit of the just-climbed Crestone Needle. It was almost dark as the pair passed under the buttress, but Ellingwood searched for a possible route, hoping they would return. It was to be nine years, however, before the two climbers once again stood under the face.

Prior to World War I, Ellingwood had studied at Oxford as a Rhodes scholar, yet he somehow found the time to learn to climb in England's famous Lake District. After returning to Colorado to be a professor of political science, he found he was the only climber in the area who could handle a rope with any degree of skill. Indeed, his 1916 ascents in the Crestone group were, as climbing historian Chris Jones has put it, "probably the first rock climbs in the United States where a conscious effort was made to belay." In succeeding years Ellingwood established an enviable climbing record, making among other Colorado climbs the first ascent, in 1920, of

Lizard Head, still regarded as the state's most difficult summit to attain. Three years later, he and Eleanor Davis climbed in the Teton Range, making the first ascents of the South and Middle Tetons. The pair also made the fourth ascent of the Grand Teton, with Davis becoming the first woman to stand atop the highest point in that range. By 1925 Ellingwood was quite likely the finest mountaineer in the land, and Eleanor Davis was undoubtedly the most experienced American female climber. In August of that year the pair decided to attempt the buttress remembered from their 1916 trip and organized a foursome for the ascent.

Camping at the windswept lake below the Crestone Needle, the two climbers studied possible routes with their companions, Stephen Hart and Marion Warner. The lower part of the buttress was sliced by many ledges, some of which even contained grassfields. They weren't too concerned about this section, but as Ellingwood later wrote in his account of the climb, "there were pessimistic doubts expressed as to the last five hundred feet, where the precipice seemed to attain verticality, and near the top of which a huge boss of well-polished rock was certain to force us into an enormous overhang from which we could discern no avenue of escape."

As predicted, the forty-five-degree lower section proved easy, though a slip, according to the professor, would result in "deliberate suicide, and there are easier ways." A hail-storm arose just as the foursome reached the upper "delectable and dubious cliff." Though brief, the storm left quantities of hail on every ledge, and the climbing was slowed while the mountaineers scraped away the ice and thrust cold hands into warm pockets. A long chimney system, visible from the ground, led up just to the right of the buttress, and the party soon was spread out over hundreds of feet. This section, in the words of Ellingwood, was a "diddle-diddle-dumpling sort of climb—one foot in and one foot out, and hands usually clawing at such minute molecules of rock as have survived the process of erosion." The chimney was not difficult, but the tiny belay ledges, the hail-covered rock, and the altitude—13,700 feet—conspired to use up several hours. Eventually the climbers reached a wide ledge, directly on the prow. Above was "an obviously invulnerable" wall, so they set out on an upward traverse which led around a corner on the left. This easy pitch brought the foursome to the now-famous Head Crack, the crux of the climb. Ellingwood struggled up a short chimney, his head awkwardly ensconced in the crack. A delicate move to the right soon had the professor spread out "like a skin stretched to dry." From this compromising position he finally was able to grasp a small hold and pull himself onto easier ground.

Elated, the party regrouped at the top of the Head Crack pitch, but a bit higher another possible cul-de-sac—this one a chimney "almost wide enough to drive a wagon through"—confronted the tired mountaineers. The resourceful Ellingwood stemmed up as far as possible, then transferred to an easier crack on the right. The shorter members of the group found the stem a few inches too wide, and for a few feet they needed help from the rope. Conditioned by this point to expect another impasse, the four climbers were surprised to see the summit ridge only a hundred feet above them. It was late in the afternoon when they celebrated their success around the cairn Ellingwood and Davis had built nearly a decade before.

As on the earlier descent, the irrepressible Ellingwood kept gazing at the battlements for other routes, and he later indulged in word play: "One of the famous problems of the Middle Ages was to ascertain the exact number of angels who could sit upon the point of a needle. I would adapt it and propound a question both more interesting and more answerable: From how many angles can the Needle's point be reached?"

Ellingwood died at the early age of forty-six, but before his death he highly recommended the climb to his protégé, Robert Ormes. In July 1937, Ormes—later to write the definitive *Guide to the Colorado Mountains*—and a companion made the second ascent of the route, naming it the Ellingwood Ledges in

memory of the professor. (Later this was corrupted to the Ellingwood Arête, a misnomer since the ridge is not sharp.) Like the first-ascent party, the 1937 team took four hours to overcome the "delectable" upper section. To preface Ormes' article in *Trail and Timberline*, the journal of the Colorado Mountain Club, the editor wrote: "Ormes' own account of the second ascent . . . draws deserved attention to a long neglected field for those who appreciate the weird contortions of Acrobatic Alpinism."

Despite an ever-increasing number of climbers who stealthily practiced "weird contortions," the next ascents did not take place until the early 1950s. Later, however, the route became so popular that it was not uncommon for several parties to mingle on a pleasant summer day, enjoying not only the fine climbing but also the remarkable views of the massif.

One of the highlights of the route is the quality of the rock. The sedimentary conglomerate, formed during the early Paleozoic Era, bristles with so many knobs that it is confusing to know which one to grab. Some of the pinkish-colored knobs appear on the verge of being expelled from the matrix, but Ellingwood discovered they were so firm that they must have "roots ten feet long." Climbing on this unique rock is a pleasure that few climbers ever forget, and many return for additional doses of knob climbing in an alpine setting.

First ascent

Albert Ellingwood, Eleanor Davis, Stephen Hart, and Marion Warner. The ascent was made in August 1925, though several accounts claim it was made the previous year.

Elevation

The summit is 14,197 feet above sea level. The face is approximately 2000 feet high.

Difficulty

III, 5.7.

Time

Most parties take about six hours from the lake to the summit. Allow two hours for the descent.

Maps

USGS quadrangles: Beck Mountain (for the road approach) and Crestone Peak. The scale for both is 1:24,000.

Useful reference

Guide to the Colorado Mountains.

Route description

From the town of Westcliffe, some fifty miles west of Pueblo, drive south on Colorado Highway 69 for four-and-a-half miles to Colfax Lane. Turn right and drive five-and-a-half miles until the road ends at a crossroad. Turn west toward the mountains and follow a dirt road straight toward the first trees. Park shortly after this point. (Jeeps and tough passenger cars can be driven farther.)

Hike up the road toward the South Colony Lakes, which are about five miles away. Camp at either the lower or the upper lake; the latter is at 12,000 feet and closer to the face.

From the upper lake ascend a short talus slope to the face. The first steep section can be climbed near its left edge. Next, zigzag up ledges and short cracks, aiming eventually for the buttress on the right. This thousand-foot-plus section is mostly class 3. When the steep upper section is reached, ascend a chimney system which rises just right of the prow. There actually are several chimneys; take either the central or right-hand one. After 200 feet, climb an easy gully which leads up and left to a large ledge on the very prow of the buttress.

Work up and left around a corner to a ledge at the base of the Head Crack, which is the crux pitch (5.7). Climb a short, awkward crack for a few feet until it is possible to stem right onto small holds. Continue up and right to easier climbing. Higher is a wide slot which is stemmed until it becomes feasible to exit right to a crack. Shortly above here the difficulties end.

The descent is easy but tricky. From the summit, scramble down the southeast ridge a short distance and enter a shallow gully. Follow this down about 500 feet to its bottom, a wide ledge. Then scramble down along the ridge, past several notches, until it seems obvious to drop down toward the lower lake. This area is all class 3, but soon talus is reached and the problems are over.

Equipment

Carry a selection of ten chocks. Fixed pitons are located at key sections.

Hallett Peak Northcutt – Carter Route

It is not unusual for a climber to become obsessed with a certain peak or route. Edward Whymper's fixation with the Matterhorn is well known to climbing-history buffs. Less renowned is Gaston Rébuffat's infatuation with the north face of the Grandes Jorasses, a fierce wall he dreamed about and attempted over a four-year period before his final success. North America also has had its share of climbing compulsives, and during the 1950s one of them was a physical-fitness devotee named Ray Northcutt. While he was in the army in Colorado, Northcutt took note of the forbidding and unclimbed north side of Hallett Peak, a 12,713-foot-high mass in Rocky Mountain National Park. Although this face was less than 1000 feet high, it was steep, complex, and rarely saw the sun. Spying a potential route on the third, or westernmost, of several separate buttresses, Northcutt predicted that a

◀ *The north face of Hallett Peak. The Northcutt–Carter Route lies near the right skyline.* Ed Cooper.

remarkable route could be established. He had voraciously read all the books dealing with the great north walls of the Alps, and here in his backyard was a miniature Cima Grande. A fellow climber–soldier, Harvey Carter, also had been thinking about the face, and they agreed it was time for a reconnaissance.

In early August 1954, adhering to *Nordwand* tradition, the two men grimly approached the face with packs containing outrageous quantities of pitons and ropes. To their surprise—and probable disappointment—the lower pitches were hardly alpine in character; indeed, the climbing was straightforward and moderate fifth class. Knowing that European climbers always left their pitons fixed in place, Northcutt and Carter did the same, a practice made easier by the fact that they had access to an endless supply of army pitons. (The vast majority of American climbers, concerned with the scarcity and expense of pitons, conscientiously removed their iron so they could reuse it.) By late in the day the two climbers were nearly halfway up the face, but above them loomed overhanging walls and obvious routefinding problems. Having left fourteen pitons in place, the pair rappelled to the talus.

At this point Northcutt's obsession really took hold, for he knew that even if the route were not an Eiger, it was one that could emerge as the hardest and finest in the state. Two more attempts, in 1954 and 1955, achieved relatively little, for sick-

ness, lack of time, and respect for the wall resulted only in an additional 200 feet. "I must admit," wrote Northcutt in an account of the climb, "that after the third try I was somewhat discouraged, for upon looking out and up from beneath the huge overhang where we had quit that day, all I could see was hundreds of feet of some of the smoothest looking walls I had ever seen."

In July 1956, Northcutt and Carter once again returned to the face. This time waning light would not make retreat mandatory, for the pair carried bivouac gear and enough food for a three-day effort. The men climbed rapidly over the familiar rock, finding and testing their rusted pitons. By noon they were at their previous high point, a small slab enveloped by ceilings and bulging walls. Moving delicately across a steep face at one moment and thrashing up a narrow chimney the next, the leader weaved his way through the maze. One overhang required a direct-aid piton, a move which left the climbers grumbling, for so far the route had gone free—a feat which had appeared impossible from the ground. "I was certain," wrote Northcutt, "that this could be done without tension; however, as we still had a lot of climbing ahead of us, we were quite concerned about saving time and energy."

Disconcerting rumblings to the west reminded the pair that the usual afternoon thunderstorm was approaching. This didn't unduly worry the Colorado climbers, especially since the climbing had eased somewhat and more obvious crack systems could be followed. Nearing the summit ridge in a slight drizzle, Carter appeared to be having trouble in one spot. Northcutt, out of sight below, heard mutterings turn to curses, snarls fade into a frightening silence. Soon, though, the rope began to snake upward once again, and the perplexed Northcutt relaxed. Within a few minutes a belay was established and Northcutt worriedly began to follow. Halfway up the pitch he wriggled around a corner and to his wonderment saw a solitary boot wedged in a crack. Realizing the cause of the delay, he hammered out the boot and stowed it in his pack. Soon Carter was regaling Northcutt with the story. He had been jamming nicely when his right foot refused to come out of the crack. At first merely an annoyance, it quickly became a nightmare as his arm strength began to fail. Finally, perched in a precarious position, he managed—during the ominous silence Northcutt had noted—to unlace his boot, remove his foot, and proceed, unable even to retrieve the boot.

By this time, with the storm having passed and easy climbing ahead, the boot incident was vastly amusing. Lapsing into the black humor climbers appreciate, the two men indulged in elaborate speculations as to Carter's fate had he not been able to extricate his foot. At dusk they stood jubilantly on the summit ridge building a huge cairn. Lightning flashes illuminated the shadowed ridges outside Estes Park, and the climbers knew it was time to hasten back to civilization.

Because of a lack of communication among climbers in various parts of the United States, Carter was largely ignorant that far more difficult climbs had been made in Yosemite and the Tetons. He began broadcasting the "north-wall" characteristics of Hallett to anyone who would listen, and the climb quickly acquired a formidable reputation. The rumor that Colorado finally had a climb to compare with other areas reached Yvon Chouinard and Ken Weeks in 1959. On their way to the Tetons, they thought, why not stop in Colorado for a few days and attempt the fabled route. As they leisurely hiked in toward their bivouac at the foot of the wall, they had the bright idea of climbing a few pitches in the afternoon to get an idea of the route's problems. Roping up in mid-afternoon, the two men left most of their gear behind. Encountering no major difficulties, they raced to the halfway point and, finding no reason for rappelling from that high up, continued. At dark two incredulous climbers stood at the

Bob Culp leads a relatively easy pitch low on the route during an early ascent. Huntley Ingalls.

cairn: so much for Colorado's hardest route. This ascent forever put the climb into proper perspective, for although it was a superb route and one well worth doing, it was hardly a significant breakthrough in American rockclimbing.

Within a few years the face was climbed numerous times. Northcutt returned with Layton Kor, and they were able to equal the fast time of the second-ascent party. Kor, Colorado's finest climber in the 1960s, later soloed the route in an astounding ninety minutes.

Northcutt and Carter had wandered back and forth on their ascent, trying to follow the path of least resistance. However, later climbers discovered that the peculiar granitic schist permitted climbing almost anywhere, and the most obvious crack systems weren't necessarily the easiest. Many hopelessly confused climbers established variations on their ascents, but finally a standard route evolved, one much more direct and a bit easier than the original line.

By the late 1970s about ten routes had been established on the north side of Hallett Peak, several of which are similar in length and difficulty to the Northcutt–Carter Route. While there is heated controversy concerning which of these fine routes offers the most enjoyable climbing, there is little discussion about which one has the most fascinating history. Late on a summer day, surrounded by shrieking winds and darkening clouds, one still can be transported back a quarter of a century and hear Northcutt comparing his wall to other, more remote, north faces.

First ascent

Ray Northcutt and Harvey Carter. July 27 or 28 (accounts differ), 1956.

Elevation

The summit is 12,713 feet above sea level. The climbing route is approximately 800 feet long.

Difficulty

III, 5.7.

Time

A fast party of two can race up the route in a few hours, but larger and less skilled parties require a day.

Map

USGS quadrangle: McHenry's Peak, scale 1:24,000.

Useful reference

A Climber's Guide to the Rocky Mountain National Park Area. Although the author has with admirable consistence misspelled the name of the peak, the route description is adequate.

Route description

From the Bear Lake parking area, some eleven miles southwest of the village of Estes Park, follow the trail to Emerald Lake, two miles distant. From here, head up to a scree-covered bench which runs under the broad north face of Hallett. Follow this bench past the first two buttresses (actually flat faces) to the third buttress, which lies to the right of the Slit, a narrow chimney capped with a smooth overhang.

On the lower left side of the buttress is an overhanging white scar, several hundred feet high and equally wide. Ascend broken, class 3 rock just to the right of the scar to the rope-up spot at the base of steeper rock. An easy class 5 pitch ascends the right system of two obvious crack systems; a chimney on this pitch may be avoided by face climbing on its left. A fine grassy ledge 140 feet up marks the end of the first pitch. Next, climb more or less directly up a dihedral and then a 5.5 face. Belay on a poor ledge which lies just right of the overhangs at the upper right edge of the white scar.

Finding the route on the third pitch is the key to a pleasurable ascent. Climb past the overhangs until about 20 feet above them; then make an inobvious 5.6 traverse left. Angle up and left toward a large, prominent dihedral, but before reaching it, ascend a 5.4 crack which leads up to a belay pillar. Two mistakes often are made on this pitch: missing the traverse and continuing straight up; and going all the way into the dihedral. Both errors lead to difficult climbing on substandard rock.

From the pillar, climb 140 feet of 5.5 rock to a cramped belay alcove beneath a 5-foot overhang. The fifth pitch begins by climbing around the overhang on its right side. After turning it, start upward immediately rather than making a more obvious traverse to the right. This 5.7 section is the crux of the climb. A large, grassy ledge is reached 140 feet out.

The final two pitches are fairly obvious from here. Pitch six diagonals up and right, past a second grassy ledge, to a conspicuous overhang. Turn this on the left (5.6) and belay higher. The last pitch ascends 5.5 chimneys and cracks to broken, class 3 rock just below the summit ridge.

To descend, walk west along the ridge toward the summit for a few hundred feet to a notch. Although the actual summit of Hallett is a thirty-minute walk from here, most climbers prefer to start their descent from this notch. Descend an unpleasant gully on the north side of the peak for about 500 feet. When a drop-off is imminent near a fork in the gully, climb up and left a short distance to a small saddle. From here a talus slope leads to the floor of the canyon.

Equipment

Carry a selection of fifteen small- to medium-sized chocks.

Remarks

Register for this climb at the Bear Lake Ranger Station.

Cheryl Wiggins follows a difficult pitch midway up the exposed wall.   Dean Tschappat.

194

Petit Grepon
South Face

34

Invisible from standard viewpoints in Colorado's Rocky Mountain National Park, the 800-foot-high fang of the Petit Grepon can be appreciated from only one spot: Sky Pond. This deep, timberline lake lies at the head of Loch Vale, a beautiful forested valley visited by many hikers. Standing on the rocky southern shores of the lake, the climber can hardly fail to be impressed by his or her first glimpse of the needle. Like most pinnacles, the Petit Grepon has both a spectacular aspect—in this case, the south side as viewed from the lake—and a less formidable back side. Although the Petit Grepon's north side is sheer and thin, it is only 100 feet high. An unknown party, probably in the mid-1950s, ascended this short problem, finding moderate difficulty in an airy location.

To imaginative viewers, the south side of the peak (in actuality the southeast side, but climbers prefer simple designations) is shaped much like the Eiffel Tower, for the ridges on either side of the main face steepen in gentle curves until at the very summit their angles ap-

This view of the south side of the peak shows its Eiffel Tower—like shape. Earl Wiggins.

proach the vertical. The south face, the location of the first two-thirds of the classic route, also gradually steepens, and the climber standing at the base of the wall is overwhelmed by the great curving lines which converge at the overhanging summit blade.

Climbers familiar with the Chamonix *aiguilles* will recognize the derivation of the name of this striking formation. Although A. F. Mummery's legendary exploits on the Grépon far outshine the almost nonexistent climbing history of the pinnacle's Colorado namesake, those who have done both routes agree that the climbing on the smaller pinnacle is just as stimulating as that on the larger formation. Moreover, the Petit Grepon is nestled in an unspoiled region, free of *téléphériques* and hordes of mountaineers.

In the summer of 1961 Bill Buckingham and Art Davidson completed a first ascent on the south side of the spire. Their description, however, makes it clear that they avoided the main face, preferring to climb mostly on the ridge which borders its left side. Later climbers whose names are unknown pieced together the line which is now the *voie normale* on the main south face. It is not unusual for a minor climb to have a murky history regarding its first ascent, but since the Petit Grepon is both a great-looking climb

◄ *The Petit Grepon as seen from the southeast.* Mike Covington.

and a great climb, it is curious that the first climbers who thought they might be number one on the face didn't inform the climbing public. One possible explanation is that since most climbers were vaguely aware that Buckingham and Davidson had been somewhere on the south face, the true first ascenders assumed that the main face already had been climbed. They also may have found pitons from early attempts, thus strengthening this conviction.

Naturally, at some point, probably in the mid-1960s, climbers came back from the ascent raving about it, but mentioning fixed pitons as proof that they weren't first. During the next fifteen years, the route on the main south face achieved an excellent reputation. By present-day standards it is not difficult, and even guided parties (shades of Chamonix) find the climb rewarding. With superb rock, continuously exciting climbing, and, finally, a remarkable summit, it is no accident that the route has become one of the most sought-after in the park.

The route begins on low-angled slabs directly beneath the beetling summit prow. Wandering up a 200-foot, class 4 section, a climbing party is struck immediately by the character of the rock. Not only is the granite colored a beautiful orange and black, but the perfectly shaped and sized holds seem designed for rockclimbers. This condition, which all mountaineers appreciate, persists for most of the climb.

Soon a wide ledge is reached, a fine spot to remove sweaters, have a late breakfast, and sort gear for the more demanding section above. The angle steepens subtly at this point, and a wide, easy chimney evolves into a narrow, left-slanting crack which provides the first real challenge. The lead climber must struggle to avoid being torqued out of the awkward, leaning slot. Eventually reaching another wide ledge, he or she can easily pick out the next part of the ascent, a wide gash in the wall. Although it is thrilling to watch the leader spread-eagled across this slot, with his or her rope dangling free below, this section isn't particularly difficult. Soon the route angles up and right toward the right skyline, and evidence of harder climbing is manifest as the angle steepens yet again and the holds, perfect until now, seem to withdraw into the stone.

The crux pitch is next, and early parties undoubtedly used aid over a short stretch. Even though the pitch currently is rated 5.8, the crux moves are inobvious and awkward, as one well-known climber once discovered. This man, who wishes to remain anonymous since he is embarrassed at having almost popped off a "mere" 5.8 move, describes his emotions and tactics on the upper part of the pitch:

I was so engrossed with looking up at the 5.8 part that I nearly forgot to concentrate on the 5.7 wall below it. The holds were there, all right,

but they were tilted and spaced crazily. At one point I felt crucified—my
left toes were twisted painfully into a
thin crack, and my right foot was
way off to the side, perched on a tiny
ledge at thigh level; my left hand
was clawing a lieback flake, and two
fingers of my right hand were piled
into an inch-wide jamcrack. I was so
spread out that I could hardly heave
myself up onto my right foot.

It took a few more minutes to get to
the crux, which is this big bulge on an
already horribly steep wall. After a
while it was apparent that I had to
slither around to the left, but the
footholds were damned sloping, and
my right handhold—the only one
available—would be okay only for
the first part of the slither. So the
trick was to ooze around slowly, hoping to grab a left handhold before the
right one gave out. I was getting pretty tired by this time, and my right
arm started to cramp. With protection right there, I quickly made my
bid rather than study it carefully.
Well, I must have levitated, because I
was aware that all four appendages
were slipping at once. But my shoe
caught on a microflake, and my left
hand lunged into a small slot and I
got across, snorting like a grizzly
in rut.

The leader moves up the left-slanting crack about a third of the way up the route.   Steve Roper.

The panting leader doesn't have far to go before reaching belay ledges on the right-hand ridge. A new and fascinating landscape opens up at this point; it is like turning a corner on the Eiffel Tower and gazing at a different aspect of Paris. To the northeast is the immense, chockstone-filled gash which rises between the Petit Grepon and the Saber. Above, on the Grepon, lies a steep, yellow face, the left side of which is the by-now vertical prow at the junction of the south face and eastern escarpment. From the ledges, the mirrorlike surface of Sky Pond lies more than 1000 feet below.

Steep and continuous climbing is the lot of the climbers in the next few hundred feet. The route remains close to the junction of the south and east faces, and in one stretch the climber must make a series of complicated 5.7 moves on the fearsomely exposed south face. Directly beneath one's legs at this point lie the early pitches of the route. Higher, a pull-up onto the summit ridge ends the major difficulties.

Yvon Chouinard has remarked that although he has done a number of routes which approximate the excellent climbing found on the Petit Grepon, it is the "incredible position" of the latter which makes it such a special climb. The climber creeping along the summit ridge is certainly very much aware of this. Barely six feet thick, the long summit blade drops off vertically into evil-looking gullies on either side. And rising to the north are the vertigo-inducing walls of the Sharkstooth and Saber.

On a typical summer day towering cumulus clouds enhance the wild setting, and the rumble of thunder is a sign that climbers must not ignore—the overhanging rappel, the ten-minute scramble up to a notch, and the talus- and slab-covered descent soon must be undertaken.

First ascent

Unknown, but unquestionably in the early 1960s.

Elevation

The summit is 12,100 feet above sea level. The south face is approximately 800 feet high.

Difficulty

III, 5.7.

Time

Four to six hours.

Map

USGS quadrangle: McHenry's Peak, scale 1:24,000. The "a" in "Sharkstooth" marks the location of the Petit Grepon.

Useful reference

A Climber's Guide to the Rocky Mountain National Park Area.

Route description

Park at a hairpin turn half a mile below the end of Bear Lake Road and follow a marked trail about four miles to Sky Pond. Steep talus leads to the rope-up spot at the base of the wall. Several enjoyable and easy pitches (many different routes may be taken) bring one to a deep, wide chimney. Climb this and belay near the point where the chimney ends and a left-slanting crack begins. This crack provides an excellent,

Mike Covington finds a foothold on the steeply angled crux pitch.   Allen Steck.

steep, 5.6 pitch. Another easy chimney lies above a large ledge; from its top, move up and right to belay ledges. The crux lead is next: work right a few feet, then climb very steep rock to a bulge. Turn this on the left (5.8) and move up onto the ridge. The next few hundred feet of climbing lie close to the junction of the south and east faces, though most of the route is on the latter. There are several variations in this area, but at least once the climber must make difficult moves on the exposed south face. Once the summit ridge is attained, the route is clear.

A 125-foot rappel down the back side of the spire leads to a talus gully. A short class 4 section lies just above, and a broad notch is soon reached. From here, descend slabs and talus due north to Andrews Creek and the trail.

Equipment

A selection of fifteen chocks up to two-and-a-half inches is sufficient.

Longs Peak
The Diamond

35

Climbing regulations in the United States fortunately have been confined to a few national parks and monuments. In certain of these areas one must register for climbs, and although solo climbing occasionally has been forbidden, outright bans on climbing have been rare indeed. One of the most curious bureaucratic prohibitions concerned the east face of Colorado's Longs Peak during the 1950s. Though mountaineers had an abiding interest in this precipitous flank of the 14,251-foot peak, all of them carefully avoided the 1000-foot central section known, because of its shape, as the Diamond. Their reluctance is easy to understand, for the wall is perpendicular and virtually ledgeless, and vicious storms often rake the face. There is no more imposing alpine wall in the lower forty-eight states.

An oblique view of the Diamond.   Ed Cooper.

By the early 1950s, however, certain Colorado climbers thought they were ready for an attempt on the state's most visible unclimbed wall. In 1954 Dale Johnson applied to the officials of Rocky Mountain National Park for permission to climb. He was surprised when permission was declined on the grounds that the climb was too dangerous. If the climbers were to get into trouble, reasoned the rangers, who could get them out of their predicament? Certainly not the rangers, whose climbing experience was severely limited. Although Johnson had assembled a support party of experienced mountaineers, the officials still stubbornly declared the Diamond off-

limits. Various generations of park officials refused further applications from Johnson, Ray Northcutt, Richard Pownall, and others during the remaining years of the decade.

Meanwhile, in Yosemite Valley, demonstrably more difficult climbs had been accomplished with no constraints upon climbers. Ironically, it was the first ascent of the Nose Route on El Capitan in 1958 which entrenched the position of the National Park Service. This historic ascent, described later in this book, resulted in an edict from Washington barring "stunt and daring trick climbing." This absurd phrase infuriated responsible members of the climbing community, but there was little to do except write letters. Luckily, more lucid governmental minds prevailed by the summer of 1960, and the ambiguous proclamation was set aside. By comparison, the new guidelines were quite liberal: a party could attempt big-wall climbs in the park system if certain requirements were met. Not only would mountaineers have to show they were competent, but support teams composed of highly qualified climbers would have to be present in case of trouble.

Rangers at Rocky Mountain National Park informed all prospective Diamond climbers of the new re-

◄ *The east face of Longs Peak. The climbing route on the Diamond begins at Broadway, the prominent ledge located one-third of the way up the face.* Ed Cooper.

quirements. Northcutt couldn't get away from his job; Johnson was out of shape and lacked big-wall experience; and Layton Kor, by far the finest Colorado climber at that time, was sitting out foul weather in Canada. Two candidates from California, however, rushed to Colorado.

Dave Rearick, a bashful mathematician, had done most of his climbing in California. A gymnast by avocation, he was envied his skill at balance climbing. His schoolteacher partner, Bob Kamps, was a man for whom the word "wiry" might have been invented. While at home on big walls, he abhorred bivouacs (years later he was to specialize only in short, fierce climbs, a pursuit which at least got him into a sleeping bag or bed at night). The two men had made the fifth ascent of the north face of Yosemite's Sentinel Rock in 1958 and in the course of this grueling crack climb discovered that they made a cohesive and fast team. In the early summer of 1960 Kamps had participated in the first ascent of the north face of Yosemite's Higher Cathedral Rock, a sinister wall which was identical in height and verticality to the Diamond. At the same time, Rearick was climbing the awesome face of Half Dome with Royal Robbins; this marked the third ascent of the wall, and the two men were able to accomplish the climb with only one bivouac.

Though Rearick and Kamps knew they were qualified, perhaps even overqualified, for the Diamond

climb, they also realized that the provincial rangers might not know enough about Yosemite climbs to be impressed with their credentials. To rectify this situation, the pair made the second ascent of the Diagonal, a climb on the smooth wall below and to the left of the Diamond. This difficult and circuitous route had been put up the previous year by Northcutt and Kor, who had established fixed ropes for most of the route. The fired-up team of Rearick and Kamps blitzed the route in a remarkable twelve hours. This fast ascent was made possible, in part, by the unseasonably dry rock—usually it was dripping with water and slime—but few climbers were not dazzled by the feat. The rangers, too, were impressed and in late July gave the Californians permission to attempt the Diamond.

On the drizzly afternoon of July 31, Rearick and Kamps, with a support party in tow, arrived at Chasm Lake, the usual campsite for east-face climbs. The misty wall above them was split by dozens of vertical cracks systems, and the pair decided on the prominent one which ran straight to the apex of the Diamond (their route later would be named D-1, an abbreviation for "Diamond One"). The choice of route settled, the climbers sat back to wait for a break in the weather. Rearick later wrote that "the grim aspect of the Diamond looming over us, veiled in clouds and weeping streams of water, did little for our morale."

203

But the morning of August 1 brought a surprise, for it was cold and clear. By mid-morning the Californians had become the first ever to set foot on the wall, a memorable experience indeed. Because of the seven-year ban, Rearick later reflected, the Diamond had "gradually assumed the distinction of being the most famous unclimbed wall in the United States."

A pitch-by-pitch account of the route would make tedious reading, for the climbing itself turned out to be a routine, 1960-style rockclimbing adventure. Instead of encountering fascinating climbing, the two men found the aesthetics of the route particularly invigorating. Their position was comparable to that of window washers on a sky-scraper placed in an outstanding natural environment. Several thousand feet below was Chasm Lake, black in its basin of talus. Mills Glacier, directly under the wall, was a reminder that climbing on Longs Peak was not the same as climbing in Yosemite Valley.

The two pioneers used direct aid for much of their upward progress, since the wall actually overhung slightly in the 400-foot central region—a fact of which they were constantly reminded by a small waterfall that drifted silently behind them during the many hours it took to overcome this section. Occasionally, the cracks widened enough to allow free climbing, and the pair would quickly gain a few more feet. The granite, excellent on the lower part of the route, became decom-

posed and blocky midway up, and the climbers moved gingerly up the fragile aid cracks. The team rarely found comfortable platforms, so belays in slings or on book-sized ledges were unavoidable. Mossy rock hindered progress at times, and huge chunks of ice blocked a chimney high on the route, adding an alpine touch.

On their first day the Californians accomplished only four pitches, so they rappelled to the base of the route, concerned about the weather, which again looked threatening. They spent the second night on a perfectly flat, two-by-seven-foot ledge two-thirds of the way up the wall; Rearick sat cross-legged while Kamps managed a modified supine position. It was early afternoon on August 3 when the climbers emerged from the final dank chimney onto the talus just below the summit. On hand to greet them were support-team members, Bonnie Kamps, and a few hardy reporters. The climb had attracted an unusual amount of publicity, and the group met other newsmen, in various stages of altitude sickness, as they meandered down the trail.

The following week was a busy one for the climbers, for their notoriety made public appearances obligatory. They appeared in a local rodeo parade, responded politely to the inevitable "Why did you do it?" questions on a television show, and stuffed themselves at a banquet. What a striking contrast, they must have felt, to the solitude and discomfort of the preceding days.

The Diamond is renowned for its steep, continuous cracks; here, a climber's haul rope indicates the verticality. Mike Kennedy.

The next party to ascend the route received no such accolades. Royal Robbins and Layton Kor made the climb in 1963, taking but a single day. During the next fifteen years nearly twenty routes and major variations were established on the Diamond. While D-1 is not climbed as frequently as the much easier 1966 route known as D-7, the directness of the route, along with its note-worthy history, continues to attract mountaineers. In 1978 the route was climbed free for the first time, an event which typifies the irreverent attitude of modern rockclimbers to-ward big walls. Treating the over-hanging central section as if it were merely a series of marginal boulder problems, Billy Westbay and John Bacher encountered four 5.11 pitches. One wonders what the next "first" will be on the wall where for seven years potential first ascenders struggled against bureaucrats in-stead of overhangs and liebacks.

First ascent

Dave Rearick and Bob Kamps. August 1–3, 1960.

Elevation

The summit is 14,251 feet above sea level. The climbing route is slightly less than 1000 feet.

Difficulty

V, 5.7, A4. Done free, the climb is 5.11.

Time

A fast party of two can do the route in one day.

Map

USGS quadrangle: Longs Peak, scale 1:24,000.

Useful reference

A Climber's Guide to the Rocky Mountain National Park Area.

Route description

From Estes Park drive south on Colorado Highway 7 for about ten miles. Turn west on the short road which leads to the Longs Peak Ranger Station. Follow a marked trail for about four miles to Chasm Lake, at 11,800 feet.

Walk up talus to the Mills Glacier and ascend it to the North Chimney, a prominent diagonal cleft directly below the center of the Diamond. Three moderate class 5 pitches, in-volving loose and wet rock, lead to Broadway, the conspicuous ledge which runs across the entire face. Move left a short distance to the rope-up spot.

Broadway also can be reached, with less trauma, from the Longs Peak Trail. Follow this from the ranger station to Boulderfield, at the 12,800-foot level. Head up a trail toward the base of the north face of the peak; then walk up talus a short way to Chasm View, a notch over-looking the Diamond. Make three rappels to Broadway and then follow it across to the start of the route, just left of the point where the North Chimney Route meets Broadway.

In the following description, aid climbing is indicated whenever the majority of climbers use it; as men-tioned above, the climb has been

done all free. An easy pitch on the left side of a small buttress leads 130 feet to a belay ledge. From here, climb up to a right-diagonaling overhang and nail it to a point where one can go free again to a grassy belay platform.

Next, climb a difficult corner for 30 feet; then nail a dihedral a short dis-tance to a large ceiling. More nail-ing above this ceiling leads to a belay bolt. Pitch four leads 80 feet to the conspicuous and sloping Ramp. Belay on a better ledge 20 feet higher. Two more pitches of aid lead up an overhanging wall for 200 feet to a very flat belay ledge.

The seventh pitch ascends blocky overhangs for 130 feet and ends at a tiny belay alcove on Table Ledge. At this point, instead of ascending the prominent chimney above, move left about 6 or 8 feet to a perfect crack. Nail this for 130 feet to a small belay spot. On the final pitch, traverse right into the prominent chimney and ascend it to the top of the route.

A good trail descends from the summit to the ranger station.

Equipment

Carry a rack of thirty chocks. Most climbers also will want a selection of twenty pitons, varying from knife-blades to two-and-a-half-inch angles.

Remarks

Register for this climb at the Longs Peak Ranger Station.

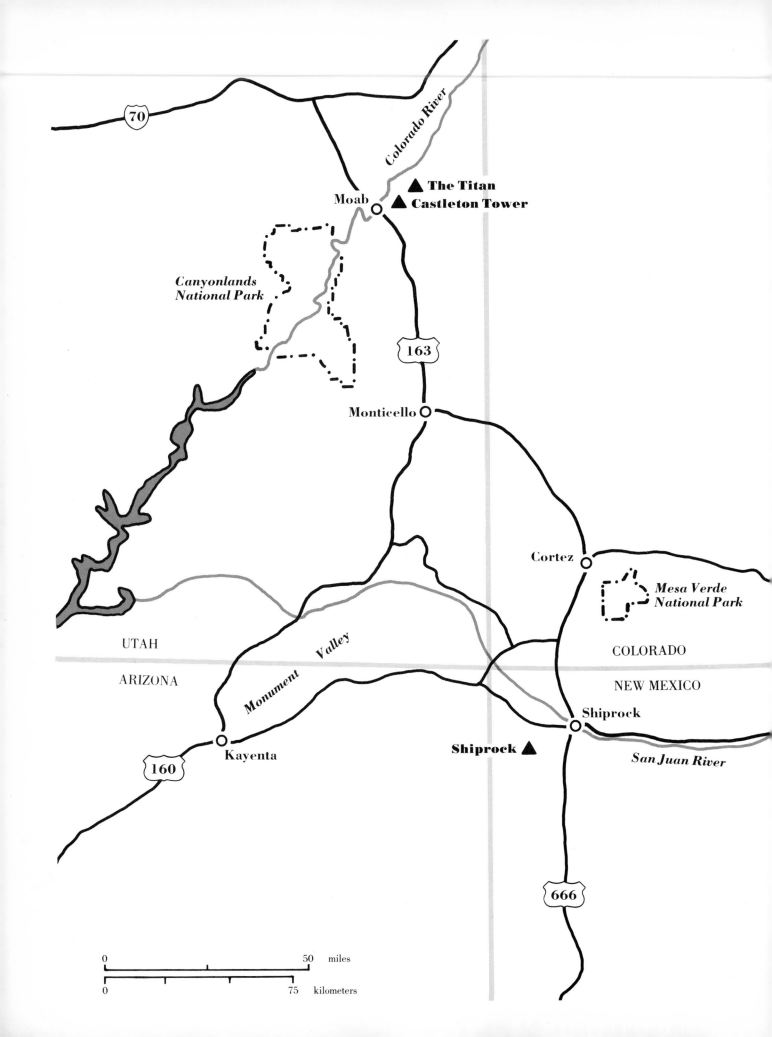

The Southwest

Twenty thousand square miles of alluring canyon country containing hundreds of beautiful sandstone spires lay virtually uncharted until the uranium boom of the early 1950s. Including parts of Utah, Colorado, New Mexico, and Arizona, the southwest desert is so topographically convoluted that even today's detailed maps sometimes prove inadequate to the wanderer. The vast area known as Four Corners remained *terra incognita* to rockclimbers—with the exception of Shiprock and a few minor climbs—until 1956, when Yosemite-trained experts scaled Spider Rock, a fabulous 800-foot pillar which would have been included in this book had the Navajo Tribal Council not placed it permanently off-limits. Realizing the first-ascent potential in the desert, climbers from California and Colorado quickly began ascending such dramatic pinnacles as the Totem Pole and Standing Rock.

The decade following the first ascent of Spider Rock rightly may be called the golden age of desert climbing, for adventurers who thrived on vertical red sandstone were able to select their first ascents from hundreds of untouched pinnacles. From then on, the likelihood of discovering virgin spires diminished each year, of course, and present-day climbers must be satisfied with establishing new routes on previously ascended monoliths or seeking out canyon walls, where literally thousands of short crack climbs await those rockclimbers capable of 5.10 and higher. Utah's Zion Canyon, the desert equivalent of Yosemite Valley, contains innumerable excellent, untouched routes; yet climbers traditionally have been lured by pinnacles, those free-standing formations that offer no easy routes of ascent. Thus, in recent years, rockclimbers have been infiltrating the desert in order to repeat the noteworthy early routes, several of which offer unique and rewarding climbing.

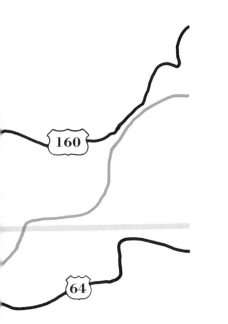

The Southwest has a well-deserved reputation for its soft and crumbly rock, and climbers must choose their routes with care. As Chuck Pratt, a desert aficionado, has written: "Why the desert should exert such a fascination on a handful of climbers is a mystery to those who are not attracted to it, for the climbs in Four Corners, with a few remarkable exceptions, have little to recommend them. They are generally short —often requiring less time than the approaches—the rock at its best is brittle and rotten and at its worst is the consistency of wet sugar. . . . To gain any lasting worth from what the desert has to offer, we had to learn to put our pitons and ropes away and to go exploring in silence, keeping our eyes very open. It wasn't easy. We wasted a lot of time climbing until we got the knack."

Shiprock

On a clear New Mexican day one can see it for forty miles—a massive, full-rigged barkentine sailing serenely and incongruously through a desert so unattractive that highway travelers can pass close by the rock without even seeing it, so intently are their dulled eyes affixed to the white line. But climbers, most of whom have driven many hundreds of miles for the prize of its summit, strain for their first glimpse of Shiprock. They can identify its individual summit towers from twenty miles distant and impatiently while away the remaining miles speculating about famous sections of the standard route.

The east side of Shiprock. The lower part of the route ascends the hidden west side to the prominent notch; from this point the Rappel Gully drops to the Traverse Pitch. Higher, on the skyline, lies the Horn. Ed Cooper.

To take a two-hour walk around the base of Shiprock is to experience more convoluted geology and more stupendous walls than the mind can fathom. Great fluted grooves rise for many hundreds of feet without noticeable change; cracks which from a distance appear to be a few feet wide and thus climbable turn out to be ten-foot-wide slashes. Afternoon lighting reveals buttresses, ramps, and towers which were indiscernible a few hours earlier.

Several writers have made the mistake of referring to the "sandstone" of Shiprock, but its yellowish-tan rock is actually tuff-breccia: tiny, sharp-angled fragments of feldspar and other minerals cemented into a matrix of volcanic material. Shiprock is the plugged vent of a volcano which was active about forty or fifty million years ago. The black basalt dikes and gullies which are so striking from below were formed from dark magma that cut into the solidified tuff-breccia during later eruptions.

Both types of rock present problems for the climber. The basalt is fine-grained and hard, yet it is highly fractured. Frost action has caused many blocks to fall and has rendered others precariously balanced. The tuff-breccia, on the other hand, is monolithic, and the few cracks that occur are flared and bottomed. The decomposed outer shell of this rock often has handhold-sized flakes which prove to be loose.

Up until the late 1920s none of the spectacular rock formations in the southwestern desert regions had been thought of seriously as summits worthy of attainment. American climbing was done in mountain ranges, not on isolated monoliths. Yet when Albert Ellingwood, whose fine route on Crestone Needle is discussed earlier in this book, drove by Shiprock around 1930, he paused, for here was a *mountain*. It had ridges, couloirs, and buttresses. Walking around the mass, studying it with his field glasses, he tried to pick out a route. Most peaks have an obvious easy way up, or at least an obvious hard way up. But Shiprock appeared to have *no* way up. Ridges could not be followed, for they were too steep and had deep, impassable notches. True, there were gullies and low-angled areas high on the peak, but they had no bottom—only horrifying blank walls. Chimneys were gigantic troughs, smooth and overhanging.

Asking locals about the formation, Ellingwood discovered that the Navajos, on whose reservation the rock stood, called the peak Tsa-Beh-Tai, the Rock with Wings. According to their legends, a giant bird once flew their people from the north country to their present sun-baked homeland. Shiprock was a remnant of that bird.

A few years later Ellingwood suggested to his young climbing protégé, Robert Ormes, "Now that you've polished off the best climbs in Colorado, why not go down to New Mexico and have a look at

Shiprock?" More years passed, and before long so many climbers had heard about the peak that, even without a serious recorded attempt, the unclimbed summit became known as "the number one climbing problem in America." Fearful that easterners or Sierra Club climbers would snatch the prize, Ormes and a friend drove to Shiprock in the spring of 1936.

When the pair reached the northwest side of the rock, they immediately were taken with a wide basalt gully which, though somewhat hidden from below, appeared to lead to the summit towers. Perhaps this was the key to the route, thought Ormes; it had to be, for other possibilities seemed nonexistent. The two men saw that the summit ridge of the mountain ran north to south and had three conspicuous towers astride it. Their proposed route would not take them to the middle, highest summit, but rather to a notch just north of the north summit. Perhaps a route could be worked out from there. The pair climbed slowly into what now is called the Basalt Gully, gaining 500 feet of elevation. But at the base of a steep, fractured headwall, sapped by debilitating heat and out of water, they turned back.

Returning in the cool autumn of 1937, Ormes brought more supplies and three experienced companions: Bill House, Mel Griffiths, and Gordon Williams. This group soon reached the notch atop the Basalt

The Traverse Pitch. Above and to the right of the belayer rises the dark slot known as the Rappel Gully. Steve Roper.

Gully. Above lay a 150-foot tower which they knew to be the north summit. If they reached this point, could they then work their way over to the main summit? No other alternative presented itself, so they set to work. Piton cracks were poor, and the rock was steep; the foursome traded leads several times. Suddenly, as Ormes tried to stretch across a difficult section, a foothold broke and he plummeted backward. His twenty-foot fall was held safely by House, but the demoralized team soon retreated.

Notes in mountaineering journals concerning these attempts, plus an article about the impregnability of the peak in the *Saturday Evening Post,* spurred a group of Californians into action. In mid-October 1939, four Sierra Club climbers arrived at the rock with the latest in climbing equipment, including expansion bolts. These small devices, never before used in American climbing, obviated the need for piton cracks. By hand-drilling an inch-and-a-half-deep hole, the climber could place a bolt in blank rock and then proceed in complete security.

Trained on the great walls of Yosemite Valley, the team was well qualified in the art of difficult climbing. Dave Brower was along because of his mastery of delicate friction climbing; Bestor Robinson because of his self-proclaimed equipment fetish; Raffi Bedayn because of his well-known belaying capabilities; and John Dyer for a rather practical reason—weighing only 135 pounds, he was to be positioned at the front end of the rope whenever it seemed the pitons were about to pop loose. Bedayn could hold Dyer easily, they thought.

When the four men reached the Colorado group's notch, they were appalled by the upward view. Rather than waste time on what seemed to be a futile effort, they decided to investigate a relatively low-angled gully which dropped from the notch into the deep recesses of the east face. The Coloradans also had noticed this gully, thinking that if they rappelled it, perhaps they could traverse around the north tower rather than climb over it; however, they did not try it. After one rappel and some scary downclimbing, the Californians reached a small bowl and were pleased to see that a lower-angled section of tuff-breccia did indeed lead around the tower. Brower's ability paid off, and a hundred feet of new terrain—the now-classic Traverse Pitch—was overcome. With daylight ebbing, the men returned to the ground.

Belayed by Steve Roper, Dick Long gingerly moves up the bypass to the Double Overhang.   Allen Steck.

The following day Robinson and Dyer labored on the strenuous Double Overhang, a spectacular thirty-foot-high obstacle which blocked the entrance to the bottom of a large and obviously easy bowl. After making only twenty feet, the team once again made the long journey back to the ground.

Returning to the ground each afternoon was taking so long that on the third day the group carried bivouac gear. It took half a day to finish the overhang, but the class 3 and 4 terrain above allowed the climbers to scramble quickly to the base of the final problem, the middle summit. A false start on the north side of this tower ended the day's climbing, and the group settled into one of the many shallow caves dotting the bowl.

Early on the fourth morning the Californians attacked the fearsomely exposed ridge on the south side of the tower. Later to become well known as the Horn Pitch, this section, like the Double Overhang, required intricate and innovative piton work. It proved to be the last major difficulty, and the four men reached the "mainmast" summit at noon on Columbus Day—a fitting touch for those who are metaphorically inclined.

A climber works his way up the Horn Pitch, the most continuously difficult section of the route. Steve Roper.

Four bolts had been placed on Ship-rock, two for belay anchors and two for safety. Pitons had been used for direct aid, of course, but ethical concerns led the team to avoid bolts for aid. Robinson later wrote: "We agreed with mountaineering moralists that climbing by the use of expansion bolts was taboo. We did believe, however, that safety knew no restrictive rules. . . ."

Not until 1952 did the next ascent of Shiprock take place, and by that time many American climbers were using bolts indiscriminately. Ship-rock's second-ascent party began the "unnecessary bolt syndrome" by placing several anchor bolts, missing or ignoring the cracks the first-ascent team had used. Ten years later one could count thirty expansion bolts in place; ludicrously, some rappel stations had four bolts. In 1963 an antibolt fanatic from California decided to remove all but the original bolts and, having done so, pontificated in the summit register that the climb had been returned to 1939 standards. Repeating the route a few years later, the same climber was amused by the graffiti that had been added next to his 1963 entry. One comment was brief: "Fink!" A second read: "Unfortunately, didn't take long for all that iron to reappear."

It was not until 1959—during the forty-fifth ascent—that a free variation was found which rendered the awkward and time-consuming Double Overhang obsolete. Two decades earlier, Dave Brower had walked along a ledge for fifty feet past the overhang and reported that the route beyond wouldn't go. Pete Rogowski discovered that it would. One necessary safety bolt was placed on this short, moderately difficult section. Higher, Rogowski led the Horn Pitch without direct aid, thus accomplishing the first free ascent of Shiprock.

The route became increasingly popular in the 1950s; its reputation as a varied and intricate climb in a bizarre landscape attracted most of the active American climbers of that time. During this decade the rock was ascended forty-six times; in the 1960s ninety more parties signed the historic register.

Other routes were done on the peak. Inevitably, the route the Coloradans had attempted (now called Ormes' Rib) was completed—it was climbed with aid in 1957 and done free a short time later. Multi-day and even multi-week aid routes eventually were established on those same "impossible" walls that the early climbers had shunned with such horror.

On the thirtieth anniversary of the first ascent, Will Siri, a director of the Sierra Club, stood on the lonely summit blocks and noticed darkened skies to the east. In the distance he saw the grotesque stacks of the controversial Four Corners Generating Station. Coal-laden smoke, drifting over thousands of square miles, had replaced the once-famous clear air of the region. Never again would Shiprock climbers have hundred-mile visibilities. But then, with the recent action of the Navajo Tribal Council, perhaps there won't be too many summit climbers to miss the clear skies.

The conflict between the Navajos and the climbers began in the early 1960s, as climbing on the various towers and buttes on the Navajo reservation was becoming popular. A new awareness of their changing role in American society caused the Navajos to reconsider letting outsiders defile their sacred rocks. In 1962 Spider Rock and the Totem Pole, two of the finest sandstone towers in the world, were place off-limits to climbers. Citing not only religious reasons, a Navajo official blustered, "Those iron spikes you use have shortened the life expectancy of the Totem Pole by 50,000 years."

For some arcane reason, Shiprock was not included in the ban until the spring of 1970, when signs announcing "Absolutely No Rock Climbing" appeared around the rock. Another reason for the "absolute and unconditional" ban was that two climbers had been killed on Shiprock. One tribal official wrote that "because of the Navajo's traditional fear of death and its aftermath, such accidents and especially fatilities often render the area where they occur as taboo, and the location is sometimes henceforth regarded as contaminated by evil spirits and is considered a place to be avoided."

At the present time the ban is still in effect, though many clandestine ascents have been made. If a responsible and influential group made an effort to negotiate with tribal officials, perhaps some sort of an agreement could be worked out so that climbers once again could be allowed on the formation.

First ascent

Dave Brower, Bestor Robinson, Raffi Bedayn, and John Dyer. October 9–12, 1939.

Elevation

The summit is 7178 feet above sea level. The rock rises approximately 1700 feet above the desert floor.

Difficulty

III, 5.7, A2. Done free, the route is 5.9.

Time

Four to eight hours for the ascent; half as long for the descent.

Map

USGS quadrangle: Shiprock, scale 1:24,000.

Useful reference

Guide to the New Mexico Mountains.

Route description

From the town of Shiprock drive seven miles south on U.S. Highway 666 to a junction. Turn right onto a paved road which leads toward Red Rock and drive eight miles until reaching the dike which radiates south from the rock. A poor dirt road on the eastern side of this dike takes one close to the monolith.

Walk north along the western base of Shiprock until almost at the northwest corner; then ascend talus upward to the base of the black Basalt Gully. A cave blocks easy entrance to the gully, but a 5.8 move (or a shoulder stand) at the far left allows one to reach easy scrambling. A few class 4 pitches, interspersed with talus, are encountered next; soon one arrives at the base of a shattered basalt headwall. There are several ways to go from here. The object is to reach a notch which can be seen up and to the right. This small notch lies at the base of a thin basalt rib which shoots up through the tuff-breccia. Be careful of the rock in this area, for it is dangerously loose.

From the notch, called the Colorado Col, the famous Rappel Gully winds down to the east. A 100-foot rope must be left fixed over the first rappel to facilitate return. Lower in the gully, a 20-foot piece of rope should be left in place through a tunnel in some chockstones. A hundred feet below this, the class 3 and 4 gully widens into a spacious bowl.

A friction ledge now leads south around a rounded corner. This is the beginning of the Friction Traverse, 125 feet of delicate climbing. The first third of the traverse is essentially level; the remainder slants distinctly downward. Beware of getting too high. From the ledge at the end of the pitch, climb a short wall (5.9 or A1) to another ledge. A few steps to the left lies the Double Overhang, festooned with pitons and bolts. Continue down the ledge to its end, step around an exposed corner, and make a few 5.6 moves which lead into a huge bowl. Four hundred feet of class 3 and 4 climbing leads to a prominent, exposed notch just below and left of the Horn, a well-named formation which juts against the left skyline. The Horn Pitch, by far the most continuously difficult pitch of the route, can be climbed with a short stretch of aid or else free (5.7). This superb pitch ends on a ledge with a ring bolt, the only original bolt left on the current route. From here, traverse up and right around a corner to a short step which is either 5.9 or A1. Easier climbing leads 100 feet to the summit.

The Horn, in this view resembling a sightless reptile, provides exposed and difficult climbing. Ed Webster.

Descent is via the same route as the ascent, with two important exceptions. Rappel directly over the Double Overhang. And from the Colorado Col, instead of rappelling the basalt headwall directly, peer over a small notch to the west. Down about 25 feet is a mass of rappel slings. A 100-foot rappel takes one to a class 3 gully which leads into the upper portion of the Basalt Gully.

Equipment

Carry five chocks and five pitons. Also take two extra ropes, or pieces of rope, to leave fixed in the Rappel Gully.

Remarks

Summer temperatures can be torrid, and winter storms can deposit several inches of snow. The best months to climb are April and October.

Castleton Tower Kor – Ingalls Route

37

A dozen miles northeast of Moab, Utah, lies remote Castle Valley, a feature offering a splendid introduction to the varied topography of the Four Corners area. The lower end of the valley intersects the Colorado River at 4100 feet, and at the confluence of Castle Creek and the Colorado, one looks out upon a pure desert environment. The vegetation is sparse; the summer heat is debilitating; and rattlesnakes seek shelter in the talus lying beneath the bluffs bordering the river. From the Colorado one must travel a few miles through rugged country to reach the main part of Castle Valley. Six miles of relatively flat terrain follow, the desert giving way gradually to grasslands dotted with pinyon pine and juniper. Fifteen miles after leaving river level, Miner's Basin is reached at 9600 feet; here nuthatches and chickadees flutter among ponderosa pine. A short distance beyond the basin lie the 12,000-foot peaks of the La Sal Mountains, and although

The south side of Castleton Tower. Ed Webster.

one may start out in shirtsleeves at the river, a sweater will be needed while wandering among snowfields. Thus, in a single morning's traverse of the valley from its lowest to its highest point, one passes through an incredibly wide range of climatic zones.

Part way up Castle Valley, perched atop a gigantic talus cone, stands Castleton Tower. The truncated spire resembles Wyoming's Devil's Tower in shape, but the similarity ends here; for Castleton is brick red rather than buff, and instead of hundreds of cracks from which to choose a route, there are only three or four. One of these cracks, located on the south face of the monolith, attracted Layton Kor and Huntley Ingalls, the first climbers to visit the area.

At this stage of desert climbing history—1961—Kor was a newcomer to sandstone climbing. Although he was Colorado's finest climber, his experience had been limited to climbs on solid rock and on alpine walls, neither of which had prepared him for the loose, brittle quality of sandstone. Yet those who followed Kor's meteoric career in the early 1960s had little doubt that the gangling and compulsive giant would succeed in whatever climbing endeavor he put his mind to. Winter bricklaying jobs in Colorado were Kor's means of making a living and of keeping in shape, while each spring the restless twenty-two-year-old made a frenetic Grand Tour of North American climbing centers. After a few

months in Yosemite Valley, Kor would gravitate first to the Wind River Range, then to the Tetons, and finally to Canada. In late summer he usually made his way back to Yosemite for a few culminating climbs before driving home to Colorado.

In mid-September 1961, the insatiable Kor decided to prolong his climbing season even further by visiting the Four Corners area. Finding that desert temperatures had dropped sufficiently to make climbing comfortable, Kor arranged to meet three of his climbing friends in Moab. Huntley Ingalls, an astrophysicist who had accompanied Kor on many difficult routes in Colorado, arrived quickly. Realizing that they had several free days before Fred Beckey and Harvey Carter were due to arrive, the two Coloradans perused postcards and tourist guidebooks in search of possible climbing goals. Photographers, they knew, had covered the remote desert areas far more thoroughly than climbers had. The two men were fascinated by photographs showing dramatic pinnacles but found the captions frustratingly vague concerning the names and locations of the formations. Studying one striking photo, however, Kor recognized the shape and name of Castleton Tower from conversations with friends who had once seen the spire.

217

On September 15, after learning from townspeople the exact location of the pinnacle, Kor and Ingalls began driving east along the meandering Colorado River. Thirty minutes later the pair turned south on a rough dirt road; five miles from the river the two excited climbers turned a corner and saw the huge, red shaft outlined against the morning sky. Having decided that a casual reconnaissance, rather than a summit bid, was in order for the first day, the two men leisurely hiked up loose scree slopes under the south face of the pinnacle. Kor already had picked out a system of conspicuous dihedrals on the face; it was the only obvious route.

As Kor began the first pitch—two short, easy dihedrals—he was surprised to discover firm, reliable rock. Having heard rumors that desert sandstone was so soft that a climber could drive pitons straight into the rock, Kor yelled down to Ingalls that progress was far more pleasant than he had expected. On a spacious ledge 100 feet above the base, Kor anchored his rope to a large block and shouted to his companion that it was his turn to climb. In the late afternoon Kor led another pitch; this one was much more intimidating than the first. Resorting to direct-aid techniques, the leader placed large angle pitons back to back to surmount a three-inch-wide crack. Superb, exposed crack climbing followed, and before long Kor arrived at another large platform.

On the second pitch of the route, the leader struggles up a flared chimney.
Ed Webster.

The two men rappelled from the second ledge, leaving their climbing ropes fixed to the spire. Although they had accomplished more than half the projected route, they were well aware that the crux pitch would have to be faced early the following day: above the second ledge rose a long, foot-wide chimney which tapered to a jamcrack at one ominous, bulging section.

In the morning, after the two climbers had prusiked to their high point, Kor attacked the worrisome section. The lanky Coloradan ascended forty feet on direct aid to the base of the slit; then, eschewing aid slings, he began wriggling up the crack by means of the strenuous and time-consuming heel-and-toe method. When Kor finally reached the bulge, he discovered he was far too massive to fit inside the crack. He could not jam it either, for the wall seemed too steep for this committing technique. Thus, out came the bolt kit and in went two bolts for aid. With this problem neatly overcome, Kor soon was thrashing up the squeeze chimney above. As he pulled onto a wide ledge ninety feet below the summit, he saw that the major difficulties were over. By mid-afternoon he and Ingalls stood on top.

A thunderstorm was brewing as the two men hurriedly built a cairn and set up a rappel station. The top of an isolated desert pinnacle, thought Kor, could hardly be considered a haven during a wild electrical display. Fortunately, the nucleus of the storm passed to the south of the successful climbers, and they were able to take their time on the airy descent. The following day Kor and Ingalls joined Beckey and Carter in Moab and surged on to other first ascents.

Kor raved about Castleton Tower to many climbers during the next few years, but there were so many untouched pinnacles in the area that rockclimbers preferred establishing new climbs rather than repeating old ones. Californians Chuck Pratt and Steve Roper were looking for classic routes when they arrived in Moab in October 1963 and, after seeing Castleton, decided it would make a perfect warm-up climb. Pratt was able to lead the crux pitch without direct aid, jamming smoothly past Kor's two bolts. Greatly impressed with the quality of the climb and delighted to have made the first free ascent, the two men emerged onto the thirty-by-forty-foot summit.

At the summit a remarkable sight greeted the climbers, for scattered randomly over the flat surface were dozens of pieces of lumber. The puzzled men sat down at the summit cairn to try and figure out an explanation for the wood's mysterious presence. Surely Kor and Ingalls had not been so perverse as to have hauled the wood up as a practical joke. Neither could nonclimbers have carried the timber up an easy route, for there was none. An airplane never could have dropped the lumber so accurately on the summit. "Hold it!" Pratt exclaimed. "Wasn't there an advertisement last year that showed a new model car on top of a pinnacle?" Pratt's hypothesis was later verified in Moab. A helicopter had lowered several men onto the summit, where they built a crude wooden platform. After a car was lowered into position, the men were replaced by a young woman, who—nervously, we may presume—posed for spectacular aerial photographs. When the modeling session was over, the wood was not removed. Who would ever see it? the crew must have reasoned. Roper spelled out a few obscene words in five-foot-high wooden letters to inform pilots of his displeasure with such esoteric littering. Soon the two climbers were rappelling joyfully to the ground.

Scores of rockclimbers have stood on the summit of Castleton Tower after ascending the most popular short climb in the Southwest. The summit lumber has disappeared slowly over the years, for climbers are inordinately fond of casting any summit debris—rock or wood—into the abyss. Thus, the summit today looks much the same as it did when Kor and Ingalls pulled over the top in 1961. The extensive panorama of red desert, bordered on one side by the Colorado River and on the other by the La Sal Mountains, also looks the same, for man has made few encroachments upon this wild region. It seems certain that the overall experience of climbing the Kor–Ingalls Route will be as rewarding for the hundredth party as it was for the first.

First ascent

Layton Kor and Huntley Ingalls.
September 15–16, 1961.

Elevation

The summit is 6656 feet above
sea level.

Difficulty

III, 5.9.

Time

Four hours.

Map

USGS quadrangle: Castle Valley,
scale 1:62,500. Although the local
name for the pinnacle is Castleton
Tower, the official name, as shown
on the map, is Castle Rock.

Route description

From Moab, Utah, drive north on
the main highway for a few miles to
the Colorado River; then turn right
onto a paved road on the south side
of the river. After following the road
for about sixteen miles, turn right
onto the road to Castleton. The spire
will come into view after four or five
more miles.

The leader nears the crux moves of the route.   Ed Webster.

Hike up the huge talus cone to the
base of the tower's south face. The
route is quite obvious since it stays
in or close to major dihedrals. To
descend, rappel the route.

Equipment

Carry a few wide chocks in addition
to standard rockclimbing gear.

Remarks

Spring and autumn are the best times
to climb the pinnacle.

The Titan

38

Eroded by wind and storms, the Fisher Towers, near Moab, Utah, prove to be a startling sight to those who seek them out. One must take a half-hour detour from U.S. Highway 160, the main tourist artery of the region, even to glimpse the towers. A rough dirt road traverses the last few miles to a parking area, and from this vantage point half a dozen spires loom like skyscrapers. The first thing a visitor notices, besides the brilliant coloration, is the delicate, curtainlike appearance of the Moenkopi sandstone. Every wall is covered with a unique patina of mud over scoured grooves. Nowhere else in the Four Corners area do similar formations occur. What caused these great fluted ripples? The answer is relatively simple: even by desert standards the rock is quite soft, and since the Fisher Towers abut the 12,000-foot-high La Sal Mountains, they receive far more precipitation than do most of the other desert areas. Rain courses down the flanks of the spires, carrying abrasive red mud with it, and deep ruts are carved into the weak rock. As the rock dries, the viscous liquid slows until curtains of mud

The first pitch. Ed Webster.

are frozen in place to await the next rains and eventual reduction to piles of red grit at the base of each wall. Wind, too, has contributed considerably to the shaping, for the unsheltered towers are exposed to fierce drafts which in certain seasons sweep the La Sal slopes.

Upon first touching this bizarre rock, the climber is astounded to discover that fingernails can easily gouge the mud which appears to have been laid on by a drunken mason. One can knock off hunks of stone with a strong kick, and even children can pry off flakes. Debris lies in disturbing mounds below the awesome grooves. How is it possible, wonders the prospective climber, to make any headway on this nightmarish rock?

The Titan commanded the attention of the first climbers to visit the area, for it was the tallest spire—900 feet on its downhill side—and it was free-standing, in contrast to some of the area's other spires, which were partially connected to nearby buttes. Layton Kor and Huntley Ingalls were the first climbers to discover the Titan, having spotted it from Castleton Tower, six miles away. On a reconnaissance shortly thereafter, they outlined a possible route on the 650-foot-high northeast side of the monolith. Examining the rock, they

found that an inch or so under the dried mud lay much more dependable rock. Still, they realized that even this loose outer shell of stone would pose problems with both man-caused rockfall and the placing of bolts in obvious blank sections.

In the spring of 1962 Kor decided that a desert first ascent might be a marvelous way to begin the climbing season, and he approached Ingalls. Always in need of extra cash, they hatched a clever plan: perhaps they could interest someone in sponsoring the venture. Ingalls queried the National Geographic Society regarding an article about the ascent of the Titan. He knew that for years the organization had published articles about the hidden canyons and Indian ruins of the Four Corners. Knowing also of the Society's growing interest in mountaineering, Ingalls anticipated a positive reply. Word arrived in a few weeks: the Society indeed was interested in publishing such an article and would assign a staff photographer when the time came for the summit push.

Kor and Ingalls next persuaded George Hurley, a mild-mannered English instructor at Colorado University, to accompany them. A party of three, they reasoned, not only would be safer but would allow more exciting photographs to be taken. In early May, having only a weekend available, the three men drove to the rock to establish a high point.

As they roped up on a clear May morning, the climbers all felt that singular combination of emotions peculiar to those who engage in dangerous activities. The challenge was obvious, and the men were excited and curious about what lay ahead. At the same time, however, they were apprehensive, if not fearful. Rational thought suggested that the ascent should progress without incident—after all, they were experienced at what they were doing. But other thoughts intruded, especially in those lonely hours before daybreak: What would happen if the leader pulled off a flake onto those below? What if he ripped out a long string of pitons and smashed into a ledge? Keeping such thoughts to oneself was the rule in the masculine world of rockclimbing, so the talk at the rope-up spot was jocular and laced with obscenities.

Kor and Hurley climbed about 200 feet the first day, slowed by the unfamiliar vertical rock. Since they were able to follow a continuous crack system, few bolts were necessary. Rather than spend the night on a foot-wide ledge, they rappelled to the base at sundown. The following day it was Ingalls' turn to belay Kor, who was to lead the entire route. The aid climbing was unique, and in his article for *National Geographic* magazine, Ingalls wrote that "sometimes Kor had to probe the caked

The Titan as seen from the northwest. The upper part of the route follows the left skyline. Ed Cooper.

mud with a long piton or excavate with his hammer to find a crack, showering dust and small rocks down upon me. At times he had to drive a long piton directly into the mud and gingerly trust his weight to it." Progress was slow, and the pair accomplished only two pitches that second day. As he watched the climbers rappel the fixed lines, Hurley reflected that the ropes were strung barely halfway up the tower, an inauspicious start, for it was the upper section which looked toughest. Since the climbers had to return to jobs in Colorado the next day, they left their ropes dangling and planned to return the following weekend.

Accompanying the three climbers on their return drive to the Fisher Towers was *National Geographic* photographer Barry Bishop, soon to become famous in the mountaineering world as one of the first Americans to climb Everest. Bishop's task on the Titan was to shoot telephotos from the ground and also to obtain aerial photographs. The climbers themselves would document the route at close range.

Barry Bishop took this aerial photo showing three members of the first-ascent party on the final pitch. Copyright by the National Geographic Society.

On May 12 all three climbers ascended the fixed ropes to their high point 350 feet above the ground. Kor began work on the next section, which proved to be difficult free climbing up cracks. A short while later the three adventurers were resting on the best ledge of the route. Cold winds had risen, and swirling red dust permeated clothes and equipment. The climbers' eyes were becoming inflamed, but there was little to do about the problem except face away from the gale. Kor led one more pitch in late afternoon, placing nine aid bolts because of the paucity of cracks. Fortunately, however, the rock on the upper section was far better than the rock below, and even though the summit area bristled with overhangs, it was clear that the route would go. Rather than rappel to the ground 500 feet below, the climbers prepared their bivouac.

The wind remained gusty all night, and the temperature dropped into the thirties. One disadvantage of having the six-foot-five Kor along, ruminated Hurley, was that he took up so much room on the bivouac ledge! The ledge, which had looked so spacious in the afternoon, was perceived by dawn as a sloping, lumpy ramp. But all bivouacs do come to an end, and the sun mercifully struck the eastern side of the tower with early warmth.

Layton Kor on the last difficult pitch of the route; George Hurley belays. The climbers are in the same position as in Bishop's aerial photograph. Huntley Ingalls.

Kor soon began drilling his way up the next section—the pitch was another which lacked cracks for pitons—but it wasn't long before he shouted down that he was on easy ground just below the summit. Bishop chose this moment to have his chartered plane make a close pass, and for a few seconds the climbers forgot their own precarious position as the plane banked frightfully close to the rock.

By noon the climbers were eating lunch on the mesa-like summit, trying to relax before facing the frightening rappels. Only a few of the rappels were routine; most had pendulums at the bottom or transfers at hanging bolt stations. By dark, three tired men had reached the welcome, flat earth.

Fifty-two expansion bolts had been placed, half for direct aid and half for anchors. Most of the belay stations had three anchor bolts, which may seem overly cautious to climbers unfamiliar with sandstone. But Kor had climbed enough in the Southwest to realize that a few extra minutes of drilling meant a distinct increase in peace of mind.

"We Climbed Utah's Skyscraper Rock" appeared in the November 1962 issue of *National Geographic*. While written for the layman, Ingalls' article managed to capture much of the flavor experienced by first ascenders on unknown sandstone. Whether the article itself caused a renaissance in desert climbing is not clear, but hundreds of climbers soon ventured to the desert. The Titan route became the most popular of the major desert climbs, even though only about ten ascents were made in the decade following the first ascent.

On the third ascent, three climbers put up with a steady drizzle throughout the upper pitches and the descent. Observing at first hand how the mud curtains were formed, these highly experienced big-wall men practiced extra caution on the descent. It was not until reaching the ground that one of the climbers noticed to his horror that grooves had been cut halfway through his rappel carabiners by the abrasive red mud which had been forced against the aluminum by the pressure of the sliding rope. The unusable carabiners now hang in ceremonial display at the climber's house as a reminder of the unexpected dangers of rockclimbing.

The Titan is much more than loose rock, sand in the eyes, shifting pitons, drizzles, and dangerous rappels, however. Anyone who walks in its vicinity will be awed by its multitude of bizarre rock forms, startling colors, and fascinating vegetation. Those who climb the Titan may find the landscape and climbing so different from that found in other areas that the experience becomes distinctly unearthly. Equally dramatic is the contrast between the glaring midday sun and the soft light from a full moon, which renders the region hauntingly beautiful. The convoluted rock casts a network of eerie shadows at such a time, and the howl of the coyote seems eminently appropriate.

First ascent

Layton Kor, George Hurley, and Huntley Ingalls. May 12–13, 1962.

Elevation

The summit is approximately 5600 feet above sea level. The climbing route is about 650 feet long.

Difficulty

IV, 5.8, A3.

Time

The route can be done easily in one day by experienced sandstone climbers, but many climbers have bivouacked at the ledge 500 feet up.

Map

USGS quadrangle: Castle Valley, scale 1:62,500.

Route description

From the town of Moab drive north on the main highway for a few miles to the Colorado River. Turn right on a paved road which goes along the south side of the river. Follow this road twenty-one miles to a turn-off marked "Fisher Towers." Take the dirt road two miles to its end.

A path wanders south around the bases of various towers for about two miles. Shortly after passing underneath the west face of the Titan, leave the trail and work around benches which lead to the east side of the monolith. Climb gullies and benches to the notch which separates the Titan from the bluff to the northeast.

The first 300 feet of climbing lie in an obvious crack system, and the belay spots are easy to locate. This steep section is mostly artificial climbing. From a belay station below a blank wall, traverse right on bolts, under an overhang, for 15 feet to a slot. Mixed aid and free climbing leads to a notch.

Next, climb 5.8 cracks (with some aid) to a rounded arête, a fine belay spot. Traverse left on a friction ledge until it is possible to climb 5.6 cracks which lead to the bivouac ledge. Step right around a corner from this ledge and nail 30 feet up to the main arête of the Titan. Ascend a 70-foot bolt ladder to a wild belay station. Continue on bolts and pitons past the summit overhangs to a good ledge. A hundred feet of class 4 scrambling leads to the summit.

The descent follows the climbing route and is time-consuming. A short rope should be fixed over the bolt traverse after the initial 300-foot aid section. This greatly facilitates the descent, although it is not absolutely necessary.

Equipment

Carry a selection of twenty pitons (up to three-inch) and a standard rack of chocks. As mentioned above, take along a short rope to leave fixed at the bolt traverse.

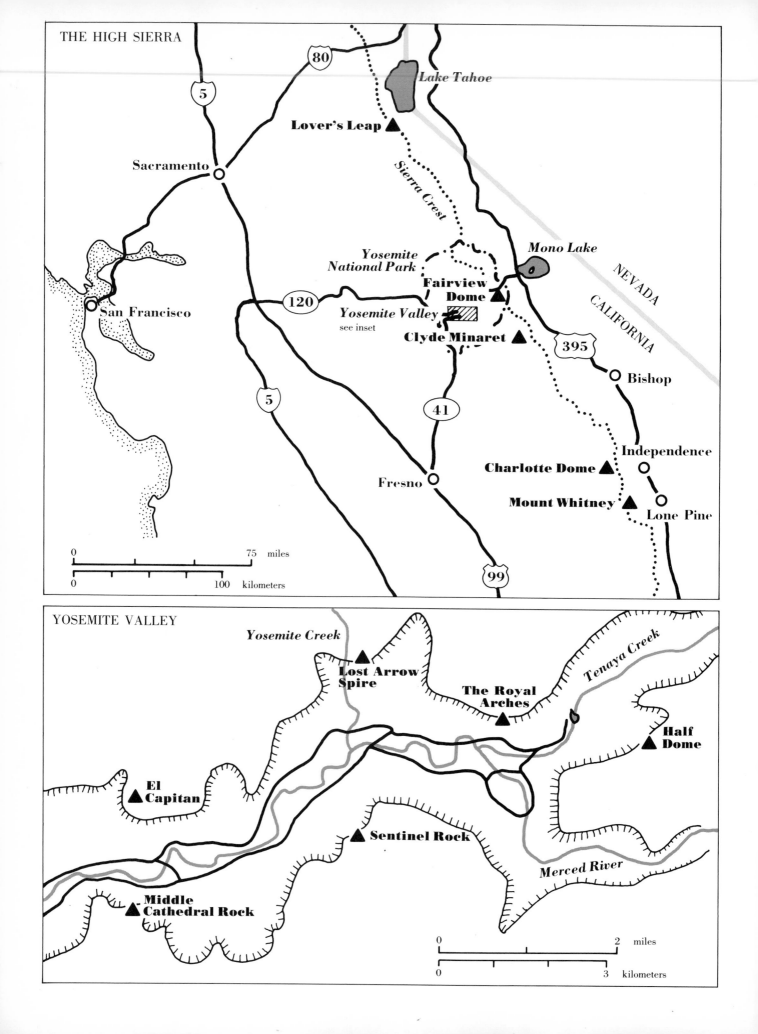

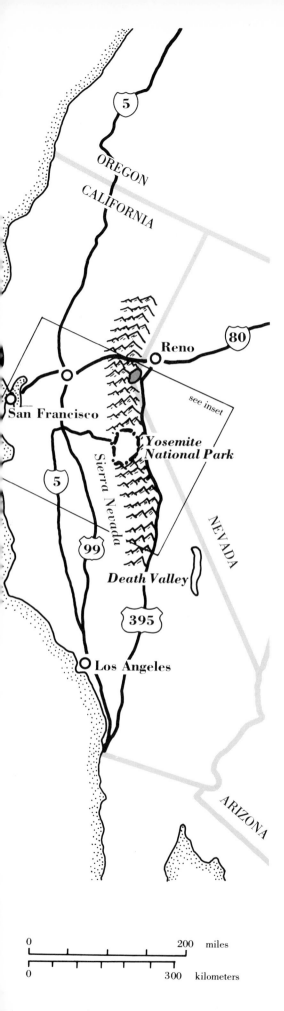

0   200   miles

0   300   kilometers

California

The phrase "sunny California" is not unfounded; the Golden State has such a benign climate that even in midwinter there are long periods during which no precipitation is recorded in the High Sierra. It therefore should come as no surprise to find that there are no substantial glaciers in the state. If neophytes wish to master snow and ice techniques, they are well advised to head north. Rockclimbers, however, flock to California by the thousands to enjoy the state's fine weather and high-quality granite. This gratifying combination exists nowhere else on earth, and appreciative climbers can be observed clinging to steep, warm rock during every month of the year. The popularity of California climbing is a fairly recent phenomenon, however, for it demands the employment of rope techniques which were virtually unknown half a century ago.

Rockclimbing began surprisingly late in California in comparison to many other North American climbing areas. In the summer of 1931 a cadre of young and enthusiastic Sierra Club climbers were trained in rope management by the noted Harvard climber Robert Underhill. Two years later a small band of these San Francisco–based adventurers felt ready to tackle the intimidating walls of Yosemite Valley; during the remainder of the decade they established many excellent routes.

Following World War II, a new generation of climbers, better equipped and more daring than their predecessors, accomplished Yosemite climbs considered to be impossible just a decade earlier. Skilled parties soon ascended the fearsome faces of Half Dome and El Capitan. With the development of durable chrome–moly pitons and wide-angle pitons in the early 1960s, even more dramatic routes were established, and word of Yosemite's high-level rockclimbing soon began to spread worldwide.

During much of this frenetic activity in the "granite crucible"—as Chris Jones has called Yosemite Valley—other climbing areas in California were somewhat neglected. Not until the 1960s did enterprising mountaineers ferret out the hidden walls of the High Sierra, discovering magnificent climbing in a remote setting. Other formations on the periphery of the High Sierra, such as Lover's Leap, also were explored during this period.

With such an enormous number of classic California routes available, we agonized over which routes to include. Making our choices for Yosemite Valley, which now has more than 800 routes, proved especially frustrating. While we were reluctant to omit such wonderful climbs as Higher Cathedral Spire and Half Dome's Snake Dike, we feel confident that our seven Valley selections not only are superb routes but also represent the evolution of Valley climbing in its first thirty years.

The Royal Arches

On a recent autumn morning, on a wide ledge 600 feet above the just-awakening campgrounds of Yosemite Valley, an unlikely assortment of rockclimbers briefly intertwined ropes and conversation before dispersing. Most impatient to get on were two young men from Munich; after a few minutes of halting English and rapid-fire German, they attacked the wall above and quickly disappeared. Taking things a bit more leisurely, the author of the Valley guidebook and the editor of *Ascent* chatted with two people, one a forty-five-year-old woman who recently had returned from the Karakoram. The *Ascent* editor recalled that he actually had crossed paths with the woman in that far-off place, much as they were presently doing. As the guidebook writer mumbled something about it being a small world, voices rose from below,

◀ *The Royal Arches. The climbing route ends at the Jungle, a large grove of trees from which the Royal Arch Cascade emerges.* Steve Roper.

and in a few minutes a party of three reached the ledge and joined the conversation. One of the newcomers, a stocky old man nursing a muscle he had pulled on the first pitch, spoke no English, and it took a few minutes before the others realized that he happened to be one of the legendary climbers of all time, Riccardo Cassin. Thoughts of the Walker Spur, the Piz Badile, and McKinley's Cassin Ridge passed through each climber's mind as the group prepared for the next pitches.

Why had such a diverse assortment of characters assembled in one place? What was the lure? Was this ledge located on the Lost Arrow, Half Dome, or El Capitan?

The answer will surprise many climbers: the "lowly" Royal Arches route was the scene of this brief encounter. Extremely popular during the 1950s, this long and varied route fell into some disrepute in the next two decades because of its relative ease. Formerly used by resident climbers as an early-season conditioning climb, it came to be considered by these climbers as a route for "duffers." Perhaps this judgment is accurate, but if so, the climb must be one of the best duffer routes in the United States.

The route's name is something of a misnomer, for the spectacular and unique formation known as the Royal Arches lies hundreds of yards

east of the climbing route and is so imposing that no direct route was made on it until 1960. But in 1935, with no routes to the rim ever having been done in this vast section of wall, "Royal Arches" was the most obvious geographical name for the route described here. In that year Morgan Harris and two other Sierra Club climbers made the first attempt, having picked out a route which contained many trees and ledge systems. One cause for concern was the 200-foot blank section which would have to be traversed two-thirds of the way to the rim; the massive arch which dominated the wall above certainly would prove an impossible obstacle.

On Harris' first attempt this blank area wasn't even reached, for waning light made it necessary to retreat. Harris and his companions returned in the spring of 1936 and were able to climb a few hundred feet higher. To his surprise, instead of 200 feet of smooth rock, Harris found an unexpected and very welcome ledge which ran across the face. There was just one problem: a fifteen-foot blank section would have to be crossed before the ledge could be reached. However, the resourceful climbers managed to swing across, dangling from a piton driven higher on the wall. The now-famous First Pendulum Pitch was a key one, and the climbers rappelled, convinced the route would go.

On October 9, 1936, Harris was joined by a companion from the previous trip, Ken Adam, and a newcomer to the route, Kenneth Davis. The climbers quickly retraced the familiar terrain and soon were standing forlornly at the far end of the key ledge. Another surprise: the ledge ended once again at a blank spot. Nevertheless, the same swinging technique used earlier worked once more, and the three men soon faced a perplexing problem that has amused, frightened, and captured the imagination of the thousands of climbers who have followed them. Across an otherwise insurmountable chasm lay a thirty-foot pine tree, dead for many years, but forming a perfect bridge to the easier upper section of the route. Less than a foot in diameter and only vaguely attached to the remnant of its trunk, the tree had fallen as if directed by the god of rockclimbers. The three pioneers shinnied and squirmed up the tilted log and within a few hours had reached a point just below the rim.

Progress directly upward once again was barred by giant overhangs, but the climbers could look across an improbable slab toward a heavily forested area which they knew marked the end of the difficulties. Although this slab was nearly 200 feet across, its angle was only about thirty degrees. What bothered the three men most was the lack of protection, for the slab was totally

The Royal Arches Route lies near the shadowed ribs at left center of photograph. The northwest face of Half Dome rises in the background. Ed Cooper.

crackless. Realizing that retreat was out of the question because of the traverses, the men pondered the situation for several minutes. Gingerly, Harris began to traverse the slab, finding few protuberances for his feet. Pine needles covered the lower-angled spots on the slab and had to be carefully brushed aside. As Harris traversed farther and farther from the safety of his belay, his partners became intensely watchful and silent. At last they saw Harris disappear into the forest. Somewhat shaken by the potential danger involved, Adam and Davis were belayed across. Soon, surrounded by enormous incense

cedars, Douglas firs, and ponderosa pines, the three climbers were relaxing at the welcome year-round spring near the unroping point.

The dead tree, now known as the Rotten Log, was mentioned only casually in the first-ascent party's write-up as "an old tree-trunk." In the second-ascent party's account of the route, the log is referred to simply as a "dead-tree bridge." But by the mid-1950s, when the climb had become *de rigueur* for all Valley climbers, the Rotten Log was by far the most talked-about pitch. As the years passed, the log naturally continued to rot, and its imminent demise was predicted annually. Nowadays the infamous trunk has taken on a leprous appearance, and it vibrates wildly with every passage. It seems a safe bet that when it finally goes, there will be a climber astride it. No one looks forward to this possibility.

Over the years other pitches have gained notoriety. The Bear Hug Pitch, at the one-third point, is well named, for three cracks split an otherwise holdless section, and the climber must thrust hands and feet into various cracks while hugging the intervening ribs. Although not especially difficult, this pitch has given some Valley newcomers trouble, since the required hand jams and friction-stemming seem endemic only to Yosemite.

The First Pendulum Pitch was climbed free in the late 1950s. With solid protection well above the climber, it is one of the safest 5.9 pitches in the valley, and even though only a minority of climbers make it across the short section of minuscule holds, it is certainly fun to try. The exposure and beauty of the monolithic slab make the lead a thrilling one, even for spectators. The Second Pendulum Pitch also has been climbed free, and yet because of its less exposed position, it lacks the character of the first and does not linger so long in the memory.

Using cross-pressure techniques, Brock Wagstaff works up the Bear Hug Pitch. Steve Roper.

At the end of the route, the now-heralded Traverse into the Jungle continues to provide the excitement and terror encountered by the first ascenders. As with the Bear Hug Pitch, the traverse gives pause to Valley neophytes. The successful traverse depends upon mastery of the deceptively simple "trick" of keeping the weight directly over the feet. There are no handholds whatsoever, yet many climbers lean in and try to dig some in the granite. As they do so, their feet begin to ooze off the slab. Since protection is nonexistent, and since the leader and follower are in much the same boat, the tension which accrues at the end of the long route is nearly palpable. Yet few tumble, and the spring and surprisingly lush vegetation make the unroping ritual especially memorable.

With the enormous summit arch looming overhead, the leader moves across the First Pendulum Pitch. Steve Roper.

First ascent

Morgan Harris, Ken Adam, and Kenneth Davis. October 9, 1936.

Elevation

The climb is approximately 1300 feet in length, and the unroping spot is 5400 feet above sea level.

Difficulty

III, 5.6, A1. Two 5.9 pitches are encountered if the route is done totally free.

Time

The route has been soloed in less than an hour, but the usual range of times runs from four hours for a strong party to a very long day for a large group. Many parties have bivouacked.

Map

A special USGS topographic sheet, Yosemite Valley, with a scale of 1:24,000, is excellent for identifying valley features.

Useful references

Climber's Guide to Yosemite Valley. A schematic drawing of the route is included in *Yosemite Climbs*.

Route description

From the Ahwahnee Hotel parking lot, walk toward the cliff until a wide path is found; take this east for a few hundred feet to a stream bed. Follow the stream bed up to the cliff and walk east along it to an obvious, slanting chimney. The walk from the parking lot takes less than five minutes.

The 5.5 chimney is harder than it looks, and the rock is quite polished. From the top of this first pitch continue east along a series of huge "steps"; these contain a few short class 5 sections. From the top of the highest step, some 600 feet above the valley floor, climb more or less straight up for about five pitches. This section is rather obvious; simply follow crack systems and trees.

The next four pitches also are easy to follow: a pendulum (or free); an easy ledge traverse; another pendulum (or free); and the Rotten Log. Little vertical elevation is gained on these four pitches. From the ledge above the Log, climb up about 250 feet to a huge tree. The next pitch diagonals up and left and ends on ledges at the east edge of the Traverse into the Jungle. There are several ways to go in this area, but they all present about the same difficulty. An intermediate belay spot can be arranged about fifty feet out.

From the unroping spot in the Jungle, a trail can be followed up and west for 100 feet or so until it becomes obvious to clamber over a

Riccardo Cassin ascends the shaky Rotten Log.   Steve Roper.

cliff band onto the slopes above. Easy and rapid progress can be made east across slabs and brush to the Washington Column, a distance of half a mile. From the saddle between the Column and the slope to the north, a faint trail can be followed east. This trail descends slightly but primarily contours for several hundred yards, remaining above cliffs. When safely past these cliffs, slabs are reached. At this point turn in the direction of Glacier Point and descend class 2 and 3 granite to the forest below.

Equipment

The climb can be accomplished easily using chocks (carry ten) and the fixed pitons which are found at key sections.

Remarks

In springtime copious quanties of water pour over the area just beyond the First Pendulum Pitch, so it is wise to check this from the ground before proceeding.

Lost Arrow Spire

40

Richard Leonard, a key figure in early American roped climbing, and his elite group, known as the Cragmont Climbing Club, ventured to Yosemite Valley in 1933 to try their skills on its awesome granite cliffs. During the next two years they established several excellent routes, including ascents of the two Cathedral Spires, near-vertical pillars which demanded bold climbing and meticulous planning. It was the glamorous pinnacles, rather than the walls, which attracted early adventurers, and the existence of the Lost Arrow did not escape Leonard. Located a few hundred yards from the wondrous drop of Upper Yosemite Fall, the Arrow's summit was at the same level as the canyon rim but was separated from it by a horrific gap of 125 feet. The slender and monolithic spire joined the cliff at an airy notch 250 feet below rim level.

◀ *A climber makes the airy tyrolean traverse from the Lost Arrow Spire during the twentieth-anniversary ascent. Another climber can be seen halfway up the right edge of the pinnacle. Ed Cooper.*

In 1935 Leonard and several others used a rope to descend exposed slabs which overlooked the notch far below. Later Leonard recorded his impression of this day: "We obtained a view that was terrifying even to those who had climbed the Cathedral Spires. It was unanimously agreed that we would never attempt it." Although he kept that promise, Leonard retained quite an interest in the proposed climb, for two years later he referred to it as "probably the most fascinating unsolved problem in the state." And in 1941 he called the spire "the nightmare of all those who have inspected it closely."

In the 1930s a few desultory attempts were made to reach the notch from below, using the long slit now known as the Lost Arrow Chimney. But these forays failed not far off the ground, even though Leonard had once called the route "terrifyingly clear." By the start of World War II no real progress had been made, and the Lost Arrow stood as alone as it had been on the day when the Indian maiden Tee-hee-neh supposedly was lowered on joined pine saplings into the Arrow notch to recover the corpse of her lover, who had lost an arrow and then his footing on the treacherous rounded rim.

A new breed of climbers emerged after the war. Less conservative and better equipped than Leonard's generation, these climbers soon began thinking seriously of the Arrow. Among the newcomers was a forty-seven-year-old Swiss blacksmith named John Salathé, who only recently had learned to climb. Salathé had arranged to meet two companions on the rim above the Arrow one mid-August day in 1946, but through a misunderstanding his friends failed to show. Rather than waste the day, Salathé made an astonishing decision: he would rappel to the notch and take a close look at the pinnacle. An hour later he became the first man ever to stand amid the shattered blocks which separate the Arrow from the rim. As expected, the side of the formation facing the rim was blank, but Salathé noted a thin ledge which ran around the east side. He fastened safety ropes to boulders in the notch and edged out toward the end of the ledge. In the words of Anton Nelson, who later figured prominently in the Arrow saga, "it was like stepping out of a window from the hundredth floor of the Empire State Building onto a window ledge." The 1400-foot drop didn't faze Salathé, and he slowly began pounding pitons into an incipient crack which led upward for a few feet. Instead of using the soft iron pitons his peers used, Salathé had hand-forged his own pitons from Model-A axles. Instead of buckling when hammered into imperfect cracks, these excellently crafted pitons could be forced into narrow and bottomed cracks since they were so much tougher than ordinary pitons. Salathé slowly worked up to a ledge thirty feet above. To his delight, another crack appeared where least expected, and though it was overhanging and rotten, he soon pulled onto the four-foot-wide ledge which now bears his name. He was seventy-five feet above the notch, and his position on the outer face of the spire was as wild and lonely as any Yosemite climber had ever experienced. But daylight was failing, and Salathé realized he should call a halt to his venture.

A week later Salathé returned with San Francisco climber John Thune. The two men quickly ascended to Salathé Ledge. Difficult and time-consuming direct aid led upward for eighty feet, and the blacksmith's miraculous pitons continued to do their job well. But once again darkness was near, and Salathé decided to retreat when he realized that the remaining fifty feet consisted of blank granite which would require many expansion bolts.

Meanwhile, other climbers had watched Salathé's progress with intense and envious eyes. As Nelson later coyly wrote, "it must be admitted that competition is the essence of sport and the spur to thought." A week later, on August 31, Nelson, Jack Arnold, Fritz Lippmann, and Robin Hansen hiked to the rim with a clever plan: if a rope could be thrown from the rim over the top of the spire, it might be possible to reach the rope from the other side and use it for aid. Why did the four-some come up with this novel method of climbing the Arrow,

The Lost Arrow, its summit barely protruding above rim level, casts a distinctive shadow on the cliff. To the left is Upper Yosemite Fall, framed by sheets of rime.   Ed Cooper.

especially knowing that Salathé had been within a few feet of the top? First, it must be remembered that only Salathé had the miraculous pitons. In addition, the Arrow's legend of invulnerability must have negatively influenced the more traditional climbers. And, of course, that last fifty feet of "flint-hard and flawless" granite, to which Nelson later referred, seemed to justify the controversial measure.

By late afternoon Hansen, after numerous tries, managed a perfect toss—the light line, weighted with lead sinkers, snaked over the minuscule summit and fell swiftly onto Salathé Ledge. The first stage of the plan had worked.

Nelson and Arnold began the climb the following morning, while the other two climbers prepared for their own crucial role: setting up a complex system of ropes and anchors. Using traditional soft pitons, the climbing team was nearly stymied on the first aid section. Nelson ruefully wished for the pitons of his predecessor. In a later statement, which should serve forever as an example of what *never* to say in print, Nelson wrote: "As we further diminish the crack's possibilities, it becomes doubtful that many others will ever climb the Lost Arrow." By the end of the day the pair had gained only thirty feet, something of an embarrassment. On the following day progress was halted completely—they could not repeat Salathé's route to the next ledge. Yet, showing the same originality that had characterized the over-the-top strategy, the two men lassoed a horn twenty feet above them and prusiked onto Salathé Ledge. What skill couldn't conquer, ingenuity could. The light line which had swayed in the wind for forty hours awaited them, as well as the cairn built by Salathé on his startling solo effort.

The climbers carefully pulled nylon ropes over the summit and anchored them to blocks on the ledge. Finally a means to the summit was open: by using prusik knots the two men could mount the rope with confidence. Arnold was chosen to go first, since, as Nelson put it, "the stern code of the climber decrees that the lightest man shall lead doubtful pitches." Arnold furiously

With Upper Yosemite Fall in the background, a climber moves up the third pitch. Bill Feuerer.

smoked three cigarettes, then placed his weight on the rope and moved upward on his lonely odyssey to the Arrow's summit. Would the rope stay put, he wondered, or would it pop off the narrow, rounded tip? Even though he was belayed from both the ledge and the rim, no one was certain what Arnold's fate would be if the rope slipped off. However, there were no incidents, and as the late afternoon sun turned the walls golden, Arnold pulled onto the incredibly exposed summit. Soon Nelson joined him and yodels reverberated from the cliffs.

The climb was not over, however, for the game plan called for an aerial traverse back to the rim. Hours went by as deep holes were drilled for the summit anchors. Ropes were hauled back and forth, and belays were arranged. It was pitch black when Arnold—the lightest-man rule being in force once again—cast loose from the Arrow tip for the 125-foot journey. Those on the rim had a momentary scare when curses and grunts were heard from the void, but Arnold merely had encountered a minor complication and soon stood among his friends on the rim. Lippmann desired to visit the summit as a reward for his unsung role, so he traveled quickly across the "Lost Arrow Trolley and Scenic Railway," touched the spire's summit, and then returned. Robin Hansen, whose toss of the light line had ensured success, declined the

offer—it was very late and a job in the city awaited him the next morning. Soon Nelson had returned and the umbilical cords were coiled; the Arrow stood alone once again.

The Arrow had been climbed—or had it? As Nelson later wrote, "spectacular and effective though [the 1946 ascent] was, this maneuver required very little real climbing; it was in effect an admission of the Arrow's unclimbability." The top had succumbed to a rope trick, but could it be climbed by conventional methods? On Labor Day weekend in 1947, Salathé returned to the Arrow with Nelson. Their objective was a bold one: the ascent of the Lost Arrow Chimney. In four days of arduous climbing, by far the most extreme ever done in America up until that time, they attained the Arrow notch. Above, they followed Salathé's cracks to the final blank section, where about eight bolts had to be placed to reach the summit.

During the next eight years approximately ten more ascents followed: two parties proceeded via the Arrow Chimney; the remainder climbed just the free-standing spire. Nine bolts were added on the pinnacle when various climbers found the aid cracks unusable. In 1956 a party led by Mark Powell, uneasy at this demeaning of Salathé's great route, made a decision which was to have significant implications. Using pitons, Powell bypassed the non-Salathé bolts; then the second man chopped the offending nine bolts. While this act upset the less talented Valley climbers, it pleased

many of the hard-core ones. Many fanatical American climbers were to emulate Powell's act over the next decade, thus confirming the basic ethic of leaving a route the way the first ascenders "created" it. For those who carried their courage in their rucksacks, as Reinhold Messner so aptly put it, this dictum was infuriating, and splinter groups broke away from the mainstream climbing community and placed bolts without regard to popular opinion. Does climbing have "rules"? The debate still goes on, in one form or another.

The next chapter in the Arrow saga is a sad one. In March 1960, Irving Smith, a seventeen-year-old from Fresno, California, fell from the Arrow notch 500 feet into the Arrow Chimney. He was the first of his group to rappel into the notch and thus was out of sight when the fall took place. What happened never will be known with certainty, but it seems probable that Smith either rappelled off the end of the rope or lost his balance while making the tricky transition from the rappel onto unstable blocks in the notch. Rangers deemed the body irrecoverable and closed the Arrow Chimney to climbers for a year out of respect.

When Yvon Chouinard and Steve Roper made the ninth ascent of the Arrow Chimney in May 1961, they found the remains, barely recognizable as those of a human, on a large chockstone. Not surprisingly, during the first solo ascent of the Arrow Spire a few months later, Roper checked his rappel setup so carefully and so often that he nearly gave up the attempt before setting foot on the actual climb.

By the mid-1960s the climb of the Lost Arrow Spire was almost mandatory for serious rockclimbers. When out-of-state mountaineers drove into Yosemite Valley, it was invariably El Capitan which first attracted their attention, but next on their tour of the area was the notorious Arrow. Of the many hundreds of ascents made during these years, the vast majority were of the Arrow Spire only. (By this time the Arrow Chimney had been climbed free, but the rock was decomposed and the climbing unpleasant.) Few made the aerial traverse to the rim, since two rappels and a straightforward prusik back to the rim seemed just as fast and far less complicated. On the twentieth-anniversary ascent, however, fifteen climbers did the route, and all returned via the spectacular tyrolean traverse.

The leader surmounts the final obstacle on the last pitch.   Don Lauria.

241

What is the route like today? Nelson felt he had destroyed the cracks in 1946, but in actuality he simply altered them, as did all subsequent parties. In the late 1950s prospective Arrow climbers knew they had to include "sawed-off horizontals" in their piton selection. These non-tapered, truncated stubs of iron worked perfectly in the quarter-inch-wide bottomed cracks. But soon, because of wear in the cracks, "sawed-off angles" were needed. With the advent of chrome—moly pitons the cracks sometimes became wider than they were deep. Angle pitons two inches wide were pounded into shallow holes, tied off with webbing close to the rock to reduce leverage, and used for upward progress. Recent climbers, using chocks, have stopped the wear and tear on the cracks, but the scars will remain forever. Using these scars, modern climbers have managed to climb much of the route free, and two 5.10 pitches are encountered. Most climbers use aid, however, and even with the mutilated rock, the climb—or the feeling of the climb—is still much the same as it was in John Salathé's day.

First ascent

Anton Nelson, Jack Arnold, Robin Hansen, and Fritz Lippmann. August 31–September 2, 1946. The first true climbing ascent of the spire was made by Nelson and John Salathé on September 3, 1947.

Elevation

The summit is about 6900 feet above sea level. The climbing route is approximately 200 feet long.

Difficulty

III, 5.5, A3. Done mostly free, the rating is 5.10, A2.

Time

Allow a full day from the rim back to the rim.

Map

Special USGS topographic sheet: Yosemite Valley, scale 1:24,000.

Useful reference

Climber's Guide to Yosemite Valley.

Route description

Follow the Yosemite Falls Trail to Yosemite Point and then walk a few hundred feet west along the rim. From a good-sized pine, rappel 130 feet to a small alcove behind a flake. Another rappel, this one about 115 feet, brings one to the notch. Both rappel ropes must be left in place to facilitate the return (unless one is returning via a tyrolean traverse).

Walk out a narrow ledge on the east side of the pinnacle; then, using some aid, attain a good ledge 30 feet above. Traverse left around a rotten corner and nail 20 feet to Salathé Ledge. The next pitch is the crux: traverse left a few feet, nail for about 20 feet, move left again, and nail to a sling belay from bolts. This 80-foot pitch has been done all free. Ascend a bolt ladder to a steep step leading to a friction slope and the summit. Two rappels (125 feet and 70 feet) lead back to the notch.

Equipment

Carry a selection of fifteen chocks, up to two-and-a-half inches, in addition to five pitons. Take two extra ropes to leave in place over the rappels to the notch.

Sentinel Rock
Steck – Salathé
Route

The leader moves up the flared, overhanging slot known as the Wilson Overhang. Mike Kennedy.

Every mountaineer has favorite routes to which he or she invariably returns. They may be short, easy climbs which afford enjoyable introductions to beginners, or they may be annual classics which provide early-season conditioning. However, rare is the route which attracts distinguished climbers for repeated ascents throughout their careers. The long and difficult north face of Yosemite's Sentinel Rock is just such a route. Chuck Pratt participated in an early ascent of the intimidating wall in 1959, completed his twelfth climb of the face in 1979, and hopes to return a dozen more times. Royal Robbins took part in five of the first sixteen ascents. Allen Steck has done the route only three times, but his ascents spanned a quarter of a century. What is the magic that attracts so many repeaters?

Because the 1600-foot-high north wall of Sentinel lies directly across the valley from the traditional climbers' camp, it is likely that its crack systems, ledges, and buttresses have been studied more carefully than any other cliff in Yosemite.

Seen in the morning, the wall appears essentially featureless, for in the shade the granite takes on a uniformly gray color, creating the false impression that the face is nearly as smooth as that of El Capitan. When the sun strikes the wall obliquely in the early afternoon, however, the face's thousands of cracks and ledges emerge in bold

relief. The formation comes alive as shadows race across the wall, merging and vanishing. In the late afternoon the yellowing light bathes the valley, and the north face becomes fixed in tone, the shadows stabilized. In a short while the sun's golden hues steal the show. Finally, as the sun drops through the haze of the Central Valley, alpenglow briefly floods the wall before the rock once again becomes just another drab cliff.

Sierra Club climbers perused the wall in the 1930s and even made forays to the base of the steep section of cliff. However, although pre–World War II Yosemite rock-climbers were adventurous indeed, they were neither experienced enough nor bold enough for such an awesome undertaking. The most logical way up the north face was never in doubt, for on the right side of the wall climbers saw the 800-foot-high Flying Buttress, and a continuous crack system was easily discerned on its right side. Although the buttress was steep, it was clear that the ascent to its top was possible. In the upper section of cliff, beginning a few hundred feet above the top of the Flying Buttress, lay a long, dank slot—the Great Chimney—which never saw the sun. The smooth middle section which rose above the buttress to the chimney was called the Headwall, and it was this relatively short stretch which bothered those potential climbers who viewed it from the campground. How blank was it?

Various attempts by Allen Steck and others in the late 1940s failed low on the route. The first substantial success came in May 1950, when Bill Long and Phil Bettler managed to reach the top of the Flying Buttress. The pair took two days for the ascent, finding the climbing strenuous and time-consuming. They needed direct aid on almost every pitch, although not continuously.

◀ *The north face of Sentinel Rock.* Steve Roper.

The Headwall revealed a few disconnected hairline cracks, but it looked grim indeed. Without even trying it, Long and Bettler retreated, fully satisfied with their exploration.

Allen Steck, the instigator of the early attempts, had spent the summer of 1949 in Europe and had been the first American ever to climb one of the fabled north walls of the Alps. Steck thus was aware of the complexities of big-wall climbing and knew that Europeans had been doing routes the caliber of Sentinel for two decades. Unable to participate in the May 1950 venture, Steck knew after that climb that the time had come: he soon would be off to Mount Waddington for a month and realized the prize would be lost if he hesitated. The Fourth of July weekend was the next possible date, but Long, his preferred companion, couldn't make it then. Quickly going through a mental list of climbing partners, Steck came up with no one until he remembered John Salathé.

Salathé, whose adventures on the Lost Arrow are recounted earlier in this book, was then fifty-one years old. His hand-forged pitons, so welcome on the Arrow, could prove useful on the Headwall, and Steck had little trouble persuading the blacksmith to accompany him.

The afternoon air was stifling as Steck and Salathé drove into the valley. Tourists thronged the campgrounds, played in the Merced River, and overabsorbed the burning rays of the sun. It was not an auspicious time to begin a multi-day

ascent. As they packed, Steck noticed an odd two-gallon tin in the pile. Informed that it contained dates and little else, he remembered that his partner was regarded by some as an eccentric. But as they progressed smoothly up the steep cracks of the Flying Buttress, it became evident that the two men were a well-matched team, if not in matters of food ("Allen, if only you had not eaten meat it would go better for you"), then surely in what counted— the climbing. By the second night they had reached the top of the buttress and the base of the dreaded Headwall.

For much of the third day Salathé labored on this problem, pounding his superb pitons into bottomed cracks. Late in the day the pair moved across the steep and difficult slab which separated them from the Great Chimney. Once in this slot, Steck made a dramatic lead up a narrow jamcrack which widened into a severely flared and terrifying chimney. He collapsed onto a belay ledge, out of breath and very thirsty. The climbers had taken only eight quarts of water, and with the precious fluid almost gone, Steck stared at the swimmers 2000 feet below. If only they would stop splashing, he thought, as he pressed his lips to moist, mossy patches in the recesses of the slot. It was a short while before he thought to study the terrain above, and to his dismay there was no route! Eighty feet above his head a jutting ceiling on one wall sealed

245

the chimney and appeared to bar further progress. The outside of the chimney, which seemed to overhang the swimmers below, was far too wide to stem. The team appeared to have reached an impasse.

The two climbers endured a cramped and depressing bivouac, mitigated only by the balmy temperature. Throughout the night Salathé munched on his dates; Steck's food was far too salty to be palatable without liquid. Before the next climb, Steck reflected, perhaps he would give more thought to his cuisine.

In the morning a short pitch took the climbers to a belay stance just below the obstruction. Chimneying out as far as possible to take a look, Salathé discovered a thin, intermittent crack in the ceiling which appeared to lead around the outside of the slot. Placing pitons back to back, and upside-down as well, he miraculously disappeared around the corner, shouting down after an interminable time that the route was clear. It was a brilliant lead, and it assured success. The remaining 400-foot section was easier, even though slow and awkward aid climbing delayed the men's progress.

A fourth bivouac was no more comfortable than the previous ones, but around noon on the fifth day they finally emerged onto the isolated,

sandy summit. By this time even the imperturbable Salathé was parched ("Al, if only I could have just a little orange juice"). Far below, in a brush-filled side canyon, was a trace of white which indicated a stream, and the climbers quickly descended toward it. Steck, the impatient youth, surged ahead. Brought up short by a huge drop-off, he cursed and struggled back upward, finally catching up with his partner, who was carefully weaving his way through a labyrinth of gullies. Bursting ahead once again, Steck plowed through a brushfield and plunged fully clothed into a shallow pool. He vividly recalled this scene for many years.

Steck later would regret a sentence in his fascinating account of the climb in the *Sierra Club Bulletin*: "The second ascent should do better, if there should ever be one." As he reveled in the pool that sultry afternoon, he surely did not envision himself ever again struggling up those flared chimneys. How could he have predicted that times would change so radically that by his third ascent the wall would have been climbed by perhaps three hundred parties? When Salathé was told many years later that the route had been climbed in an astonishing three-and-a-quarter hours, he shook his head without comprehension, declaring, "Oh, no, perhaps three days now that all the bolts are in."

Present-day rockclimbers look upon the route as an excellent, long free climb noted for its varied and unrelenting crack climbing. By 1960

A climber wedged in the Narrows, the most notorious section of the route. Mike Kennedy.

246

bold climbers had eliminated direct aid from every pitch but the Head-wall, and even this obstacle now can be bypassed by a difficult variation. Of the sixteen ropelengths comprising the route, eleven are rated 5.7 or higher, and three are 5.9. Yet it is not the lure of a pure struggle which attracts so many, for there are far more demanding routes even on the same cliff. Why, then, are so many drawn to the climb? The glamour lies mainly in the quality of several pitches which rank among Yosemite's best in terms of enjoyment, safety, and historical interest.

Who would not savor, for instance, the Wilson Overhang? Named for Jim Wilson, who participated in several of the earliest attempts, the fourth pitch is an awesome sight from below. A radically flared and overhanging slot pierces a 110-degree wall, and it is easy to see why it was first climbed with aid. Led free, as it was on a very early ascent, the pitch is both strenuous and delicate. Luckily, an offset crack on one wall lies in exactly the correct place for the feet and also offers bombproof protection.

The Narrows, the most notorious pitch of the route, is the site of Salathé's key lead on the fourth day, yet paradoxically his route never has been repeated. On the second ascent, in 1954, Royal Robbins discovered an elliptical hole, three feet by one foot, in the ceiling above the belay spot. Struggling through this slit and the sinuous, claustrophobic chimney above, he found himself nearing daylight. After threading

through a few more holes, Robbins was atop the pitch—sixty feet had been climbed quickly and without direct aid. Every subsequent party has used this route, though many a cowed climber has wondered what he or she was doing in such a spot. Only after the upper part of the body has been thrust into the hole does the excitement begin, for the legs are still locked in four-foot-wide chimney position. The awkward and strenuous transition moves which are required to raise the legs into the narrow crack above are deemed "interesting" in climbers' parlance.

Pitches such as these are what attract climbers to Sentinel, and the list could go on—there are five or six memorable leads which are not as well known but which still offer safe and rewarding climbing.

Back in camp, the successful Sentinel climber can relax against a tree and watch the light play across the rock's face. Remembering with pleasure the flared slots and endless cracks, and disregarding the sore knees and bashed knuckles resulting from the encounter, the climber knows he must return.

First ascent

Allen Steck and John Salathé. June 30–July 4, 1950.

Elevation

The summit is 7038 feet above sea level. The north face is approximately 1600 feet high.

Difficulty

V, 5.9, A3.

Time

Although the route has been soloed by Henry Barber in slightly more than two hours, most parties presently take a long day to make the climb. Those desiring a more leisurely ascent will find an adequate bivouac spot atop the Flying Buttress.

Map

Special USGS topographic sheet: Yosemite Valley, scale 1:24,000.

Useful references

Climber's Guide to Yosemite Valley. A schematic drawing of the route can be found in *Yosemite Climbs.*

Route description

Walk up the Four-Mile Trail for about·one mile to a major stream crossing (usually dry by August). Ascend talus and brushy slopes to the north face; then walk up an obvious ramp which diagonals up and right. Follow this ramp and a few class 3 continuations to a large sloping area just short of the junction of the north and west faces.

Rope up and climb a few feet into a squeeze chimney; from here move up and left to a steep lieback corner. Belay at its top. Two pitches lead straight up to the base of the Wilson Overhang, a prominent flared slot. Once this problem is overcome, more crack climbing leads to an alcove. Above lies the strenuous fifth pitch, a 5.9 squeeze chimney. Three more pitches, containing many 5.7 cracks, lead to the top of the Flying Buttress.

The Headwall Pitch, the ninth, is next. Mixed climbing, including several bolts and horns for aid, leads upward for 45 feet; then traverse left to a belay ledge on a steep slab. (To avoid the Headwall, and thus do the climb free, either climb or rappel 60 feet down the east side of the Flying Buttress; then ascend 5.9 rock until reaching the belay ledge on the slab.)

A difficult and devious pitch wanders up the steep slab to the base of the Great Chimney. A 5.8 jamcrack is followed by a spectacular flared chimney. The Narrows Pitch is next, and part way up the slit one can either stay inside or move to the outside, where bolts protect 5.7 face climbing. A relatively easy chimney comes next, and this is followed by a nondescript section which leads to one of the most difficult pitches of the climb—a steep wall broken by narrow cracks which prove especially difficult for a tired climber. A final crack problem leads to ledges next to an enormous tree. The easiest pitch of the route leads to the summit from here.

To descend, walk down brush and boulders to the notch separating Sentinel from the rim. Then follow a large gully down to the east; subgullies containing short drop-offs can make the routefinding tricky. Eventually, one comes to a stream which can be followed (some class 3) to the trail.

Equipment

The climb has been done many times using only chocks (a selection of twenty up to three inches) and the fixed pitons and bolts along the route.

Middle Cathedral Rock
East Buttress

Whenever climbers gather around a campfire in Yosemite Valley, the conversation includes many diverse topics, only ninety percent of which concern rockclimbing. One subject, discussed countless times, relates to the changing popularity of those routes which have been—or are now—the most desired of Yosemite's many hundreds of climbs. Certain routes fashionable in the 1950s, for instance, are done rarely nowadays, and even routes in vogue five years ago have faded from present-day climbers' repertory. It is probably the capricious nature of climbers which accounts for the rise and fall in popularity of these routes; for as attitudes and techniques change, the majority of Yosemite rockclimbers easily switch their allegiance from one set of routes to another more suited to their latest style of climbing.

For a climb to remain in favor for twenty years is as exceptional as a Hollywood marriage surviving the same time span. One such route,

however, actually seems to *gain* repute with each passing year. Recognition of the excellence of the East Buttress Route of Middle Cathedral Rock certainly was not instantaneous; in the five years following its first ascent in 1955 it was done fewer than half a dozen times. Yet by the late 1970s, half a dozen parties were climbing the buttress each *week* during the height of the climbing season.

The route which has attracted so many for so long is not especially striking from the valley floor, largely because of Middle Cathedral's two dominating features, the northeast face and the north face. These walls, among Yosemite's most dramatic, tend to distract mountaineers from the subtle intricacies of the massive rock. Overshadowed by the grandeur of the north side of the rock, the east buttress forms the left-hand skyline when viewed from the Merced River. Although the rounded line of the buttress is steep and clean for 1000 feet, the upper section leading to the summit degenerates into an amorphous, brushy ridge. Because of this, a few purists insist the buttress is unaesthetic when viewed from afar. Pragmatists, however, realize that superb climbing often is found on ugly-looking routes. In any case, the lack of a continuous line to the top hasn't seemed to bother the thousand-plus climbers who have accomplished the ascent.

Is the route so popular because of its climbing history? It is well known that routes with a noteworthy

Dick Long moves up the bolt ladder low on the route. Lower Cathedral Spire dominates the background. Allen Steck.

past often lure climbers who wish to share, however vicariously, the adventures of its pioneers. For example, climbing the Matterhorn without reflecting on the Whymper party's tragic fall would be impossible. Similarly, the climber hanging in slings on the Lost Arrow Spire

surely recalls—and appreciates—John Salathé's laudable exploits. That the memory of such events adds immeasurably to the overall experience of a climb is indisputable. However, this theory does not explain the enduring popularity of the East Buttress Route on Middle Cathedral, for there is a dearth of information about the first few ascents, and only a handful of anecdotes have survived to the present generation.

Although many of the climbs described in this book are important in climbing history as either the most difficult or the most influential of their respective eras, the same cannot be said of the East Buttress Route. In 1955 Yosemite Valley already contained a handful of equally difficult routes, and several were far more consequential. The first ascenders of the east buttress neither advanced the level of free climbing nor developed new aid techniques. Not surprisingly, the climb which was to become so coveted merited only a laconic phrase in a single climbing journal: "New climbs included . . . the east buttress of Middle Cathedral Rock by Warren Harding, Jack Davis, and Bob Swift."

The East Buttress Route, as stated, is not especially commendable from

◀ *The northeast side of Middle Cathedral Rock. Numerous routes lie on the face to the right of the East Buttress Route. Ed Cooper.*

a distance, nor has it had a momentous history. If the route is truly a classic, then there is only one thing left to recommend it—the quality of the climbing. And, indeed, it is this characteristic that makes the climb so special, as will be made evident later. Warren Harding, however, was not concerned with the route's future popularity; he just wanted to climb it.

Harding is a slight, wild-eyed climber who bears, in Chuck Pratt's words, a "legendary resemblance to the traditional conception of Satan." In 1952, on one of his first climbs, he apparently had been the weakest member of a guided party on Wyoming's Grand Teton. This story, repeated around many a climbers' camp, could well be apocryphal, for Harding's endurance is renowned today.

During the spring of 1954 Harding became fascinated with the gigantic, untouched northern side of Middle Cathedral Rock. In May, he and three others established a three-day route up the 2000-foot-high north buttress, a fine route which is climbed frequently today. Encouraged by this success, Harding immediately decided to investigate the east buttress.

The first pitch of the projected route proved to be trivial, but soon Harding and his two companions, Bob Swift and John Whitmer, were slowed by strenuous climbing and tricky routefinding. By mid-morning the three men stood on a narrow ledge now known as Ant-Tree

Ledge. Compared to such notorious Yosemite problems as 100-degree summer heat, rattlesnakes, and slippery jamcracks, biting ants are a minor inconvenience. But the singular ferocity of the insects inhabiting a small tree and the surrounding rock were to arouse emotional responses from nearly everyone who later did the route. Swift and Whitmer endured a few miserable hours screaming invectives at the creatures while Harding labored above. No longer under attack, Harding paused several times to admonish his belayer, who was jerking like a marionette. The unique stench of formic acid from the slain ants permeated the area, adding to the unreality of the situation. Not knowing whether to laugh or cry, the three adventurers realized that at the very least the incident would make a decent campfire tale.

Not far above Ant-Tree Ledge, the trio reached a comfortable ledge at the base of an utterly blank wall. Forty feet higher were cracks which continued upward, so out came the bolt kit. Taking turns drilling inch-and-a-half-deep holes, the three men labored until sunset. Work resumed at daybreak, but before they finished their task the bolt supply ran low. Weary of the strenuous and boring drilling, the climbers were not unhappy to head for home. Even if they had made only 450 feet, it was a beginning, and they had seen crack systems above which meant the route was possible.

251

Unconcerned about competition—there was remarkably little in those days—Harding waited a full year before returning, this time with Swift and Jack Davis. After finishing the bolt ladder (all told, about eight bolts were placed) and nailing over an awkward ceiling above, the pioneers encountered free climbing of a quality they could hardly believe. A long, serrated flake shot up the seventy-degree wall, and the orange-colored granite was dotted liberally with knobs. It was the type of climbing every mountaineer enjoys: it was not hard, but certainly not trifling; one could rest on knobs, but just barely; the exposure was tremendous, yet the protection was excellent. Fifty feet above the ceiling the ecstatic leader stepped onto a beautifully shaped ledge.

Up and to their left the three men could see a long crack system composed largely of flared chimneys. Harding and his companions took another day and a half to work their way up this mostly free section. Finally, they unroped on a brushy shoulder 1000 feet above their rope-up spot. Rather than continue up the vegetated, slabby slopes above, the men traversed off the buttress by means of the Kat Walk—a broad, easy ledge which had been reached in the 1920s. This rapid descent route has been followed by most subsequent east buttress climbers.

In 1961, the year the east buttress was "discovered" by Yosemite climbers, Yvon Chouinard and Mort Hempel deviated from Harding's route, and their major variation became the standard way up the buttress. From the ledge above the ceiling (which by then was free) the two climbers spotted a crack system up and to the right. Deciding they had nothing to lose by exploring new ground, they delicately worked their way across a crackless but knobby wall and after a hundred feet reached their immediate goal, a steep dihedral. Higher, they climbed a pitch which would always stand out in their memories: the V-Slot Pitch. This 100-foot flared groove required every technique except pure friction climbing. A lieback move was followed by a strenuous handjam; a delicate face-climbing maneuver evolved into a wild stem. Many 5.7 moves were interspersed with minuscule resting stances where the leader could smash a piton into the perfect crack in the back of the groove. Some climbers consider the V-Slot to be the most entertaining 5.7 pitch in Yosemite Valley.

Chouinard and Hempel continued to the brushy shoulder, encountering several more interesting pitches. Their variation soon attracted the majority of east buttress climbers, although some deviates who thrived on chimneys continued to follow the original upper route, which also offers magnificent climbing. Perhaps the 1955 route will become more popular in the future as climbers tire of queuing up for the now-standard route.

First ascent

Warren Harding, Jack Davis, and Bob Swift. 1955. The variation which is now standard was pioneered in 1961 by Yvon Chouinard and Mort Hempel. The first free ascent, which involved free climbing the bolt ladder (5.10), was made by Frank Sacherer and Ed Leeper in 1965.

Elevation

The 1000-foot route ends at about the 5400-foot level.

Difficulty

IV, 5.9, A1. Done free, the route is 5.10.

Time

Six to eight hours for the ascent; one-and-a-half hours for the descent.

Map

Special USGS topographic sheet: Yosemite Valley, scale 1:24,000.

Useful references

Climber's Guide to Yosemite Valley. A schematic drawing is included in *Yosemite Climbs.*

Route description

The approach is obvious and takes about twenty minutes. Rope up at a wooded shelf at the very base of the buttress and climb 150 feet of class

Following the long flake above the bolt ladder, Allen Steck begins to mantle onto a comfortable hold.   Steve Roper.

4 rock to a bushy ledge beneath overhangs. Turn these overhangs on the right via awkward 5.8 moves; then head up and right to Ant-Tree Ledge. Next, climb steep, strenuous lieback flakes to a small ledge; a smooth dihedral just above involves 5.7 liebacking. Another short pitch leads up and left to the bolt ladder.

Climb the bolts (A1 or 5.10) and then move left a few steps. Lieback over a ceiling (5.8 or 5.9) to a long, enjoyable lieback flake with good holds. Belay on a small ledge 50 feet above the ceiling. The routefinding on the next pitch is tricky:

ascend about 30 feet on rounded knobs; then begin working right toward a conspicuous ledge. A delicate 5.7 move or two is found shortly before reaching the ledge.

From the ledge ascend obvious dihedrals to a tiny stance just right of a solitary tree. The extraordinary V-Slot rises above and ends on ledges about 120 feet above the belay spot. Next, move left a few feet and ascend a shallow, 5.7 dihedral to another belay ledge. A strenuous pitch, the second most difficult of the route, lies above, and the routefinding once again becomes tricky. Easier climbing above leads to the end of the route.

After unroping, scramble upward several hundred feet; then follow a faint path which leads south along the Kat Walk. Upon reaching the main couloir, turn left and downclimb (some class 4) to the forest.

Equipment

Carry a selection of twenty chocks.

Half Dome Northwest Face

43

"It is a crest of granite . . . perfectly inaccessible, being probably the only one of all the prominent points about the Yosemite which never has been, and never will be, trodden by human foot." With these words, so ludicrous today, the 1865 report of the California Geological Survey dismissed forever the climbing possibilities on Half Dome.

It took only ten years, however, for the prediction to be disproved. A Scottish trail-builder and carpenter named George Anderson spent several weeks in October of 1875 drilling six-inch-deep holes into the smooth eastern flank of the peak. Pounding iron pegs into these holes and fastening ropes to them, Anderson was able to ascend the 300-foot, forty-five-degree slab which had stymied previous climbers.

◀ *The northwest face of Half Dome. The final part of the route curves left around the Visor. Ed Cooper.*

Tens of thousands of hikers reached the summit of Half Dome in the next seventy years, but every one of them followed Anderson's route, over which cables had been placed. It was not until 1946 that skilled rock-climbers established another route to the top by climbing the longer and steeper southwest face. If two sides of the "inaccessible" dome had been found climbable, what about the other sides? To the immediate post-war generation, the south face was regarded as a scenic wonder, not a climbing goal. It was so huge and smooth that many bolts would have been required, and this was in the days before indiscriminate bolting became popular. The northwest face was equally impressive, for this was the side which had been sliced by glaciers into the startling and world-renowned half-dome shape. The resulting face—"a frightful amputation" in the words of J. S. Chase—was 1800 feet high and tilted at an angle of more than eighty degrees. It is hardly surprising that climbers shunned this great wall, considering it the epitome of un-climbability.

Because of its apparent invulner-ability, the wall was not even studied closely by climbers until 1954. In that year Dick Long, Jim Wilson, and George Mandatory ventured onto the face, choosing a route at the junction of the smooth part of the huge wall and the more broken area to its left. It was the obvious place to begin, and the group had expecta-tions of making a bold attempt. But

the technical problems of steep aid climbing on the enormous monolith were such that only a pitiful 200-foot section was explored.

The next climbers who felt ready to attempt the face were Royal Rob-bins, Jerry Gallwas, Warren Hard-ing, and Don Wilson. Although all four men had climbed either the Lost Arrow Chimney or the Steck–Salathé Route on Sentinel Rock, the northwest face of Half Dome was so much higher in caliber that a three-day effort in 1955 ended at the 450-foot mark, far below what ap-peared to be the major difficulties.

By this time the projected route was fairly clear: after ascending 800 feet up the left margin of the smooth face, a team of climbers would have to move up and to the right across a questionable blank section leading to a prominent chimney system. From the top of this system, at the 1300-foot level, flakes shot upward nearly to the awesome summit over-hang known as the Visor. This close to the top, climbers would have to cleverly weave their way over or around this obstacle. It was obvious from the ground that much of the upward progress would be by means of direct aid. At a rate of 150 feet a day on the relatively easy lower section, how much time would be needed for the horrendous upper section?

No attempts were made on the face in 1956, perhaps because of these logistical problems. But in 1957, having gained two more years of experience, Robbins and Gallwas decided that another try was in order. Robbins was just fifteen years old when he had begun climbing in 1950 and became within a few years the finest free climber in the country. Gallwas and Mike Sherrick, the third man chosen for this next attempt, were both well-known rockclimbers from Southern California and, like Robbins, had accomplished many difficult routes.

Aware that other climbers, especially Warren Harding, also coveted the face, Robbins and his group made plans for an early summer ascent, a tactic they hoped would surprise the competition. (At that time Yosemite climbers spent at least the first month of their three-month season getting into condition.) On June 23, 1957, the three adventurers made the long approach to the wall. A friend named Wayne Merry volunteered to help transport loads until the climbers left the trail, after which he would ascend the Anderson Route to post a sign warning hikers that rocks dropped off the Visor—a favorite pastime in those days—might strike climbers below. Yosemite Valley is a climbing area renowned for its lack of natural hazards, but rocks thrown by tourists created a distinct peril.

Progress on the first day was uneventful, although the pioneers were pleased to be moving rapidly and efficiently. Knowing that extra-

Low on the route, Doug Robinson jumars upward. The slightly concave northwest face curves toward the background.   Galen Rowell.

256

heavy loads could inhibit their advance, the team had decided to carry minimum gear for a five-day effort and kept their haul bag to a weight of sixty pounds. Only fourteen quarts of water were taken, an absurdly small amount by modern standards. Just above the high point of two years earlier, the three men reached a sloping ledge. Here they established an uncomfortable bivouac and consumed a traditional climbers' meal of dates, raisins, tuna, and chocolate.

Much easier climbing the second day brought the trio to the route's first major obstacle, the blank section which led across the smooth wall to the chimney system. The Robbins Traverse, as it is now called, required the drilling of holes for seven bolts, several hard-to-place pitons, and finally a spectacular pendulum. This pendulum proved to be the longest and most difficult yet tried in Yosemite; a small ledge far to the right was the immediate goal. Back and forth Robbins swung, missing the ledge first by a few feet and then by a few inches. As Sherrick and Gallwas watched in absolute silence, Robbins had them lower him another foot so that he was then forty feet below his shaky pendulum piton. With an explosive burst of energy he ran far to his left, paused momentarily, and then charged back across the blank wall, his legs churning. Just as he lost momentum, his fingers curled over the ledge and he heaved himself onto it. The most difficult part of the Robbins Traverse had been completed.

Belayed by Dick Long, John Evans ascends the bolt ladder at the start of the Robbins Traverse. The Visor dominates the top of the wall, 1000 feet above the climbers. Allen Steck.

Early the next morning the climbers reached the chimney system and found that, while the route was clear, it also was strenuous and time-consuming. By mid-afternoon Robbins faced an appalling obstacle now known as the Undercling Pitch. Sherrick later described it in his article in the *Sierra Club Bulletin:* "The chimney is filled with very large blocks of rock. One of them sticks out of the chimney about 8 to 10 feet at a distance of 6 inches from the wall. . . . At the bottom of this block, with a secure piton in place, Robbins grasped up underneath the

inside edge of the bottom of the block and 'walked' out the vertical face of the cliff. . . ." This strenuous section, rated 5.9, has engaged the full attention of every one of the hundreds of climbers who have repeated Robbins' "walk."

Not far above the Undercling Pitch the climbers bivouacked behind a huge formation which later parties named Psyche Flake. This forty-foot-high blade of granite was perched alarmingly atop a narrow ledge, and the area of contact between the two was only a few square feet. One vertical side of the flake seemed attached to the main cliff;

the other was separated from it by a four-foot gap perfect for chimneying. On the morning of the fourth day, as the lead climber rapidly gained elevation by means of the back-and-foot method, those below were vaguely aware of rattling noises in the depths of the slot. This phenomenon, which many later climbers commented upon, indicated that the flake was unstable: wedged stones were shifting and dropping as the flake was pried outward. Although scary, the flake was the only possible route. (The formation vanished from the wall in the winter of 1966–67, a victim of frost action combined with a little help from dozens of climbers, many of whom shuddered upon hearing of the flake's demise, remembering how cavalierly they had thrust their legs outward against it.)

"By this time," Sherrick later wrote, "lack of sufficient water, food, and sleep, plus the enervating hot sun rays had fatigued us." Robbins was especially affected, and Sherrick had been intimidated early on by the magnitude of the wall. Thus it was Gallwas who pioneered much of the strenuous section known as the Zigzag Pitches. The nearly vertical wall was distinguished by overlapping and disconnected flakes, which, as Sherrick described them, gave the effect of "climbing one overhang of about 30 degrees for about 20 to 40 feet with angle pitons driven straight up, then up a 60-degree sloping ledge with pitons driven down . . . and so on."

Three tired men spent the fourth night in a tiny niche midway up the Zigzag Pitches, some 1500 feet above the ground. By mid-morning on the fifth day they gathered together on a small ledge at the base of an utterly blank wall leading up to the Visor. They had been concerned about this section for days, but to their delight a ledge, hidden from below, shot fifty feet left toward a crack system. This foot-wide formation, named Thank God Ledge by Sherrick, easily was the most spectacular pitch of the route. Although skillful balance climbers have since inched across the ledge "no hands," the first-ascent party, as well as most of those who followed, used a combination of hand-traversing and crawling. The exposure was astonishing, and even though the group had become inured to such sights for five days, they blanched at the 1600-foot drop unblemished by a single ledge.

A few more pitches led around the Visor, and by early evening the trio stood on the flat summit, where they were greeted by none other than Warren Harding, who, disappointed that he had not been asked on the climb, nevertheless hiked eight miles to congratulate his fellow climbers.

Three years passed before Chuck Pratt, Joe Fitschen, and Tom Frost made the second ascent, a feat accomplished with only two bivouacs. This rapid ascent spurred Robbins into competitive action, and a week later he and Dave Rearick sped up the wall in a day and a half. The

Although this double-crack pitch looks intimidating, hidden holds inside the slot allow the leader to move easily and quickly.
Galen Rowell.

next logical achievement, a one-day ascent, was not made until May 7, 1966, when Jeff Foott and Steve Roper began in the half-light of dawn and, with little energy remaining, coiled their rope just as full darkness blanketed the Sierra.

Few subsequent climbers were able to accomplish a one-day ascent, but other "firsts" soon followed. Eric Beck made the first solo ascent in 1966, a two-and-a-half-day climb audacious for that era. A seven-day ascent by Greg Lowe and Rob Kiesel in January of 1972 marked the first time the great wall had been ascended in winter. The two men were caught by a severe storm near the summit, and their last day became an Eiger-like epic, complete with shrieking winds, rime, and nearly frozen hands. Another evolutionary advance concerned direct-aid pitons, of which the first-ascent party had placed nearly two hundred. As the years went by and the number of ascents approached a hundred, more and more of these pitons were eliminated by talented climbers. Finally came the inevitable ascent in which the last three or four aid pitons were bypassed, and aid slings became dispensable. With a clean ascent in 1973, pitons also could be left behind, as chocks and fixed pitons proved sufficient.

Thus, in the remarkably short span of two decades, the Northwest Face Route on Half Dome had evolved from America's most demanding climb to a route which could be done free and clean in a single day. Although some modern climbers regard the route as merely a conditioning climb to be tackled before moving on to El Capitan, another segment of the climbing community envisions Half Dome as an ultimate goal. Those climbers who choose the route as the sole Grade VI of their careers can hardly have made a finer

The Thank-God Ledge narrows at the spot where the climber is pausing; at this point, most climbers drop to hands and knees to continue. Galen Rowell.

259

selection. If bivouac gear and a few pitons are taken, the pace can be slowed so that the climb becomes sublimely enjoyable. The route is particularly suitable for experienced weekend mountaineers. Although twenty-five pitches long, it is safe, varied, and lacks "horror" pitches; its ledges are adequately sized for belaying; and three or four sites offer superb bivouacking.

A few words of advice may soothe nervous Half Dome aspirants. If the Undercling Pitch, which appears frightening from the entire lower section, proves too difficult, consider the possibility of using an aid sling. If the Zigzag Pitches are too strenuous, persevere for a few minutes until a low-angled ramp is reached. If Thank God Ledge seems like a bad joke played on tired climbers, remember that hundreds have scuttled across to easier ground. Finally, if the very magnitude of the wall is oppressive, calm down and savor the startling location—an "impossible" climb on an "inaccessible" dome.

First ascent

Royal Robbins, Jerry Gallwas, and Mike Sherrick. June 24–28, 1957.

Elevation

The summit is 8842 feet above sea level. The face is 1800 feet high.

Difficulty

VI, 5.9, A3. Done free, the route is 5.11.

Time

Allow two days for the ascent.

Map

Special USGS topographic sheet: Yosemite Valley, scale 1:24,000.

Useful references

Climber's Guide to Yosemite Valley. A schematic drawing of the route is included in *Yosemite Climbs.*

Route description

The start of the route can be reached from Mirror Lake by scrambling up 3000 feet of slabs and brush. A longer but easier method is to follow the Half Dome Trail to the base of the subdome just east of Half Dome. At this point, drop down steep slopes to the northwest to the base of the climb.

Rope up the junction of the great smooth wall and the more broken area to its left. Three long pitches, mainly free, lead to a belay flake below a right-curving crack. Follow this crack and the bolts above; then nail or free climb a long crack. Two easier pitches end on a large, sloping platform.

Three relatively easy pitches take one up and slightly right to small ledges at the base of the bolt ladder which marks the beginning of the Robbins Traverse. Climb the bolts and then pendulum right to a small belay ledge. A devious pitch leads over to the base of a long, prominent chimney system. Ascend obvious cracks and chimneys for four pitches to an excellent ledge.

Move a few steps to the right along the ledge and climb double cracks to Sandy Ledge, an excellent bivouac site. Nail or free climb (much 5.11) three easy-to-follow pitches—the strenuous Zigzag Pitches—to Thank God Ledge. From its left end, climb a slot to a belay ledge. Next, work left on aid, nail a low-angled slab, and belay at its top. Scramble down and left 120 feet; then wander up a 5.5 slab to the summit.

An eight-mile trail down the east side leads to the valley floor.

Equipment

Carry fifteen pitons and approximately forty chocks.

El Capitan
The Nose Route

High on the Nose Route of El Capitan is a ledge known as the Glowering Spot. Six feet long and eighteen inches wide, the platform provides a dramatic and unexpected belay stance. An object tossed from here will plummet nearly 1500 feet before brushing the slabs which form the lower section of the monolith. Above the ledge the view is extraordinary, for vertical walls of gray and orange granite converge in pure geometric lines. It is like being inside a cut diamond.

The Glowering Spot—a strange name for such an entrancing location? Indeed it is, unless one considers the personality of the man who first climbed the route, naming this ledge along with many other features. Warren Harding has long been an enigma, for while he loves climbing immense granite walls, he doesn't care to admit to his contemporaries that he is doing anything out of the ordinary. Deriding the "spiritual" aspect of climbing, which

many mountaineers insist is a large part of their experience, Harding would have us believe that his exploits are about as significant as walking a dog. It is not only modesty which accounts for his prosaic attitude about rockclimbing, but also a deeply rooted distrust of anything that hints of intellectualism. When a climber compares a Yosemite setting to Mozart's music, as a well-known Valley climber once did, Harding's response is to bestow such names as Guano Ledge and the Glowering Spot on his own routes. Harding thus has become a hero to some and a pariah to others.

Early in his climbing career, Harding displayed a remarkable determination to succeed, and it was this trait, along with his legendary endurance, which were to become renowned. By the summer of 1957 Harding felt ready for a big effort, and of all the untouched faces of Yosemite, the great cleft face of Half Dome cried out to be climbed. However, as related in the preceding account, Harding was beaten to the prize by a trio of Southern Californians. Predictably, he drove to the other end of the canyon and stared at the next "great problem"—the 3000-foot bulk of El Capitan. Climbers traditionally had shunned the massive formation, for they had noted the numerous blank sections lying between obvious crack systems and concluded that excessive bolting would be required to climb them. Because of this, the route would take far too long, posing insuperable logistical problems.

Not far above Sickle Ledge, the leader must pendulum far to the right to reach another crack. Jim Stuart.

These sobering facts bothered Warren Harding only briefly as he pieced together a devious path up the very nose of the monolith. He realized immediately that his patience and endurance could overcome the problems; all that remained was to interest other determined men in the adventure. This proved to be easy, since Mark Powell and Bill "Dolt" Feuerer also had been studying Half Dome and were upset when it had been "taken away" from them. They agreed to begin the climb as soon as possible.

Knowing that five or six days was the maximum that a self-contained climbing team could remain on a wall during a torrid Yosemite summer, the newly formed El Cap team planned on a long-term siege effort from the very beginning. Fixed lines would be strung as the ascent progressed, thus forming a supply line to a support team on the ground. As Harding later put it: "Our technique was to be similar to that used in ascending high mountains, with prusiking and rappelling gear replacing ice axe and crampons as aids for traveling, and winch and hauling lines instead of Sherpas."

The climbers quickly began gathering and borrowing equipment. A thousand feet of rope was acquired,

The south side of El Capitan. To the left of the Nose Route, on the shadowed wall, lies the Salathé Wall Route. Ed Cooper.

along with many pitons and expansion bolts. The most unusual items to be included were four ungainly pitons which a friend had roughed out from the legs of an old stove. It was hoped that these devices would fit into the wide cracks which were obvious even from the ground. Only six days after the Half Dome ascent, all was ready. Little did the three men know that the hastily conceived siege would stretch out for nearly eighteen months.

The first ledge of the climb lay about 500 feet above the ground, and several days were spent attaining it. Sickle Ledge became Camp I, the staging area for the frightening and ledgeless section above. Not far past the ledge, an awesome pendulum had to be made to reach a long crack system. This section had looked questionable from the ground, and the skeptics below were impressed as the leader finally gained purchase in the crack. But even this victory was minor relative to the task at hand. Rappelling each night from their high point to their airy campsite, the team soon became aware that progress was going to be even slower than expected. Hauling supplies from the ground was taking too much time, and each morning two men had to make the tedious prusik to the top of their fixed rope. Retreat each afternoon was faster, of course, but still involved an hour or so. It was becoming quite clear that the climbers had underestimated the problems.

The cracks above the pendulum were wider and more continuous than expected, and the stoveleg pitons were receiving a rough initiation. In one 300-foot section, now known as Stoveleg Crack, the fissure was so uniform that the indispensable pitons had to be leapfrogged time and again. With long, pitonless sections thus stretching between the belayer and leader, an element of danger was introduced. Too long a pitonless section was foolhardy, thought Harding, so he placed bolts every so often for added protection.

At the end of seven days the pitons were mangled, supplies were low, and the weather was sweltering. It was time for retreat, and the climbers returned extremely pleased to have overcome a 1000-foot section. During the last few days on the wall, Harding had wondered about the traffic jams on the road below. The men weren't on the ground long before the park's chief ranger informed them that the problem had occurred because of the spectacular nature of the ascent. Henceforth no climbing was to be allowed during the summer tourist season. With their enthusiasm at a high point, this was disheartening news to the climbers. But, they reasoned, the time certainly could be used to make improvements in their equipment.

Powell, by far the finest climber of the trio, badly injured his ankle in September, and for the remainder of 1957 the others accomplished little. Dolt Tower, at the 1200-foot level, was reached at Thanksgiving. The highlight of this effort was the turkey and chablis hauled by the team to Sickle Ledge! Harding and his group had completed more than a third of the route, but blank walls and overhangs loomed ahead, and it was obvious to all that the logistical problems were just beginning. The only feasible way the climbers could take gear up the face was to carry it on their backs or haul it hand over hand from higher ledges. Both methods were strenuous and limited the gear carried to sixty or seventy pounds. Also, as the ropes stretched higher and higher, a hauler's increasing need for food and water proportionately decreased the amount of supplies he could carry to the climbers far above.

During the spring of 1958 bad weather hampered the team, still composed of Harding, Powell, and Feuerer. By the time the summer ban came around, they had managed to string ropes only as far as Boot Flake, a sixty-foot-high, hollow-sounding formation about 1700 feet up. The chief ranger, upset about the traffic problem even in the off-season, told the climbers they could have only the twelve weeks between Labor Day and Thanksgiving to finish the route, though, as Harding later wrote: "I have never understood how this was to have been enforced." Still, the pressure was on for the autumn climbing season. By then, however, dissension had sprung up among the team, sparked largely by Harding's conviction that Powell's crippled

ankle was impeding the group's progress. Powell, realizing he wasn't the dynamic climber he had once been, finally decided to drop out, and Feuerer did the same.

The resourceful Harding soon recruited other Valley climbers, some of whom already had served as haulers. By mid-October the high point had been pushed nearly to the Great Roof, the enormous ceiling so prominent from the valley floor. Camp IV, not far below the roof, was heavily stocked by now, and the men realized they were finally ready for the push to the summit.

On November 1 the climbing team, now composed of Harding, Rich Calderwood, George Whitmore, and Wayne Merry, prusiked 2000 feet to the scattered ledges comprising Camp IV. The climbing began in earnest the following morning, and day after day the party placed its ropes higher. The discovery of the spacious and aesthetic Camps V and VI provided the team with a necessary morale boost, but soon a strange monotony set in, with each day seeming to blend into the next. Calderwood fled to the ground after a week—"an attack of nerves" Harding called it. Whitmore patiently hauled loads as Harding and Merry nailed up perfectly formed cracks in the vicinity of the Glowering Spot. Nearly all the climbing in this upper section was artificial, and the verticality made the going strenuous. A brief storm on the ninth day permitted the team to rest, a welcome break from the hammering and hauling.

Chuck Pratt leads a crack above Dolt Tower on the second ascent of the route in 1960. Tom Frost.

By the middle of the eleventh day the men realized that they had been on the wall twice as long as any American had ever spent on a rock climb. The rim was just a few hundred feet above them at this point, and at dusk on November 11, Harding found himself staring at the final horrifying obstacle: an overhanging wall devoid of cracks on its upper part. Rather than retreat to Camp VI, 350 feet below, Harding made the decision to press on. The night of November 11–12 has become one of the best remembered Yosemite epics, for the tireless Harding drilled twenty-eight holes on a wall which in certain spots overhung ten degrees. The eastern sky was graying with dawn as Harding heaved himself onto the summit slabs. He was later to write: "It was not at all clear to me who was conquerer and who was conquered: I do recall that El Cap seemed to be in much better condition than I was."

Forty-five days of hard labor had spanned nearly one-and-a-half years; 700 pitons had been placed; and 125 bolts had been inserted. With Harding's pull-up that dawn, a new era in North American rock-climbing was born, for never again could climbers consider a huge rock wall unclimbable.

In both 1957 and 1958 a tremendous amount of publicity accompanied the climb. Much of the information printed in newspapers was supplied by members of the support

Shari Kearney moves toward the Great Roof.   Alan Kearney.

team, with Harding's blessing. Metropolitan dailies, including the *Oakland Tribune* and the *San Francisco Chronicle*, dwelled on the climbers' progress throughout the final push and plastered photos on their front pages. This great clamor displeased many people. Some nonclimbers were convinced that the ascent was nothing more than a gigantic publicity stunt; others thought the climbers had been inconsiderate of possible rescuers, who might risk their lives attempting to get an injured man off the wall. Nor were some climbers especially pleased with the attention received by Harding and his group. Although many criticisms certainly could be explained as sour grapes, a responsible segment of the

climbing community believed that the sport of climbing had been demeaned by such commercial exposure. Many felt that the public, already convinced of the madness of climbers and the death-defying aspect of the sport, hardly would be enlightened by the emphasis on climbers cheating death once again. Not surprisingly, Harding was scarcely concerned with such misgivings, and he reveled in the discomfiture of his peers.

Who would be next on El Cap? Everyone knew that the second ascent could go much faster. The bolts were in place; the route was known; and, perhaps most important, the knowledge that the difficulties were surmountable would add greatly to the psychological confidence of the next group. Still, many climbers questioned whether enough food and water could be carried to make the route in one push, and all were wary of the long-term logistics ordeal involved in using fixed ropes.

The summer of 1960 proved to be a vintage year for Yosemite climbing, and many excellent climbers did a great number of difficult, multi-day routes. By Labor Day, Royal Robbins, Chuck Pratt, Tom Frost, and Joe Fitschen were ready to cap off the magnificent season by attempting the climb of their lives: the Nose in one continuous push. Loaded down with an arsenal of ironware (including many specially designed wide-angle pitons) and sixty quarts of water, enough for ten days, the superbly conditioned climbers moved rapidly up the wall. Two climbers swung leads while the other pair struggled with the haul bags, which weighed 200 pounds at the start. On alternate days the teams traded chores. Nights were spent at each of the previously numbered camps, all of which were roomy enough for the four men to more or less stretch out in their light sleeping bags.

Certain pitches would stand out forever in the climbers' memories. The three exceptional pendulums of the route were difficult and terribly exposed. The nailing of the detached Boot Flake impressed the men so much that Robbins placed a bolt halfway up it, on the off chance that the two-foot-thick sliver might decide to part company with the mother rock. The Great Roof was simple nailing, but the climbers agreed that it was easily the most spectacular pitch in Yosemite. And, finally, all believed the the upper 1000-foot dihedrals contained some of the most dramatic and aesthetic climbing they had ever experienced. Wildflowers grew out of perfect cracks, and ledges appeared just when it seemed a sling belay would be necessary. Robbins called the seven-day ascent "the most magnificent and complete adventure of our lives." He also thought that "the day will come when this climb will be done in five days, perhaps less. . . ."

No one felt qualified for the third ascent until 1963, when a party of three sped up the route in three-and-a-half days, sleeping at the even-numbered camps. This fast time was to remain an excellent one for the next ten or fifteen ascents. By the spring of 1970 those who kept track of the ascents gave up at twenty-one, for relatively unknown climbers were coming into Yosemite, doing the route quickly, and departing unheralded.

Three-quarters of the route has been climbed free, and today's climbers flash up the Stoveleg Crack with quiet confidence. Several solo ascents have been made, and teams with scant big-wall experience somehow have made the rim, though, tragically, five men have been killed in falls. Perhaps the most memorable ascent took place in 1975, when a party of three climbed the Nose in one long day. Although the climbers knew the route intimately and benefited immeasurably from the fixed pitons (more than a hundred were in place) their remarkable effort demonstrates that climbing in Yosemite is still an evolving art.

First ascent

Warren Harding, Wayne Merry, and George Whitmore. The rim was reached on November 12, 1958.

Elevation

The cliff is 2900 feet high. The rim is 7050 feet above sea level and the rounded summit 500 feet higher.

Difficulty

VI, 5.11, A3. If done with as much free climbing as possible, there are twenty pitches rated 5.9 or higher.

Time

Though at least three one-day ascents have been made thus far, most parties plan on two to five days for the climb.

Map

Special USGS topographic sheet: Yosemite Valley, scale 1:24,000.

Useful references

Climber's Guide to Yosemite Valley. A schematic drawing of the route is included in *Yosemite Climbs.*

Against the monolithic granite of El Capitan, two climbers are just visible to the right of the conspicuous Great Roof.   Jim Stuart.

267

Route description

A short stretch of class 3 rock leads to the rope-up ledge. Climb a long, obvious crack to a ledge. From its right side climb a corner; then pendulum right to another crack and follow it for 200 feet. When almost level with Sickle Ledge, make two short rope-traverses to reach it. These four pitches to Sickle have been done mostly free; if aid is used, there will be some A3 pins. An easy pitch leads up the curve of the ledge. Climb a short bit of 5.9; then make a long pendulum right to a 5.8 crack which leads to Dolt Hole, a small belay alcove. More 5.9 leads to a bolt ladder, and from its top make another wild pendulum to reach the notorious Stoveleg Crack. This 400-foot section leads to Dolt Tower and can be done all free (5.10).

Move right from the top of the tower and reach a conspicuous crack system; follow it a few hundred feet (all free, 5.9) to El Cap Tower, an excellent ledge. A short crack then leads to the chimney behind Texas Flake; belay at its knife-edged top. Bolts lead up and left to Boot Flake, which is either easy aid or desperate free climbing. A giant double pendulum leads left around the corner. Ascend not-too-pleasant rock for a long pitch; then pendulum left to a long ledge. One more pitch leads up and left to the ledges known collectively as Camp IV.

From the ledges, climb up and right over a 5.9 pitch. The obvious Great Roof Pitch is next and ends at a tiny ledge just right of the lip. The Pancake Flake is next (A2 or 5.11). Another hard pitch brings one to Camp V, a multi-level series of ledges. An easy aid pitch then leads to the Glowering Spot. Two more leads end at Camp VI, a small, triangular platform which usually reeks of feces (a problem encountered more and more on popular routes). Four or five easy-to-follow pitches are encountered next; these are steep and mostly free, and they bring the climber to the base of the awesome summit cap. No one has ever gotten lost at this point.

From the unroping area, climb slabs to the summit of El Capitan. A trail is found here which eventually leads either west to the Tamarack Road (about four miles) or east to Yosemite Lodge via Yosemite Falls (about six miles). The fastest descent, if one is familiar with it, is as follows: from the unroping spot, walk along the rim of El Cap downward and east until above the El Cap East Buttress Route. A wide, brushy ledge can be followed down and east until it narrows. Two 150-foot rappels lead to the forest.

Equipment

Many chocks up to three-and-a-half inches should be taken, and although the route has been done clean, it is advisable to carry a dozen pitons.

El Capitan
Salathé Wall

It has been called the finest rock climb in the world—thirty-six rope-lengths of superb, varied, and unrelenting climbing on a near-vertical wall in one of nature's most masterful canyons. Is it any wonder that climbers from all over the world have come to try the Salathé Wall?

Yosemite's El Capitan is supposedly the largest mass of exposed granite on earth, but even if it ranked one-hundredth, its shape alone still would be awesome to both tourists and climbers. Few protuberances interrupt the sweeping lines of the light-colored Salathé Wall, which lies to the left of the Nose, that perfectly proportioned buttress discussed earlier.

The name Salathé Wall is misleading. To begin with, the term "wall" in this instance refers not to an entire face, but rather to a particular route. Moreover, John Salathé, who took part in two of the climbs discussed in this book, did not name or climb this route. Around 1960, Yvon Chouinard, a mountaineer, inventor, and hero worshipper, decided that the by-then legendary

Salathé merited a significant named feature—after all, Yosemite already had a Washington Column, a Rixon's Pinnacle, and a Harris's Hangover. Mesmerized by the great unclimbed southwest face of El Cap, Chouinard realized that somewhere on the broad wall there had to be a route, and he began referring to the entire face as the Salathé Wall. When the first route on the face was done, however, the route itself came to be called Salathé Wall.

Yosemite climbers had always stared longingly at El Cap, of course, but after the revolutionary ascent of the Nose in 1958, they actively began seeking other possible routes. Many climbers of varying abilities dreamed of a second route, but the next explorers to hammer pitons into an unknown section of the monolith were Royal Robbins, Chuck Pratt, and Tom Frost. All were well-known Yosemite climbers, and all had spent many days struggling up the vertical walls of the Valley. Along with Joe Fitschen, the three men had made the second ascent of the Nose in 1960, and they were ready for a still greater challenge. What better prize than a new route on El Cap?

No new climb the length and difficulty of El Cap's southwest face ever had been done in one push without fixed ropes, those lifelines to the ground that enable climbers high on a wall to replenish supplies at will

Swinging across a blank wall during the first ascent, Royal Robbins begins to reach for the crack leading to Hollow Flake Ledge. Tom Frost.

and to retreat in a matter of hours. While taking much of the commitment out of climbing, fixed ropes seemed the only way to tackle such smooth, massive cliffs. Hoping to minimize the stringing of ropes, the three men, after much deliberation, decided they would fix the first third of the route, descend for more

supplies, and then boldly set forth on the upper 2000 feet with no fixed ropes. The loads for this upper push, which they thought might take six days, would be monstrous: sixty-five pounds of water, twenty-five pounds of food, extra ropes, sleeping gear, and a huge quantity of aluminum and steel. Never had three American climbers accomplished such a task.

On September 12, 1961, Robbins and Frost began the adventure, while Pratt, having lost the coin toss, hitchhiked to the city for additional supplies, including bolts. Roping up just a short distance to the left of the Nose, the two men planned to work further to the left and eventually link disconnected crack systems by means of questionable traverses. By proposing this somewhat circuitous route, they hoped to avoid excessive bolting. Five hundred feet above the ground, however, they came up against a 100-foot blank section. To their relief, the angle was only fifty-five degrees, and very tenuous free moves on microflakes kept the number of bolts to thirteen. Still, it was not a propitious beginning for climbers to whom bolts were anathema.

The southwest face of El Capitan. The Heart, one-third of the way up the Salathé Wall Route, can be seen easily. The Nose lies on the right. Ed Cooper.

For two days Robbins and Frost climbed tricky crack systems until establishing a high point about 600 feet above the ground. Having used up their food, as well as their entire supply of bolts, the two retreated to await Pratt's return. Several days later all three returned to the task and succeeded in reaching and naming Mammoth Terraces, 1000 feet above the starting point. From here they rappelled 150 feet to the base of the Heart—an enormous, indented feature of the southwest face. Caching much of their hardware at this point, the trio then rappelled 800 feet down an appallingly blank wall to the talus, leaving their ropes in place. With the first section of the route completed, the climbers relaxed and bought new supplies.

On September 19, the three men prusiked with great loads to Heart Ledge, casting their fixed ropes to the ground. The committing adventure was about to begin. Not far above Heart Ledge, the climbers tried connecting crack systems by means of a spectacular and difficult pendulum. Climbers on the ground were charting the day's progress while this "king swing" took place, and a long silence ended with cheers and yodels as the leader, after several wild attempts, finally swung his body into a narrow jam-crack. A few hundred feet above this point the angle steepened to vertical, thus severely limiting the free climbing. Pitch after pitch of strenuous artificial climbing became

routine for the next few days. But at least the regular appearance of ledges every 400 to 500 feet made the nights fairly comfortable.

Great orange facets and pillars constantly came into view, and the climbers weaved cleverly among them. So far the three men had followed a line picked out many weeks earlier, but on the fourth day radical and crackless overhangs forced them onto territory which had not been studied carefully from the ground. This new line brought the trio to an intimidating obstacle which afterward became known simply as the Roof. Sticking out horizontally for fifteen feet, the obstacle was overcome slowly by Frost's adroit use of pitons. Perched in their aid slings, Robbins and Pratt watched fascinated as the leader's contorted body stretched sideways to make long reaches. Eventually, only Frost's legs were visible, then a wildly gyrating foot, and finally just the tail of an aid sling. Above the Roof, Frost discovered he was at the base of a 200-foot, ninety-five-degree wall broken only by a curving, bottomed, and discontinuous crack. As Frost hung suspended just above the lip of the ceiling, those on the ground who had been in similar situations sighed and were silently thankful for their present location.

271

By late afternoon on the sixth day the three pioneers stood on a small ledge just below the rim. The final obstacle, a narrow slit which led through an overhang, was overcome with alacrity by Pratt. It proved to be one of the hardest free pitches of the route.

It was over! Five nights had been spent on the final push, and Robbins wrote later that it had been "the most rewarding climbing we had ever done." Especially gratifying was the fact that the team had not placed a single bolt on the final push; Pratt's trip to the city fortunately turned out to be a wasted one. High on the route the climbers had accomplished some very demanding aid climbing, and several times the placing of a marginal piton had taken longer than simply placing a bolt. But drilling, they reasoned, made the ascent less challenging and certainly was work fit only for drones.

Royal Robbins relaxes at one of Yosemite's finest bivouac sites, the flat summit of El Cap Spire. Tom Frost.

Displeased with having fixed the lower part of the route, Robbins and Frost returned the next year and made the first continuous ascent in a remarkable four-and-a-half days. Because of the forbidding appearance of the wall and the respect Valley climbers had for Robbins, Pratt, and Frost, the next ascent was not made until 1966. By 1970, however, the face had been climbed eleven times, and by the end of the 1970s the Salathé Wall was one of the most popular of the two dozen or so routes on El Cap, with one knowledgeable observer estimating the total number of Salathé ascents at 120.

Perhaps the chief reason for the route's popularity is the challenge of engaging in so much varied climbing on such a huge wall. Although no one climbs the Salathé Wall for the pleasure of a single pitch, some sections remain indelibly recorded in the climber's memory. Chimney specialists savor the Ear—a nasty, bottomless slot midway up the route—and exult over the hidden gash behind El Cap Spire, an eighty-foot-high detached pinnacle. Lovers of sublime belay ledges also appreciate the latter pitch, for the top of El Cap Spire could well be Yosemite's most spectacularly situated ledge. Ten feet square and perfectly flat, the airy platform is so spacious and comfortable that some parties plan their ascent so that they are certain to spend a night on this incomparable site. For aid climbers, the section surrounding the Roof is as marvelous a setting to practice this art as anywhere on the planet.

On the pitch above El Cap Spire, Chuck Pratt encounters a perfect crack on a monolithic wall.   Tom Frost.

Those who prefer jamcracks can hardly wait for the summit pitch, though it is but one of many strenuous slits. Liebacks and small-hold climbing also are present for aficionados of these techniques.

As the route becomes more and more popular, it is undergoing significant changes. For example, a tremendous amount of the climb has gone free. Most of the lower-angled section on the first third of the route can be climbed by small-hold techniques; six of the ten pitches to Mammoth Terraces are rated 5.10 or higher. And, amazingly enough, the perpendicular cracks in the central section of the wall can be jammed and liebacked. Only the area around the Roof remains mostly aid, but it is just a matter of time before some 5.12 climber alters this situation.

273

One deplorable change that has taken place is the proliferation of bolts along the route. The third-ascent party admirably preserved the route in its original state by excluding a bolt kit from their gear. Soon afterward, however, the leader of another party placed a bolt at a spot where he was stymied. His act set a precedent which far too many climbers have emulated. When Royal Robbins made his third ascent of the face in 1976, he found forty-two aid and anchor bolts in place, a sad commentary on the thoughtlessness of a few hurried climbers.

In recent years the Salathé Wall has attracted many foreign mountaineers, including Doug Scott, Peter Habeler, and a crack Soviet team. Articles extolling the virtues of the climb have appeared in many journals, and it seems certain to remain one of the world's most sought-after big-wall rock climbs.

First ascent

Royal Robbins, Chuck Pratt, and Tom Frost. First effort, September 12–16, 1961; final push, September 19–24.

Elevation

The cliff is approximately 2900 feet high, and the rim is 7050 feet above sea level.

Difficulty

VI, 5.10, A3.

Time

Two to five days.

Map

Special USGS topographic sheet: Yosemite Valley, scale 1:24,000.

Useful references

Climber's Guide to Yosemite Valley. A schematic drawing of the route can be found in *Yosemite Climbs*.

Route description

From the base of the Nose, walk up and to the left for several hundred feet to a recess. Two pitches of very difficult free climbing lead up cracks on the right side of the recess to a sling belay beneath a small ceiling. Nail right under this; then ascend a solitary crack for about 200 feet. From the crack's end, work up and left to a series of bolts. Move right from the last bolt on difficult friction and belay on a tiny ledge.

More bolts are found on the sixth pitch, and soon a pleasant ledge is reached. A straightforward, but very difficult, pitch leads to a belay spot below the formation known as the Half Dollar. Turn this on the right and ascend a corner to a good belay ledge. Two more pitches lead to Mammoth Terraces. From a tree on the west end of the ledges, rappel 150 feet onto Heart Ledge. From here a complex pitch goes up and left (a short pendulum is necessary) to Lung Ledge. The following pitch is class 4. Next comes one of the most spectacular pitches: work up a bit, then make a giant pendulum left to a long flake. Climb this flake (5.8) to Hollow Flake Ledge.

Three pitches of obvious, mixed climbing lead up crack systems to the notorious Ear—an overhanging, bottomless chimney. Climb the Ear (5.7) and enter the long, steep Double Cracks. Two pitches of very strenuous free and aid climbing end at the Alcove, a block-filled terrace. Next, chimney to the top of El Cap Spire. Four easy-to-follow pitches, all with some aid, lead to the Block, an excellent ledge. The next pitch is complicated: climb a short crack; nail a black flake; tension-traverse left to a small ledge; and finally nail up to Sous Le Toit Ledge, an exposed and disappointingly small belay spot.

Two pitches of mostly artificial climbing end at a wild belay spot just under the Roof. Nail this obstacle and belay in slings on the overhanging wall above. Two pitches of fast and easy nailing end at Long Ledge, the finest ledge since the Block.

Begin the next pitch in an aid crack at the far right end of Long Ledge; a decent belay ledge is found a short distance higher. A mixed free and aid pitch leads more or less straight up to the final, obvious pitch: a 5.9 chimney and jamcrack.

Descend via one of the three routes described in the Nose Route account.

Equipment

Carry a selection of thirty pitons, varying from a rurp to a three-inch angle. Many chocks up to three inches also should be included.

Chuck Pratt stares upward at the solitary crack which splits the ninety-five-degree Headwall.   Tom Frost.

Mount Whitney East Face

46

Mount Whitney is not a distinguished peak from most sides, and
even the east face—its only noteworthy feature—does not dominate
the landscape. Many travelers on
U.S. Highway 395, ten miles east of
Whitney and ten thousand feet
below it, mistakenly identify
neighboring peaks as the highest
point in the lower forty-eight states.
One should not deride these
tourists, however, for during the
1860s and 1870s there was a certain
confusion about which was the highest peak. In 1864 Clarence King,
while surveying with the California
Geological Survey, spied a cluster of
high peaks twenty miles distant. In
an epic five-day journey with
Richard Cotter, he tried to reach the
high point already named for Survey
leader Josiah Whitney. Standing
atop a high peak, the pair were dis-
concerted to see the real Whitney

◀ *The east face of Mount Whitney.*
Jim Stuart.

several miles away. A second try a
few weeks later also failed. Seven
years passed before King returned to
his nemesis. Clouds obscured the
crest during his approach from the
east, but soon he stood atop another
high peak—surely this was it! He
returned satisfied that he had
reached his goal. Two years later
other explorers discovered that King
actually had climbed Mount Langley, a rounded hump five miles
south of Whitney and a few hundred
feet lower. King entrained from New
York when he heard this news, but
it was too late: America's true high
point had been ascended several
times in the preceding month. Francis Farquhar, the noted Sierra historian, wrote that King was "either a
very clumsy mountaineer or a victim
of hallucinations."

The 14,494-foot-high mountain
soon attracted various agencies and
individuals. For a twenty-year
period the summit area was the most
curious military reservation in the
land, established for the purpose of
conducting high-altitude research
into solar radiation. In 1909 a stone
hut, which still serves as a summit
shelter, was erected by the Smithsonian Institution to protect members who were to determine if Mars
had water vapor in its atmosphere.
A few years later a biplane flew over
the summit, establishing an American altitude record. This event occurred just three days before a significantly more world-shaking one at
Sarajevo, and the story of Whitney
lay quiescent for more than a decade.

By the late 1920s the peak had a
good trail up its easy side, and the
summit was not a lonely place on a
summer day. All ascents, except
one, had been via the easy south
and west flanks. Oddly enough, the
exception (which had not been repeated for more than half a century)
was John Muir's 1873 solo ascent
of a steep, narrow couloir just north
of the imposing eastern escarpment.
Although Muir had warned that
"soft, succulent people should go
the mule way," his couloir, now
known as the Mountaineer's Route,
is not difficult and presently is used
more often as a descent route than
as a way up the peak.

The 2000-foot-high east face was
never considered as a climbing
route in the old days, but it definitely attracted attention during 1931,
when organized roped climbing
made its debut in California. Francis Farquhar had met Robert
Underhill in Canada in 1930 and
had been impressed with his com-
mand of technical climbing. Farquhar cajoled Underhill into visiting
California the following year to in-
struct local climbers on how to use
ropes for safety. As recounted earlier, Underhill had enjoyed a pro-
ductive summer in the Tetons during
1931, and less than two weeks after
his bold ascent of the north ridge of
the Grand Teton, he was teaching

belaying and rappelling to members of a Sierra Club outing in Yosemite. About ten of the most interested climbers migrated south after this introduction, and, with Underhill, made several first ascents in the central Sierra. Whitney's untouched east face was next on their list.

The climbing group had dwindled to five by the time they began the arduous approach to the base of the wall. With Underhill and Farquhar were Jules Eichorn and Glen Dawson, two young men who had never set eyes on the mountain, as well as the already legendary Norman Clyde, a forty-five-year-old climber who was well known both for his multitude of Sierra first ascents and for the monstrous loads he carried in the high country. Underhill later remarked that Clyde's pack was "an especially picturesque enormity of skyscraper architecture."

It was mid-morning on August 16, 1931, when the five men stood at Iceberg Lake, just below the cliff. The true east face lay to their left; it was so sheer and unbroken that they didn't even consider it. But the right side of the face, above the lake, looked more promising. "Suddenly I saw what seemed a just possible route," wrote Underhill in his account of the climb, "and simultaneously Dawson and Eichorn exclaimed to the same effect. It turned out that we all had exactly the same thing in mind. Through the field-glasses we now examined it in detail as well as we could, noting that much of it seemed possible, but

Poised above an 800-foot drop, a climber contemplates the rounded holds of the Tower Traverse. A strip of snow marks the base of the peak. Steve Roper.

that there were several very critical places. Rating our chances of success about fifty-fifty, we were eager to go ahead with the attempt."

Farquhar, out of shape, opted to climb the Mountaineer's Route and meet the victorious climbers on top. The others quickly ascended 600 feet of talus and class 3 rock until they reached ledges leading left onto the main face. After a short delay because of routefinding problems, they reached the Washboard, a rippled section of tiered slabs which proved easier than expected. Four

hundred feet of class 3 and 4 rock were rapidly overcome, and the foursome soon reached an exposed wall which offered no immediate way up. The two younger climbers suggested a frontal attack, but, as Underhill put it, "before such a *tour de force* was undertaken Clyde and I urged that a traverse, which we had all already noticed out to the left, be investigated." Clyde later wrote that this traverse "proved to be one requiring considerable steadiness, as the ledges were narrow and there was a thousand feet of fresh air below." The now-famous Fresh-Air Traverse generally is regarded as the crux of the route.

Higher lay the Grand Staircase, a 400-foot section consisting of easy slopes interspersed with short, vertical steps. At the 14,200-foot level, the climbers emerged into an area of excellent, broken rock. Unroping, they wandered individually up the final few hundred feet, pausing when out of breath to gaze at the astonishingly clear vista. Underhill later wrote that "even the Californians did not succeed in remaining impeccably *blasé*" about the view.

Soon the four climbers were shaking hands with Farquhar. The ascent had taken just three-and-a-quarter hours, a time that is rarely equaled today. While by no means as hard as some of the 1931 Teton routes, it was a memorable ascent and remained the most difficult High Sierra climb throughout the 1930s. Underhill graciously observed that "the beauty of the climb lies chiefly in its unexpected possibility, up the apparent precipice, and in the intimate contact it affords with the features that lend Mount Whitney its real impressiveness."

Eichorn and Dawson soon became leaders in Yosemite Valley rock-climbing, and while they put up many routes more difficult than Whitney, they did not forget their historic climb of the east face. Dawson participated in the second ascent in July 1934, and a month later Eichorn also reascended the wall, inaugurating a variation which has

Moving up the Washboard toward an enormous, shaded alcove, the climber eventually reaches the notch at the upper left.   Steve Roper.

since become the standard first pitch of the route. This variant, known as the Tower Traverse, is located a short distance below the original party's traverse to the Washboard. The Tower Traverse, although short, is terrifically exposed and requires delicate footwork; many climbers consider this 5.3 pitch to be the finest of the route.

Other variations have been made. Two in the vicinity of the Fresh-Air Traverse are named Shaky-Leg Crack (the one considered in 1931 by Eichorn and Dawson) and the Direct Crack, climbed in 1953. Many other routes have been done on the eastern escarpment, and the true east face finally was climbed in 1959.

The summit of Whitney no longer is a place meant for reflection. The park service has erected a second structure, California's highest outhouse, and other agencies have set various benchmarks and plaques into the rock. One nonsensical plaque informs us that the height of the peak is 14,495.811 feet. This figure was established by the U.S. Coast and Geodetic Survey in 1928 and was modified almost immediately to another absurd figure: 14,494.777 feet. Fortunately, no sign has yet been placed to tell us of this change. But if the east-face climber walks west for a few hundred feet, over the remnants of the sixty-million-year-old pre-uplift landscape, he or she can ponder thousands of square miles of pure wilderness. Nothing manmade disturbs the view, and even the ever-present jet contrails can be imagined as mare's-tail cirrus.

First ascent

Robert Underhill, Norman Clyde, Jules Eichorn, and Glen Dawson. August 16, 1931.

Elevation

From the first roped pitch—the Tower Traverse—to the summit is about 1100 feet. The summit is 14,494 feet above sea level.

Difficulty

III, 5.4.

Time

A small, strong party can do the climb easily in a day starting from the car, but this effort involves a round trip of sixteen miles and an elevation gain of more than 6000 feet. The advantages of a one-day trip are twofold: light packs and, with no high camp to pick up at the base of the east face, an easy descent via the south-side trail. In early season or after autumn storms, the trail is preferable because the top of the Mountaineer's Route faces north and can be snow-covered or icy. Most parties, however, take two days, returning to a camp on the north fork of Lone Pine Creek. The climb itself, from Iceberg Lake, usually takes from three to six hours. Under good conditions, allow one-and-a-half hours for the return to the lake.

Maps

USGS quadrangles: Lone Pine (for the approach) and Mount Whitney. The scale for both is 1:62,500.

Useful reference

The Climber's Guide to the High Sierra.

Route description

From Lone Pine, on U.S. Highway 395, drive up the paved road leading west to Whitney Portal, at 8400 feet. Follow the Whitney Trail for half a mile until it crosses the second creek. Above, there is a gorge with very steep walls. A path leads up the south side of the creek—the north fork of Lone Pine Creek—for a long quarter-mile. Cross the creek just as it becomes choked with alder and zigzag up ledges on the north side of the gorge until 150 feet above the creek. Follow ledges and paths back west to stream level and ascend decreasingly steep slopes to Clyde Meadow.

Recross the creek and follow a path to a large talus slope. Cross the creek again when a quarter of a mile above the meadow and ascend slabs almost to Upper Boy Scout Lake. Head due south from here, up slabs and talus. Soon a valley is reached; follow it upward toward the Whitney massif, which is visible for the first time. A steep and slabby talus slope finally leads north to the shores of Iceberg Lake.

Climb talus and broken slabs for about 500 feet to a notch behind the obvious First Tower. Rope up here and ascend a system of steep steps for 50 feet to the Tower Traverse. At its end, climb a short squeeze chimney onto the Washboard and ascend this undulating feature hundreds of feet to the small bowl at its head. Next, climb a short but very steep headwall on the left. This brings one to a ridge. Drop over the south side for 40 feet and continue to a huge corner.

Scramble up the corner for a few feet; then move left toward the start of the inobvious Fresh-Air Traverse. Exposure, not difficulty, is the chief problem here, and soon a broken, decomposed chimney is reached. Ascend this for a few feet; then move up and right onto ledges at the base of the Grand Staircase. The route from here is fairly obvious—the final "step" is surmounted by a foot-wide crack on the left. Various class 4 routes lead to the summit.

To descend the Mountaineer's Route, walk several hundred feet west along the edge of the north face; then drop down steep blocks (sometimes icy) to a notch at the 14,000-foot level. Head down and east from here—the steep couloir is not difficult, merely tiring.

Equipment

Pitons are not necessary; chocks work extremely well, and a selection of six to eight is sufficient.

Allen Steck moves across the Fresh-Air Traverse, the most famous section of the East Face Route.   Steve Roper.

Fairview Dome North Face

47

Tuolumne Meadows, located in California's Yosemite National Park, was known among mountaineers in the late 1950s principally as a beautiful base camp from which nearby mountains could be climbed. Every peak in the Tuolumne area had been long since overcome, and some, including John Muir's Cathedral Peak, were so popular that climbers had developed a blind spot regarding the conspicuous domes and walls bordering the narrow and tortuous Tioga Pass Highway, which winds through the area. Many of these formations have indefinite summits, which indicated to mountaineers of the era that they were mere outcrops or cliff bands. Because superb rock climbs were available in nearby Yosemite Valley, Tuolumne's bluffs were ignored. Even prominent Fairview Dome, hardly a bluff, remained untouched except for a scrambling route on its south side.

◀ *The north face of Fairview Dome.* Steve Roper.

Lying only half a mile from Tioga Pass Highway, Fairview is the preeminent dome in a region geologists claim has the highest proliferation of granitic domes on earth. The symmetrical, 900-foot-high north face displays fascinating evidence of exfoliation, and whoever compared this geological process to the peeling of successive layers of an onion must have conceived the analogy after seeing Fairview. Enormous overhangs and arches clearly demonstrate that for millennia the outer shell of rock has been peeling off as the elements prey at natural flaws. Although there were obvious ways to bypass the curving overhangs, the face remained untouched as late as 1958.

Few mountaineers have the good fortune to stumble upon a climbing area as undeveloped as Tuolumne Meadows was in 1958. One such lucky person was Wally Reed, who felt like a child turned loose in a toy store as he puzzled over which should be the first big climb of the region. Since previous climbers had established only a few routes—all of them of the one-pitch variety—Reed had his choice of many prominent, multi-pitch climbs.

During the course of several fishing trips to the Tuolumne area, Reed had noticed half a dozen intriguing route possibilities, but his thoughts kept returning to the largest dome, Fairview. On its steep north face were two long, conspicuous cracks; the right-hand one looked promising, for it shot up 300 feet and ended in broken rock. At the 450-

foot level was a huge, crescent-shaped ledge, and if it could be reached, the remainder of the route looked easier. Reed's proposed route was the longest and most striking of the region, and he knew it was unusual in climbing history for the most notable climb in an undeveloped area to be done first. But he also was confident that it wouldn't be as difficult as a few of the climbs he had been accomplishing quietly in Yosemite Valley for several years.

Unheralded in his own era and virtually forgotten by present-day climbers, Wally Reed is an anomaly in the climbing world: a superb rockclimber with little historical reputation. To be sure, observant readers of the Valley guidebook will catch sight of his name, usually in the company of such better-known climbers as Warren Harding and Mark Powell. But his name rarely appears in climbing histories, and few anecdotes about him are told around campfires. In the late 1950s Reed worked as a night clerk and accountant at Yosemite Lodge, tasks which not only gave him free time for climbing but also allowed this exceptionally bashful man to avoid people. Perhaps his obscurity can be explained by his dislike of casual social chatter, including climbing conversation. When pressed to say something about one of his fine new routes, Reed would blush, stare at the ground, and

murmur that Powell might be a better person to contact. In a world of
breast-beaters, Reed's excessive
modesty meant that he was easily
forgotten: "Did you hear about that
great new route Powell and some
guy just finished?"

Early in the summer of 1958, Reed
met nineteen-year-old Chuck Pratt
and asked if he would be interested
in making an attempt on the north
face of Fairview. Pratt agreed immediately, flattered that a man who
had labored on El Capitan with
Warren Harding would ask him
along on a new route. As they drove
to Tuolumne Meadows, Reed found
that his new partner also was a
quiet, modest lad. A particularly
long silence was broken by Pratt,
who was having second thoughts
about the route. He confessed to
Reed that he had been climbing less
than a year, although the book
Annapurna had once stirred him to
experiment on a small Washington
crag armed with just a clothesline
and a few lag screws. (He often
wondered what benevolent god had
spared him on that occasion.) But
Reed was not troubled by Pratt's
admission of inexperience, for he
had heard rumors that the powerful-
looking youth was a rising star in the
Yosemite climbing scene.

*The first pitch, an easy-looking set of cracks, proves troublesome for many
climbers.* Steve Roper.

When Pratt saw the route that Reed had picked out, he knew at once that it had the ingredients of a memorable climb. For one thing, it was marvelously direct—no one ever could say they had avoided the main problems of the wall. The aesthetic lower crack, unsullied by broken rock or ledges, also made a favorable impression on Pratt, who had been influenced by countless mountaineering photographs to appreciate direct and pure lines. Recalling Emilio Comici's credo—"Where the drop of water falls from the summit; that is the line I wish to climb"—Pratt thought the great Italian climber would unquestionably approve of their projected route.

The first pitch of the climb, consisting of a pleasant double crack which converged toward the main crack, went free and fast. But higher, as the cliff steepened, the two men were forced into direct-aid techniques, and progress was hampered by quantities of dirt in the cracks. One of the disadvantages of climbing on a north face, the two men realized, was that it remained wetter and colder than a south-facing cliff. Because of their dankness, north walls often contain decomposed rock and excessive vegetation. The dirt on Fairview, which had accumulated throughout the centuries, made it necessary for the leader to probe and "garden" the crack before inserting a piton. Occasionally, an especially large clump of earth would provide a resting place, but these tenuously attached hummocks quivered under a person's weight, and it was clear they could not survive the passage of many climbers. Luckily, the problem with the vegetation was short-lived, for Pratt had other concerns.

Since he had never done such extensive aid work, Pratt regularly tangled his feet in his aid slings, much to the amusement of Reed, who was completely at home on a long piton ladder. Twice it was necessary to belay in slings, an awkward technique Pratt had done only on practice climbs. So attentive were the two men to their world of stone that when the sun disappeared behind a nearby ridge, they were caught by surprise. From a small ledge 400 feet above the ground the pair hurriedly abandoned the face, satisfied that the route was feasible at least as far as what they called Crescent Ledge.

It was not until August that the two climbers found time to return. They decided to carry bivouac gear on this attempt, which was a wise decision, for it was dusk when they reached Crescent Ledge, and the temperature quickly plunged to the freezing point. Insulated from the cold by their sleeping bags, the pair watched the moon rise over the Sierra crest and illuminate a world glowing with granite.

Early the next morning Reed and Pratt began noticing subtle changes in the character of the rock. On the lower part of their route the granite had been smooth and monolithic, similar to that in Yosemite Valley. But in the vicinity of Crescent Ledge, flakes and knobs began to appear, and the excited climbers stowed their aid slings and rapidly gained elevation. A four-foot-wide ceiling which cut across the face at the 600-foot level looked formidable, but hidden, juglike holds permitted the obstacle to be free climbed easily. Above this outstanding pitch the rock became even more convoluted; weathering had carved the granite into remarkably varied shapes. By noon the two men had reached the rounded summit, amazed by the fact that they had covered the final 500 feet so easily.

Wally Reed became so enamored with "his" area that he went on to pioneer several more sterling routes, encountering everywhere the weathered, knobby granite he had enjoyed on Fairview. Word of this high-quality rock spread quickly throughout the climbing community, so that within two decades there were about 150 established routes in Tuolumne, many of them far more difficult than the Fairview climb. But none were as long, and few were so pleasing from afar.

The troublesome dirt which had hindered the first ascenders was worn away slowly by the numerous piton placements and scuffling feet of the next half a dozen parties. In 1962 climbers found that the newly revealed cracks could be done without direct aid. Protection at the relatively few difficult sections was perfect for free climbers, and this fact, as well as the dome's spectacular location, guaranteed that the climb would become increasingly popular.

Many more routes have been established on Fairview, and some presently are considered equal to the hardest free climbs anywhere. Even 5.11 climbers need a vacation, however, and it is not unusual to see a pair of heavily muscled climbers roping up for the original route as late as noon. These modern adventurers carry little else besides a rope and a dozen chocks; their daypacks certainly lack sleeping bags. Such a carefree and unburdened ascent could not have been imagined by Reed and Pratt in 1958.

Though he is well known for repeating favorite climbs, Chuck Pratt oddly has never repeated Fairview; perhaps he wishes to savor the memory of his earliest significant climb, one which launched him into a lifestyle totally committed to climbing. Wally Reed, on the other hand, vanished from the world of high-level rockclimbing as unobtrusively as he had participated in it.

Dick Long ascends a dihedral above Crescent Ledge.   Allen Steck.

First ascent

Chuck Pratt and Wally Reed. August 1958.

Elevation

The summit is 9731 feet above sea level. The face is approximately 900 feet high.

Difficulty

III or IV, 5.9.

Time

Five to eight hours.

Map

USGS quadrangle: Tuolumne Meadows, scale 1:62,500.

Useful reference

The Climber's Guide to the High Sierra.

Route description

Fairview Dome is located a few miles west of Tuolumne Meadows and is prominent from the Tioga Pass Highway. The obvious approach from the road takes about twenty minutes.

The most striking features of the lower north face are two very similar, parallel cracks about 300 feet in length. Climb the right-hand crack for three pitches. The crux of the route—and its only 5.9 section—is found near the top of the third pitch.

Pitch four leads up and slightly right for 150 feet to Crescent Ledge. From here follow a conspicuous ramp up and left 150 feet to a belay spot. Midway on the following pitch is a ceiling; this can be surmounted at a knobby area. Belay about 50 feet higher. Finally, a long pitch diagonals up and right to a bushy ledge. Increasingly easier slab climbing leads to the summit.

Descend via class 3 friction slopes on the south side.

Equipment

Carry a selection of fifteen chocks.

Clyde Minaret Southeast Face

4 8

More than one hundred years ago, the surveyor Clarence King explored an alpine region in the central Sierra Nevada, attempting and naming its highest peak, Mount Ritter. In the official account of this reconnaissance, Josiah Whitney, leader of the California Geological Survey, wrote that to the south of Ritter were "some grand pinnacles of granite, very lofty and apparently inaccessible, to which we gave the name of 'the Minarets.' Here are numerous peaks, yet unscaled and unnamed, to which the attention of mountain climbers is invited." No one accepted this invitation, and for half a century not a single serious attempt was made on any of the ten-odd summits which comprise the serrated ridge.

In the early 1920s Charles Michael, the postmaster of nearby Yosemite National Park and a mountaineer who thrived on class 3 and 4 solo climbing, managed to reach the top of what he believed to be the highest

◀ *The southeast face of Clyde Minaret.* Steve Roper.

pinnacle. When Michael Minaret later was shown to be about forty feet below the actual high point, Michael had no regrets: "Whether my peak was the highest or not does not matter to me so much, for I can at least recommend it as a grand and thrilling climb." It remained for the remarkable Norman Clyde to climb, in 1928, the highest summit, which, like most of the other Minarets, has been named unofficially for its first ascender. Clyde had been climbing in the Sierra since 1914 and already had garnered an enviable number of first ascents. Like Michael, Clyde also loved solo climbing, and his class 4 route on Clyde Minaret was exposed, loose, and, in his words, "somewhat arduous." Even today many climbers uncoil their rope somewhere on this climb.

At 12,281 feet, Clyde Minaret is a peak of many shapes. On the northeast—the site of Clyde's route—it rises boldly from a minuscule glacier, and though it is the most massive of the Minarets, it does not protrude significantly above the median level of the sawtooth ridge. Several deep chutes, separated by razor-thin arêtes, lie on the northeast side of the peak, and they are filled with shadows and snow for much of the year. Other facets of the Minaret are not especially striking, and the climber's eyes pass quickly to other formations.

When viewed from the southeast, however, the *real* Clyde Minaret looms forth. The daggerlike southeast face forms an enormous isosceles triangle whose apex appears so sharp that it is difficult to envision a person standing safely atop it. Nearby spires are so humbled by Clyde that they hardly seem worth looking at, let alone climbing. From Minaret Lake, the best campsite for climbs in the southern Ritter Range, the dagger dominates the scene much as the Matterhorn overshadows Zermatt.

Despite the fact that by the late 1930s all the Minarets had been climbed by various routes, Clyde, being the highest summit, remained the most popular. Indeed, it had four separate routes by 1960. Because of the structure of the rock, most routes in the area ascended either ridges or gullies. The notable lack of prominent faces made the southeast wall of Clyde even more conspicuous. Why, then, wasn't it climbed until 1963? The proximity of Yosemite Valley may well be the reason, for most climbers of the late 1950s and early 1960s were so infatuated with Valley climbing that they rarely left Yosemite. (One punster named the valley the "Great Rut.") And when Valley regulars did leave, it was to head for recognized ranges such as the Tetons. The Sierra was thus a neglected range, one which contained scores of undiscovered climbs equal to those in the Tetons.

Luckily for the sport of mountaineering, there are always climbers more interested in pioneering new routes on high mountains than in pure rockclimbing. All four men who approached the southeast face of Clyde Minaret in June 1963 were superb rockclimbers, but all preferred the isolated mountains to overcrowded Yosemite, an airy class 5 ridge to a flared chimney choked with bay trees, and the howl of a coyote to the howls emanating from radios. Allen Steck had been climbing in the Ritter Range for many years and often had wondered whether a route could be forced up Clyde's imposing southeast face. His trusted climbing partner, Dick Long, was making the difficult career transition from carpenter and climbing equipment manufacturer to physician. Long had climbed in many of the western ranges and was perhaps the finest unheralded climber in the land. But despite his power, he looked emaciated beside the third man, John Evans, who had wrestled alligators the previous few summers at Reptile Gardens in South Dakota. The final member of the party, Chuck Wilts, was the engineer who ten years earlier had invented the knife-blade piton, a tiny piece of chromium—molybdenum alloy which could be hammered into incipient cracks. This invention, one of the first chrome—moly pitons ever made, had sparked a revolution in Yosemite aid climbing. Ironically, the reserved Wilts was not known as an aid man; instead, he had made his reputation as a superb free climber.

At their Minaret Lake campsite the four men discussed possible routes and strategies. Even from a distance

John Fischer begins a pitch low on the route. Allen Steck.

290

the upper section of the face appeared obviously climbable, for it had several large dihedrals. But the broad lower part of the wall, at least from the climbers' vantage point, looked rather featureless. Some of the team members were concerned enough about this nebulous lower section to suggest carrying bivouac gear. The bolder climbers pointed out that since they all were in good shape, the climb surely could be done during one long June day. But the four men also knew that June was not yet summer in the High Sierra, and the nighttime temperature at 12,000 feet would be well below freezing. In the end, those who wished to avoid being benighted without bivouac gear overruled those who disliked the idea of carrying cumbersome packs.

The climbers set out on the hour-long approach to the base of the 1000-foot face during that quiet and hauntingly beautiful time between first light and sunrise. No one spoke much as they trudged up talus- and snow-covered slopes, but by the time they reached the base of the cliff it was clear to all four men that they would rope up in the talus and begin a long upward traverse to the right. This pitch would lead to ledges from which steep and disconnected cracks could be seen leading erratically toward the summit dihedrals. Long and Evans decided to take on the task of finding the route; Steck and Wilts would have an absorbing job of their own—taking eight-millimeter movies of the ascent.

The climb progressed smoothly, as is often the case when competent climbers get together. Signals and commands were low-keyed and brief; belayers made sure the rope wouldn't snag on flakes; and the leader's occasional "watch me here" was uttered without a hint of panic. There was time for laughter, basking in the sun, and movie-making. A sharp contrast, thought Steck, to his first big climbs, when there was more struggling than humor, more panic than meditation.

Suddenly a mishap shattered the blissful mood. Somehow a pack broke loose and plunged 600 feet into the talus. The supercompetent team had been a bit too casual, and their food, water, and most important, their bivouac gear, was gone. The easygoing atmosphere of the climb vanished, ironically just at the point where the climbing became serious as well. Although the situation wasn't too desperate, a race with the sun was on. Long got down to business and made several brilliant and rapid leads up 5.8 corners.

Even though the pace of the climb had intensified, all four climbers knew that they were pioneering an exceptional route. For one thing, the rock of Clyde Minaret was solid and seemingly designed for climbers. Josiah Whitney had been mistaken in calling it granite. The hard,

On the fourth pitch Allen Steck grasps the angular holds typical of the Minarets. Dick Long.

dark-gray stone actually was ancient lava, which, metamorphosed beyond all recognition, still proved as firm as granite. The foursome reveled in superb handholds, perfect liebacks, and wild stemming maneuvers across dihedrals. Evans, new to High Sierra climbing, wondered aloud how such a fine route could have remained unclimbed for so long. His partners sternly warned him not to reveal the existence of this and similar projected climbs. If these matters were kept quiet, the virgin walls and ridges would be left to them alone. Let the others go to the Tetons!

The views were marvelous that June day, and southern Sierra peaks fifty miles distant looked to be only half as far. Just below the peak was Cecile Lake; the older climbers remembered that its previous name had been Upper Iceberg Lake, a far more appropriate name, the men thought, since ice blocked all signs of water. A glance at the base of the wall revealed the telltale blue of the lost pack, a reminder that eyes should be directed upward. The sun set just as the climbers pulled onto the summit ridge, and Steck's yodels reverberated across arêtes and amphitheaters. The fortunate four knew the descent route perfectly, and when darkness coincided with the freezing point, they were chattering happily around a campfire.

Not until the late 1960s did big-wall climbing in the High Sierra become popular, with dozens of difficult routes established. In the quest for first ascents, most climbers ignored previously done routes, even those of Clyde's quality. But this condition was temporary, and the Clyde route became a desirable goal for many during the 1970s. When Long and Steck reclimbed the route fifteen years after their first ascent, they found it just as hard and as beautiful as they remembered. They noted traces of many climbers: bent pitons, some from the original ascent; rappel slings draped over blocks; and nearly invisible chocks left behind in the depths of cracks.

In 1970, trying for the third ascent, a young climber took a short fall onto a ledge at the two-thirds point. To his surprise and horror he discovered he had snapped his right femur. The resulting rescue effort, conducted by guides from Yosemite, was the most complex yet made in the High Sierra. The lessons learned about lowering a litter down 600 feet of steep and broken rock soon proved useful in far more dramatic rescues in Yosemite Valley.

The route on the southeast face is not particularly difficult, and climbers interested solely in superhard routes still remain sequestered in Yosemite. But for well-rounded mountaineers who do not mind a six-mile approach, who appreciate an excellent climb in a splendid setting, and who can sit mesmerized on a historic summit while gazing over the Range of Light, this is *the* climb of the region.

First ascent

Allen Steck, Dick Long, John Evans, and Chuck Wilts. June 22, 1963.

Elevation

The summit is 12,281 feet above sea level. The face is just over 1000 feet high.

Difficulty

IV, 5.8.

Time

A long day usually is required for the round trip from Minaret Lake.

Map

USGS quadrangle: Devil's Postpile, scale 1:62,500.

Useful reference

The Climber's Guide to the High Sierra.

Route description

From the resort village of Mammoth Lakes drive over Minaret Summit and follow signs to Red's Meadow. A marked trail leads from here to Minaret Lake, some six miles to the northwest.

From the lake's major inlet follow a path northwest along the creek to Cecile Lake; then head up talus to the base of the face. Allow an hour from Minaret Lake to the rope-up point.

An inobvious upward traverse (5.6) leads across 130 feet to large ledges. Moderate class 5 climbing, with many minor routefinding problems, leads up chimneys and broken rock for about four long pitches. There are many small variations to be found in this section, but during the last two pitches bear distinctly up and right. Aim for a shallow dihedral, a prominent feature on the central part of the face.

The dihedral is the first hard pitch: 5.8 face and crack climbing lead to a belay alcove near the top of an open book. The next pitch also is difficult and ascends a steep face immediately left of an obvious white scar visible from the ground. This pitch ends on large ledges at the base of the conspicuous summit dihedral.

Climb the dihedral for about 90 feet to a small belay ledge; then leave the dihedral and move 40 or 50 feet left across improbable rock. Climb straight up 90 feet to a small ledge. One more pitch leads to the summit ridge, and the summit cairn is just five minutes away.

To descend, scramble north along the crest for several hundred feet; then drop down the second gully encountered. Soon one reaches a ledge system which runs across the face to the notch between Clyde and the next formation south. From the notch, downclimb and rappel a steep couloir to the rope-up spot for the route. Allow about one hour for the descent to this point.

Equipment

Although the climb usually is done clean, it is advisable to carry five pitons in addition to a standard selection of twenty chocks.

Stemming across a dihedral, a climber works his way toward his companions. Steve Roper.

Charlotte Dome South Face

One of the pitfalls of writing about a climb is the overwhelming tendency to make predictions about its future popularity. Even if phrases are qualified with a "perhaps" or a "probably," some statements inevitably will haunt the writer later. Yosemite's Sentinel Rock and Lost Arrow would never have second ascents, according to the authors of the first-ascent write-ups. Of Yosemite's Ahwahnee Buttress, a writer had this to say: "It is difficult to conceive of an ascent . . . being completed in less than two days of sustained climbing." The second ascent was made in eight hours, and the route later was done in half that time.

In Kings Canyon National Park there stands an imposing formation known among climbers as Charlotte Dome. Chris Jones, a member of the first party to ascend its 1000-foot-high south face, later wrote that if

◀ *The southeast side of Charlotte Dome. The South Face Route lies in the conspicuous grooves near the left skyline.* Allen Steck.

the climb were in Yosemite, it "would be recognized as one of the best in the Valley." But, he prophesied, since it was "in the backcountry it will probably remain unknown." Today the route is far from unknown; it is one of the most desired High Sierra climbs, with the total number of ascents conservatively estimated at sixty. An article glorifying the route recently appeared in a national climbing magazine. Consequently, on a September weekday in 1978, two parties happened to meet on the first pitches of the climb, a sure sign that the "unknown" route had been discovered.

Jones' assessment of the route's quality, however, was uncannily accurate, for without exception those who have done it have been thrilled with the climb. Jones wrote: "We were rewarded with some of the finest climbing we had ever done anywhere, all free and on wonderful rock. . . . Every pitch was excellent, none easy, all interesting." If indeed the climb were located in Yosemite, it certainly would average five parties a day. (This is an example of an unchallengeable prophecy, since it is quite unlikely that anyone will move the dome north!)

It is unusual in North American climbing history for the first ascent of a climb of this quality to come as late as 1970, especially since Charlotte Dome was one of the first monoliths noted in the High Sierra. During the summer of 1864, members of the California Geological Survey camped just below the dome

at Charlotte Creek. Charles Hoffmann sketched the peak, and William Brewer, the field leader of the survey, described it in his journal as "a grand smooth granite rock."

Generations of John Muir Trail backpackers have seen the dome from the Glen Pass region, some twenty miles north of the Mount Whitney massif. Among these walkers must have been hundreds of rockclimbers, who surely commented upon the formation only two miles distant. Yet for some reason Peak 10,690 remained for decades just a designation on the map rather than an entry in a climbing guide. Perhaps the idea of carrying a pack full of iron for ten miles—the nearest road is that far—discouraged would-be pioneers. After all, closer chunks of granite beckoned.

When Jones, Fred Beckey, and Galen Rowell approached Charlotte Dome in October 1970, they carried heavy packs indeed, for a previous long-distance reconnaissance had indicated a long, steep, and blank wall. With only a weekend at their disposal, it was obvious to the trio that they would have to make a one-day effort or none at all. With the short autumn days, this limitation posed a potential problem. When the climbers arrived under the face, they blanched, for there were absolutely no continuous crack systems, and the wall approached verticality in several places. Bolt ladders might be necessary, they thought, and the climb could take several days. To the side of the south face, however, the cliff looked more feasible, and Beckey insisted that this was the logical way to go. Reluctantly, the other two agreed.

When the three men actually set foot on the rock, they were pleasantly surprised, for the golden granite bristled with flakes and "chickenheads," the doorknob-like protrusions which occur on certain types of weathered granite. Although Beckey remained committed to his proposed route, Rowell and Jones thought they could piece together a direct line up the south face, hoping that blank-appearing walls would yield knobs. Jones later wrote that they felt it was "better to retreat off a good climb than to succeed on an indifferent one." With this noble attitude, the threesome roped up.

After a few easy pitches on the apron at the base of the face, the climbers encountered the first problematical section, a steep headwall capped with a short vertical step. The first part of this obstacle was overcome by means of copious hidden holds. And just when these vanished, cracks appeared, and a few 5.7 moves led through the impressive step. By the time the pioneers had gathered atop this pitch, they

The south side of Charlotte Dome is sliced by hundreds of furrows and cracks; the route wanders up the center of the wall. Galen Rowell.

realized that they had discovered a real gem of a climb. But with three climbers the going was slow, and the sun already was at its zenith. Beckey, still unhappy about the rash decision to push for a direct route, volunteered to jumar up a fixed rope, thus freeing the second man to belay the leader. Self-belayed, Beckey could proceed at his own pace. The climbers thought this clever idea might just get them back to warm sleeping bags that night.

Several pitches higher the incredulous climbers, almost sated with chickenheads, came up against a fabulous wall which is known now as the Furrow Pitch. This steep, 100-foot section dominates the central part of the route and hovers ominously over the lower-angled slabs below. Great grooved ruts, some of them three feet deep, scar the otherwise monolithic granite, as if some gigantic feline had sharpened its claws there during primordial times. The Furrow Pitch is not difficult—the only real problem is choosing the easiest slit—but it is the most memorable of many sterling pitches.

An enormous ledge not far above this pitch proved perfect for a brief lunch stop, brief because the sun was sinking disturbingly low in the west. Several more pitches, liberally sprinkled with knobs, went quickly, and soon Rowell's shouts told the others he was on top. The splendid summit boulders were still aglow when Jones and Beckey arrived, though Charlotte Creek already was cloaked in shadow. Fortunately, the

descent proved easy and rapid, and the pessimistic Beckey was amazed as they strutted into camp before pitch dark.

Although word of the fabulous route quickly spread through the California climbing community, the long approach still discouraged many interested climbers. However, after a few parties came back raving about the chickenheads, the law of geometric progression took over: three successful climbers told nine prospective climbers; nine pleased climbers convinced twenty-seven others; and so on. Finally came that September day when two parties met by accident at the beginning of the climb. One party's surprise was greater than the other's, however, for one of the groups was composed of two women.

When the women saw three men approaching the rope-up spot, they must have groaned with disappointment, for Charlotte Dome was to be their first climbing venture away from the familiar and crowded Southern California rocks where they had learned to climb. Now they would have to share the route with climbers who surely (they thought) would be faster and who would secretly criticize them for their uncertainty. They also knew that they would be subject to another, more subtle form of criticism: that age-old tradition that climbing was a man's sport. When, in answer to a yelled

Low on the route, Allen Steck ponders his next moves. Steve Roper.

question from one of the women, one of the men shouted unthinkingly, "What did you say, honey?" the women girded themselves for an unpleasant day on the rock.

Although women have been climbing just about as long as men, their role until the last ten years or so has paralleled their role in society as a whole: they were relegated to being followers of mostly easy routes.

Many male climbers, of course, also fit into this category, but usually they were called "inexperienced," not "boy climbers." (One never hears the phrase, "He's pretty good for a boy.") The myth that women don't have the physical or emotional strength to ascend the bigger climbs was as old as the concept of roped climbing itself. But lately women have been gaining experience leading—the only skill they previously lacked. True, many females may be stymied by 5.12 overhangs, but so are the authors of this book, along with many of their macho climbing partners. Charlotte Dome, however, holds no such obstacles, and during that September ascent the battle of the sexes was forgotten in the course of superb climbing, with both parties gathering congenially on the summit following their respective efforts.

First ascent

Chris Jones, Galen Rowell, and Fred Beckey. October 1970.

Elevation

The summit is 10,690 feet above sea level. The south face is approximately 1000 feet high.

Difficulty

III, 5.7. The route was overrated by the first ascenders, and this mistake was perpetuated in the climber's guide.

Time

Five to eight hours from the campsite below the dome.

Maps

USGS quadrangle: Mount Pinchot, scale 1:62,500. If one approaches from the west, take along the Marion Peak quadrangle.

Useful reference

The Climber's Guide to the High Sierra.

Route description

From the town of Independence, on U.S. Highway 395, drive west to the roadhead at Onion Valley. Hike over Kearsarge Pass (11,760 feet) and follow marked trails three more miles to Charlotte Lake. From its west end follow a faint path downstream for several miles until below the obvious dome. Allow a full day for this ten-mile approach.

An alternate approach, equally long, begins on the west side of the Sierra at the end of Kings Canyon Highway. Take the marked trail up Bubbs Creek for eight miles or so; then follow Charlotte Creek steeply upward to the base of the dome.

The south face is more correctly a rounded buttress, especially on its lower part. Ascend brushy slopes and steep slabs to a huge bowl left of this buttress. A choice of class 4 pitches takes one onto the actual buttress. Continue up class 4 rock, working diagonally right at times, to a steep section. Several cracks split its upper part; the easiest is the most prominent and most fearsome-looking. This 5.7 slot is probably the hardest part of the climb.

On the next pitch, work up and slightly right to another steep step, which is climbed by a 5.7 dihedral. This pitch ends on small belay ledges. The next lead—the fifth if one counts the two class 4 approach pitches—meanders back and forth over small knobs. Midway on this pitch is a 30-foot traverse to the right.

The Furrow Pitch is next, and one can belay in any of the numerous alcoves at its top. A long, steep, easy pitch then leads to a huge ledge. Above this is one of the finest pitches, a steep 5.5 face with orange knobs. Shortly above the end of this lead is the summit ridge.

The descent is easy to describe and equally easy to make. Drop down the class 3 north ridge of the dome to easier ground; then descend low-angled slabs down and east to brushy slopes and the creek.

Equipment

No pitons ever have been driven on this climb, and it is the only route included in this book which always has been done clean. Chocks work perfectly in this type of granite, and flakes offer superb protection. Carry a standard selection of fifteen chocks.

Dick Long ascends the knob-covered granite near the summit.   Allen Steck.

299

Lover's Leap
Traveler Buttress

50

California is justly famous among climbers for the quality of its rock. Yosemite Valley's ultrasmooth, monolithic granite, of course, is coveted—and feared—by climbers from all over the world. Nearby Tuolumne Meadows is noted for its unique knobby granite, which permits free climbing of a remarkably high standard on blank-appearing walls. Not quite so well known internationally is Tahquitz Rock, the haunt of rockclimbers who practice the sport in the southern part of the state. This striking dome offers more than a hundred routes, and its orange-colored granite is renowned for its soundness. Many climbers gravitate automatically to these three areas, neglecting a 700-foot-high wall near Lake Tahoe called Lover's Leap, a formation composed of a type of granite unlike any found elsewhere in North America.

◀ *The central section of Lover's Leap. Main Ledge can be seen one-third of the way up the route.* Steve Roper.

Because of a freakish interaction of geology and weathering, the fantastic granite of Lover's Leap is a rockclimber's paradise. Running across the entire half-mile width of the near-vertical cliff are thousands of dikes—or sills—which provide not only hand- and footholds but even belay stations. Spaced from one to eight feet apart, these countless, minuscule ledges form a veritable ladder to the top of the cliff. Climbing difficulties arise whenever the dikes merge into the matrix for a few feet, resulting in a smooth surface devoid of alternate holds. Some sections of the cliff are blessed with more dikes than others; the difficulty of a prospective route usually can be judged from afar by studying the number and configuration of the dikes.

Perhaps because the name Lover's Leap is such a cliché, climbers throughout the years have chosen more imaginative names for the various routes on the cliff, including Eeyore's Ecstasy, Craven Image, Bear's Reach, and Surrealistic Pillar. The name of the finest climb on the cliff—Traveler Buttress—at the very least demonstrates the involuted workings of one person's mind. On a climbing trip to the area in June 1966, Steve Roper noticed a pink-colored patch of granite part way up a 600-foot-high buttress. It reminded him that pink, or pinko, was the pejorative word attached to some of his heroes during the

McCarthy era. In a flash, "pinko" had traversed Roper's brain circuitry and emerged as "fellow traveler," a synonomous but more pleasing term. "Fellow Traveler Buttress" seemed awkward, so Roper shortened it; thus ten seconds after the initial sighting of the pink rock, a route name was born. None of Roper's companions on that trip were as enamored as he with the derivation of the name, but with the subsequent publication of Roper's brief climbing guide to Lover's Leap, the name Traveler Buttress became permanently entrenched in the climber's lexicon.

Traveler Buttress lies just to the left of the tallest section of the cliff. Although Roper and his partners, Gordon Webster and Steve Thompson, knew that the upper two-thirds of the buttress—the section rising above wide, bushy Main Ledge—had been climbed by an unknown party, they were fascinated by the 160-foot, dead-vertical wall leading from the ground to Main Ledge. This imposing face is rippled with dikes and displays a few vertical crack systems. If the face could be climbed, the men thought, it would be a logical and aesthetic start to the route on the upper buttress. The climbers uncoiled their ropes on Tombstone Ledge, upon which a cluster of granite obelisks stands. Joking about what it would be like to plummet onto such spikes, the climbers readied their gear.

Roper won the coin toss to determine who would lead the first pitch, but within minutes he was wishing he had lost the honor. The climb began abruptly with a series of mantelshelf moves which had to be made quickly to avoid severely straining one's arms. The wall was so steep that finding adequate resting spots proved difficult for Roper, whose arm strength was not exceptional. Protection also proved problematic, for it was difficult to let go long enough to search for a piton crack. Fortunately, twenty feet above the ground Roper encountered an eight-inch-wide dike and was able to flatten himself against the cliff and free both hands. Having relaxed his nearly cramped arms, he realized protection had priority and therefore was pleased to find that an intermittent dike at eye level had weathered into a collection of jug-like knobs. Wrapping a sling tightly around one of these knobs, Roper affixed his rope with an audible sigh. Moments earlier the granite spikes below had seemed as threatening as a shark's gape; from this new position, they appeared tiny and benign.

The first pitch of Traveler Buttress is steep, but the conspicuous dikes provide holds as well as resting places. Gordon Webster.

The remainder of the eighty-foot pitch was somewhat easier, though still complicated and time-consuming. Roper established his belay on an airy, foot-wide dike, using three knobs to anchor himself. On the next lead Thompson faced an imposing overhang not far above the belay dike. Luckily, a jamcrack provided key footholds, and the tall, agile leader was able to surmount the obstacle quickly. Two hours after they began climbing, the three men stood on Main Ledge, gazing upward at their next challenge.

A series of fixed pitons midway up the smooth, pink wall indicated to the three young climbers that direct aid had been used by previous groups. They knew the pitch had been climbed free only once, when Dick Long had wriggled up a strenuous squeeze chimney, rating a ten-foot section 5.9. Because there were no dikes on this section, Long had compared the obstacle to a typical, smooth Yosemite crack.

At this point it was Webster's turn to lead, and since he was a seasoned Yosemite crack climber, he overcame the slot with minimal grunting and swearing. The upper part of the pitch consisted of a two-inch-wide crack that proved ideal for hand-jamming, and Webster surged up the crack to a belay ramp 100 feet above Main Ledge.

Thompson insisted on the next lead, feeling that each of his partners had led a superlative pitch while his single effort had been middling by comparison. Making several difficult moves look trivial, Thompson disappeared around a corner. Immediately the belay rope began snaking out rapidly; Roper and Webster stared at one another and at the diminishing pile of rope. It was not until Webster had turned the corner that he discovered the explanation: the dikes were so large and plentiful that there was no need to pause, even though the rock lay at an angle of seventy degrees. Although the exposure was tremendous, the climbing on the rococo wall proved facile. Thompson was grinning like a Cheshire cat when Webster reached the foot-wide belay dike, and the two men agreed that it had been a fitting pitch for Thompson to have accomplished. After another hundred feet of easy climbing, the three men reached the top of the cliff, realizing instinctively that Traveler Buttress was destined to become a frequently climbed route.

Steve Roper searches for a hold during the first ascent of the lower section of the buttress. Gordon Webster.

303

Upon publication of Roper's guide to Lover's Leap in the 1967 issue of *Ascent,* rockclimbers began flocking to the cliff, establishing dozens of first-rate routes. Of all the difficult climbs, however, Traveler Buttress became the most popular. Royal Robbins—who was so impressed with Lover's Leap that he founded a climbing school at the rock in the late 1960s—later wrote a tribute to the route: "Personally, I think the best route on Lover's Leap is Traveler Buttress. It takes first place for quality of climbing, variety, situation, and length. The first pitch is steep, intricate, and sustained. Although the technical difficulty is only 5.7, that moderate rating belies the difficulty, which is greater, for the leader at least, because of the problems of 'putting it together.' Traveler is a great route. . . ."

At the top of the dike-covered first pitch, the leader, visible at center of photo, sets up a belay.   Gordon Webster.

First ascent

The steep section leading to Main Ledge was first climbed by Steve Thompson, Gordon Webster, and Steve Roper on June 26, 1966. Although the first ascent of the upper part of the buttress is unknown, Dick Long and Allen Steck made the first free ascent of this section in 1965.

Elevation

The top of the cliff is approximately 6900 feet above sea level.

Difficulty

II, 5.9.

Time

Three hours.

Map

USGS quadrangle: Pyramid Peak, scale 1:24,000.

Useful reference

Climber's Guide to the Tahoe Region.

Route description

Lover's Leap is located on U.S. Highway 50 a short distance southwest of Lake Tahoe. Park at Strawberry Lodge, a small resort lying nine miles east of the town of Kyburz.

Cross the bridge over the American River and follow a poor road which leads east toward the obvious cliff. Upon reaching the main section of the cliff, leave the road and ascend talus to the base of Traveler Buttress, which lies just to the right of a huge gash that splits the formation.

On the first pitch, more or less follow the left-hand crack of two parallel cracks; then belay just beneath an overhang. Turn this obstacle on either side and then continue to Main Ledge.

The spectacular crux pitch (5.9) is next and needs no description. Belay 100 feet above Main Ledge, just right of a small ceiling. Next, climb a 5.8 ramp; then turn a corner and wander up enjoyable, high-angled rock to the rim.

The easy and rapid descent leads down to the east, paralleling the rim.

Equipment

Carry a small selection of chocks up to three inches; pitons are not necessary.

Remarks

The climbing season in the Lake Tahoe region runs from April to November, although winter climbing is becoming popular. Beware of rattlesnakes in the area.

Gordon Webster reaches for a piton as he contemplates the crux crack on the third pitch. Steve Roper.

An Explanation of the Rating System

The system used to rate the difficulty of individual pitches on the climbs described in this book was developed by European mountaineers in the 1920s. Refined in California after World War II, the Sierra Club System separates those climbs which can be accomplished without artificial aids into the five categories explained below.

Class 1 climbing requires only simple hiking. Class 2 encompasses rough, off-trail hiking where the hands occasionally are used for balance. Class 3 climbing requires the use of handholds and footholds; the consequences of a fall are such that an unsteady climber will feel more secure if he or she uses a rope.

Class 4 usually involves steep rock, much smaller holds, and great exposure. Whereas a class 3 fall may result in a broken leg, an unroped fall on a class 4 section may well be fatal; therefore ropes should be carried and used. A thorough knowledge of knots, belay techniques, and rappelling is obligatory.

Class 5, which for the rockclimber is subdivided into thirteen categories of increasing difficulty (5.0, 5.1 . . . 5.11, 5.12), consists of difficult climbing requiring protection. This protection can take the form of the flakes and natural projections common on most high-mountain routes, where the rock often is severely weathered. On more monolithic rock, such as that found in Yosemite Valley, chocks or pitons must be placed in cracks. In general, a class 5 climb is quite steep, and the available holds, often less than an inch wide, must be searched out. Jamming and liebacking techniques come into play, and proficient rope management is mandatory. No climber should venture onto such a climb unless he or she has received proper instruction in belaying.

As mentioned earlier, the class 1–5 system is used only to rate free routes—those done without direct aid. To rate individual aid pitches, the letter "A" is used in conjunction with a numeral from 1 to 5. A1 designates the easiest type of aid climbing, where pitons or chocks can be inserted rapidly into perfectly shaped cracks. A5 involves difficult and insecure placements, and the chances of a piton or chock slipping out when the climber's weight is applied are extremely high.

A third type of rating also is applied to climbs. Roman numerals from I to VI designate the Grade of a route; a Grade number gives a rough indication of the overall difficulty to be found. Such factors as route length, commitment, strenuousness, and continuity are taken into consideration. Grades I and II are relatively easy and can be accomplished in a few hours. Grades III and IV indicate committing routes which generally take most of a day. Grades V and VI are extreme "big-wall" climbs usually requiring several days. Developed in Yosemite Valley in the late 1950s, this overall rating system works well for pure rock climbs. Several guidebook writers have used the system to indicate the difficulty of snow-and-ice climbs as well, though some confusion has resulted from this practice. For example, should one compare a route on El Capitan with a route on Mount McKinley when the climbing problems and dangers differ so radically? Many climbers believe one should not, and therefore we have not rated the snow-and-ice climbs in this book (primarily those in Alaska and the Yukon). Perhaps a different and more accurate system for grading alpine routes will be developed in the future.

Notes on Sources

Listed below are the sources of quotations appearing in this book. Other works researched also are listed. Much of the information in the climbing accounts is derived from the personal experience of the authors. Other sources of information, not listed in this note, include the various climbing guidebooks applicable to specific geographical areas. A few abbreviations are used: *AAJ (American Alpine Journal)*; *AJ (Alpine Journal)*; *APP (Appalachia)*; AS (Allen Steck); *CAJ (Canadian Alpine Journal)*; *SCB (Sierra Club Bulletin)*; SR (Steve Roper).

Alaska and the Yukon

A major source of information for all the accounts in this section was two comprehensive articles by Terris Moore and Kenneth Andrasko in the 1976 *AJ* and the 1978 *AJ*.

The remark by Vitus Bering in the Mount Saint Elias account is reported by Francis P. Farquhar in the 1959 *AAJ*. The quotes attributed to Filippo de Filippi come from two sources: the 1898 *AJ* and *The Ascent of Mount St. Elias (Alaska)*. Other sources include *A History of Mountaineering in the Saint Elias Mountains*, by Walter A. Wood, and Israel Russell's article in the May 1891 issue of *National Geographic*.

The many Carpé quotes in the Mount Fairweather account are taken from the 1931 *CAJ*. The quote "The Fairweather Range is subject . . ." is from an article by Walter Gove and Loren Adkins in the 1969 *AAJ*. Ladd's comment is reported by J. Monroe Thorington in the 1950 *AAJ*. Paddy Sherman's book *Cloud Walkers* also proved useful, as did a conversation between Bradford Washburn and AS (December 1978).

The comments by Beckey in the Mount Hunter write-up are from his article in the 1955 *AAJ*. Another helpful source for this account was Bradford Washburn's article in the 1953 *AAJ*.

The Drasdo remark in the Mount McKinley account first appeared in the 1974 *Ascent*. Washburn's comments come from the 1956–57 issue of *The Mountain World*. Maraini's quotes can be found in the 1963 *AJ*. The Cassin quote comes from his article in the 1962 *AAJ*.

Welsch's remark in the Moose's Tooth account comes from his article in the 1965 *AAJ*. Another useful source was Anthony Smythe's note in the 1963 *AAJ*.

In the Mount Huntington write-up, the Terray quote comes from the 1965 *AAJ*. All remarks attributed to Roberts can be found in his book *The Mountain of My Fear*.

The Russell quote in the Mount Logan account comes from his article in the June 1892 issue of *Century* magazine. Long's remark stems from a conversation with AS (November 1978). The comments by Evans come from his unpublished diary and his article in the 1966 *AAJ*. Steck's quotes come from his unpublished diary and his article (revised by author) in the 1967 *Ascent*. Paddy Sherman's *Cloud Walkers* and Walter A. Wood's *A History of Mountaineering in the Saint Elias Mountains* also proved useful.

DeMaria's remarks in the Middle Triple Peak write-up are taken from the 1966 *AAJ*. The Embick quotes are from the 1978 *AAJ*.

Western Canada

The remark by Tewes in the Mount Sir Donald account is paraphrased from the original German by an unknown author in the May 1906 issue of the *AJ*. The phrase "cannot be considered difficult . . ." is by an anonymous writer in the February 1910 issue of the *AJ*. Other sources used were the 1936 *AAJ* and J. Monroe Thorington's original guide to the Interior Ranges.

All of the Kain quotations in the Bugaboo Spire account can be found in his book *Where the Clouds Can Go*. In a letter to SR (February 1979) David Isles described his memories of the first ascent. Also helpful was John Turner's note in the 1959 *AAJ*.

In the South Howser Tower write-up, Beckey's article in the 1962 *AAJ* provided valuable information and all the quotes. His article in the 1962 *CAJ* also was useful.

Kain's quote "God made the mountains . . ." in the Mount Robson account is reported by Dmitri Nabokov in the 1954 *AAJ*. Mike Sherrick reports Kain's phrase "I see more glaciers . . ." in the 1956 *SCB*. Darling's remark comes from the 1915 *CAJ*. All comments by Sherrick can be found in the 1956 *SCB*. The Claunch quote comes from the 1956 *AAJ*. In addition to the above sources, Kain's *Where the Clouds Can Go* proved helpful.

The Chouinard quotes in the Mount Edith Cavell account come from his article in the 1962 *AAJ*. The comment by Eberl is found in the 1967 *AAJ*. A conversation between SR and Chouinard (April 1977) resulted in his recollection of the sports jacket incident.

The Collie quote in the Mount Alberta account comes from the book he co-authored with H. E. M. Stutfield: *Climbs and Explorations in the Canadian Rockies*. The Palmer quotes are taken from the February 1926 issue of *APP*. The four Weber comments (with spelling modernized by authors) can be found in the 1953 *AAJ*. The Maki register quote is reproduced photographically in the 1949 *CAJ*. Oberlin's comment is found in the 1949 *AAJ*. Other sources used were the December 1948 *APP* and the 1959 *CAJ*.

All comments by Wittich in the Mount Temple write-up are from his article in the 1932 *CAJ*. The Jones quote comes from a conversation with SR (March 1979). Further information was obtained from a conversation between SR and Glen Boles (February 1979).

In the Mount Waddington account, the two Munday quotes come from the 1933 *CAJ*. Robinson's comment is taken from the 1936 *SCB*. Wiessner's remark is from the 1936 *CAJ*. Beckey's comment can be found in his book *Challenge of the North Cascades*. Culbert's quote comes from his *A Climber's Guide to the Coastal Ranges of British Columbia*.

Beckey's opening remark in the Devil's Thumb account has been paraphrased by SR from a statement reported by Dick Culbert in the 1971 *CAJ*. The remaining Beckey quotes come from his article in the 1947 *AAJ*. Culbert's two quotes can be found in the 1971 *CAJ*. Donaldson's comment appears in the May 1972 issue of *Summit*. Other sources used were the 1972 *CAJ* and the 1972 *AAJ*.

McCarthy's remarks in the Lotus Flower Tower write-up are from the 1969 *Ascent*. The numerous quotes attributed to Bill come from his article in the 1969 *AAJ*. Wexler's comment is from the 1956 *AAJ*. Buckingham's remark is found in the 1961 *AAJ*. Levin's statement comes from the 1978 *AAJ*.

The Pacific Northwest

Molenaar's remarks in the Mount Rainier account are taken from his book *The Challenge of Rainier*. The comments by Campbell can be found in the same book, quoted by Molenaar. Other sources include Francis P. Farquhar's article in the 1960 *AAJ* and Will Borrow's article in the December 1935 issue of the *Mountaineer*.

The Ulrich quote in the Forbidden Peak account comes from his article in the 1936 *AAJ*. All of Beckey's remarks are found in his *Challenge of the North Cascades*. The lengthy quote at the end of the account comes from a letter from Martha Higgenbotham to AS (January 1979).

The two Manning remarks in the Mount Shuksan account come from Tom Miller's *The North Cascades*. Beckey's remarks can be found in his *Challenge of the North Cascades*. The Curtis quote is found in the 1907 *Mountaineer*.

Beckey's remarks in the Slesse Mountain write-up can be found in his *Challenge of the North Cascades*. Other sources are Paul Starr's article in the 1970 *CAJ*, conversations with Starr and Alan Kearney (by AS, January 1979), and Eric Bjornstad's article in the January–February 1964 issue of *Summit*.

Beckey's comment about Russell in the Mount Stuart account comes from his *Cascade Alpine Guide: Climbing and High Routes, Columbia River to Stevens Pass*. The two quotes by Rusk are found in his book *Tales of a Western Mountaineer*.

The remark by Davis in the Liberty Bell Mountain account is from the 1938 *SCB*. The two Beckey quotes come from his *Challenge of the North Cascades*. Jones' comment is from his *Climbing in North America*.

Wyoming

In the Devil's Tower account, the quote "by driving pegs . . ." is from Ray Mattison's *Devil's Tower National Monument: A History*. "There will be plenty . . ." comes from the same source. The Butterworth quotes are taken from the June 1938 issue of *APP*. Another source perused was Lawrence Coveney's article in the December 1937 issue of *APP*.

Underhill's comments in the Grand Teton–North Ridge write-up come from his article in the 1931 *CAJ*.

Sources for the Grand Teton–Direct Exum Ridge account are Kenneth Henderson's article in the December 1936 issue of *APP* and Fritiof Fryxell's article in the June 1932 issue of *APP*.

The Chouinard quote in the Grand Teton–North Face account is from his book *Climbing Ice*. The Garner quote comes from the 1951 *AAJ*. Other information was obtained in conversations (February 1979) with the late Willi Unsoeld.

Emerson's remark in the Mount Moran account can be found in the 1954 *SCB*. Another useful source was Leigh Ortenburger's article in the 1963 *AAJ*.

Yensen's comment in the Pingora write-up comes from the 1963 *AAJ*. A letter from Harry Daley to SR (October 1978) also proved helpful.

Some of the ideas expressed in the Wolf's Head account were suggested by Wilfrid Noyce's *The Springs of Adventure*.

Colorado

In the Crestone Needle account, the first nine quotes by Ellingwood come from his article in the November 1925 issue of *Trail and Timberline*. The final Ellingwood quote, "roots ten feet long," is found in the June 1925 issue of *Trail and Timberline*. Jones' comment is from his *Climbing in North America*. The phrase "Ormes' own account . . ." is by an anonymous editor in the September 1937 issue of *Trail and Timberline*. The July 1955 issue of the same journal also proved useful, as did a conversation (July 1977) between SR and the late Shirli Voigt.

The comments by Northcutt in the Hallett Peak account can be found in the January 1957 issue of *Summit*. Also used as a source was Northcutt's article in the 1959 *AAJ*. A conversation (April 1977) between SR and Yvon Chouinard also was helpful.

Information on the Petit Grepon climb came from the authors' conversations with Bill Buckingham, Yvon Chouinard, Mike Covington, and Steve Komito.

The two Rearick quotations in the Longs Peak account come from his article in the 1961 *AAJ*. A conversation (September 1978) between SR and Billy Westbay concerning the first free ascent also proved useful.

The Southwest

Ellingwood's remark in the Shiprock account is reported by Robert Ormes in the July 22, 1939, issue of the *Saturday Evening Post*. David Brower's article in the February 3, 1940, issue of the same magazine is the source of the quote "number one climbing problem. . . ." Robinson's comment is taken from the 1940 *SCB*. "Those iron spikes . . ." comes from a conversation between SR and a Navajo tribal ranger at Monument Valley, Utah, in October 1969. "Because of the Navajo's traditional fear . . ." is contained in a letter to SR (December 4, 1969) from Sam Day III, Director of the Navajo Parks and Recreation Department. Other sources include the 1940 *AAJ*; letters to SR from Dr. Ernest Anderson of Los Alamos, New Mexico; and the typescript of a film clip shown on KOB-TV, Albuquerque, New Mexico, on October 13, 1969 (Siri's view of the smoke).

Sources for the Castleton Tower write-up include Ingalls' note in the 1963 *AAJ* and correspondence between SR and Ed Webster (February 1979).

The Ingalls quote in the Titan account is from his article in the November 1962 issue of *National Geographic*. Another useful source was Ingalls' note in the 1963 *AAJ*.

California

Harris' note in the 1937 *SCB* proved helpful in the writing of the Royal Arches account.

The three Leonard quotes in the Lost Arrow write-up come from, respectively, the 1936, 1938, and 1941 *SCB*. Nelson's comments can be found in his articles in the 1947 and 1948 *SCB*. Mark Powell's note in the 1957 *SCB* also proved helpful.

Steck's comment in the Sentinel Rock account is taken from his article in the 1951 *SCB*. Salathé's statement comes from a conversation with SR (May 1966).

In the Middle Cathedral Rock account, the phrase "new climbs included . . ." is from Hervey Voge's note in the 1956 *AAJ*. Pratt's comment about Warren Harding (slightly revised by the author in 1979) first appeared in the 1965 *AAJ*.

The opening quote in the Half Dome write-up is reported in the 1954 edition of *A Climber's Guide to the High Sierra*. J. S. Chase's phrase "frightful amputation" is reported by François Matthes in *The Incomparable Valley*. All three comments by Sherrick can be found in his article in the 1958 *SCB*. Other sources include the 1973 *AAJ* and the March 1967 issue of *Summit*.

The Harding quotes in the El Capitan—Nose Route account come from his article in the 1959 *AAJ*. Robbins' quote comes from his article in the 1960 *SCB*.

Robbins' comment in the El Capitan—Salathé Wall write-up is taken from the 1963 *AAJ*. His note in the 1962 *SCB* also was helpful.

Farquhar's reflection about Clarence King in the Mount Whitney account comes from his article in the 1929 *SCB*. Muir's remark is reported by Farquhar in the 1935 *SCB*. The five Underhill quotes are from his article in the 1932 *SCB*. Clyde's comment is taken from his *Norman Clyde of the Sierra Nevada*.

Two sources proved useful for the Fairview Dome write-up: Reed's note in the 1959 *SCB* and the recollections of Chuck Pratt as reported to SR in 1978.

Whitney's comment in the Clyde Minaret account is cited in Francis Farquhar's article in the 1964 *AAJ*. Michael's remark is from the 1930 *SCB*, as is the Clyde quote. Other sources include Allen Steck's note in the 1964 *AAJ* and Bruce Kinnison's article in the January—February 1971 issue of *Summit*.

In the Charlotte Dome account, the sentence "It is difficult to conceive . . ." is from George Sessions' note in the 1960 *SCB*. All of Jones' remarks come from his note in the 1971 *AAJ*.

The remark by Robbins in the Lover's Leap account comes from *Climber's Guide to the Tahoe Region*.

Bibliography

Guidebooks

Alaska Alpine Co. *Mount McKinley Climber's Guide*. Anchorage: Alaska Alpine Co., 1976.

American Alpine Club. *Climber's Guide to the Cascade and Olympic Mountains of Washington* (based on a previous edition by Fred Beckey). New York: The American Alpine Club, 1961.

Beckey, Fred. *Cascade Alpine Guide: Climbing and High Routes, Columbia River to Stevens Pass*. Seattle: The Mountaineers, 1973.

————. *Cascade Alpine Guide: Climbing and High Routes, Stevens Pass to Rainy Pass*. Seattle: The Mountaineers, 1977.

Bonney, Orrin H., and Lorraine G. Bonney. *Field Book: The Wind River Range*. Houston: Orrin H. Bonney and Lorraine G. Bonney, 1968.

Culbert, Dick. *A Climber's Guide to the Coastal Ranges of British Columbia*. Banff: The Alpine Club of Canada, no date.

Dexter, Greg; Rick Sumner; John Taylor; and Bill Todd. *Climber's Guide to the Tahoe Region*. Modesto, California: Mountain Letters, 1976.

Fricke, Walter W., Jr. *A Climber's Guide to the Rocky Mountain National Park Area*. Boulder: Paddock Publishing, 1971.

Kelsey, Joe. *A Guide to Climbing and Hiking in the Wind River Mountains*. San Francisco: Sierra Club Books, forthcoming.

Meyers, George. *Yosemite Climbs*. Modesto, California: Mountain Letters, no date.

Nesbit, Paul W. *Longs Peak: Its Story and a Climbing Guide*. Colorado Springs: Paul W. Nesbit, 1963.

Ormes, Robert. *Guide to the Colorado Mountains*. Chicago: The Swallow Press, 1970.

Ortenburger, Leigh. *A Climber's Guide to the Teton Range*. San Francisco: Sierra Club, 1965.

315

Putnum, William L. *A Climber's Guide to the Interior Ranges of British Columbia*. New York: The American Alpine Club, 1971.

Putnum, William L., and Glen W. Boles. *Climber's Guide to the Rocky Mountains of Canada—South*. New York: The American Alpine Club, 1973.

Putnum, William L.; Robert Kruszyna; and Chris Jones. *Climber's Guide to the Rocky Mountains of Canada—North*. New York: The American Alpine Club, 1974.

Roper, Steve. *Climber's Guide to Yosemite Valley*. San Francisco: Sierra Club Books, 1971.

———. *The Climber's Guide to the High Sierra*. San Francisco: Sierra Club Books, 1976.

Rypkema, Terry, and Curt Haire. *A Climber's Guide to Devil's Tower National Monument*. Devil's Tower, Wyoming: Terry Rypkema and Curt Haire, 1977.

Ungnade, Herbert E. *Guide to the New Mexico Mountains*. Albuquerque: University of New Mexico Press, 1965.

Histories and Memoirs

Abruzzi, Duke of the. *The Ascent of Mount St. Elias (Alaska)*. Narrated by Filippo de Filippi. New York: Frederick Stokes Co., 1899.

Beckey, Fred. *Challenge of the North Cascades*. Seattle: The Mountaineers, 1969. Memoirs of a fabled mountaineer.

Browne, Belmore. *The Conquest of Mount McKinley*. 1913. Reprint. Boston: Houghton Mifflin, 1956.

Bueler, William M. *Roof of the Rockies: A History of Mountaineering in Colorado*. Boulder: Pruett Publishing, 1974.

Clyde, Norman. *Norman Clyde of the Sierra Nevada*. San Francisco: Scrimshaw Press, 1971. Twenty-nine essays.

Collie, J. Norman, and H. E. M. Stutfield. *Climbs and Explorations in the Canadian Rockies*. London: Longmans, Green, and Co., 1903.

Farquhar, Francis P. *History of the Sierra Nevada*. Berkeley, Los Angeles, and London: University of California Press, 1965.

Godfrey, Bob, and Dudley Chelton. *Climb!* Boulder, Colorado: Alpine House Publishing, 1977. A history of Colorado rockclimbing.

Harding, Warren. *Downward Bound: A Mad! Guide to Rock Climbing*. Englewood Cliffs, New Jersey: Prentice-Hall, 1975. Memoirs and advice by a noted Yosemite rockclimber.

Jones, Chris. *Climbing in North America*. Berkeley, Los Angeles, and London: University of California Press, 1976. A comprehensive history.

Kain, Conrad. *Where the Clouds Can Go*. Edited by J. Monroe Thorington. Boston: Charles T. Branford Co., 1954. Memoirs of the most famous guide of the Canadian Rockies.

Miller, Tom. *The North Cascades*. Seattle: The Mountaineers, 1964. Many photographs of the region, with accompanying text by Harvey Manning.

Molenaar, Dee. *The Challenge of Rainier*. Seattle: The Mountaineers, 1971. A record of explorations and ascents of the Northwest's greatest peak.

Munday, Don. *The Unknown Mountain*. London: Hodder and Stoughton, 1948. Early explorations in the Mount Waddington region.

Roberts, David. *The Mountain of My Fear*. New York: The Vanguard Press, 1968. A personal account of the first ascent of the west face of Mount Huntington.

Rowell, Galen, ed. *The Vertical World of Yosemite: A Collection of Photographs and Writings on Rock Climbing in Yosemite*. Berkeley: Wilderness Press, 1974.

Rusk, C. E. *Tales of a Western Mountaineer*. 1924. Reprint. Seattle: The Mountaineers, 1978. Early adventures in the Cascades.

Sherman, Paddy. *Cloud Walkers: Six Climbs on Major Canadian Peaks.* Toronto: Macmillan of Canada, 1965.

Watson, Sir Norman, and Edward J. King. *Round Mystery Mountain.* London: Edward Arnold and Co., 1935. Early ski adventures in the Mount Waddington region.

Wood, Walter A. *A History of Mountaineering in the Saint Elias Mountains.* Vancouver: Yukon Alpine Centennial Expedition, 1967.

Books on Technique

Blackshaw, Alan. *Mountaineering: From Hill Walking to Alpine Climbing.* London: Kaye and Ward, 1965.

Chouinard, Yvon. *Climbing Ice.* San Francisco: Sierra Club Books, 1978.

Climbing Committee of the Mountaineers. *Mountaineering: The Freedom of the Hills.* Seattle: The Mountaineers, 1960.

Robbins, Royal. *Basic Rockcraft.* Glendale, California: La Siesta Press, 1971.

————. *Advanced Rockcraft.* Glendale, California: La Siesta Press, 1973.

Periodicals

The Alpine Journal. An annual record of mountain adventures and scientific endeavors. Published by the Alpine Club (London).

The American Alpine Journal. An annual compendium of accounts of new routes. Published by the American Alpine Club (New York).

Appalachia. Two major issues a year contain accounts of new climbs. Published by the Appalachian Mountain Club (Boston).

Ascent. A collection of mountaineering experiences in word and image. Published annually by the Sierra Club (San Francisco) from 1967 to 1974, then sporadically.

The Canadian Alpine Journal. A well-illustrated annual emphasizing Canadian mountaineering. Published by the Alpine Club of Canada (Banff).

Climbing. A bi-monthly magazine devoted to climbing news and articles. Published in Aspen, Colorado.

Mountain. A bi-monthly magazine emphasizing European and British climbs. Published in Sheffield, England.

The Mountaineer. Published by The Mountaineers (Seattle), this monthly (semi-monthly in June and July) reports climbing news pertaining to the Cascades.

The Mountain World. Informative volumes containing accounts of major expeditions and scientific observations. Published annually by George Allen and Unwin (London) from 1953 to 1955, then bi-annually to 1965.

Off Belay. A bi-monthly magazine emphasizing climbs in the Northwest. Published in Renton, Washington.

Sierra Club Bulletin. The annual issues, published by the Sierra Club (San Francisco) from the 1890s to 1963, contain hundreds of interesting articles about North American mountaineering. The Club's magazine is known now as *Sierra*.

Summit. A bi-monthly climbing magazine published at Big Bear Lake, California.

Trail and Timberline. The monthly magazine of the Colorado Mountain Club (Denver).

Index

Abruzzi, Duke of the, 5
Abruzzi Ridge, Mount Saint Elias, 4–8
Adam, Kenneth, 133, 232–34
Agassiz Glacier, 5–8
Ahwahnee Buttress, 295
Airoldi, Luigi, 21–24
Alaska Range, 3, 15
Alberta, Mount, 75–79
Alippi, Gigi, 21–24
Alley Camp, 32, 35
Alpine Club of Canada, 68
Amedeo, Prince Luigi, 5, 8
Amphitheater Lake, 149, 152
Anderson, George, 255
Anderson, Lloyd, 113–16
Angel Glacier, 70–74
Ann, Lake, 121
Ant-Tree Ledge, 251–53
Arnold, Jack, 238–42
Astoria River, 74
Athabasca River, 75, 77
Ayres, Fred, 78

Bacher, John, 205
Bacon, Paul, 38–40
Bad God's Tower, 141
Baer, Hans, 126
Baird Glacier, 95
Baker, Mount, 122, 125, 126
Baker, Robert, 27
Barber, Henry, 247
Bartleet, A.M., 54
Basalt Gully, 210–15
Bear Hug Pitch, 233
Bear Lake, 193
Bear Prairie, 107
Bear's Reach, 301
Beck, Eric, 259
Beckey, Fred, 15–18, 27, 31, 61–64,
    71–74, 90, 93–97, 105, 113–16,
    120–26, 129, 130, 133, 135, 174,
    217, 295–98
Beckey, Helmy, 90, 113–16
Bedayn, Raffi, 211–14
Berg Lake, 67, 68
Bering, Mount, 7
Bering, Vitus, 5
Bernd, Ed, 32–35
Bertulis, Alex, 135, 136
Bettler, Phil, 245–47
Bierl, Klaus, 27–29
Big Sandy Lake, 171, 176
Big Step, 83, 84
Bill, Sandy, 99–103
Bishop, Barry, 224, 226

Bishop, Captain Robert, 87
Bisserlich, 43
Biven, Barrie, 25, 27
Bjornstad, Eric, 27, 125, 126
Black Dike, 157
Black Dike Route, Mount Moran, 81, 165
Black Face, 153, 156, 157
Black Ice Couloir, 152
Black Pyramid, 111
Black Towers, 80–84
Bohren, Christian, 51–54
Bona, Mount, 11
Bonney, Orrin, 171, 175
Boot Flake, 264, 266
Borrow, Jim, 108–10
Boston Basin, 113–16
Boston Glacier, 113
Botta, Erminio, 5, 8
Boulder Camp, 57–59
Bravo Glacier, 87, 90
Brewer, Mike, 147
British Columbia, 49, 51
British Columbia Mountain Club, 88
Broadway, 205
Brower, David, 211–14
Brown, Donald, 93
Bryan, Jack, 126
Buckingham, William, 179–82, 197
Buckskin Glacier, 25
Bugaboo Spire, ix, 49, 55–59
Butterworth, Harrison, 141–45

Cagni, Umberto, 5, 8
Calderwood, Rich, 264
Campbell, Arnie, 108–10
Campbell River, 91
Canada Rockies, 49
Canadian Pacific Railroad, 49, 51, 52, 55
Canali, Giancarlo, 21–24
Carbon Glacier, 108–11
Cariboos, 51
Carpé, Allen, 9–13
Carpé Ridge, Mount Fairweather, 9–13
Carter, Harvey, 191–93, 217
Cascade Pass, 113
Cascade Range, 105, 113
Cassin, Riccardo, 21–24, 231, 235
Cassin Ridge, Mount McKinley, 19–24,
    231
Castle Creek, 217
Castle Valley, 217, 220
Castleton Tower, 216–20
Cathedral Peak, 283
Cecile Lake, 292, 293
Charlet, Armand, 149

Charlotte Dome, 294–99
Chase, J. S., 255
Chasm Lake, 203–5
Chelan, Lake, 133
Chilcotin Indian tribe, 87
Chiliwack Group, 123
Chockstone Chimney, 150–52
Chouinard, Yvon, 61–64, 71–74, 135,
    159, 192, 199, 241, 252, 269
Cirque of the Towers, 171–75, 177, 183
Cirque of the Unclimbables, 99, 103
Claunch, Don, 67–69, 130, 131
Cle Elum, 129, 131
Clyde Meadow, 280
Clyde Minaret, 288–93
Clyde, Norman, 278, 289
Coale, Frank, 38–40
Coleman, Edmund, 107
Collie, J. Norman, 77
Collins, Dave, 125
Colorado Col, 214, 215
Colorado Mountain Club, 185, 188
Colorado Mountaineering Club Route,
    Mount Moran, 170
Columbia Icefields, 75
Columbia River, 75
Comici, Emilio, 285
Continental Divide, 49, 177
Cook, Captain James, 5, 9
Cotter, Richard, 277
Coveney, Lawrence, 141
Covington, Mike, 200
Craft, Dave, 58, 59
Cragmont Climbing Club, 237
Craig, Bob, 93–97
Craven Image, 301
Crescent Ledge, 285–87
Crestone Needle, 185–89
Crillon, Mount, 12
Crooks, Jim, 113–16, 144
Croux, Antonio, 8
Crystal Glacier, 121, 122
Culbert, Dick, 95–97
Culp, Bob, 185, 192
Currens, Ken, 90
Curtis, Asahel, 119
Curtis Ridge, 108
Cussing Crack, 145
Cutthroat Peak, 133

Daiber, Ome, 108–10
Daley, Harry, 173–75
Darling, Basil, 67
Davidson, Art, 197

Davis, Eleanor, 187–89
Davis, Jack, 251, 252
Davis, Kenneth, 133, 232–34
Dawson Creek, 99
Dawson, Glen, 278–80
Deborah, Mount, 15
Decker, Don, 167–69
DeMaria, Alvin, 44
Denali National Monument, 29
Devil's Thumb, 49, 92–97
Devil's Tower, xi, 58, 139–46, 217
Diamond, Longs Peak, 185, 201–5
Dias Glacier, 85–91
Dickey, Mount, 44
Direct Exum Ridge, Grand Teton, 153–58
Direct South Buttress, Mount Moran,
        165–70
Dolt Hole, 268
Dolt Tower, 263, 264
Donaldson, Greg, 96
Doody, Dan, 71–74
Double Cracks, 274
Double Overhang, 211, 212, 214
Double-Pendulum Pitch, 168, 169
Douglas, Fred, 95–97
Drasdo, Harold, 19
Durrance, Jack, 141–45, 155–57, 159
Durrance Route, Devil's Tower, 58, 140–46
Dyer, John, 211–14

Ear, the, 273, 274
Early Winter Spire, 133
Early Winters Creek, 133
East Buttress: Middle Cathedral Rock,
        249–53; Middle Triple Peak, 42–47
East Face, Mount Whitney, 276–81
East Nooksack Glacier, 119
East Ridge: Bugaboo Spire, 55–59; Devil's
        Thumb, 92–97; Mount Temple,
        80–84; Wolf's Head, 177–83
Eberl, Dennis, 72
Edith Cavell, Mount, 49, 61–64, 70–74
Eeyore's Ecstasy, 301
Eichorn, Jules, 278–80
El Capitan, 135, 229, 307: Nose Route,
        203, 261–68; Salathé Wall, xi, 151,
        262, 269–75
El Cap Spire, 272, 273
Eldorado Canyon, 185
Eldorado Peak, 113
Ellingwood, Albert, 185, 187–89, 209
Ellingwood Ledges, Crestone Needle,
        186–89
Embick, Andy, 43–46
Emerald Lake, 193

Emerson, Richard, 162, 163, 167–69
Emmons Glacier, 111
Emperor Falls, 69
Englishmen's Col, 25, 28, 29
Evans, John, 38–40, 257, 290–92
Exum, Glenn, 153, 154

Fairview Dome, 282–87
Fairweather Fault, 13
Fairweather Mount, 9–13, 95
Fairy Meadow, 99, 100, 103
Fan Glacier, 69
Farquhar, Francis, 277–79
Fay, Mount, 81
Feuerer, Bill, 263, 264
Feuz, Edouard, 51–54
Filippi, Filippo de, 5, 6, 8
Firestone, Harvey, 58, 59
First Pendulum Pitch, 231, 234
Fischer, John, 290
Fisher, C. A., 119
Fisher Chimneys Route, Mount Shuksan,
        119, 121, 122
Fisher Towers, 221, 227
Fitschen, Joe, 258, 266, 269
Flood Lake, 97
Flying Buttress, 245, 248
Foott, Jeff, 258
Forbidden Peak, 105, 112–17
Forgotten Peak, 113
Four Corners, 207
Franklin Glacier, 87, 88, 91
Fraser River Valley, 105
Fresh-Air Traverse, 278–81
Friction Pitch, 155, 158
Friction Traverse, 214
Frost, Tom, 99–103, 258, 266, 269–75
Fryxell, Fritiof, 149–51
Fuhrer, Hans, 87, 108
Fuhrer, Heinrich, 78, 79
Furrow Pitch, 297–99
Fury, Mount, 105
Fynn, Val, 54

Gallwas, Jerry, 255–60
Garner, Ray, 161–64
Garnet Canyon, 157
Gerhardt, Clark, 132
Ghiglione, Piero, 21
Gibraltar Route, 107, 108, 110
Gilkey, Art, 161–64
Glacier Bay National Monument, 9, 13
Glacier House, 51, 52

Glacier Lake, 99, 103
Glen Pass, 295
Glowering Spot, 261, 268
Goat Pass, 130, 132
Gonella, Francesco, 5, 8
Goode, Mount, 105
Graber, Mike, 43–46
Grandes Jorasses, 191
Grand Staircase, 279–81
Grandstand, 149, 152
Grand Teton, x, 139: Direct Exum Ridge,
        153–58; North Face, 159–64; North
        Ridge, 147–52
Granston, Bill, 120–22
Great Chimney, 245–48
Great Gendarme, 131, 132
Great Line, 101–3
Great Roof, 264–68
Great White Headwall, 61–64
Greenwood, Brian, 79, 83
Griffiths, Mel, 210
Guano Chimney, 161–64
Guano Ledge, 261

Habeler, Peter, 274
Hale, Matt, 31–35
Half Dome, 203, 229, 254–60
Hall, Henry, 87
Hallett Peak, 190–94
Hanging Glacier, 119
Hansen, Robin, 238–42
Harding, Warren, 251, 252, 255, 258,
        261–68, 283
Harrer, Heinrich, 15–18
Harris, Morgan, 231–34
Harris's Hangover, 269
Hart, Stephen, 187–89
Harvard Route, 34
Hasenkopf, Arnold, 27–29
Hashimoto, S., 79
Hatano, M., 79
Hayakawa, T. 79
Hayes, Mount, 15
Head Crack, 188, 189
Headwall, 245–48
Heart, the, 270, 271
Heart Ledge, 271–74
Heller, Sam, 144
Hempel, Mort, 252
Henderson, Kenneth, 139, 147, 155–57
Hendricks, Sterling, 159
Hennig, Andy, 119
Hickson, Joseph, 77
Higher Cathedral Rock, 203
Higher Cathedral Spire, 229

Hoffmann, Charles, 295
Hollow Flake Ledge, 269–74
Homathko Valley, 87
Hood, Mount, 105
Hopkins, George, 144
Hopkins Rescue, 144
Horn Pitch, 212–14
House, William, 88–91, 141, 210
Howser Spire, 56, 61
Hummingbird Ridge, Mount Logan, 36–41
Hunter, Mount, 14–18, 71
Huntington, Mount, 30–35
Hurley, George, 223–27

Iceberg Lake, 278–81
Icefall Point, 91
Ice Nose, 12, 13
Icy Bay, 5, 7
Illecillewaet Glacier, 52, 54
Ingalls Creek, 129, 131
Ingalls, Huntley, 217–20, 223–27
Inter Glacier, 111
Ipsut Creek, 110
Isles, David, 57–59
Isosceles, 113
Italian Alpine Club, 21

Jackson Hole, 139
Japanese Couloir, 19, 23, 24
Japanese Route, Mount Alberta, 75–79
Jasper Park Lodge, 71
Jeanette, Mount, 7
Jenny Lake, 153
Jensen, Don, 31–35
Johnson, Dale, 201
Jones, Chris, 83, 135, 187, 229, 295–98
Jungle, the, 230, 235

Kahiltna Glacier, 15–19, 21, 24
Kahiltna Notch, 24
Kain, Conrad, 55–59, 65, 77
Kaisergebirge, 88
Kamps, Bob, 203–5
Kamps, Bonnie, 204
Karakoram Range, 21
Karstens, Harry, 3
Kat Walk, 252, 253
Kate's Needle, 93
Kautz, August, 107
Kearney, Shari, 127, 130, 265
Keith, William, 108
Kennedy, John F., 23
Kiesel, Rob, 259

King, Clarence, 277, 289
King Col, 37, 41
Kinney Lake, 69
Kitchatna Range, 43, 44
Knight Inlet, 87, 91
Kohler, Hans, 79
Kor–Ingalls Route, Castleton Tower,
    216–20
Kor, Layton, 185, 193, 203, 204, 217–20,
    223–27
Kronhofer, 43

Ladd, William, 9, 11
Lakes. See names of individual lakes
Langley, Mount, 277
La Sal Mountains, 217, 221, 222
Lassen, Mount, 105
Leaning Column, 143–46
Leeper, Ed, 252
Leigh Canyon, 165, 167, 169, 170
Leonard, Richard, 237
Les Courtes, 81
Levin, Steve, 103
Liberty Bell Mountain, 133–37
Liberty Cap, 108–11
Liberty Crack, 133–37
Liberty Ridge, Mount Rainier, 105–11
Lind, Dave, 113–16
Lippmann, Fritz, 238–42
Lithuanian Roof, 133, 136
Lituya Bay, 9, 10
Lizard Head, ix, 171, 187
Loch Vale, 195
Lofthouse, Dick, 79
Logan, Mount, 6, 7, 36–41
Logan Mountains, 99
Logan, Sir William, 37
Lone Pine Creek, 280
Lonesome Lake, 171, 176
Long, Alan, 43–46
Long, Bill, 245
Long, Dick, 38–40, 135, 168, 169, 171,
    211, 249, 255, 257, 286, 290–92,
    299, 303–5
Long Ledge, 274
Longs Peak, 185, 201–5
Lost Arrow Spire, xi, 236–42
Lotus Flower Tower, 49, 98–103
Louise, Lake, 49, 81–84
Lover's Leap, 229, 300–305
Lowe, Greg, 259
Lower Cathedral Spire, 249
Lower Saddle, 152, 153, 157, 158
Lung Ledge, 274

MacCarthy, Albert, 37
McCarthy, Jim, 99–103
Machler, 43
McKinley, Mount, 3, 19–25, 231, 307
McKinley Range, 15
McLean, Russ, 45
McPherson, Don, 135–37
Main Ledge, 300, 301, 303, 305
Maki, Yuko, 77–79
Malaspina Glacier, 6, 8
Mammoth Terraces, 271, 273
Mandatory, George, 255
Manning, Harvey, 119
Maquignaz, Antonio, 8
Maraini, Fosco, 21
Marblemount, 113, 116
Marts, Steve, 125-26, 135–37
Mateo Tepee, 141
Mauri, Carlo, 21
Mazama, Washington, 137
Meadows, the, 143–46
Merry, Wayne, 256, 264–67
Messner, Reinhold, 240
Meybohm, Henry, 15–18
Michael, Charles, 289
Middle Cathedral Rock, 249–53
Middle Teton Glacier, 157
Middle Triple Peak, 42–47
Miller, Maynard, 7
Miller, Tom, 119
Mills Glacier, 204, 205
Miner's Basin, 217
Mita, Y., 79
Mitchell, Steve, 133, 137
Molenaar, Dee, 107
Monashees, 51
Moore, Terris, 11–13
Moose's Tooth, 25–29
Moraine Lake, 81, 82, 84
Moraine Park, 111
Moran, Mount, 82, 165–70
Mountaineer's Route, Mount Whitney, 277,
    278, 280
Mountain of the Spiral Road, 69
Mountains. See names of individual
    mountains
Muir, John, 108, 277
Mummery, A. F., 197
Munday, Phyllis, 85, 87
Munday, W. A. D., 85, 87
Mystery Mountain, 87

Nabokov, Dmitri, 65
Narrows, the, 246, 247
Navajos, 209, 213

Neave, Ferris, 87
Neave, Roger, 87
Needles, x, 144
Nelson, Anton, 237–42
Nenana River Valley, 15
Nesakwatch Creek, 125–27
Newton Glacier, 5–8
Newton, Mount, 6
Nooksack Cirque, 119, 120
Nooksack River, 122
North Chimney, 205
Northcutt–Carter Route, Hallett Peak,
    190–94
Northcutt, Ray, 185, 191–93, 203
Northeast Buttress, Slesse Mountain,
    123–27
Northeast Face, Pingora, 171–76
North Face: Fairview Dome, 282–87; Grand
    Teton, 159–64; Mount Edith Cavell,
    70–74
North Ridge: Grand Teton, 147–52; Mount
    Stuart, 128–32
Northwest Arête, Mount Sir Donald, 51–54
Northwest Face, Half Dome, 254–60
Nose, the, 32, 33, 35
Nose Route, El Capitan, 203, 261–68

Oberlin, John, 78
Oily Lake, 8
Okabe, N., 79
O'Neill, Jerry, 133
Ormes' Rib, 213
Ormes, Robert, 188, 209, 210
Ortenburger, Leigh, 139, 163, 167–69
Owen–Spalding Route, 139, 152, 153, 155,
    158, 164

Palmer, Howard, 77
Pelisier, Andrea, 8
Pendulum Pitch, 162–64, 167
Perego, Romano, 21–24
Perley Rock, 54
Petigax, Giuseppe, 8
Petit Grepon, ix, 195–200
Petzoldt, Paul, 153, 155, 159, 161
Picture Lake, 119
Pigeon Col, 61–64
Pike's Peak, 185
Pingora, 171–76
Piz Badile, 231
Plummer, William, 179–82
Porter, Charlie, 23, 45
Powell, Mark, 240, 263, 264, 283
Pownall, Richard, 161–64, 203

Pratt, Chuck, 207, 219, 243, 251, 258,
    264, 266, 269–75, 284–87
Price Glacier, 118–22
Price, W. M., 119
Psyche Flake, 257, 258
Ptarmigan Ridge Route, 105, 110
Purcells, 51, 57

Rainier, Mount, 105–11
Rappel Gully, 209, 214
Rating system, 306, 307
Rearick, Dave, 203–5, 258
Rébuffat, Gaston, xiii, 191
Reed, Wally, 283–87
Reichegger, Alfons, 27–29
Riesenstein, 43
Ripley, Willard, 141
Ritter, Mount, 289
Rixon's Pinnacle, 269
Robbins, Royal, 72, 203, 204, 243, 247,
    255–60, 266, 269–75, 304
Robbins Traverse, 257–60
Roberts, Dave, 31–35
Robinson, Bestor, 88, 211–14
Robinson, Doug, 256
Robinson, Mark, 103
Robson, Mount, 49, 55, 65–69
Rock with Wings, 209
Rogers Pass, 51
Rogers, William, 141
Rogowski, Pete, 213
Roof, the, 271–74
Roper, Steve, xii, 114, 168, 211, 219, 241,
    258, 301–5
Rotten Log, 232–35
Rowell, Galen, 295–98
Royal Arch Cascade, 230
Royal Arches, the, 133, 230–35
Rupley, John, 130, 131, 174
Rusk, C. E., 129
Russell Col, 5, 6, 8
Russell, Israel, 5, 37, 129
Ruth Amphitheater, 25
Ruth Gorge, 25

Saber, 199
Sacherer, Frank, 252
Saint Elias, Mount, 4–8, 37
Saint Elmo Pass, 111
Saint Paul, 9
Saint Peter, 5
Salathé, John, 237–42, 245–47, 269
Salathé Wall, El Capitan, 151, 262,
    269–75

Samovar Hills, 8
Sangre de Cristo Range, 187
Schauffelberger, Walter, 67, 69
Schmidtke, Cliff, 93–97
Schunk, George, 43–46
Schwabland, Jack, 120–22
Scott, Doug, 274
Secord, Campbell, 87
Selkirks, 51–54
Sella, Vittorio, 5, 7, 8
Seneca Rocks, x
Sentinel Pass, 84
Sentinel Rock, 243–48
Seward Glacier, 6, 37, 38
Shakes Lake, 97
Shaky-Leg Crack, 279
Sharkstooth, 199
Shawanagunks, x
Sheldon, Don, 25, 27
Sherman, Paddy, 12
Sherrick, Mike, 68, 69, 256–60
Shiprock, 207–15
Shuksan, Mount, 118–22, 125
Sickle Ledge, 261, 263, 268
Sierra Club, 88, 90, 210, 229, 245
Silver Star Mountain, 133
Sir Donald, Mount, 49, 51–54
Siri, Will, 213
Skagit River, 116
Sky Pond, 195, 199
Slesse Mountain, 105, 123–27
Sluiskin, 107, 108
Smith, Dean, 34
Smith, Irving, 240
Smithsonian Institution, 277
Smythe, Frank, 27
Smythe, Tony, 25, 27
Snake Dike, 229
Snoqualmie Pass, 113
Snow Dome, 75
Snowpatch Spire, ix, 59, 61, 64, 68
Sous Le Toit Ledge, 274
South Colony Lakes, 189
Southeast Chimney Route, Mount
    Waddington, 90
Southeast Face, Clyde Minaret, 288–93
South Face: Charlotte Dome, 294–99;
    Mount Robson, 69; Mount
    Waddington, 85–91; Petit Grepon,
    195–200
South Howser Tower, 56, 60–64
Spearin, E. P., 119
Spider Rock, 207, 213
Standing Rock, 207

Stanley, Fred, 135–37
Starr, Paul, 95–97
Steamboat Prow, 111
Steck, Allen, xii, 38–40, 114, 144, 165, 243, 245–47, 253, 281, 290–92, 297
Steck–Salathé Route, Sentinel Rock, 243–47
Stegmaier, Otto, 82–84
Stegosaur, the, 32, 35
Stettners' Ledges, 185
Stevens, Hazard, 107
Stevens Pass, 129
Stewart, Sandy, 103
Stikine River, 93–97
Stoveleg Crack, 263, 266, 268
Stuart Glacier Couloir, 129
Stuart, Mount, 128–32
Stuck, Reverend Hudson, 3
Sunshine Glacier, 43, 44, 46
Sunwapta Pass, 79
Surrealistic Pillar, 301
Swift, Bob, 251, 252
Sykes, Dick, 57–59
Symmetry Spire, 155

Table Ledge, 205
Tackle, Jack, 90
Tahoma Glacier, 108
Tahquitz Rock, 301
Talkeetna, 24, 29, 46
Tatina Glacier, 46
Tatina Spire, 44
Tatlayoko Lake, 87
Taylor, Andy, 9, 11
Teanaway River, 131
Teewinot Mountain, 159
Temple, Mount, 80–84
Terray, Lionel, 27, 31
Teton Glacier, 152
Teton Range, 81, 139, 187. See also Grand Teton
Tewes, E., 51–54
Texas Flake, 268
Thank God Ledge, 258–60
Thompson, Gray, 72
Thompson, Steve, 301–5
Thorington, J. M., 77
Thor Peak, 170
Thumb Rock, 109–11
Thune, John, 238
Tiedemann Glacier, 87
Tiger Tower, 183
Tioga Pass Highway, 283, 287
Titan, the, 221–27

Tokositna Glacier, 32, 35
Tombstone Ledge, 302
Topham, W. H., 5
Totem Pole, 207, 213
Tower Traverse, 278–81
Traveler Buttress, Lover's Leap, 300–305
Traverse Pitch, 209–14
Triolet, 81
Trott, Otto, 119
Tsa-Beh-Tai, 209
Tuolumne Meadows, 283, 301
Turner, John, 58, 59

Ulrich, Louis, 129
Ulrich's Couloir, 129, 131, 132
Ulrichs, Hermann, 113, 133
Undercling Pitch, 257, 260
Underhill, Robert, 139, 147–51, 155, 229, 277–80
Unsoeld, Willi, 150, 163, 167
Upper Boy Scout Lake, 280
Upper Yosemite Fall, 237–39
Uto Peak, 51, 54

Valhalla Traverse, 152
Vancouver, George, 107
Van Trump, Philemon B., 107
Vaux Glacier, 54
Verdant Creek, 74
Victoria, Mount, 81
Visor, the, 254, 255, 257, 266
Vowell Glacier, 64
V-Slot Pitch, 252, 253

Waddington, Alfred, 87
Waddington, Mount, 16, 49, 85–91
Walker Spur, 231
Wall Street, 153, 154, 156, 157
Waputik Icefield, 83
Warbonnet, 171
Warner, Marion, 187–89
Washboard, the, 279, 281
Washburn, Bradford, 3, 11, 31, 15–19, 31, 108
Washington Column, 269
Washington Pass, 133, 135, 137
Watson, Dwight, 114
Watson Lake, 99, 102, 103
Weber, Jean, 78, 79
Webster, Gordon, 301–5
Weeks, Ken, 192
Wehman, Bruce, 34
Welsch, Walter, 27–29

Welsh, Chuck, 133
Wenatchee Mountains, 129
Westbay, Billy, 205
West Buttress Route, Mount McKinley, 23, 24; South Howser Tower, 60–64
West Face, Mount Huntington, 30–35
West Ridge: Forbidden Peak, 112–17; Moose's Tooth, 25–29; Mount Hunter, 14–18
Wexler, Arnold, 99
Whitmer, John, 251
Whitmore, George, 264–67
Whitney, Josiah, 277, 289
Whitney, Mount, 276–81
Whymper, Edward, 191
Wiessner, Fritz, 88–91, 93, 141, 151
Wiggins, Cheryl, 194
Wilcox, Alanson, 88
Williams, Gordon, 210
Willis Wall, 108, 109
Wilson, Don, 255
Wilson, Jim, 38–40, 255
Wilson Overhang, 243–48
Wilts, Chuck, 290–92
Wind River Range, 139, 171
Winthrop Glacier, 111
Wishbone Arête, Mount Robson, 65–69
Wittich, Hans, 82–84
Wolf Jaw Col, 181, 183
Wolf's Head, 177–83
Woolley Col, 79
Woolley, Mount, 79
Woolsey, Betty, 88
Wrangell Mountains, 3

Yakutat Bay, 5–7
Yensan, Jim, 173–75
Yoho National Park, 83
Yokum Ridge, 105
Yosemite Valley, 229, 231, 306, 307

Zigzag Pitches, 258–60
Zion Canyon, 207
Zucchi, Annibale, 21–24